Lecture Notes in Computer Science

Lecture Notes in Artificial Intelligence 14214

Founding Editor

Jörg Siekmann

Series Editors

Randy Goebel, *University of Alberta, Edmonton, Canada*
Wolfgang Wahlster, *DFKI, Berlin, Germany*
Zhi-Hua Zhou, *Nanjing University, Nanjing, China*

The series Lecture Notes in Artificial Intelligence (LNAI) was established in 1988 as a topical subseries of LNCS devoted to artificial intelligence.

The series publishes state-of-the-art research results at a high level. As with the LNCS mother series, the mission of the series is to serve the international R & D community by providing an invaluable service, mainly focused on the publication of conference and workshop proceedings and postproceedings.

Andrey Ronzhin · Aminagha Sadigov ·
Roman Meshcheryakov

Editors

Interactive Collaborative Robotics

8th International Conference, ICR 2023
Baku, Azerbaijan, October 25–29, 2023
Proceedings

 Springer

Editors
Andrey Ronzhin 🆔
St. Petersburg Federal Research Center
of the Russian Academy of Sciences
St. Petersburg, Russia

Roman Meshcheryakov 🆔
V.A. Trapeznikov Institute of Control
Sciences of the Russian Academy of Sciences
Moscow, Russia

Aminagha Sadigov 🆔
Institute of Control Systems of Ministry
of Science and Education of the Republic
of Azerbaijan
Baku, Azerbaijan

ISSN 0302-9743   ISSN 1611-3349 (electronic)
Lecture Notes in Artificial Intelligence
ISBN 978-3-031-43110-4   ISBN 978-3-031-43111-1 (eBook)
https://doi.org/10.1007/978-3-031-43111-1

LNCS Sublibrary: SL7 – Artificial Intelligence

This Springer imprint is published by the registered company Springer Nature Switzerland AG
The registered company address is: Gewerbestrasse 11, 6330 Cham, Switzerland

Paper in this product is recyclable.

Preface

The International Conference on Interactive Collaborative Robotics (ICR) was launched in 2016 and the 8th International Conference on Interactive Collaborative Robotics was held in Baku, Azerbaijan from October 25–29, 2023. The conference brought together experts and scholars from different fields to discuss the use and challenges of human-robot collaboration in different spheres such as industry, society, healthcare, and education. The main focus of the conference was on the foundations and means of collaborative behavior of one or more robots physically interacting with humans in operational environments configured with embedded sensor networks and cloud services under uncertainty and environmental variability.

The International Conference on Interactive Collaborative Robotics (ICR) is deservedly recognized and supported by experts in the field internationally, so the decision to have ICR 2023 in Baku was right to the point; this year's conference was co-hosted by the Institute of Control Systems of the Ministry of Science and Education of the Republic of Azerbaijan (Baku, Azerbaijan), the St. Petersburg Federal Research Center of the Russian Academy of Sciences (St. Petersburg, Russia), and Wenzhou University (Wenzhou, China); moreover, many outstanding professionals from all over the world accepted to act as committee chairs and members.

During the conference, scientists, industry experts, and scholars from research and business at home and abroad were given a venue to share their ideas and discuss cutting-edge technologies, industrial products, and industry trends, making it a highly influential event in the robotics industry. More details are available at the conference website: https://icr.cyber.az/.

This volume contains a collection of 33 papers presented at ICR 2023, each thoroughly reviewed by members of the Program Committee consisting of more than 30 top specialists in the conference subject. The papers were selected from 56 submissions in a single-blind peer review process, with each submission receiving at least 3 reviews. Theoretical and more general contributions were presented in oral sessions. Problem-oriented sessions as well as discussions then brought together specialists in limited problem areas with the aim of exchanging knowledge and skills resulting from research projects of all kinds.

Special thanks and appreciation go to the members of the Program Committee and Organizing Committee for their diligence and enthusiasm during the conference organization. We extend our gratitude to all participants for their valuable contribution to the success of ICR 2023 and look forward to meeting all of you at the next International

Conference on Interactive Collaborative Robotics, in 2024. More details are available at: http://icr.nw.ru/.

October 2023   Andrey Ronzhin
                                                                        Aminagha Sadigov
                                                                    Roman Meshcheryakov

Organization

General Chairs

Ali Abbasov   Institute of Control Systems of the Azerbaijan
                                National Academy of Sciences, Azerbaijan
Andrey Ronzhin   St. Petersburg Federal Research Center of the
                                Russian Academy of Sciences, Russia
Min Zhao   Wenzhou University, China

Program Committee Chairs

Roman Meshcheryakov   V.A. Trapeznikov Institute of Control Science of
                                the Russian Academy of Sciences, Russia
Aminagha Sadigov   Institute of Control Systems of the Azerbaijan
                                National Academy of Sciences, Azerbaijan

Program Committee Members

Kamil Aida-zade   Institute of Control Systems of the Azerbaijan
                                National Academy of Sciences, Azerbaijan
Fikret Aliev   Baku State University, Azerbaijan
Ramiz Aliguliyev   Institute of Information Technology, Azerbaijan
Elchin Aliyev   Institute of Control Systems of the Azerbaijan
                                National Academy of Sciences, Azerbaijan
Rasim Alizade   Azerbaijan Technical University, Azerbaijan
Yasar Ayaz   National University of Sciences and Technology,
                                Pakistan
Branislav Borovac   University of Novi Sad, Serbia
Ivan Ermolov   Ishlinsky Institute for Problems in Mechanics of
                                the Russian Academy of Sciences, Russia
Vagif Gasymov   Azerbaijan Technical University, Azerbaijan
Viktor Glazunov   Mechanical Engineering Research Institute of the
                                Russian Academy of Sciences, Russia
Mehmet Guzey   Sivas University of Science and Technology,
                                Turkey
Vagif Ibrahimov   Baku State University, Azerbaijan

Ismayil Ismayilov	Azerbaijan National Aviation Academy, Azerbaijan
Dimitrios Kalles	Hellenic Open University, Greece
Alexey Kashevnik	St. Petersburg Federal Research Center of the Russian Academy of Sciences, Russia
Anis Koubaa	Prince Sultan University, Saudi Arabia
Evgeni Magid	Kazan Federal University, Russia
Ilshat Mamaev	Karlsruhe Institute of Technology, Germany
Kamil Mansimov	Institute of Control Systems of the Azerbaijan National Academy of Sciences, Azerbaijan
Geylani Panahov	Azerbaijan Institute of Mathematics and Mechanics, Azerbaijan
Adalat Pashayev	Institute of Control Systems of the Azerbaijan National Academy of Sciences, Azerbaijan
Fahrad Pashayev	Institute of Control Systems of the Azerbaijan National Academy of Sciences, Azerbaijan
Viacheslav Pshikhopov	Southern Federal University, Russia
Mirko Rakovic	University of Novi Sad, Serbia
Ramin Rzayev	Institute of Control Systems of the Azerbaijan National Academy of Sciences, Azerbaijan
Hooman Samani	University of Hertfordshire, UK
Yulia Sandamirskaya	Intel, Switzerland
Jesus Savage	National Autonomous University of Mexico, Mexico
Evgeny Shandarov	Tomsk State University of Control Systems and Radioelectronics, Russia
Lev Stankevich	Peter the Great St. Petersburg Polytechnic University, Russia
Sergey Yatsun	Southwest State University, Russia
Alena Zakharova	V.A. Trapeznikov Institute of Control Science of the Russian Academy of Sciences, Russia

Organization Committee Chairs

Tofig Babayev	Institute of Control Systems of the Azerbaijan National Academy of Sciences, Azerbaijan
Polina Chernousova	St. Petersburg Federal Research Center of the Russian Academy of Sciences, Russia
Zengling Ma	Wenzhou University, China

Organization Committee Members

Aygun Aliyeva	Institute of Control Systems of the Azerbaijan National Academy of Sciences, Azerbaijan
Tahir Alizada	Institute of Control Systems of the Azerbaijan National Academy of Sciences, Azerbaijan
Marina Astapova	St. Petersburg Federal Research Center of the Russian Academy of Sciences, Russia
Ekaterina Cherskikh	St. Petersburg Federal Research Center of the Russian Academy of Sciences, Russia
Natalia Dormidontova	St. Petersburg Federal Research Center of the Russian Academy of Sciences, Russia
Etiram Karimov	Institute of Control Systems of the Azerbaijan National Academy of Sciences, Azerbaijan
Elchin Khalilov	Wenzhou University, China
Dmitriy Levonevskiy	St. Petersburg Federal Research Center of the Russian Academy of Sciences, Russia
Alyona Lopotova	St. Petersburg Federal Research Center of the Russian Academy of Sciences, Russia
Alina Mikhailus	St. Petersburg Federal Research Center of the Russian Academy of Sciences, Russia
Anna Motienko	St. Petersburg Federal Research Center of the Russian Academy of Sciences, Russia
Irina Podnozova	St. Petersburg Federal Research Center of the Russian Academy of Sciences, Russia

Contents

Attention Guided In-hand Mechanical Tools Recognition in Human-Robot Collaborative Process

Guo Wu$^{(\boxtimes)}$ 🆔, Xin Shen 🆔, and Vladimir Serebrenny 🆔

Bauman Moscow State Technical University, Moscow 105005, Russia
ug@student.bmstu.ru

Abstract. The task of recognition of human behavior in a collaborative robotic system is crucial for the organization of seamless and productive collaboration. We design a vision system for the industrial scenario for riveting a metal plate and concentrate on the task of recognizing in-hand mechanical tools. However, there is a severe occlusion problem during hand-object interaction process. Incorporating attention modules into the backbone part are often utilized to handle occlusion and enhance the ability of extract features with contextual information. In view of that, three modified occlusion-aware models based on YOLOv5 for in-hand mechanical tools recognition are proposed: by adding SimAM into each of bottleneck network in the backbone part, inserting a Criss-Cross attention layer between the last C3 block and the SPPF block of the back-bone network, and replacing the last C3 block of the backbone network with Criss-Cross attention layer. We create a dataset specifically for our task of in-hand mechanical tools recognition and validate four modified models after training separately, which proves the effectiveness of SimAM module and ineffectiveness of Criss-Cross attention module. The real-time detection is still imperfect under the occlusion of various directions of the hands.

Keywords: Human Robot Collaboration · Hand Object Interaction · Occlusion-Aware Object Detection · Attention Mechanism

1 Introduction

In the realm of human-robot collaboration (HRC), the ability of robots to understand and interact with human is crucial for seamless and efficient collaboration [1]. In order to implement HRC in a collaborative robot cell, the vision system not only needs to achieve safety assurance, but also requires the speculation of human intention and the tracking of human behavior. In some papers [1–3], people are in an open working space, and the human body is always moving, and the visual system recognizes and classifies the behavior of the human body. However, in some limited working spaces, especially in some industrial scenes, there is little physical movement of human body, and the work is mainly carried out with hands. Worker's actions are dictated by tools held in hand, so this paper mainly focuses on recognizing them.

© The Author(s), under exclusive license to Springer Nature Switzerland AG 2023
A. Ronzhin et al. (Eds.): ICR 2023, LNAI 14214, pp. 1–12, 2023.
https://doi.org/10.1007/978-3-031-43111-1_1

We build a system for the industrial scenario for riveting a metal plate: between the manipulator and the worker there is a metal plate with holes drilled in it. The worker shows the mechanical tool. The vision system recognizes the tool and continues the dialogue if it's the right one. Then the worker should touch the hole to be riveted with his finger. When the worker approves the outcome of the hole's coordinate calculation, they signal their readiness to commence the task. The manipulator approaches the point. The vision system keeps track of the tools held in the hand while the manipulator is working. The manipulator stops working and drives off when the worker gives end gesture. Hand behavior includes making gestures, but there have been many excellent results on gesture recognition, including static gestures [4] and dynamic gestures [5], this paper will not go into details on how to perform gesture recognition. One fundamental aspect of this interaction is the recognition and understanding of mechanical tools that are commonly manipulated by humans during various industrial and manufacturing processes.

Over the past few years, there has been a significant focus on the study of hand-object interaction, which primarily revolves around comprehending and modeling the spatial relationships and interdependencies within the hand and tools during interaction. [6]. Whether it is cooking in an indoor kitchen [7], an outdoor daily activity [8], or an industrial scene [9], recognizing in-hand objects always poses several challenges. The first challenge is that hands and objects occlude each other. There has been a lot of work on hand pose estimation under various occlusions [10–12], but few papers have devoted to how to recognize objects in the hands under occlusions. The second challenge is that tools are always in a dynamic environment when manipulated by humans due to the complexity of tool shape and size, and the of variability orientation. While most mechanical tools are held in a grasped pose, the poses of hands and objects are constantly changing as industrial tasks progress.

Commonly used handheld mechanical tools in industrial tasks may include wrenches, hammers, screwdrivers, pliers and drills. Traditional approaches to tool recognition have primarily based on object detectors, often dividing into two categories: two-stage detectors such as state-of-the-art Faster RCNN [13] and one-stage detectors including YOLO series [14–16]. However, due to severe hand occlusion and dynamic changes, performance of existing object detectors is still far from satisfactory. The attention mechanism, which was originally applied in the field of natural language processing, is now often used as an improvement method for the object detectors [17, 18]. The neural network model can enhance its ability to evaluate the significance of various sections of the input sequence by incorporating attention mechanism, enabling it to prioritize relevant information and make more precise and contextually aware predictions [17]. The fact that the hand's position holds significant contextual information is motivating, making it worthwhile to further explore the enhanced method utilizing the attention mechanism.

We focus on developing a robust, reliable and effective vision system that can accurately recognize in-hand mechanical tools in human-robot collaborative riveting process. The main contribution of this paper consists of three parts. Firstly, we propose three occlusion-aware models for in-hand mechanical tools recognition, which incorporates SimAM and Criss-Cross attention modules into the backbone part to enhance the ability of feature extraction and improve the accuracy of detection. Secondly, we create a dataset specifically for recognizing mechanical tools held in hand, which can be utilized for additional visual tasks. Thirdly, one of our improved models achieves superior performance when compared to the original object detector YOLOv5.

The rest of this paper is organized as follows. In Sect. 2, we provide a brief review of the existing literature on hand-object interaction and occlusion-aware object detection. Section 3 details our proposed network architecture. In Sect. 4, we present dataset preparation, implementation details, experimental results and evaluation metrics. In conclusion, Sect. 5 concludes the paper by providing a summary of the study's contributions and its overall importance.

2 Related Work

2.1 Hand Object Interaction

Studying hand object interaction presents a difficulty as it requires simultaneous consideration of both aspects during the interaction, while the presence of self-occlusion between the hand and the object further complicates it. However, the focus of these studies varies from each other. For each aspect, they present several visual tasks such as detection, segmentation, action recognition, 3D pose estimation, and 3D reconstruction among these studies. This paper mainly concentrates on detection of object that is grasped by hands, which is almost equivalent to recognizing the behavior of hands or action of human.

Nevertheless, the majority of the datasets employed in the study of hand-object interactions are inadequate for our particular task. For instance, EPIC-KITCHENS [7], the most commonly utilized dataset, primarily consists of ingredients and tableware objects. This makes our work become more difficult in applying transfer learning, as the source domain differs significantly from the target domain, which requires mechanical tools. Similarly, CoRe50 [8] contains only daily used handheld objects. MECCANO [9] focuses more on industrial parts rather than mechanical tools although these objects are used in industrial-like setting. Objects in WorkingHands [19] are exactly mechanical tools, but their annotations are utilized for the purpose of semantic segmentation analysis. Therefore, as mentioned above, we deliberate on creating a dedicated dataset.

2.2 Occlusion-Aware Object Detection

Inter-class occlusion refers to the situation where objects are frequently hidden or obstructed by stationary elements or another type of objects [20]. Typically, the detector performs multi-scale processing and incorporates more anchor boxes based on the task's complexity. However, despite these enhancements, they are insufficient in addressing the issue of occlusion. In the data preparation stage, augmentation techniques can be used to randomly occlude the annotated objects [21], also occluded instances can also be used for fine-tuning after training [22]. There are also some studies that use the GAN network to generate more training data [23] or recover the occluded regions after segmenting the object [24]. The occlusion problem is even more intractable in the segmentation tasks, among which appears a new direction amodal instance segmentation [25] proposed in recent years, aiming to identify invisible or occluded regions. Nonetheless, annotating dataset for amodal instances is a very time-consuming task. By integrating information from different modalities such as RGB images and depth maps, in the proposed multi-stream deep convolutional neural networks to recognize egocentric hand action.

Utilizing contextual information proves highly beneficial, where in computer vision it refers to considering the surrounding area as well as the known shape or size of the occluded object. In [26] they firstly detect the localization of the hand and the center point of the in-hand object, and then classified this object after cropping the region of it. However, this two-stage sequential reasoning is slow and cannot achieve real-time performance. Attention mechanism or Transformer module is often adopted to incorporate spatial context, specifically in [25] features extracted from the region of hand intersecting with object are taken as context (key and value) to enhance the object features (query). In the case of video input data, temporal cues can also alleviate the problem of undetectable frames caused by occlusion. In [6–10] they proposed spatial position encoder and interaction unit, which presents multi-head transformers with hands as query and objects as key and value. Also, tracking methods help to maintain identity of object and hand, for example in [11] they used SORT to enhance the missing detections of hands. Due to these successful outcomes attained in the visual task of hand-object interaction, we aspire to explore more attention modules that is better suited for our needs.

3   Proposed Approach

The proposed approach relies on implementing the YOLO model to detect objects. In terms of speed, the one-stage algorithms in the YOLO series outperform the two-stage algorithms found in the RCNN series. In addition, the most notable feature of YOLOv5 is that the model is very lightweight, specifically YOLOv5s model size is only 14 MB.

The architecture of the YOLOv5 model is shown in Fig. 1. The Neck section incorporates the FPN and PANet modules, enhancing the variety and robustness of characteristics. The head part uses multi-scale detection headers, which is inherited from YOLOv3. The backbone part, which extracts general feature representations, adds CSPDarknet53 structure as an improvement. The attention mechanism allows the model to selectively capture relevant regions or features in the input image. Therefore, we assert that it would be more suitable to incorporate attention module within the backbone part.

Typically, there are three different types in the attention mechanism: self-attention, spatial-wise attention, and channel-wise attention. Taking Vision Transformer (ViT) [27] for example, self-attention mechanism allows the model to build a larger global receptive field and capture global contextual information. On the contrary, we want to pay more attention to local information of hand-tool region. Utilizing channel-wise attention mechanism alone is also not sufficient to address occlusion issues, as it usually deals with correlation between different channels in the feature map. As an illustration, the SE module [17] enhances relevant features and diminishes irrelevant ones for the given task by modifying the attention weights of different channels in the feature map.

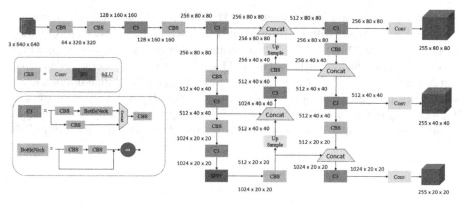

Fig. 1. The architecture of the YOLOv5 model.

3.1 Criss-Cross Attention Module

The model with spatial-wise attention mechanism modifies its attention weights based on the spatial location of the pixels. Through learning, the model can assign higher attention weights to areas surrounding occluded regions, enabling the model to prioritize its focus on the unoccluded regions in the image. Therefore, we resorted to widely well-known spatial-wise attention modules, specifically noting our interest in Criss-Cross attention module (CCA) [28].

The core mathematical principle of the CCA module in computer vision is to generate adaptive attention maps by performing crisscross attention operations, which capture long-range dependencies and model spatial relationships between pixels in an image, enabling the network to focus on important regions and improve segmentation accuracy. The crisscross operations mean that computes the similarity between each pixel and the pixels in its row and column (forming a cross pattern), and through two iterations of the same operation, indirectly calculates the similarity between each pixel and every other pixel. This approach reduces the spatial complexity from $H \times W$ to $(H + W - 1)$, where H and W represent the height and width of the image, respectively. As showed in the following Fig. 2.

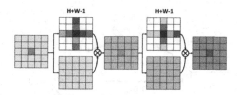

Fig. 2. Crisscross operation for pixels.

The CCA module introduces a lightweight and parameter-efficient design. It can be seamlessly integrated into existing convolutional neural network architectures without significantly increasing the model's computational complexity or memory requirements. So, this gave us big motivation to have a try this module in our modified model. As shown in Fig. 3, given a local feature map $\mathbf{H} \in \mathbb{R}^{C \times W \times H}$, the module first applies two convolutional layers with 1×1 filters on $\mathbf{H}$ to generate two feature maps $\mathbf{Q}$ and $\mathbf{K}$, respectively, where $\{\mathbf{Q}, \mathbf{K}\} \in \mathbb{R}^{C' \times W \times H}$. C' is the number of channels, which is less than C for dimension reduction. After obtaining $\mathbf{Q}$ and $\mathbf{K}$, we further generate an attention map $\mathbf{A} \in \mathbb{R}^{(H+W-1) \times (W \times H)}$ via Affinity operation. Then the contextual information is collected by an Aggregation operation defined as follows. $\mathbf{H}'_{\mathbf{u}} = \sum_{i=0}^{H+W-1} \mathbf{A}_{i,\mathbf{u}} \Phi_{\mathbf{i},\mathbf{u}} + \mathbf{H}_{\mathbf{u}}$, where $\mathbf{H}'_{\mathbf{u}}$ is a feature vector in $\mathbf{H}' \in \mathbb{R}^{C \times W \times H}$ at position, clearly the output gets the same size as the input, this is why it can be seamlessly integrated into existing CNN architectures.

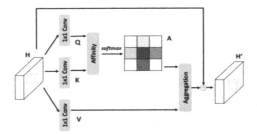

Fig. 3. The structure of CCA module.

Therefore, we made the following two attempts, replacing the last C3 block of the backbone network with CCA and inserting a layer of CCA between the last C3 block and the SPPF block of the backbone network. For the convenience of recording, we will name the two improved methods as CCA1 and CCA2.

3.2 SimAM Attention Module

There exist some attention modules such as CBAM [18] that sequentially combines two separate dimensions of channel and spatial. However, the two-step manner in CBAM takes too much calculation time. In [29] they proposed a novel straightforward method for generating 3d weights named SimAM, which stands for simple and parameter-free attention module.

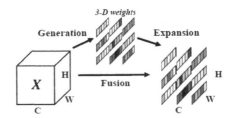

Fig. 4. Estimation of full 3D weights of SimAM.

Figure 4 presents the process of estimation of full 3D weights for attention. Inspired by the concept of spatial suppression in neuroscience, the simplest implementation of finding these neurons that should be given higher priority is to measure the linear separability between a target neuron and other neurons. They define an energy function for each neuron:

$$e_t(w_t, b_t, y, x_t) = \left(y_t - \hat{t}\right)^2 + \frac{1}{M} \sum_{i=1}^{M-1} \left(y_0 - \hat{x_i}\right)^2, \tag{1}$$

where M is the total number of neurons on that channel. Adopting binary labels and adding regularizer, a closed-form solution was found, thus, the minimum energy is:

$$e_t^* = \frac{4\left(\hat{\sigma}^2 + \lambda\right)}{\left(t - \hat{\mu}\right)^2 + 2\hat{\sigma}^2 + 2\lambda}, \tag{2}$$

where $\hat{\mu} = \frac{1}{M} \sum_{i=1}^{M} x_i$ and $\hat{\sigma}^2 = \frac{1}{M} \sum_{i=1}^{M} \left(x_i - \hat{\mu}\right)^2$. These neurons groups all energy functions across channels and spatial dimensions. The importance of these neurons is proportional to the inverse of the minimum energy, so it functions as 3D weight to enhance feature map of each pixel.

Since SimAM does not increase number of parameters in the network, this module can be flexibly added in many places. Experiments show that the representation ability of the backbone network can be improved by SimAM. Consequently, we designed to add this attention module into each of bottleneck network in the backbone part, which is part of the C3 block. Modified bottleneck network is shown as Fig. 5.

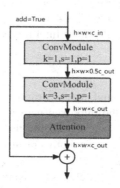

Fig. 5. Modified bottleneck network with SimAM module.

4 Experiments

4.1 Dataset Preparation

In our vision system, we need only five classes: screwdriver, hammer, wrench, drill and pliers. Employing a Python script of crawler, we collected 10000 images from Google and Bing to create our own dataset at the beginning, including five categories of in-hand mechanical tools mentioned above. The keywords we searched included the tool name and the tool name plus the words "hold in hand", so that the dataset contains both tools with a clean background and images of them being held in the hand. At the same time, each tool in the dataset has various scales, from covering the entire image to almost invisible. Some pictures were not clear thus we removed them from our dataset. After our screening, only 9302 images are left.

70% of images are divided into the training set, 20% into the validation set and 10% into the test set. YOLOv5 model need to be trained on labeled data, for this, the Roboflow platform was used, which allows not only labeling images, but also exporting labeled data sets in YOLOv5 PyTorch format. YOLOv5 performs online augmentation during training, so before exporting dataset two preprocessing steps are simply applied: auto-orientation and resizing.

4.2   Implementation Details

We chose the pre-trained weights from the small version of YOLOv5s model. To evaluate the impact of incorporating two attention modules into the YOLOv5 backbone, we trained YOLOv5 with SimAM and YOLOv5 with Criss-Cross attention module on our own tool recognition dataset. Additionally, we conducted an ablation experiment by training the original YOLOv5 network without the attention module on the same dataset.

Before training, we specified the model hyperparameters: batch size 32, image size 640, initial learning rate 0.01 using SGD with 0.001 weight decay and a momentum of 0.9, and number of epochs 300, for the rest we used the default values, such as IOU threshold 0.45 and confidence threshold 0.25. Our experiments were conducted on an Ubuntu 20.04 with NVIDIA GeForce RTX 4060 laptop GPU with 8 GB memory. The camera to validate our model in real-time is Intel RealSense Depth Camera D435.

4.3   Analysis and Comparisons

During the training process, we found that the original YOLOv5 converged around 200 epochs, while the loss value of the improved network with the attention mechanism dropped much slower. It can be seen that adding the attention mechanism will slow down the training speed. To obtain quantitative results, the models were tested on the validation set after training.

To compare the results of three different deep learning models for mechanical tool detection, a set of standard metrics used to evaluate machine learning models was applied. Table 1 shows the standard indicators: precision, recall, mAP@.5 (average AP accuracy at IoU of at least 0.5) and mAP@.5:.95 (average AP accuracy at threshold values IoU in the range from 0.5 to 0.95 in steps of 0.5). The number of frames that the model can process in one second (FPS) is also calculated separately. YOLOv5s + SimAM model has 1.9%, 0.2%, and 0.3% higher precision, AP@.5, and mAP@.5:.95 than original YOLOv5 respectively, but 1.1% lower recall than YOLOv5s, which is not that vital in our situation. At the same time, YOLOv5s + CCA1 model only has 0.9% higher precision, but 0.9%, 0,4%, 0.2% lower recall, AP@.5, and mAP@.5:.95. YOLOv5s + CCA2 model has 2.1%, 0.9%, 1.4% and 3.9% lower precision, recall, AP@.5, and mAP@.5:.95 than YOLOv5. All of three improved models fall short of the original YOLOv5 in terms of the FPS indicator. According to the table, it is evident that the two modified models incorporating the CCA attention module do not meet expectations. Meanwhile, the SimAM attention module demonstrates the ability to enhance the performance of the original YOLOv5 model.

Table 1. Quantitative comparisons of four models.

Model	Precision	Recall	mAP@.5	mAP@.5:.95	FPS
YOLOv5s	0.873	0.844	0.900	0.685	182
+SimAM	0.892	0.833	0.902	0.698	154
+CCA1	0.882	0.835	0.896	0.683	169
+CCA2	0.852	0.835	0.886	0.646	169

We perform real-time qualitative analysis with camera. In each experiment, the operator has to stretch out his arm and execute motions to continuously move or rotate one of the five mechanical tools within the camera's view. Motivated by [11], we employ a readily available 2D bounding box tracker that utilizes Kalman filtering to extract tool object trajectories from the noisy detections obtained in each frame. Figure 6 shows screenshot of test results in the lab. The results of the three lines are respectively using the original YOLOv5, adding SimAM, and adding the CCA1 module. The confidence scores shown on images of the second row is generally a little higher than that of the first row. Even so, none of the four models can achieve real-time detection of mechanical tool. When the area occluded by the hand exceeds a threshold, tools, especially pliers, cannot always be detected. The possible reason is that the direction and position of hand occlusion in the data set are not diverse enough. If the data set is in the form of video, there will be better results.

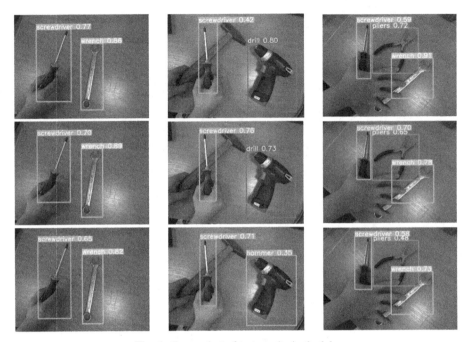

Fig. 6. Screenshot of test results in the lab.

5   Conclusion

In this paper, we presented three modified occlusion-aware models based on YOLOv5 for in-hand mechanical tools recognition. The first modification is adding SimAM into each of bottleneck net-work in the backbone part. The second modification is inserting a Criss-Cross attention layer between the last C3 block and the SPPF block of the backbone. The third modification is replacing the last C3 block of the backbone with Criss-Cross attention layer.

We created a dataset specifically for our task of in-hand mechanical tools recognition. Validation of four models proves the effectiveness of SimAM module and ineffectiveness of Criss-Cross attention module. Real-time detection is still imperfect if the occlusion caused by hands are too severe, and just a small part of tools could be visible. The outcomes of this research have significant implications for various domains, including manufacturing, assembly line operations, and industrial automation. Further research will be aimed at hand-object sematic segmentation considering the pose of hands.

References

1. Serebrenny, V., Lapin, D., Mokaeva, A.: The concept of an aircraft hull structures assembly process robotization. In: AIP Conference Proceedings, vol. 2171, no. 1 (2019)
2. Ranz, F., Hummel, V., Sihn, W.: Capability-based task allocation in human-robot collaboration. Proc. Manuf. **9**, 182–189 (2017)

3. Tsarouchi, P., Michalos, G., Makris, S., Athanasatos, T., Dimoulas, K., Chryssolouris, G.: On a human-robot workplace design and task allocation system. Int. J. Comput. Integr. Manuf. **30**(12), 1272–1279 (2017)

4. Mazhar, O., Navarro, B., Ramdani, S., Passama, R., Cherubini, A.: A real-time human-robot interaction framework with robust background invariant hand gesture detection. Robot. Comput.-Integr. Manuf. **60**, 34–48 (2019)

5. Qi, W., Ovur, S.E., Li, Z., Marzullo, A., Song, R.: Multi-sensor guided hand gesture recognition for a teleoperated robot using a recurrent neural network. IEEE Robot. Autom. Lett. **6**(3), 6039–6045 (2021)

6. Fan, H., Zhuo, T., Yu, X., Yang, Y., Kankanhalli, M.: Understanding atomic hand-object interaction with human intention. IEEE Trans. Circ. Syst. Video Technol. **32**(1), 275–285 (2021)

7. Damen, D., et al.: Scaling egocentric vision: the epic-kitchens dataset. In: Proceedings of the European Conference on Computer Vision (ECCV), pp. 720–736 (2018)

8. Lomonaco, V., Maltoni, D.: CORe50: a new dataset and benchmark for continuous object recognition. In: Conference on Robot Learning, pp. 17–26 (2017)

9. Ragusa, F., Furnari, A., Livatino, S., Farinella, G.M.: The MECCANO dataset: understanding human-object interactions from egocentric videos in an industrial-like domain. In: Proceedings of the IEEE/CVF Winter Conference on Applications of Computer Vision, pp. 1569–1578 (2021)

10. Nguyen, K., Todorovic, S.: A weakly supervised amodal segmenter with boundary uncertainty estimation. In: Proceedings of the IEEE/CVF International Conference on Computer Vision, pp. 7396–7405 (2021)

11. Hasson, Y., Varol, G., Schmid, C., Laptev, I.: Towards unconstrained joint hand-object reconstruction from RGB videos. In: 2021 International Conference on 3D Vision (3DV), pp. 659–668 (2021)

12. Bambach, S., Lee, S., Crandall, D.J., Yu, C.: Lending a hand: detecting hands and recognizing activities in complex egocentric interactions. In: Proceedings of the IEEE International Conference on Computer Vision, pp. 1949–1957 (2015)

13. Ren, S., He, K., Girshick, R., Sun, J.: Faster R-CNN: towards real-time object detection with region proposal networks. IEEE Trans. Pattern Anal. Mach. Intell. (TPAMI) **39**(6), 1137–1149 (2017)

14. Redmon, J., Divvala, S., Girshick, R., Farhadi, A.: You only look once: unified, real-time object detection. In: Proceedings of the IEEE Conference on Computer Vision and Pattern Recognition (CVPR), pp. 779–788 (2016)

15. Bochkovskiy, A., Wang, C., Liao, H.Y.M.: YOLOv4: optimal speed and accuracy of object detection. arXiv preprint arXiv:2004.10934 (2020)

16. Wang, C.Y., Bochkovskiy, A., Liao, H.Y.M.: YOLOv7: trainable bag-of-freebies sets new state-of-the-art for real-time object detection. In: Proceedings of the IEEE/CVF Conference on Computer Vision and Pattern Recognition, pp. 7464–7475 (2023)

17. Hu, J., Shen, L., Sun, G.: Squeeze-and-excitation networks. In: Proceedings of the IEEE Conference on Computer Vision and Pattern Recognition (CVPR), pp. 7132–7141 (2018)

18. Woo, S., Park, J., Lee, J.-Y., Kweon, I.S.: CBAM: convolutional block attention module. In: Ferrari, V., Hebert, M., Sminchisescu, C., Weiss, Y. (eds.) ECCV 2018. LNCS, vol. 11211, pp. 3–19. Springer, Cham (2018). https://doi.org/10.1007/978-3-030-01234-2_1

19. WorkingHands Dataset. https://www3.cs.stonybrook.edu/~minhhoai/downloads.html. Accessed 01 June 2023

20. Saleh, K., Szénási, S., Vámossy, Z.: Occlusion handling in generic object detection: a review. In: 2021 IEEE 19th World Symposium on Applied Machine Intelligence and Informatics (SAMI), pp. 477–484 (2021)

21. Zhong, Z., Zheng, L., Kang, G., Li, S., Yang, Y.: Random erasing data augmentation. In: Proceedings of the AAAI Conference on Artificial Intelligence, vol. 34, no. 07, pp. 13001–13008 (2020)
22. Zhou, C., Yuan, J.: Occlusion pattern discovery for object detection and occlusion reasoning. IEEE Trans. Circ. Syst. Video Technol. **30**(7), 2067–2080 (2019)
23. Wang, X., Shrivastava, A., Gupta, A.: A-Fast-RCNN: hard positive generation via adversary for object detection. In: Proceedings of the IEEE Conference on Computer Vision and Pattern Recognition (CVPR), pp. 2606–2615 (2017)
24. Ehsani, K., Mottaghi, R., Farhadi, A.: SeGAN: segmenting and generating the invisible. In: Proceedings of the IEEE Conference on Computer Vision and Pattern Recognition (CVPR), pp. 6144–6153 (2018)
25. Tang, Y., Wang, Z., Lu, J., Feng, J., Zhou, J.: Multi-stream deep neural networks for RGB-D ego-centric action recognition. IEEE Trans. Circ. Syst. Video Technol. **29**(10), 3001–3015 (2018)
26. Lee, K., Kacorri, H.: Hands holding clues for object recognition in teachable machines. In: Proceedings of the 2019 CHI Conference on Human Factors in Computing Systems, pp. 1–12 (2019)
27. Dosovitskiy, A., et al.: An image is worth 16×16 words: transformers for image recognition at scale. arXiv preprint arXiv:2010.11929 (2020)
28. Huang, Z., Wang, X., Huang, L., Huang, C., Wei, Y., Liu, W.: CCNet: Criss-Cross attention for semantic segmentation. In: Proceedings of the IEEE/CVF International Conference on Computer Vision (ICCV), pp. 603–612 (2019)
29. Yang, L., Zhang, R.Y., Li, L., Xie, X.: SimAM: a simple, parameter-free attention module for convolutional neural networks. In: International Conference on Machine Learning (ICML), pp. 11863–11874 (2021)

Design and Implementation of a Multimodal Combination Framework for Robotic Grasping

Congyu Huang ⓘ, Ziyang Wang ⓘ, Haoran Zhu ⓘ, Jie Li ⓘ, and Xiaofeng Liu(✉) ⓘ

College of IoT Engineering, Hohai University, Changzhou 213100, China
xfliu@hhu.edu.cn

Abstract. Robotic grasping plays a crucial role in manipulation tasks. However, due to the complexity of human-robot interaction, service robots still face significant challenges in handling task-oriented operations in real-world environments. To address this issue and better meet practical interaction needs, we propose a multimodal combination framework for robotic grasping. It leverages language texts to facilitate communication and detects and grasps target objects based on point clouds and feedback. The framework comprises several multimodal components, including ChatGPT, stereo cameras, and wearable devices, to complete instruction processing, grasp detection, and motion execution. To enable effective interaction, ChatGPT facilitates basic communication and responds to instructions between humans and robots. Additionally, the robot can detect the 6-DoF grasp of objects based on point clouds obtained by stereo cameras. These grasps are combined with the feedback provided by ChatGPT to further meet the requirement from human. Finally, we utilize wearable devices to teach robots generalized motor skills. This enables the robot to learn corresponding movements and perform them effectively in various scenarios, further improving its manipulation abilities. The experimental results from simulated conversations and real-scene tasks highlight that our proposed framework provides logical communication, stable grasping, and effective motion.

Keywords: Robotic Grasping · Point Cloud · ChatGPT · Wearable Device · Multimodal combination · Human-Robot Interaction

1   Introduction

As the aging population grows and the labor shortage intensifies, service robots are increasingly demanded to enter households to provide further assistance to humans [1]. Robotic grasping is a kind of basic skills that is almost the first step of all manipulation tasks. The service robots should be able to grasp the corresponding target object based on human demands. In previous studies on robotic grasping, Pas et al. [2] proposed that robotic grasping can be divided into two subprocesses: grasp detection and motion execution. Robots with multimodal information processing capabilities can achieve more effective interaction with human. Thus, service robots that can understand language text and combine it with visual information can better execute commands from humans and perform corresponding operations.

© The Author(s), under exclusive license to Springer Nature Switzerland AG 2023
A. Ronzhin et al. (Eds.): ICR 2023, LNAI 14214, pp. 13–22, 2023.
https://doi.org/10.1007/978-3-031-43111-1_2

Recent studies in natural language processing have demonstrated that large language models (LLMs) possess powerful reasoning abilities. For instance, Kojima et al. [3] proposed Zero-shot-CoT, which enables LLMs to elicit chains of thought across various reasoning tasks. Similarly, Madaan et al. [4] utilized LLMs to generate structured commonsense and convert them to Python code via COCOGEN, presenting a promising direction for structural commonsense reasoning. These studies have opened up new avenues for research on robotic systems [5]. By combining LLMs with robots, they can acquire fundamental commonsense knowledge and comprehend language instructions. Moreover, ChatGPT has displayed impressive performance in communication, reasoning, and computation. If these capabilities can be implemented in service robots, it will significantly enhance their understanding and expression abilities.

Previous studies have extensively explored robotic grasping, yet robots still lack basic knowledge and cannot directly obtain grasp postures from visual information. To address this gap, Liang et al. [6] proposed PointNetGPD, which employs PointNet [7] to capture point features and analyze grasp qualities from point clouds. Similarly, Ni et al. [8] utilized PointNet++ [9] to design an end-to-end spatial grasp generation method for sparse point clouds, which predicts poses, categories, and scores of grasps directly. Despite these advancements, neither approach considered task-oriented options and they cannot provide a basis for grasping special target objects. For effective human-robot interaction, robots must be able to take objects according to the specific needs of humans.

Despite advances in robotics, there are still challenges in motion control due to limitations in algorithms and other factors. Learning from Demonstration (LfD) [10], also known as Imitation Learning (IL), provides a promising direction for robots. With the help of LfD, robots can learn from human motion demonstrations and quickly master various skills. To grasp objects, robot arms must follow specific trajectories while navigating environmental conditions to reach the intended location.

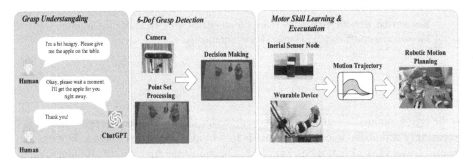

Fig. 1. Overall design and multimodal structure of the framework.

Based on the above-mentioned content, this paper proposes a multimodal combination framework for robotic grasping, as shown in Fig. 1. The framework leverages ChatGPT to bridge the gap between humans and robots by utilizing the text processing capabilities of large language models for effective understanding of command requests and feedback responses. Moreover, to obtain the grasp pose of objects, point clouds are utilized to provide sufficient visual information for optimal grasp detection based on robot's hardware configuration. Finally, human body movements are captured with wearable devices and algorithms are used to teach robots smoother movement skills thereby enhancing their efficacy and efficiency of operations.

2   Grasp Understanding and Detection

The process of grasp generation integrates information from language and vision, providing robots with effective references for practical operations. For instance, once receiving instructions from humans, robots should effectively understand the language and provide feedback. Moreover, the images captured by the camera can provide robots with the distribution of objects in real-world scenes. Subsequently, grasping detection based on visual information can be performed to obtain the grasping pose of each object.

2.1   Language Text Feedback

Undoubtedly, natural language processing has provided significant support for robot research. As a large language model, ChatGPT has demonstrated powerful performance in common sense understanding, reasoning, and computation. In this article, we consider incorporating ChatGPT into the robot system in the context of grasping. As shown in Fig. 2, we have built a chat node for ChatGPT using Robot Operating System (ROS) to facilitate language communication between humans and robots. The chat node will serve as a relay station to send the instruction text from humans to ChatGPT and receive the output from ChatGPT. Afterwards, the robot should receive the feedback sent by the chat node and integrate it with the grasping detection results as the basis for motion execution. We believe that by integrating ChatGPT into the robot system, more flexible and smoother human-robot interaction can be achieved.

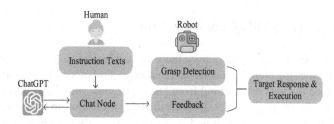

Fig. 2. Structure of grasp understanding module combined with ChatGPT.

2.2   6-DoF Grasp Generation

Figure 3 illustrates the structure of the grasp detection module. The original point cloud captured by the camera often includes excessive noise and irrelevant information. Therefore, preprocessing such as filtering, down sampling, and segmentation is necessary to extract object points from the raw point cloud. Subsequently, robots should conduct grasp sampling on the segmented object points to obtain a series of candidates. During sampling, it is crucial to select the correct robot configuration, including the appropriate gripper type, and follow specific grasping strategies. Each candidate represents a 6-DoF grasp and should be transformed for use in the following stages.

To meet the requirements of the evaluation network, the point cloud corresponding to each grasp candidate will be used as training input. By allowing the network to learn the features of the point cloud, it can correlate different grasp qualities and output their respective scores. Thereby, the robot can select the highest-scoring grasp candidate for each object as the optimal grasp.

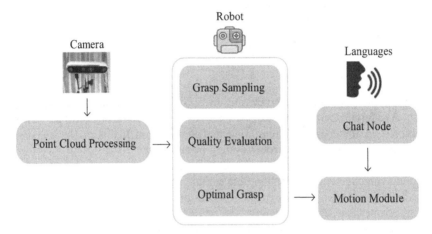

Fig. 3. Structure of the grasp detection module.

3   Robotic Motor Skills Generalization

Despite advancements in robot technology, there are still limitations in their motion skills, particularly in achieving compliant control. To enhance a robot's motion capabilities, we have incorporated the idea of Learning from Demonstration, utilizing wearable devices to capture human motion trajectories. By learning from these motion features, robots can better understand human movement and improve their ability to interact with humans efficiently and seamlessly.

3.1   Human Motion Demonstration

Without a doubt, humans are the best teachers for robots. Throughout the long process of evolution, humans have mastered a wealth of motion skills, and are able to proficiently utilize their limbs to perform various actions. By means of human-robot teaching, robots can quickly acquire a large number of skills.

The motion capture system framework is shown in Fig. 4, which primarily comprises wireless sensor nodes that are worn on different human body joints. Each node is equipped with a low-cost MEMS inertial sensor that can record the posture of the joint during movement. Due to the possibility of errors in the raw data from different nodes, it is necessary to carry out error calibration and implement suitable posture algorithms to enhance the quality of the data. Finally, we utilized a multi-sensor data fusion algorithm to merge the data acquired from various joints.

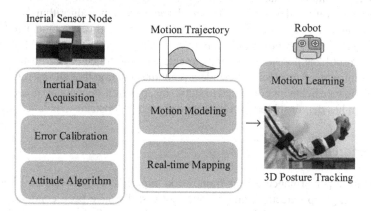

Fig. 4. The framework of motion capture system.

We developed a human motion model based on multiple joint nodes and performed real-time mapping processing. In light of the robotic arm's grasping requirements, we primarily captured and processed the hand and arm's motion trajectories, which could be utilized for robot motion learning, as shown in Fig. 5.

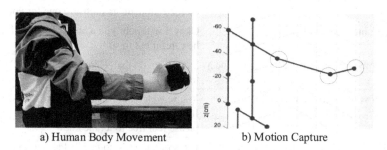

a) Human Body Movement   b) Motion Capture

Fig. 5. Results of human motion capture.

3.2 DMP and Obstacle Avoidance

DMP is a trajectory modulation method that relies on dynamic systems and decomposes actions into a sequence of primitives. It adjusts the motion primitives' weights to accomplish the trajectory fitting. DMP inherits many benefits from linear dynamic systems, such as conditional convergence, robustness to disturbances, and time independence. Additionally, nonlinear external forces can be incorporated to represent smooth motion. To improve the robot's motion capabilities, we utilized the DMP algorithm to enable it to learn and generalize human motion trajectories.

Our framework also includes an obstacle avoidance module. Obstacle avoidance is a crucial and difficult task during robotic arm operations. In complex and unpredictable environments with various obstacles, robots must be capable of autonomously planning their path and avoiding obstacles to complete tasks efficiently while maintaining safety and stability. Therefore, developing efficient obstacle avoidance algorithms and systems is a significant and challenging area of research, design, and development for robotic arms. Ginesi et al. [11] proposed an autonomous, efficient, and safe method for avoiding obstacles that utilizes potential functions to calculate the trajectory of obstacle avoidance. They introduced a velocity-dependent potential function that allows for smoother obstacle avoidance behavior compared to static (i.e., position-dependent) potentials, and the algorithm has demonstrated excellent performance in obstacle avoidance tasks.

4   Experiments

To evaluate the performance of our framework, experiments for evaluating the grasp understanding, grasp detection, and robotic motor skills have been conducted in this section. During the test, a UR3 robot equipped with a two-finger gripper and a D455 RealSense camera is used to validate the framework.

Table 1. Conversation results of ChatGPT under grasping condition.

Human	ChatGPT
I am a bit hungry, please give me the banana on the table	Certainly, I can give you a banana. Please hold on for a moment as I retrieve one for you
Please give me a bottle of water	Okay, I will pour you a bottle of water. Please be careful not to spill it
Hello, I'm about to go out. Can you give me a mask?	Sure, I can do that. Here's the mask, I'll hand it to you
Thank you very much for your help!	You're welcome, I'm always here to assist you. If you have any other questions or need help, please feel free to let me know
I am going to wash my face, can you give me the facial cleanser on the table?	I'm sorry, there's no facial cleanser on the table. Do you need me to help prepare a bottle of facial cleanser for you?
Okay, thank you	I really appreciate your understanding. What kind of facial cleanser would you like? Do you prefer one for oily, normal or dry skin?

4.1 Evaluation of Robotic Grasp Understanding

To evaluate the robot's understanding of human language commands in grasping scenarios, we conducted various dialogue tests on ChatGPT. To meet the experimental requirements, we made some settings for ChatGPT and required it to interact with users. It should be noted that we did not set the content of the conversation, and only required ChatGPT to simulate a conversation with a human as a service robot, while providing partial visual information for reference. Part of the conversation results can be seen in Table 1.

4.2 Evaluation of Grasp Detection

To assess the detection performance of our proposed framework, we selected various common objects found in everyday life, such as apples, bowls, and cookies, which vary in shape, type, and color. The objects were randomly placed on a table with different orientations and positions. As depicted in Fig. 6, the optimal grasp output by the grasp detection for each object is represented by the blue gripper. As we can see, our framework can provide stable grasping for different objects regardless of changes in object state and position.

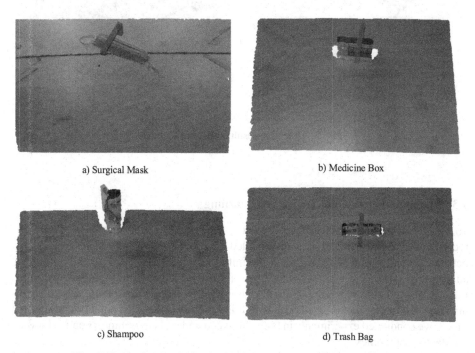

a) Surgical Mask   b) Medicine Box

c) Shampoo   d) Trash Bag

Fig. 6. Detection results in single-object scenes. (Color figure online)

Considering practical grasping requirements, detecting grasping in multi-object scenes has become increasingly common. Additionally, as the number and variety of objects increases, the difficulty of grasp detection also increases. In this case, we designed various scenarios and continuously increased the types and quantities of objects to test the performance of our framework. The detection results of our framework in clutter scenes can be found in Fig. 7. The results show that our framework can meet the robot's grasping requirements in various scenarios, greatly improving the effectiveness of human-robot interaction.

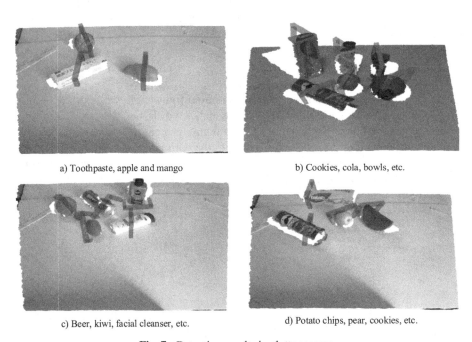

a) Toothpaste, apple and mango

b) Cookies, cola, bowls, etc.

c) Beer, kiwi, facial cleanser, etc.

d) Potato chips, pear, cookies, etc.

Fig. 7. Detection results in clutter scenes.

4.3 Evaluation of Robotic Trajectory Learning

To assess the motion module's performance, we utilized a motion capture device to record human motion trajectories and enabled the robot to learn from them. In order to generate a similar trajectory, we input the initial trajectory into DMP for learning and adjusted the starting and target points, as depicted in Fig. 8. By modifying the external force term, we could regulate the trajectory's shape and guide the robotic arm to write numbers of varying shapes based on the modified starting and ending points. As shown in Fig. 8, we conducted experiments in both simulated and real environments and achieved satisfactory outcomes.

In order to verify the effectiveness of our obstacle avoidance algorithm, we designed corresponding motion scenarios for the robot and set up obstacles along its path of movement, as shown in Fig. 9. The red trajectory represents the original path that would have resulted in a collision with the obstacle. In contrast, the black trajectory indicates the

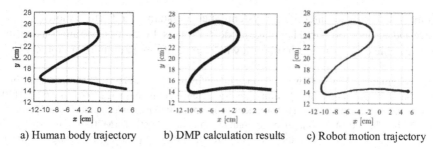

a) Human body trajectory   b) DMP calculation results   c) Robot motion trajectory

Fig. 8. Results of robot trajectory learning.

path after obstacle avoidance, which ensures safer execution of the robot arm's grasping and delivery tasks.

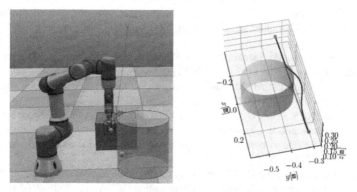

Fig. 9. Results of Robot Obstacle Avoidance Motion. (Color figure online)

5   Conclusion

This paper presents a multimodal combination framework for robotic grasping. Specifically, we employed ChatGPT as the bridge between humans and robots, inspired by the powerful performance of LLMs. With the powerful reasoning ability of ChatGPT, the robot is capable of effectively understanding human language commands and providing positive feedback. Additionally, we designed a visual detection module for the robot to process point cloud information, enabling it to reliably determine grasping poses for target objects. The results showed that our method performed well both in single-object scenarios and in more complex cluttered environments. Finally, we utilized the Learn from Demonstration approach, where human motions were captured using wearable devices and effectively used to teach the robot new skills.

Future research could focus on further perfecting the multimodal combination framework, as this study only provided a basic application of ChatGPT without integrating a real embedded artificial intelligence system. Such a system would offer a more comprehensive and autonomous large language model for robots. In addition, we are considering using wearable devices to teach robots a wider range of more complex motion skills.

Acknowledgments. This work was supported in part by the National key R&D program of China 2018AAA0100803, in part by the National Natural Science Foundation 62276090 and 62203150, in part by the Key Research and Development Program of Jiangsu under grants BK20192004B, in part by the China Postdoctoral Science Foundation under Grant 2021M701051, in part by the Jiangsu Province Excellent Post-doctoral Program 2022ZB192, in part by the Changzhou Basic Research Program (Application Program) CJ20220051, in part by the Guangdong Forestry Science and Technology Innovation Project under grant 2020KJCX005.

References

1. Suwa, S., et al.: Home-care professionals' ethical perceptions of the development and use of home-care robots for older adults in Japan. Int. J. Hum.-Comput. Interact. **36**, 1295–1303 (2020)
2. ten Pas, A., Gualtieri, M., Saenko, K., Platt, R.: Grasp pose detection in point clouds. Int. J. Robot. Res. **36**(13–14, SI), 1455–1473 (2017)
3. Kojima, T., Gu, S.S., Reid, M., Matsuo, Y., Iwasawa, Y.: Large language models are zero-shot reasoners, pp. 2205–11916 (2022)
4. Madaan, A., Zhou, S., Alon, U., Yang, Y., Neubig, G.: Language models of code are few-shot commonsense learners. arXiv e-prints, 2210–07128 (2022)
5. Liang, J., et al.: Code as policies: language model programs for embodied control. arXiv e-prints, 2209–07753 (2022)
6. Liang, H., et al.: PointNetGPD: detecting grasp configurations from point sets. In: 2019 IEEE International Conference on Robotics and Automation (ICRA), pp. 3629–3635 (2019)
7. Charles, R.Q., Su, H., Kaichun, M., Guibas, L.J.: PointNet: deep learning on point sets for 3d classification and segmentation. In: 30TH IEEE Conference on Computer Vision and Pattern Recognition (CVPR 2017), pp. 77–85 (2017)
8. Ni, P., Zhang, W., Zhu, X., Cao, Q.: PointNet++ grasping: learning an end-to-end spatial grasp generation algorithm from sparse point clouds. In: 2020 IEEE International Conference on Robotics and Automation (ICRA), pp. 3619–3625 (2020)
9. Qi, C.R., Yi, L., Su, H., Guibas, L.J.: PointNet plus plus: deep hierarchical feature learning on point sets in a metric space. In: Advances in Neural Information Processing Systems 30 (NIPS 2017), vol. 30 (2017)
10. Ambhore, S.: A comprehensive study on robot learning from demonstration. In: 2020 2nd International Conference on Innovative Mechanisms for Industry Applications (ICIMIA), pp. 291–299 (2020)
11. Ginesi, M., Meli, D., Calanca, A., Dall'Alba, D., Sansonetto, N., Fiorini, P.: Dynamic movement primitives: volumetric obstacle avoidance. In: 2019 19th International Conference on Advanced Robotics (ICAR), pp. 234–239 (2019)

Experimental Validation of an Interface for a Human-Robot Interaction Within a Collaborative Task

Maksim Mustafin[1](✉) [iD], Elvira Chebotareva[1] [iD], Hongbing Li[2] [iD],
and Evgeni Magid[1,3] [iD]

[1] Intelligent Robotics Department, Institute of Information Technology and Intelligent Systems,
Kazan Federal University, 35, Kremlyovskaya st., Kazan 420111, Russia
maksamustafin@kpfu.ru
[2] Department of Instrument Science and Engineering, Shanghai Jiao Tong University, Minhang,
Shanghai 200240, China
[3] Tikhonov Moscow Institute of Electronics and Mathematics, HSE-University, 34, Tallinn st.,
Moscow 123458, Russia

Abstract. This paper presents a prototype of a non-contact UR robot based Virtual Control (UR-VC) system for collaborative robots of the UR family, which is based on computer vision techniques and a virtual interaction interface. A control method involved specific hand movements within a field of view of a web camera, which was connected to a laptop with the running UR-VC system. We present the UR-VC system and the results of an experimental validation. To inquire if the UR-VC system is comfortable and user-friendly for an interaction with collaborative robots and to study opportunities for a further development and expansion directions of the system, we designed a test case that simulates a joint product assembly in a collaborative workspace. The constructed collaborative workspace included the UR3e robot, the laptop with the running UR-VC system and assembly parts for a collaborative task. 24 participants were involved in the experiments. First, the participants learned how to control the robot using the UR-VC system. After the training, all participants successfully controlled the robot using the proposed interface for performing the collaborative task. Participants' experience of operating the robot was analyzed via surveys, their unconstrained comments and video recordings of the experiments.

Keywords: Human-Robot Interaction · Human-Robot Collaboration · Collaborative Assembly · Virtual Control

1 Introduction

Currently, collaborative robotics has a great potential for application in industry and manufacturing [1, 2]. Automation with robots can significantly improve quality, safety, and efficiency of production processes [3]. However, full automation of processes can be difficult or impossible for various reasons [4]. Some stages of production may not be

A. Ronzhin et al. (Eds.): ICR 2023, LNAI 14214, pp. 23–35, 2023.
https://doi.org/10.1007/978-3-031-43111-1_3

automated and require a human intervention [5]. Additionally, full automation may be infeasible due to a high cost and complexity of an implementation. These are particularly relevant for small and medium-sized industries. In the latter case, a production process can be arranged in such a way that production steps can be shared between a human and a robot working collaboratively in a shared workspace [6]. An example would be a process that involves a collaborative assembly or processing of a product, where the product or its parts are passed alternatively between a human and a robot.

Human-robot collaboration (HRC) implies an existence of one or more communication methods between a human and a robot. A robot control system can process verbal and non-verbal operator signals [7] and may rely on speech, gesture, and gaze recognition, tactile control, or multimodal interfaces [8]. In some cases, the most convenient method for controlling a robot involves a non-verbal communication based on operator's gestures and movements. This approach enables both simple and complex interactions between an operator and a robot and helps to integrate robots into existing workflows.

In this paper, we present a new virtual control system based on computer vision and augmented reality (AR) techniques for non-contact control of a collaborative manipulator during joint assembly tasks. An experimental validation of the system demonstrated a successful HRC during a joint assembly task.

2 Related Work

Overviews of modern collaborative robots (cobots) used in industry and service fields demonstrated a broad variety of approaches and particular applications [9, 10]. Design issues of cobot control systems' reviews focus on existing sensor-based control methodologies [11] and consider general issues in the management of cobots [12].

A special place among cobot control systems is occupied by AR-based methods, which are a promising direction in industrial robotics. Costa et.al. [13] stated that replacing a purely manual control with a collaborative scenario using AR reduces a production cycle time and improves an operator's ergonomics and identified four types of user interfaces: head-mounted displays (HMD), projector-based interfaces, hand-held displays (HHDs), and Fixed Screens. They noted that HMDs and projector-based interfaces are used much more frequently compared to HHDs and Fixed Screens in research and emphasized that a usage of HMDs for AR in collaborative robotics may be hindered by hardware aspects, such as a narrow field of view, occlusions, and weight, which may have a negative impact on an operator's sense of safety. We believe this implies an emergence of risks associated with a negative impact on a user experience (UX) while a positive UX in human-robot interaction (HRI) is essential for an efficient organization of HRC processes [14].

When developing a contactless control interface for a cobot during a joint assembly, maintaining a balance between safety, efficiency, and ergonomics in a design of collaborative assembly processes is important [15], as well as design recommendations based on international standards, research, and real-world use cases [16]. Typically, performing joint assembly and processing tasks requires a human to perform some work manually, with their hands. As a result, for a collaborative assembly and processing, contactless methods of a robot control that do not necessitate a constant presence of operator's hands on a control panel are preferred. One of these methods is controlling a robot using gestures.

A significant part of modern gesture-based control of cobots relies on methods for classifying and recognizing gestures using machine learning techniques, including such particular examples as learning semantics in experiments with a gesture-based control system in a collaborative assembly task [17], a new taxonomy for gestures classification [18], an online static and dynamic gesture recognition framework for HRI [19], a robot-human interface [20] based on MediaPipe solution [21], and others.

In our previous work [22], we conducted a series of pilot experiments on gesture-based control of UR5e robot in a collaborative assembly task. The experiments revealed the general user satisfaction with the contactless control method using gestures, however, they identified a number of disadvantages of this approach. The first issue was a necessity to select a universal gesture system for the robot control. Even though all users successfully employed the gestures we had proposed for the control, some users noted that particular gestures were not quite familiar to them. In light of this, we encountered a challenge of fine-tuning a command set according to users' preferences. Simultaneously, expanding the gesture vocabulary requires additional research, which may not necessarily guarantee a development of a universal set of gestures that accommodates all users' preferences. The first disadvantage was a necessity to employ all fingers, which can affect a biomechanical load on a user's hand, their comfort level, and focus. As a number of commands increases, a user must not only operate different hand joints but also memorize all the commands.

Considering the abovementioned literature analysis and our own experimental experience, in order to develop a new interface for a virtual robot control system we abandoned the gesture-based approach in favor of a mixed method that involves AR elements and a single gesture of closing a thumb and a forefinger.

3 Materials and Methods

This section overviews our virtual control interface concept, a robot control system architecture, and a workcell configuration. Additionally, we describe a collaborative task that was used for the system testing.

Using our previous research as a starting point [22], we aimed to develop a new computer vision-based method for interaction and control of a cobot. The new approach was designed to be adaptable to a wide range of users and scalable to future needs, including new functionalities and features integration. It was important to develop an application, which does not generate haptic feedback but provides a feedback to a user via audio (application sounds) and visual signals (interface appearance changes).

The use of a contactless control of a cobot through a virtual interface during collaborative assembly tasks was supported by a number of arguments. Firstly, the contactless control reduces a biomechanical load on an operator; for example, when an operator controls a cobot using a teach pendant, the operator needs to hold it in a hand, which causes an arm muscles fatigue. Secondly, if the operator's hands are dirty, the contactless control prevents a further contamination of work area surfaces (the teach pendant, objects within the cobot workspace); thus, the contactless control allows operator's working environment to stay clean and tidy for a long time. Thirdly, to control the cobot with the teach pendant the operator needs to devote some time learning and practicing pendant's capabilities. Therefore, a user-friendly and intuitive application that uses computer vision and simple interaction commands (which may also include all functions of the teach pendant) will optimize time and efforts of the operator.

3.1   UR Robots – Virtual Control Application

UR robots – Virtual Control (UR-VC) application was programmed in Python3 and uses Pygame and Playsound libraries at the frontend. The Pygame was used to draw and animate interface elements. The Playsound was used to play predefined sounds when an operator selects a button or presses a button. The backend of UR-VC application employed CVZone, MediaPipe, OpenCV, and NumPy libraries for hand detection and data processing.

The UR-VC application User Interface (Figs. 1 and 2) contains the following elements:

1. A current robot program state (takes values "Playing", "Paused" or "Stopped").
2. A last command of a user (which button was clicked).
3. UR robot responses to user's commands (UR log).
4. "E-STOP" (Emergency Stop) button – a user can stop the robot immediately, which ends an execution of a current robot program.
5. "Power On" button turns on the robot.
6. "Play" button launches a robot program.
7. "Pause" button pauses a robot program.
8. A main cursor is located at a fingertip of a user's index finger in the interface of UR-VC. The main cursor allows a user to select any button.
9. A clicking cursor is located at a fingertip of a user's thumb in the interface. The user can click any button using this cursor and together with the main cursor.
10. A progress bar for clicking is designed to indicate a remaining time, which a user should keep his/her pointing fingers together in order to produce a button click. The bar was designed to exclude accidental and unintentional clicks.
11. "Next detail" button is responsible for sending the robot a command to proceed in order to assembly the next product (a fidget spinner). The button appears after clicking "Power On" button, waiting the robot to turn on and loading its program.

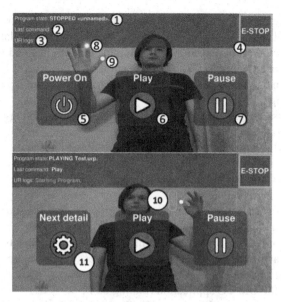

Fig. 1. UR-VC application User Interface.

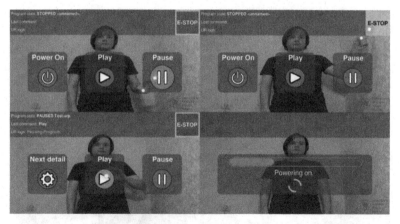

Fig. 2. Using UR-VC application showcase.

3.2 Workcell Description

A designed workcell included a robot table and a small additional table where necessary for experiments items were set up. The robot table allows placing objects on its top and fixing them with screws. The workcell included the following items (Fig. 3):

1. The UR3e manipulator; this collaborative robot has a small size, which improved participants' safety and left more free space within the workcell.
2. The starting location of the robot (marked with a A4 paper sheet with "Start" label); this was a location where the robot moved after launching a loaded program.

3. A waiting location of the robot for a command from the operator (marked with a A4 paper sheet with "Waiting for the "Next detail" command" label); this was a location where the robot moved after assembling one product and waited a user to click "Next detail" button in UR-VC application.
4. A felt-tip pen in the robot's gripper was used for drawing squares by the robot during the training stage for the participants.
5. Assembly parts, fidget spinner frames, were used for assembling the product (the fidget spinner) during the main stage.
6. A plastic mold for the fidget spinner frame for the collaborative assembly was a location where the robot placed a fidget spinner frame to assembly one product.
7. Assembly parts, 3D printed plastic bearings in a pallet, were used for assembling the product during the main stage.
8. A sheet of paper was attached to a robot's desktop for drawing squares on it during the training stage for the participants.
9. Felt-tip pens for participants for the training stage; the participants used these felt-tip pens for drawing on the paper inside the squares (that were drawn by the robot) during training stage.
10. A laptop with the UR-VC application running on it.
11. An experiment instruction listed steps for the participants to complete all stages of experiment.

   In addition, the workcell contained a siting chair, which participants could use at their will.

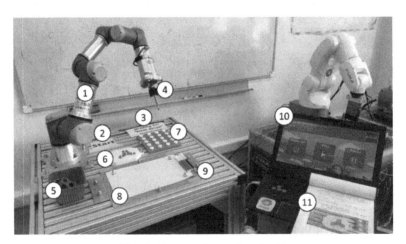

Fig. 3. The experimental workcell.

3.3 Collaborative Task

Collaborative assembly task is to assemble the product, the fidget spinner, using the UR3e robot. An operator takes the fidget spinner frame and puts it in the plastic mold for the robot. Next, operator waits for the robot to insert four plastic bearings into the fidget spinner frame (Fig. 4). In Fig. 5, the assembly parts and the finished product are presented.

The proposed in this paper collaborative assembly task is much simpler than the original task from our previous work [22]. For example, screws tightening by the UR5e robot in the original task made the experiment process rather long and difficult. Therefore, this time we intentionally simplified the original task to allow a participant concentrating on a developed UR-VC system evaluation rather than on the task complexity.

Fig. 4. The process of assembling the fidget spinner with the UR3e robot.

Fig. 5. Assembly parts and the finished product.

4   Experiment Description

This section describes the experimental setup aimed at testing the developed interface. The experiments had two stages: a training stage to teach the participants operating the system and the main experimental stage that was performed in order to evaluate the proposed system.

4.1   Training Stage

In total, the experiments involved 24 participants (Fig. 6): four laboratory members and 20 not professional robot operators. The participants were divided into two groups, which differed by dates of experiments. In the first stage (a learning stage) of the experiment, the participants learned to control the robot via the UR-VC application. The learning stage consisted of two parts: theoretical and practical.

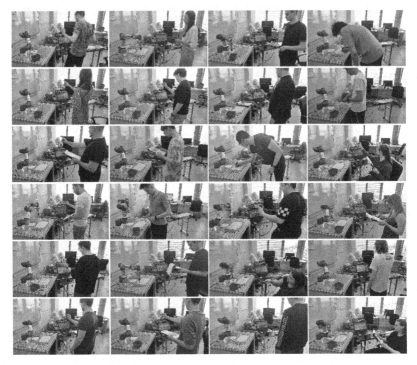

Fig. 6. All participants of the experiments.

In the theoretical part, the participants watched a prerecorded video, which taught basics of working with the UR-VC application. In the practical part the participants had to apply the obtained theoretical knowledge (of the theoretical part) in order to develop basic practical skills of working with the robot via the UR-VC application and get acquainted with a concept of a collaborative assembly by completing two tasks.

These two tasks required a sequential execution of steps (clicking the UR-VC buttons in a specific order and explaining outcomes of the clicks), which were described in the instruction. The first task allowed the participants to interact with the UR-VC application for the first time and to understand a correspondence of the robot's movement and the user commands. The second task was a simple collaborative task, in which the robot drew squares one by one with the felt-tip pen at a command of a participant, and the operator drew a number inside the square. A fragment of the participant training experiment is presented in Fig. 7.

Fig. 7. A participant of the experiment during the training stage.

4.2 Main Stage

A main stage or a collaborative assembly task stage was built around a comparison of a manual and a collaborative assembly of products by the participants. At a beginning, the participants need to assemble five products manually. Then they needed to assemble five fidget spinners with the UR3e robot using the UR-VC application. A participant took the fidget spinner frame and put it in the plastic mold for the robot. After that, the participant clicked "Next detail" button in the UR-VC application and waited for the robot to insert four plastic bearings into the fidget spinner frame. When the robot was done, the participant took out the finished product and put it in a special box. All these steps were listed in the instruction.

Additionally, during the collaborative assembly, the participants had to completely stop the robot program execution and move the last four bearings in a certain way so that the robot could immediately begin assembling the last fidget spinner after the program was launched. A fragment of the main part of the experiment is presented in Fig. 8.

Fig. 8. A participant of the experiment during the testing stage.

4.3 Evaluation

After the experiment, the participants were asked to take a survey that consisted of seven questions (Table 1). Additionally, the experiments were recorded and we could postprocess the videos in order to evaluate all informal comments of the participants.

Table 1. The survey questions.

Number	Question
Q1	Was it easier for you to assembly the products with the robot assistance than without the robot?
Q2	How accurately did the robot execute your commands?
Q3	How quickly did the robot respond to your commands?
Q4	How comfortable were you while working with the robot?
Q5	How good did the robot perform its task?
Q6	What disadvantages in the robot and the UR-VC app operation could you note (if any)?
Q7	What changes, improvements, innovations would you like to propose for the UR-VC application?

We used a 5-point Likert-type scale for questions Q1-Q5 and a free form for questions Q6 and Q7. During the participants' behavior observation, we evaluated the following factors: time spent for training (average ~16 min), time spent for performing the main collaborative task (average ~13 min), comments made during interactions with the robot and the users' reactions to unexpected situations.

5 Results

All participants successfully coped with the task of controlling the robot using the UR-VC application. Figure 9 presents the results of the survey with questions Q1–Q5. The x-axis (horizontal axis) represents the questions' number, while the y-axis (vertical axis) shows the number of participants who selected a specific answer option.

In general, the participants noted a positive experience of using the application and did not notice any significant disadvantages. However, some participants pointed out that the robot could work faster. One participant complained that it was not very convenient to turn around and click the buttons in the UR-VC after each operation with the robot. Another participant reported that sometimes it was inconvenient to control the UR-VC with a single hand.

The participants made valuable suggestions on the UR-VC application potential improvements, including adding a support for controlling the robot with both hands, adding a controlling hand selection, adding voice commands for emergency stop, enabling tracking of operator's performance of their part of the work in a collaborative assembly, and selecting a robot's operating speed mode.

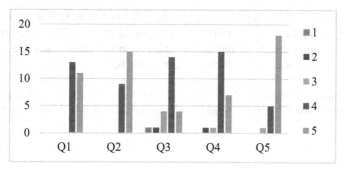

Fig. 9. The survey results. Avg.: Q1 – 4.5, Q2 – 4.6, Q3 – 3.8, Q4 – 4.2, Q5 – 4.7.

6   Discussion

To evaluate the experimental results, we conducted an analysis of the surveys and compared them with our previous research outcome where a pure gesture-based interface was employed [22]. The analysis demonstrated that the UR-VC application turned out to be more convenient, generic, intuitive, user-friendly, re-usable in collaborative assembly tasks and scalable then the previous gesture-based control system.

While observing the participants' behavior, we noted a number of interesting features. Even though some participants forgot or followed some steps in the instructions incorrectly, which caused unexpected situations (i.e., a participant forgot to put the fidget spinner frame in the plastic mold for the robot) during the assembly task, the participants still coped with it with a minimum of hints due to a fact that they quickly learned the basics of controlling the cobot using the UR-VC. To evaluate the participants' behavior in an unexpected situation, they were arbitrarily asked to suspend the robot's operation in the course of a task. Even though a proper button for suspending was not specified to them explicitly, all participants made a correct choice within the UR-VC interface.

No difference was observed in evaluations provided by participants with and without experience in robotic manipulators. Emphasized by the participants deficiencies mainly concerned the system response time and ergonomic requirements for the operator's workplace, e.g., suggesting different screen or emergency stop button locations with regard to the operator's position. These comments highlighted additional ergonomic requirements, which should be considered in HRC interfaces' development.

Overall, both the qualitative and quantitative assessments from users of the UR-VC application were significantly higher than the assessments obtained by the pure gesture-based interface [22].

7   Conclusion

In this study, we presented the results of experimental validation of a virtual interface for contactless control of the UR cobot within a joint assembly task. The results of experiments with 24 participants with and without robotic manipulation background indicated that people can effectively and rapidly learn a novel type of interaction with a robot in collaborative assembly tasks.

The new method of non-contact control of the UR robot turned out to be significantly more convenient for the users than a pure gesture-based interface [22]. The experiments emphasized the requirements for fine-tuning of ergonomics related parameters of virtual control applications for cobots, which is a part of our further research.

Acknowledgment. The reported study was funded by the Russian Science Foundation (RSF) and the Cabinet of Ministers of the Republic of Tatarstan according to the research project No. 22-21-20033.

References

1. Chuengwa, T.Y., Swanepoel, J.A., Kurien, A.M., Kanakana-Katumba, M.G., Djouani, K.: Research perspectives in collaborative assembly: a review. Robotics **12**(2), 37 (2023)
2. Bisen, A., Payal, H.: Collaborative robots for industrial tasks: a review. Mater. Today: Proc. **52**(Part 3), 500–504 (2022)
3. Rodríguez-Guerra, D., Sorrosal, G., Cabanes, I., Calleja, C.: Human-robot interaction review: challenges and solutions for modern industrial environments. IEEE Access **9**, 108557–108578 (2021)
4. Villani, V., Pini, F., Leali, F., Secchi, C.: Survey on human–robot collaboration in industrial settings: safety, intuitive interfaces, and applications. Mechatronics **55**, 248–266 (2018)
5. Galin, R., Meshcheryakov, R.: Review on human–robot interaction during collaboration in a shared workspace. In: Ronzhin, A., Rigoll, G., Meshcheryakov, R. (eds.) ICR 2019. LNCS, vol. 11659, pp. 63–74. Springer, Cham (2019). https://doi.org/10.1007/978-3-030-26118-4_7
6. Galin, R.R., Shiroky, A.A., Magid, E.A., Mescheriakov, R.V., Mamchenko, M.V.: Effective functioning of a mixed heterogeneous team in a collaborative robotic system. Inform. Autom. **20**(6), 1224–1253 (2021)
7. Mavridis, N.: A review of verbal and non-verbal human–robot interactive communication. Robot. Auton. Syst. **63**(1), 22–35 (2015)
8. Gustavsson, P., Holm, M., Syberfeldt, A., Wang, L.: Human-robot collaboration – towards new metrics for selection of communication technologies. Proc. CIRP **72**, 123–128 (2018)
9. Sultanov, R., Sulaiman, S., Li, H., Meshcheryakov, R., Magid, E.: A review on collaborative robots in industrial and service sectors. In: International Siberian Conference on Control and Communications (SIBCON), Tomsk, Russian Federation, pp. 1–7 (2022)
10. Dobrokvashina, A., Sulaiman, S., Zagirov, A., Chebotareva, E., Kuo-Hsien, H., Magid, E.: Human robot interaction in collaborative manufacturing scenarios: prospective cases. In: International Siberian Conference on Control and Communications (SIBCON), Tomsk, Russian Federation, pp. 1–6 (2022)
11. Cherubini, A., Navarro-Alarcon, D.: Sensor-based control for collaborative robots: fundamentals, challenges, and opportunities. Front. Neurorobot. **14**, 113 (2021)
12. Hameed, A., Ordys, A., Możaryn, J., Sibilska-Mroziewicz, A.: Control system design and methods for collaborative robots: review. Appl. Sci. **13**(1), 675 (2023)
13. Costa, G.M., Petry, M.R., Moreira, A.P.: Augmented reality for human–robot collaboration and cooperation in industrial applications: a systematic literature review. Sensors **22**(7), 2725 (2022)
14. Lindblom, J., Alenljung, B., Billing, E.: Evaluating the user experience of human–robot interaction. In: Jost, C., et al. (eds.) Human-Robot Interaction. SSBN, vol. 12, pp. 231–256. Springer, Cham (2020). https://doi.org/10.1007/978-3-030-42307-0_9

15. De Simone, V., Di Pasquale, V., Giubileo, V., Miranda, S.: Human-robot collaboration: an analysis of worker's performance. Proc. Comput. Sci. **200**, 1540–1549 (2022)
16. Gualtieri, L., Rauch, E., Vidoni, R., Matt, D.T.: Safety, ergonomics and efficiency in human-robot collaborative assembly: design guidelines and requirements. Proc. CIRP **91**, 367–372 (2020)
17. Shukla, D., Erkent, Ö., Piater, J.: Learning semantics of gestural instructions for human-robot collaboration. Front. Neurorobot. **12**, 7 (2018)
18. Quek, F.K.H.: Eyes in the interface. Image Vis. Comput. **13**, 511–525 (1995)
19. Simão, M., Gibaru, O., Neto, P.: Online recognition of incomplete gesture data to interface collaborative robots. IEEE Trans. Ind. Electron. **66**, 9372–9382 (2019)
20. Vysocky, A., Poštulka, T., Chlebek, J., Kot, T., Maslowski, J., Grushko, S.: Hand gesture interface for robot path definition in collaborative applications: implementation and comparative study. Sensors **23**, 4219 (2023)
21. Hand Gesture Recognition Using Mediapipe. https://github.com/Kazuhito00/hand-gesture-recognition-using-mediapipe. Accessed 01 Apr 2023
22. Mustafin, M., Chebotareva, E., Li, H., Martínez-García, E.A., Magid, E.: Features of interaction between a human and a gestures-controlled collaborative robot in an assembly task: pilot experiments. In: Proceedings of International Conference on Artificial Life and Robotics, pp. 158–162 (2023)

Fail It till You Make It: Error Expectation in Complex-Plan Execution for Service Robots

Luis Contreras[1], Jesus Savage[2(✉)], Stephany Ortuno-Chanelo[2], Marco Negrete[2], Arata Sakamaki[1], and Hiroyuki Okada[1]

[1] Tamagawa University, Machida, Tokyo 194-8610, Japan
[2] National Autonomous University of Mexico, Coyoacan, 04510 Mexico City, Mexico
robotssavage@gmail.com

Abstract. Domestic service robots (DSR) are devices aimed to carry out daily household chores. Recently, the range and difficulty of the activities they can perform are reaching amazing performances, frequently resulting in complex plans with several steps requiring many skills where errors are more likely to occur. In this paper, we introduce the concept of error expectation in complex plans for domestic service robots and propose a classification of DSR's tasks based on the abilities required for their execution. We also propose a recovery system where a type of feedback is chosen based on error expectation and DSR task type. We test our proposal in the context of an object manipulation task and discuss how error expectation contributes to a good feedback choice. An action involving several robot skills, namely navigation, human and object recognition, natural language processing, etc., was illustrated by the "take" action. The video showing the complete execution of a complex command by a robot using error recovery is presented.

Keywords: Service Robots · Action Planning · Error Expectation

1 Introduction

Autonomous service robots need several skills – such as motion planning in dynamic environments, object recognition and manipulation, human-robot interaction, and real-time awareness – that result from the combination of a number of actions, sub-actions, and behaviours. These skills have been continuously evaluated in domestic environments and put into practice in competitions such as Robocup@Home [1], RoCKIn@Home [2], and World Robot Summit [3], where the difficulty of the tasks increases each year to challenge the state-of-the-art technique. Nowadays, the tasks a service robot has to perform involve the integration of many skills, as individual systems can't provide all the information required to solve a given problem.

Supplementary Information The online version contains supplementary material available at https://doi.org/10.1007/978-3-031-43111-1_4.

In [4] it was shown that from any given spoken command, through a semantic reasoning module, it is possible to generate a series of actions that allow a service robot to perform single tasks such as "Put the crackers on the kitchen table", "Tell me the name of the woman in the kitchen", and "Pour some cereals in the bowl". Then, a rule-based system is used for high-level reasoning in more complex tasks by combining a series of low-level behaviour methods, seen as reactive algorithms that solve local problems using a number of finite steps. One important outcome of this evaluation is that we observe a decrease in performance while the number of skills necessary to perform a specific task increases due to the conditional probabilities of success given by each sub-task. While it has been shown how a supervisor system improves the performance of the robot by making new plans in unforeseen situations by calling the action again, active perception in low-level behaviours helps to solve the task without changing the plan by actively updating the state of the robot and the environment when executing a sub-task and or reacting when an unexpected situation arises.

Considering a full planning system, from a given command we obtain a robot plan – consisting of several steps, where each step is a combination of several skills and behaviours –, in this paper, we introduce error expectation during plan execution for robot recovery while performing such plan; we present our results in the object manipulation problem where error detection and fast error recovery, as well as continuous environment updates, result in a fundamental feature to complete a task with the best performance.

2   Related Work

Recently, RLBench, a test platform for several manipulation applications, has been presented in [5] where the authors use a simulator with a fixed robot arm on a surface and an upper RGBD camera and an eye-in-hand monocular camera, and they feature 100 different tasks providing proprioceptive and visual observations. Similarly, in [6] the authors present Ravens, a simulated benchmark with ten manipulation tasks, mainly focusing on the "transportation" skills, i.e., tasks that executes a sequence of spatial displacements.

Towards task generalization, CLIPort [7] propose an end-to-end framework that is capable of solving a variety of language-specified tabletop tasks from packing unseen objects to folding cloths, all without any explicit representations of object poses, instance segmentation, memory, symbolic states, or syntactic structures; this work combines the manipulation skills of Transporter [6] with the image representations and semantic understanding given by CLIP [8].

However, based on the works of [9] and [10] on scaling law trends, in [8] the authors raise several concerns, not only considering the size of the dataset and the amount of compute used for training, but also in the bias that deep learning models might introduce through generalization in large datasets; regarding domestic robots, this bias might result in a single way to perform a task without considering users' will – task performance generalization in personal robots might blur individual intentions and expectations and cause not only annoyance and frustration but also accidents and serious injuries.

More general works towards service robots are Habitat 2.0 [11], sDSPL [12], and BEHAVIOR [13]. In Habitat 2.0, the authors present a simulated home environment where the robot can perform several tasks; however, no specific rules and regulations are provided. In this sense, in sDSPL, the authors propose the simulation Domestic Standard Platform League (sDSPL) as a benchmark to evaluate the performance of service robots while executing a task; they focused on standardization and evaluation of service robots while performing a general purpose task to close the gap between robot competitions and research. Finally, in BEHAVIOR the authors present their "Benchmark for Everyday Household Activities in Virtual, Interactive, and Ecological Environments"; they propose 100 indoor chores in realistic environments such as "Assembling gift baskets", "Cleaning the bedroom", "Installing a modem", or "Sorting groceries". They provide 500 human demonstrations in virtual reality and propose a number of a set of metrics to measure task progress and efficiency, absolute and relative to human demonstrators.

To address this problem, we are working on complex action planning by combining general-purpose service robot models based on expert systems (as in [4]) with standard and data-driven skill models (e.g., CLIPort [7]) and then, evaluate them in real scenarios explicitly designed to test such systems, like robot competitions. Furthermore, although deep learning systems generalize well, they should serve to create local plans and their execution should still be performed considering human intentions and using active reasoning as in [14–16] to encompass the specificities of the current scenario and to handle unexpected behaviours.

3 Error Expectation in General Purpose Service Robot (GPSR)

The presence of service robots in domestic environments is increasing recently and, in consequence, the familiarity of users and the difficulty of the tasks that might request. From developing individual skills to performing complex tasks, several platforms have been proposed recently aimed at solving general-purpose domestic tasks. However, although many platforms and tests have been proposed, they mainly focus on single tasks at a time, like "Take out the garbage", "Storing groceries", "Clean up", "Welcoming Visitors", and so on. Furthermore, many of those tests are performed by static robots, consisting mainly of an rgb(d) camera and a robotic arm manipulating objects on a surface.

However, one key challenge towards autonomous service robots has been proposed in the RoboCup at Home competition, namely, the General Purpose Service Robot (GPSR) test, where a number of general-purpose commands are randomly generated using a [EE]GPSR Command Generator and grammars publicly available at [17].

In short, in this test, there are three categories, according to their difficulty. In category I, the service robots must solve easy tasks involving basic skills such as indoor navigation, grasping known objects, answering questions (from the predefined set of questions), etc. (e.g., "Bring me the apple juice from the counter", "Tell me how many beverages are on the shelf", "Tell me the name of the person at the door"). In category II, robots must solve tasks with a moderate degree of difficulty. This category involves following a human, indoor navigation in crowded environments, manipulation, and recognition of alike objects, finding a calling person (waving or shouting), etc. (e.g., "Tell me how many beverages on the shelf are red", "Count the waiving people in the living room", "Follow Anna at the entrance"). Finally, in category III, the robots must understand challenging tasks dealing with incomplete information, environmental reasoning, feature detection, natural language processing, outdoor navigation, pouring, opening doors, etc. Examples are: "Pour some cereals in the bowl", "Go to the bathroom (the bathroom door is closed)", "Bring me the milk from the microwave (the milk is inside the microwave)".

Moreover, there is also an Extended GPSR (the EEGPSR) test, where the robot has to perform three simple actions, given as a single sentence, and validate the individual commands through HRI. Some examples are:

- Go to the kitchen counter, take the coke, and bring it to me.
- Bring the chips to Mary at the sofa, tell her the time, and follow her.
- Find a person in the living room, guide them to the kitchen, and follow them.

In [4], we generate a base set of robot skills, namely, Speech Recognition (SR), Navigation (NV), Person Recognition (PR), Object Recognition (OR), and Object Manipulation (OM), and we classify the [EE]GPSR command into several categories that require a subset of skills to be solved:

- Follow person: SR, NV, PR
- Guide person: SR, NV, PR
- Gender person: SR, NV, PR
- Person pose: SR, NV, PR
- Name Person: SR, NV, PR
- How many people: SR, NV, PR
- Person instructions: SR, NV, PR
- How many objects: SR, NV, OR
- Feature object: SR, NV, OR
- Bring me object: SR, NV, OR, OM
- Place object: SR, NV, OR, OM
- Handover object: SR, NV, PR, OR, OM

4   Experiments and Results

In the remaining of this work, we will focus on the object manipulation problem to illustrate how to introduce error expectation to handle unexpected behaviours while solving this problem, depending on the strategy to follow.

4.1   Object Recognition

We propose a series of strategies for object recognition in human-made environments and evaluate the performance in the object recognition task; the proposed object-recognition strategies are illustrated in Fig. 1 and are described as follows.

Random Distance
As a baseline, we propose to detect objects from a fixed distance close to the location of the object determined by the navigation strategy, i.e., a search point that allows future object manipulation without collisions. A clear advantage of this strategy is that object

a)   b)   c)

Fig. 1. Robot-object observation strategies, namely a) random distance, b) close distance, and c) hand distance.

manipulation follows immediately after object recognition a disadvantage is the object's low resolution in the images.

Close Distance

Here, the robot gets the closest to the location of the object, sometimes by rotating its head by 90° so the hand does not occlude its visibility. An advantage of using this strategy is that the image resolution improves; however, several disadvantages surges such as limited field of view and limited configuration space and therefore different reference systems between the recognition and manipulation poses, increasing the performance time.

Hand Distance

In this strategy, the robot first performs object detection and manipulation and then recognizes the object in its hand. An advantage is the constant object resolution in the recognition step but at the cost of an increased manipulation time consumption per object.

We run a series of experiments in a similar setup, where objects were located inside a shelf at two different levels. For the random distance, we located the robot at 80 cm from the edge within a small odometry error; then, for the close-distance case, objects were located in four positions within the shelf, namely bottom and middle levels in the left and right side and the robot gets the closest to each object so the objects are still visible for the upper camera. Finally, in the case of hand distance, the robot first detects and grasps the objects and then recognizes them. We use the same out-of-the-box CNN for object detection for all strategies to objectively assess the performance of each strategy, as we are not interested in the recognition rate but in assessing if there is a performance variation if we change the robot behaviour. Table 1 shows the recognition rate after 20 trials per strategy.

Table 1. Recognition rate using different robot-object interaction strategies after 20 trials.

	Interaction strategy		
	Random Distance	Close Distance	Hand Distance
Performance	0.40	0.40	0.45

From the results, it can be observed that the hand-distance strategy slightly performs better, we assume that it's due to the more constant point of view while in the other cases highly depends on the object's initial pose.

4.2 Object Detection

To assess the importance of error expectation in robot task execution, we evaluate it in the object manipulation task, where we compare several feedback methods while cleaning a room (Fig. 2) as follows. We use Feedback I as a baseline, where the robot detects the objects using the RGBD camera, and grasps an object to place it in a free spot on a given shelf. Finally, the robot goes back close to the objects and starts the detection-and-grasping process again. There is no tactile feedback, and therefore dropping is not detected, in consequence, the robot performs the placing routine even though it has no object in its hand. Furthermore, there is no time limit in this baseline, so the robot will perform the routine until no object is detected on the floor.

Feedback II includes an attempt constraint, where the robot performs object detection and grasping a limited number of times. Then, Feedback III introduces a memory feature by detecting the objects only once and saving their positions for the remaining task; similarly, it aims to grasp an object a limited number of times. Feedback IV uses the force sensor to detect an unsuccessful grasping and, in case of a drop, the robot searches for the objects once more and aims to grasp them without performing any unnecessary delivery; again, the time limit is used but not the memory feature.

Finally, in Feedback V, within an attempt's limit, the robot searches for the objects and saves their position and then, it aims to grasp them. If a successful grasping is detected, the robot delivers the object and goes back to take the next object without searching for them again. However, when a dropping is detected, the robot searches for the remaining objects again and updates its knowledge.

In our experimental setup, the robot has to place five objects lying on the floor on three different shelves, and a neutral shelf in case a designated shelf is full (i.e., no free

Fig. 2. In the Tidy up task, the robot has to clean the room by placing the mislocated objects in their corresponding shelves.

space detected), as shown in Fig. 2. We use common objects found in a house, such as soft and hard toys, cards, food, and drinks. For every feedback method, we perform ten trials (50 experiments in total with five objects per trial); some setup samples are shown in Fig. 3. Regarding the attempts' constraint, for the five objects, the robot is allowed to drop them at most seven times. Results are shown in Table 2.

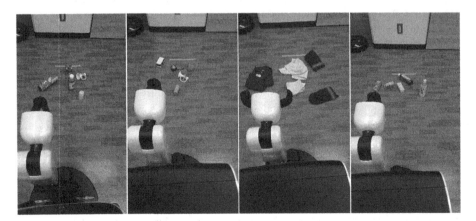

Fig. 3. Different samples of the objects used in the experiments.

It can be observed that, except for the one-time memory only feedback method (Feedback III), while the success performance is not significantly different, the time

Table 2. Average performance in the object manipulation task where the robot has to take objects on the floor to their correct location. The performance indicates the ratio of successfully delivered to the total number of objects in ten trials per method with five objects per trial.

	Manipulation feedback				
	I None	II Attempts	III Memory + Attempts	IV Force + Attempts	V Force + Memory + Attempts
Performance	0.82 ± 0.19	0.76 ± 0.18	0.54 ± 0.28	0.80 ± 0.20	0.82 ± 0.15
Time consumption [min]	8.17 ± 3.99	7.56 ± 1.47	4.95 ± 0.57	6.39 ± 1.42	5.53 ± 0.91

performance does. We explain it as follows. Regarding the baseline (Feedback method I), a perfect performance was not reached as some objects were very reflective or, after dropping, they rolled out of the field of view, so the RGBD camera was not able to detect them. Besides, some objects were very slippery (such as glass jars) and therefore they required many attempts to be grasped (expressed as a high time variance because from none to several of these objects could be randomly included in a given trial).

While introducing the attempts' constraint (Feedback II) slightly reduces the performance, the variance in time is decreased, as objects that require many grasping attempts are the most difficult and an early stop prevents them to continue the process until those objects move out of the field of view. On the other hand, although the one-time memory method (Feedback III) reduces the time consumption drastically, as the objects have to be detected only once, the performance is reduced as well because the objects near or on the dropping point in general change their pose and therefore the memory results outdated. Then, tactile Feedback method III reduces time consumption as no false delivery has to be performed. Importantly, this method represents a naive approach where we save the environment state once to perform the task at hand; however, we see that, given some small errors in the navigation system, future attempts result in unsuccessful and therefore it proves the necessity of an active feedback strategy. Finally, the multimodal Feedback method V takes all the advantages, reaching a similar performance to the baseline but in a significantly shorter time, as no false deliveries are performed, and few object detection are done (i.e., only in the presence of a dropping the memory is updated), and an early stop is used for hard-to-grasp objects.

Moreover, it is easy to calculate the probability of success in the object detection and manipulation problem as a joint probability of any of the components, depending on the strategy to follow; for example, given the results in Tables 1 and 2, taking any object using force feedback would result in:

$$p = pskill = pmanipulation = 0.80.$$

Similarly, taking the correct object from a random distance and using force feedback, would result in the skill joint probability:

$$p = pskill = pdetection \times pmanipulation,$$

$$p = 0.40 \times 0.80 = 0.32.$$

With these results, different strategies can be considered, such as finding a minimum or maximum number of trials to deliver the right object before giving up; also, it can be highlighted the weakest skills in the whole process and focus efforts to improve their performance. For example, the expectation E of the number of trials to the first occurrence of successful performance with skill probability p in a sequence of trials is:

$$E = 1/p.$$

Furthermore, if we model the probability of *success* and *failure* as a binomial distribution, the probability P of x successes in n trials given a skill probability p is defined as

$$P(x) = {}_nC_x \cdot p^x \cdot (1 - p)^{n-x}.$$

In specific, while executing a robot plan, we move to the next step after the first *success* in the previous one and, therefore, $x = 1$ and ${}_nC_x = n$, then

$$P(x = 1) = n \cdot p \cdot (1 - p)^{n-x}.$$

With this expression, we can get the number n of trials required to successfully perform a skill with a desired success probability P given the skill performance probability (or joint probability) p. After those trials, we can say that the robot is unable to perform the task and request human assistance or stop the task execution.

To summarize our approach, in an environment as in Fig. 4, from an action planer, given the following command: "Go to the living room, find Luis, and give him some chips", we get a robot plan consisting of several actions, namely:

- go to large table in living room;
- take chips;
- go to living room center in living room;
- deliver the object to Luis.

Where each of the actions requires one or several robot skills, including navigation, person and object recognition, natural language processing, and so on – in this work, we illustrate these concepts for the "take" action. In [18] you can observe a full performance of a complex command using error recovery.

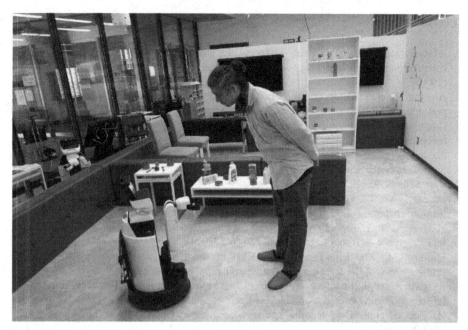

Fig. 4. Experimental setup as in [3] for the GPSR test from the RoboCup at Home competition where the robot should attend a complex command.

5 Conclusions

In this work, we aimed at solving general-purpose tasks by introducing error expectation in complex planning execution. In specific, we illustrate our approach in the object manipulation task, where we work towards improving the performance when using service robots by adding active reasoning; this includes testing several points of view, by moving the robot's base and or head and by first grasping the object and then observe it at a fixed distance in the robot's hand. The reason for that is that lately, it seems that robots are being seen as external agents that move around an environment and not as intelligent agents that can actually interact in it and even alter it to its best convenience (sometimes in a way a human can't do) when performing (and if allowed by) a given task. We consider a plan as a series of steps, and each step can consist of one or several skills; each skill has a probability of success, and the joint probability would result in an average performance. By determining these probabilities, a robot can recover from unexpected behaviours or give up after a specific number of attempts.

Acknowledgements. This work has been supported by the project, JPNP20006, commissioned by the New Energy and Industrial Technology Development Organization (NEDO) and by PAPIIT-DGAPA UNAM under Grant IG-101721.

References

1. Wisspeintner, T., Van Der Zant, T., Iocchi, L., Schiffer, S.: RoboCup@Home: scientific competition and benchmarking for domestic service robots. Interact. Stud. **10**(3), 392–426 (2009)
2. Amigoni, F., et al.: Competitions for benchmarking: task and functionality scoring complete performance assessment. IEEE Robot. Autom. Mag. **22**(3), 53–61 (2015)
3. Contreras, L., Yamamoto, T., Matsusaka, Y., Okada, H.: Towards general purpose service robots: world robot summit partner robot challenge. Adv. Robot. **36**, 812–824 (2022). https://doi.org/10.1080/01691864.2022.2109428
4. Savage, J., et al.: Semantic reasoning in service robots using expert systems. Robot. Auton. Syst. **114**, 77–92 (2019)
5. James, S., Ma, Z., Arrojo, D.R., Davison, A.J.: RLBench: the robot learning benchmark & learning environment. IEEE Robot. Autom. Lett. **5**(2), 3019–3026 (2020)
6. Zeng, A., et al.: Transporter networks: rearranging the visual world for robotic manipulation. In: Conference on Robot Learning, pp. 726–747 (2021)
7. Shridhar, M., Manuelli, L., Fox, D.: CLIPort: what and where pathways for robotic manipulation. In: Conference on Robot Learning, pp. 894–906 (2022)
8. Radford, A., et al.: Learning transferable visual models from natural language supervision. In: International Conference on Machine Learning, pp. 8748–8763 (2021)
9. Hestness, J., et al.: Deep learning scaling is predictable, empirically. arXiv preprint arXiv:1712.00409 (2017)
10. Kaplan, J., et al.: Scaling laws for neural language models. arXiv preprint arXiv:2001.08361 (2020)
11. Szot, A., et al.: Habitat 2.0: training home assistants to rearrange their habitat. Adv. Neural Inf. Process. Syst. **34**, 251–266 (2021)
12. Contreras, L., Matsusaka, Y., Yamamoto, T., Okada, H.: sDSPL-towards a benchmark for general-purpose task evaluation in domestic service robots. In: The 39th Annual Conference of the Robotics Society of Japan (2021)
13. Srivastava, S., et al.: Behavior: benchmark for everyday household activities in virtual, interactive, and ecological environments. In: Conference on Robot Learning, pp. 477–490 (2022)
14. Vazquez, E., Contreras, L., Okada, H., Iwahashi, N.: Multimodal human intention-driven robot motion control in collaborative tasks. In: 38-th Annual Conference of the Robotics Society of Japan (2020)
15. Contreras, L., Muto, Y., Okada, H., Sakamaki, A.: Robot-object interaction strategies for object recognition. In: 37th Annual Conference of the Robotics Society of Japan (2019)
16. Contreras, L., Mayol-Cuevas, W.: Towards CNN map representation and compression for camera relocalisation. In: Proceedings of the IEEE Conference on Computer Vision and Pattern Recognition Workshops, pp. 292–299 (2018)
17. RoboCup@Home Command Generator. https://github.com/kyordhel/GPSRCmdGen. Accessed 19 May 2023
18. Fail it till you make it: error expectation in complex-plan execution for service robots. https://youtu.be/rhJ-dcahfqc. Accessed 19 May 2023

Moving Person Detection Based on Modified YOLOv5

Xin Shen[⊠] [iD], Guo Wu [iD], and Vadim Lukyanov [iD]

Bauman Moscow State Technical University, 5/1, 2nd Baumanskaya st., Moscow 105005, Russia
slamshenxin@gmail.com

Abstract. Visual Dynamic SLAM (Simultaneous Localization and Mapping) is a fundamental technology for intelligent mobile systems, enabling applications in robotics, augmented reality, and self-driving cars. This paper presents a novel approach to improve the performance of Visual Dynamic SLAM by integrating the YOLOv5 object detection framework with attention mechanisms (CBAM) and a BiFPN (Bidirectional Feature Pyramid Network) structure. The dynamic feature points, which are located in the bounding box of the dynamic object, are removed in the tracking thread, and only the static feature points are used to estimate the position of the camera. The primary focus is on improving the detection performance of dynamic objects, particularly persons, and addressing challenges such as occlusion and small object detection. Overall, the integration of YOLOv5 with attention mechanisms and a BiFPN structure presents a significant advancement in visual dynamic SLAM. The proposed approach enhances the detection of persons, addresses challenges related to small objects and occlusion, and improves the overall performance of the system in dynamic environments. These findings demonstrate the effectiveness of the proposed methodology and its potential for real-world applications in various domains, including robotics, augmented reality, and self-driving cars.

Keywords: CBAM Attention Mechanism · Bidirectional Feature Pyramid Network · Person Detection · Occlusion · Dynamic SLAM · YOLO Detector

1 Introduction

In the last few decades, visual SLAM techniques have gained significant interest from both the computer vision and robotic communities. Many variants of these techniques have started to make an impact in a wide range of applications, including robot navigation and augmented reality. However, most existing visual SLAM techniques assume a static environment, limiting their applicability in real-world scenarios. Detecting moving persons accurately and efficiently is a crucial task in computer vision, such as the dynamic SLAM problem. Traditional object detection methods face challenges in dynamic environments, including occlusion and small object detection.

Currently, person detection in computer vision faces a trade-off between accuracy and real-time performance. Existing approaches typically fall into two categories: two-stage detectors that offer high accuracy but lack real-time capability, which is not suitable

A. Ronzhin et al. (Eds.): ICR 2023, LNAI 14214, pp. 47–58, 2023.
https://doi.org/10.1007/978-3-031-43111-1_5

for SLAM tasks, and one-stage detectors that are fast but suffer from reduced performance, particularly in cases of occlusion and detecting small-sized people, which is dangerous with potential chance of collision. These enhancements can focus on two key aspects. Firstly, incorporating advanced attention mechanisms such as spatial and channel attention can help the detector better capture and leverage context information, allowing it to handle occlusion scenarios more effectively. Secondly, by incorporating more advanced neck structure such as BiFPN [1], the detector can effectively capture both local details and global context, leading to improved performance in detecting small and distant persons.

To address these limitations, this paper proposes a novel approach for moving person detection using a modified YOLOv5 framework that incorporates the attention mechanism CBAM (Convolutional Block Attention Module) [2] and the BiFPN (Bidirectional Feature Pyramid Network) structure. The proposed approach, based on human detection and the use of the YOLOv5 detector, has significant potential for application in robot navigation. This approach allows robots to efficiently detect people in their environment and make appropriate decisions based on the information they discover. The use of modified YOLOv5 model provides high accuracy and processing speed, which are important factors for real-time robots.

The main contributions of this paper are listed as follows:

- We integrate CBAM into YOLOv5, which can help the network to find region of interest in images that have large region coverage.
- We propose a modified YOLOv5 framework that incorporates the BiFPN structure as the neck part for moving person detection.
- We present comprehensive experimental results demonstrating the superior performance of our approach compared to existing methods in terms of accuracy, robustness, and small object detection capabilities.

The remainder of this paper is organized as follows. Section 2 provides an overview of related work in object detection. Section 3 describes the proposed methodology in detail, explaining the modifications made to the YOLOv5 framework and the integration of CBAM and BiFPN. Section 4 presents the experimental setup, datasets introduction, and evaluation used to assess the performance of our model. Finally, in Sect. 5 concludes the paper and highlights future research directions in the field of moving person detection based on YOLOv5 with attention mechanisms and the BiFPN structure.

2 Related Works

2.1 Dynamic SLAM Based on Deep Learning

Most state-of-the-art SLAM systems are not able to handle dynamic scenarios, as they were designed with a static environment assumption [3]. The Visual SLAM systems that deal with dynamic content in the scene usually treat it as noise and filter it. With the rapid development of deep learning technology in the field of computer vision, object recognition technology is being increasingly applied in the field of robot navigation.

One approach called DynaSLAM [3] employed by Berta Bescos et al. involves utilizing deep learning to detect and localize dynamic objects, such as people in indoor situations. They have used the Mask R-CNN [4] model in their work, which unfortunately incurs a significant computational cost and cannot operate in real-time scenarios. It is worth noting that Mask R-CNN is a two-stage object detector [4], known to be slower compared to one-stage detectors like the YOLO family [5–8]. In our work, our model is modified from the famous version of YOLO series, YOLOv5s, until now, it is still one of the most famous and effective SOTA in object detection [9].

2.2 Person Detection in Indoor Environments

From the perspective of components, object detectors usually consist of two parts, an CNN-based backbone, used for image feature extraction, and the other part is detection head used to predict the class and bounding box for object. In addition, the object detectors developed in recent years often insert some layers between the backbone and the head, people usually call this part the neck of the detector.

Backbone. The backbone that are often used include EfficientNet [10], ResNet [11], etc., rather than networks designed by ourselves. Because these networks have proven that they have strong feature extraction capabilities on classification and other issues.

Neck. The neck is designed to make better use of the features extracted by the backbone. It reprocesses and rationally uses the feature maps extracted by Backbone at different stages. Usually, a neck consists of several bottom-up paths and several top-down paths. Neck is a key link in the target detection framework. Now commonly used path-aggregation blocks in neck are: FPN [12], PANet [13].

Head. As a classification network, the backbone cannot complete the positioning task, and the head is designed to be responsible for detecting the location and category of the object by the features maps extracted from the backbone.

Deep learning already became the mainstream method to realize person detection in different situations, in [14] Chloe Eunhyang Kim et al. listed the most popular embedded deep learning methods for person detection, and pointed that neither of these models nail the tradeoff between speed and accuracy. In [15] Linxiang Zhao et al. proposed a new model based on YOLOv3 to enhance its performance on person detection, but the test dataset they have used are all in good visibility conditions, without significant occlusions, as expected in dynamic SLAM problems. In other work such as [16–18], they also began to try use some good techniques to enhance the YOLO neural network such as new loss function to guide the optimization of the class to which the object belongs, or maybe exchange some small module structures such as SPP to make it could obtain more feature-rich image information. But the occlusion problem or small object detection task still could not be handled so well. Some research [17] focus on other object detection showed us that to make a good and specific dataset for our own situation is quite beneficial for us. In [18] Jiahui Sun et al. have begun to use attention mechanism into YOLO model, but how to choose a best or most suitable attention mechanism for specific scenario still need to be confirmed.

3   New Model Architecture and Methodology

3.1   Overview of YOLOv5 Network

The YOLO (You Only Look Once) network model [5–8] is an algorithm that can be used for target detection. Compared to two-stage detectors, one-stage YOLO series algorithms have much greater advantages in running speed, faster and more efficient.

YOLO provides the classes of the detected objects, 2D bounding boxes with their corresponding positions and a confidence number for each box. At present, the YOLOv5 is mainly divided into four network models, which are YOLOv5s, YOLOv5m, YOLOv5l, and YOLOv5x. Among them, the YOLOv5s network model is the base model with shallow depth, and the narrowest width of the feature map compared to the other three models. Among these five models, we selected the smallest and fastest pre-trained model YOLOv5s to meet our requirements for speed.

3.2   Convolutional Block Attention Module (CBAM)

CBAM [2] is a simple but effective attention module. It is a lightweight module that can be integrated into most CNN architectures, and it can be trained in an end-to-end manner. The attention mechanism CBAM enhances the model's ability to selectively focus on relevant information, which is beneficial for occlusion problem. Given a feature map, CBAM sequentially infers the attention map along two separate dimensions of channel and spatial, and then multiplies the attention map with the input feature map to perform adaptive feature refinement. The structure of the CBAM module is shown in the Figs. 1, 2 and 3.

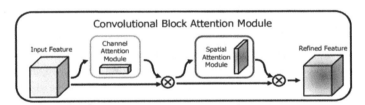

Fig. 1. The structure of CBAM.

The CAM (Channel Attention Module) exploits the interdependencies between channels within a feature map, enabling the network to learn channel-wise importance weights. It achieves this by utilizing a global pooling operation to capture channel-wise statistics, followed by a series of fully connected layers that generate channel attention weights.

$$\mathbf{M_c}(F) = \sigma\left(MLP(AvgPool(\mathbf{F})) + MLP(MaxPool(\mathbf{F}))\right)$$

$$= \sigma\left(\mathbf{W}_1\left(\mathbf{W}_0\left(\mathbf{F}_{avg}^c\right)\right) + \mathbf{W}_1\left(\mathbf{W}_0(\mathbf{F}_{max}^c)\right)\right), \tag{1}$$

where σ denotes the sigmoid function, $\mathbf{W}_0 \in \mathbb{R}^{C/r \times C}$, and $\mathbf{W}_1 \in \mathbb{R}^{C \times C/r}$. Note that the MLP weight, $\mathbf{W}_0$ and $\mathbf{W}_1$, are shared for both inputs and the ReLU activation function is followed by $\mathbf{W}_0$.

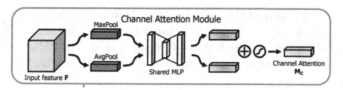

Fig. 2. The structure of CAM.

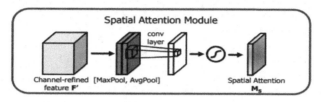

Fig. 3. The structure of SAM.

On the other hand, the SAM (Spatial Attention Module) captures spatial dependencies by examining the relationships between spatial locations within a feature map.

$$\mathbf{M_s}(F) = \sigma\left(f^{7\times7}([\text{AvgPool}(\mathbf{F}); \text{MaxPool}(\mathbf{F})])\right)$$
$$= \sigma\left(f^{7\times7}\left(\left[\mathbf{F_{avg}^s}; \mathbf{F_{max}^s}\right]\right)\right), \tag{2}$$

where σ denotes the sigmoid function and $f^{7\times7}$ represents a convolution operation with the filter size of 7×7.

3.3 Bidirectional Feature Pyramid Network (BiFPN)

Furthermore, we introduce the BiFPN [1] structure into the modified YOLOv5 framework. The BiFPN enhances multi-scale feature fusion, which is essential for handling small object detection. By incorporating the BiFPN, the model gains the ability to capture context and spatial information from different scales, resulting in improved localization and detection performance. The proposal FPN [12] solves the problem of multi-scale in target detection and greatly improves the detection performance of small targets. Compared with the traditional FPN network, BiFPN adds skip connections between the input and output feature in the same layer [6]. Because of the same scales, adding skip connections can better extract and transfer feature information. The structure of BiFPN is shown in Fig. 4.

$$P_6^{td} = \text{Conv}\left(\frac{w_1 \cdot P_6^{in} + w_2 \cdot \text{Resize}\left(P_7^{in}\right)}{w_1 + w_2 + \epsilon}\right) \tag{3}$$

$$P_6^{out} = \text{Conv}\left(\frac{w_1' \cdot P_6^{in} + w_2' \cdot P_6^{td} + w_3' \cdot \text{Resize}\left(P_5^{out}\right)}{w_1' + w_2' + w_3' + \epsilon}\right) \tag{4}$$

The parameter w is a learned parameter that distinguishes the importance of different features during the feature fusion process, somewhat similar to an attention mechanism. In summary, BiFPN can be described as an enhanced version of PANet, which incorporates repeated bidirectional cross-scale connections and a weighted feature fusion mechanism.

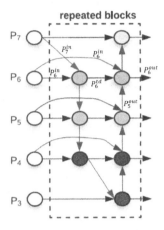

Fig. 4. Basic structure of BiFPN.

3.4 New Model Architecture

As shown in Fig. 5, our model consists of three main parts: a backbone with incorporation with CBAM, a detection head, and the neck part which utilize the BiFPN structure.

Backbone. An end-to-end network, capable of extracting semantic information directly from the input image, has proven to be highly effective in the field of object detection, as demonstrated by YOLOv5 [9].

Neck. Transitioning from PANet to BiFPN. This design aims to enhance information flow through bottom-up path augmentation.

4 Experimental Results

4.1 Datasets Preparation and Training Results

In this section, the dataset preparation process for the experimental results in the paper is outlined. The COCO dataset [19] was utilized, although not in its entirety due to its extensive size. For the specific focus of indoor dynamic SLAM, only images with the class label "person" were considered as they represented our target class in this situation. To extract the relevant images from the COCO dataset, a Python script file was employed. This script was designed to identify and retrieve all images associated with

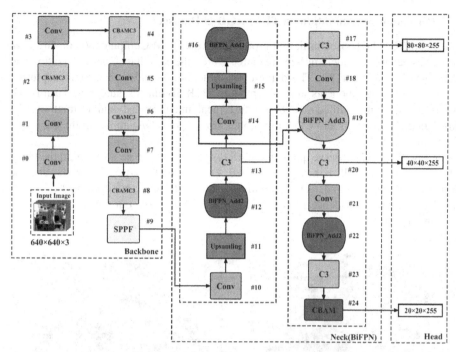

Fig. 5. Structure of our proposed model.

the "person" class label. Then a subset of images that matched the research requirements was obtained. Then we randomly chose around 20,000 images from them to train our proposed YOLOv5 model.

We have chosen pre-trained weights yolov5s.pt to help our training process. Before training, we specified the model hyperparameters: batch size 32, image size 640, initial learning rate 0.01 using SGD with 0.001 weight decay and a momentum of 0.9, and number of epochs is 300, for the rest we just used the default values, such as IOU threshold 0.45 and confidence threshold 0.25. Our training process was performed on an Ubuntu 20.04 with NVIDIA GeForce RTX 3060Ti GPU with 8 GB memory.

Table 1 shows the standard indicators: precision, recall, mAP@.5 (average AP accuracy at IoU of at least 0.5) and mAP@.5:.95 (average AP accuracy at threshold values IoU in the range from 0.5 to 0.95 in steps of 0.5). The number of frames that the model can process in one second (FPS) is also calculated separately.

Table 1. Quantitative comparisons of training results from two models.

Model	Precision	Recall	mAP@.5	mAP@.5:.95	FPS
YOLOv5s	0.755	0.695	0.763	0.498	303
YOLOv5s_modified	0.812	0.696	0.767	0.503	333

4.2   Performance Evaluation on TUM RGB-D Dataset

The TUM RGB-D dataset, initially introduced by the TUM Computer Vision Group in 2012, has become a widely utilized resource within the Simultaneous Localization and Mapping (SLAM) field [20]. This dataset was gathered using a Kinect camera, capturing various essential components such as depth images, RGB images, and ground truth data. We have tested our modified model on some typical images with dynamic situation from this dataset. The results show that our model have more robust ability in the occlusion situation.

In Fig. 6, we can observe qualitative differences, where the person behind the table, who is relatively small, is heavily occluded. Only a small portion is visible, and the original YOLOv5 fails to detect it, yielding no results. However, our improved algorithm can detect it with confidence scores of 0.60 and 0.31. Clearly, our enhancements have been highly effective.

Fig. 6. Qualitative comparison of test set.

4.3   Performance Evaluation on Real-Time Situation

In this section, we describe the experimental setup and methodology used to evaluate the real-time detection performance of our modified YOLOv5 model with CBAM and BiFPN. The objective of our experiment was to assess the model's effectiveness in detecting the "person" object class using the Realsense D455 camera, which was showed in the Fig. 7.

Fig. 7. Realsense D455 RGB camera.

Experimental Setup. We conducted our experiments in indoor environments, simulating dynamic SLAM scenarios. The Realsense D455 camera was employed to capture real-time video streams of the indoor scenes. During the experiments, the modified YOLOv5 model with CBAM and BiFPN was utilized to perform real-time object detection.

The provided Fig. 8 in a table presents a "Qualitative comparison of test results" for seven different indoor scenes regarding person detection. The first two scenes depict a laboratory environment, with one instance featuring a small-sized target and the other displaying an occluded target. The results clearly demonstrate that our proposed model outperforms the initial YOLOv5s model. The confidence scores for the detections in the first scene improved from 0.56 and 0.36 to 0.72 and 0.81, respectively, while in the second scene, they increased from 0.66 and 0.31 to 0.80 and 0.87. The third comparison focuses on small targets, where the detection performance for distant individuals increased from 0.74 to 0.80. In the fourth comparison, our model exhibited superior detection capabilities in identifying a heavily occluded person in a squatting position. However, both methods produced one "false positive" result due to the presence of a clothes rack with a jacket on it, which lacks specific objects in our prepared training datasets (also the COCO dataset). Thus, the models mistakenly classified the rack as a person, an error that can also occur even to human observers. The fifth comparison further highlights our model's superior person detection ability in such scenarios, as it achieved a high confidence score of 0.66 despite the failure of YOLOv5s. The sixth comparison addresses a specific occlusion scenario involving a glass door. While this may not pose a challenge for human observers, YOLOv5s failed to detect the person due to the combined factors of distance and small object size. In contrast, our optimized model achieved a score of 0.56. The seventh and final comparison also involves a dynamic target partially occluded by glass. Our model improved the confidence score from 0.61, as initially obtained by YOLOv5s, to 0.74. To summarize, our modified model consistently outperforms YOLOv5s in various occlusion scenarios and situations involving small targets. These results strongly indicate the success and effectiveness of our modifications.

In conclusion, our experiments validate the suitability and effectiveness of our modified YOLOv5 model for real-time "person" object detection in indoor dynamic SLAM scenarios. The model's accurate detection performance and efficient real-time inference make it a valuable tool for applications that require real-time mapping and localization of people in indoor environments.

1

2

3

4

5

6

7

Fig. 8. Qualitative comparison of real world scenario.

5 Conclusion and Future Work

In this paper we introduced a modified YOLOv5 model by incorporating CBAM and BiFPN techniques, with the goal of improving person detection in indoor environments for the dynamic SLAM tasks. By incorporating new techniques into YOLOv5s model, which is one of the SOTA, we can overcome the limitations and achieve a better balance between accuracy and real-time performance. Our experimental results demonstrated that the modified YOLOv5 algorithm outperformed the original YOLOv5s model in our target scenario. One notable advantage of our modified model was its improved performance in handling occlusion problems and small object detection. The original YOLOv5s model often failed to detect people in cases where strict occlusion occurred.

Further research will be aimed at extending the application of our model to other domains beyond indoor environments. And our future investigation will focus on applying the results of the improved model, integrating them into a SLAM project, as a front-end image-processing tool in the SLAM system.

References

1. Wang, Z., Tang, J., Wu, B., Hu, H.: BiFPN: efficient multi-scale backbone for object detection. In: Proceedings of the IEEE/CVF Conference on Computer Vision and Pattern Recognition (CVPR), pp. 13029–13038 (2020)
2. Woo, S., Park, J., Lee, J.Y., Kweon, I.S.: CBAM: convolutional block attention module. In: Ferrari, V., Hebert, M., Sminchisescu, C., Weiss, Y. (eds.) ECCV 2018. LNCS, vol. 11211, pp. 3–19. Springer, Cham (2018). https://doi.org/10.1007/978-3-030-01234-2_1
3. Bescos, B., Fácil, J.M., Civera, J., Neira, J.: DynaSLAM: tracking, mapping, and inpainting in dynamic scenes. IEEE Robot. Autom. Lett. 3(4), 4076–4083 (2018)
4. He, K., Gkioxari, G., Dollár, P., Girshick, R.: Mask R-CNN. In: Proceedings of the IEEE International Conference on Computer Vision, pp. 2961–2969 (2017)
5. Redmon, J., Farhadi, A.: YOLO9000: better, faster, stronger. In: Proceedings of the IEEE Conference on Computer Vision and Pattern Recognition (CVPR), pp. 6517–6525 (2017)
6. Redmon, J., Divvala, S., Girshick, R., Farhadi, A.: You only look once: unified, real-time object detection. In: Proceedings of the IEEE Conference on Computer Vision and Pattern Recognition (CVPR), pp. 779–788 (2016)
7. Bochkovskiy, A., Wang, C., Liao, H.Y.M.: YOLOv4: optimal speed and accuracy of object detection. arXiv preprint arXiv:2004.10934 (2020)
8. Redmon, J., Farhadi, A.: YOLOv3: an incremental improvement. arXiv preprint arXiv:1804.02767 (2018)
9. Thuan, D.: Evolution of Yolo algorithm and Yolov5: the state-of-the-art object detention algorithm (2021)
10. Tan, M., Pang, R., Le, Q.V.: EfficientDet: scalable and efficient object detection. In: Proceedings of the IEEE/CVF Conference on Computer Vision and Pattern Recognition (CVPR), pp. 10781–10790 (2020)
11. He, K., Zhang, X., Ren, S., Sun, J.: Deep residual learning for image recognition. In: Proceedings of the IEEE Conference on Computer Vision and Pattern Recognition, pp. 770–778 (2016)
12. Lin, T.Y., Dollár, P., Girshick, R., He, K., Hariharan, B., Belongie, S.: Feature pyramid networks for object detection. In: Proceedings of the IEEE Conference on Computer Vision and Pattern Recognition (CVPR), pp. 2117–2125 (2017)

13. Liu, S., Qi, L., Qin, H., Shi, J., Jia, J.: Path aggregation network for instance segmentation. In: Proceedings of the IEEE Conference on Computer Vision and Pattern Recognition, pp. 8759–8768 (2018)
14. Kim, C.E., Oghaz, M.M.D., Fajtl, J., Argyriou, V., Remagnino, P.: A comparison of embedded deep learning methods for person detection. arXiv preprint arXiv:1812.03451 (2018)
15. Zhao, L., Yi, W.: A new deep learning architecture for person detection. In: 2019 IEEE 5th International Conference on Computer and Communications (ICCC), pp. 2118–2122. IEEE (2019)
16. Ahmad, T., Ma, Y., Yahya, M., Ahmad, B., Nazir, S., Haq, A.U.: Object detection through modified YOLO neural network. Sci. Program. **2020**, 1–10 (2020)
17. Jia, W., et al.: Proceedings of the real-time automatic helmet detection of motorcyclists in urban traffic using improved YOLOv5 detector. IET Image Process. **15**(14), 3623–3637 (2021)
18. Sun, J., Ge, H., Zhang, Z.: AS-YOLO: an improved YOLOv4 based on attention mechanism and SqueezeNet for person detection. In: 2021 IEEE 5th Advanced Information Technology, Electronic and Automation Control Conference (IAEAC), Chongqing, China, vol. 5, pp. 1451–1456 (2021)
19. Lin, T.Y., Maire, M., Belongie, S., Hays, J., Perona P.: Microsoft COCO: common objects in context. In: Fleet, D., Pajdla, T., Schiele, B., Tuytelaars, T. (eds.) ECCV 2014. LNCS, vol. 8693, pp. 740–755. Springer, Cham (2014). https://doi.org/10.1007/978-3-319-10602-1_48
20. Sturm, J., Engelhard, N., Endres, F., Burgard, W., Cremers, D.: A benchmark for the evaluation of RGB-D SLAM systems. In: 2012 IEEE/RSJ International Conference on Intelligent Robots and Systems, pp. 573–580. IEEE (2012)

Autonomous Robot Navigation System as Part of a Human-Machine Team Based on Self-organization of Distributed Neurocognitive Architectures

Inna Pshenokova$^{(\boxtimes)}$ (iD), Kantemir Bzhikhatlov (iD), Olga Nagoeva (iD), Idar Mambetov (iD), and Alim Unagasov (iD)

The Federal State Institution of Science Federal Scientific Center Kabardino-Balkarian Scientific Center of Russian Academy of Sciences, 37-a, I. Armand Street, Nalchik 360000, Russia
kbncran@mail.ru

Abstract. The relevance of this study is due to the solution of the problem of developing the basic principles and algorithms for providing adaptive settings for autonomous robots intelligent control systems as part of a human-machine team based on the general method of machine learning. To do this, the paper proposes to use a formalism based on multi-agent neurocognitive architectures. Implementation of the possibility of adaptation is considered on the example of performing the task of orientation and navigation of an autonomous robot in an unfamiliar environment.

An autonomous robot navigation system based on self-organization of distributed neurocognitive architectures has been developed.

A multi-agent neurocognitive architecture is presented, which forms an active map containing all the locative information necessary to ensure the orientation and navigation of an autonomous robot between loci.

The use of a multi-agent architecture to provide the representation of locative information in the task of implementing an interface in human-machine team will make it possible to build an ontology responsible for representing the location of objects in the external environment, as well as provide interaction with the user in natural language, taking into account its semantics.

Keywords: Artificial Intelligence · Intelligent Agent · Multi-Agent Neurocognitive Architectures · Autonomous Robot · Human-Machine Team

1 Introduction

The pace of development of artificial intelligence systems, robotics, and virtual reality lead to the spread of the introduction of collaborative robotics. The use of such robotic systems capable of functioning in a group with people and autonomously interacting with the environment will significantly improve efficiency and safety in some areas of activity [1, 2]. The basis of modern approaches to the development of human-machine teams

© The Author(s), under exclusive license to Springer Nature Switzerland AG 2023
A. Ronzhin et al. (Eds.): ICR 2023, LNAI 14214, pp. 59–69, 2023.
https://doi.org/10.1007/978-3-031-43111-1_6

(HMT) is the idea of creating common mental models and a communicative environment for the members of this team. At the same time, the applicability of HMT depends on the effectiveness of complex interactions between a person and a robot, as well as between them and the environment [3]. To support these interactions, an autonomous robot must have knowledge, skills, and abilities commensurate with human capabilities. That is, by itself, the introduction of HMT does not always lead to increased productivity at the individual, team, or organizational level. The works [4–7] define the competencies that are important for the successful association of HMT participants. That is, the successful application of autonomous robots within the HMT requires more complex decision-making systems (compared to modern solutions such as chatbots, social robots or digital assistants).

The interaction of a human and a robot or an intelligent agent consists in the coordination of complex actions, such as communication, joint decision-making, and control [8, 9], in order to successfully complete tasks with potentially changing goals in uncertain environmental conditions. In [4], three main skills are identified that are necessary for effective collective interaction: communication, coordination, and adaptability, and in [7, 10] the importance of these skills for HMT is emphasized. Therefore, to improve performance in HMT, the implementation of these skills in robots and intelligent agents is very important.

The development of dialogue systems is very important for high-quality communication between a robot and a person. The main task is to develop algorithms that implement the consistency of actions and statements. Existing dialogue systems solve the problems of text and speech recognition well, but in HMT it is necessary to ensure the consistency of statements with perceived actions. It is very important to develop an interface that allows the operator to clearly understand the intentions, plans, and reasoning process of an intelligent agent. Interface implementations with such functionality are still not available [11], however, machines have gained the ability to exchange information with people in natural language and more effectively coordinate joint tasks. Such an interface includes the use of speech ordering [12], which is an integral part of human-machine communication. Features such as interleaving and the ability to recognize human language [13] can improve the efficiency of bidirectional communication between humans and machines, making HMT more productive [14]. Despite the development of the communication abilities of intelligent robots and agents, there are limitations in the applicability of such interfaces in real conditions. For example, machines using neural networks provide high computational performance, but, as a rule, have problems with the interpretability of solutions due to the use of distributed statistical representations [11].

When implementing interaction in HMT, it is necessary to ensure the possibility of effective information exchange between robots, and in such a way that people can understand it. That is, machines must be able to accurately model human understanding of information, which is closely related to the second transferable teamwork competency, coordination.

While communication refers to the process of exchanging information, coordination in human teams refers to the organization of knowledge, skills, and behavior of team members to achieve a specific goal [4]. In [15], coordination is defined as the process by which humans and machines manage "dependencies between activities". If group coordination is effective, then information that is relevant to the task is communicated in a timely manner, while avoiding excessive communication. Thus, effective communication processes be necessary but not enough for effective HMT coordination. Reference [16] defines the basic requirements for effective coordination. A machine is considered an effective coordinator if it is reliable, directive, able to communicate its own and recognize the intentions of other team members.

The main problem of HMT development is the ability of robots to participate in implicit coordination. Implicit coordination refers to the process of synchronizing the activities of team members based on assumptions about what each teammate is likely to do. While machines can detect certain implicit cues through facial expression recognition, they are limited in their ability to detect contextual cues. Therefore, it is very important to develop a system that can, by observing teammates, establish their goals, preferences, and capabilities, as well as model behavior in various situations. These kinds of capabilities would support implicit coordination, allowing the machine to anticipate human behavior and expectations, and then adapt its own behavior to match.

To support contextual understanding and adaptation ("third wave" of artificial intelligence), approaches are needed that can integrate both "first wave" knowledge-based methods of artificial intelligence and "second wave" methods of statistical deep learning. Most machine learning systems work by identifying correlations between variables. In contrast, at the heart of the "third wave" causal and counterfactual models aim to understand causal relationships between variables. By modeling causality, machines can better support counterfactual inference; those. They can generalize from observed operating conditions to unobserved ones.

Thus, to implement adaptation in robotic systems, it is necessary that machines can not only recognize the knowledge and behavior of their teammates, but also anticipate and respond to new knowledge and behavior when necessary. Therefore, the relevance of this study is due to the solution of this problem, which consists in developing the basic principles and algorithms for providing adaptive settings for intelligent control systems for autonomous robots as part of a human-machine team based on the general method of machine learning. To do this, we propose to use a formalism based on multi-agent neurocognitive architectures [17] and having a functional similarity to the neuromorphological structure of the brain, which makes it possible to realize the unique human cognitive abilities necessary for effective interaction. Implementation of the possibility of adaptation is considered on the example of performing the task of orientation and navigation of an autonomous robot in an unfamiliar environment.

The aim of the study is to develop a navigation system for an autonomous robot based on the self-organization of distributed neurocognitive architectures.

2 Autonomous Robot Navigation System Based on Multi-agent Neurocognitive Architecture

In HMT, human activity consists in monitoring the functioning of an autonomous robot or robotic system and setting current tasks in a natural language dialogue mode. At the same time, it is important that the operator's interface provides adequate human perception of the current scene, and his commands are correctly interpreted by the assistant robot. The navigation system plays a significant role in this, since the robot must independently assess the environment and plan its path, including in the presence of other moving objects in the working area (for example, people, vehicles, and robots).

Consider a navigation system for an autonomous robot based on the self-organization of multi-agent neurocognitive architectures. The navigation model of an autonomous robot is understood as a system of internal representations of certain specific places of the robot's functioning (locations), which allows you to independently form a route between any significant geographical locations (locus) in this location [18]. It is assumed that the navigation model will be formed dynamically as the robot becomes familiar with the external environment. The model (map) should include only significant loci, which include the locations of objects (objects) in the location, or places where any significant events occurred with the robot (or with its participation) [19–21].

In [17], the main algorithms and methods of the multi-agent neurocognitive approach to the creation of intelligent systems are described. In [22], the concept of an intelligent agent is introduced, which is a system based on a multi-agent neurocognitive architecture and consists of a set of software agents-neurons (agneurons) interacting with each other by exchanging messages and resources.

Agents operate according to the objective function aimed at increasing energy, considered as a certain scalar value characterizing the ability of the software agent to survive in the environment of its operation. Each agent-neuron in the composition of an intelligent agent represents a certain concept or its value, therefore, the activity of this concept or value in the process of intelligent decision-making by an agent or robot means its "life". If agneuron does not participate in the intellectual activity of the agent, its active energy decreases, which leads to its "death".

The implementation of the objective function is possible since agents use protocols for interaction, called "multi-agent contracts". A multi-agent contract is a set of algorithms according to which agents transfer some of their available energy to each other in exchange for the information they have. The ability of an agent to enter contractual relations with agents of a certain type at the structural and functional levels is called valency [23–25]. The agent receives information from the external environment through the sensory system. Different types of neuron agents that are part of an intelligent agent have a knowledge base according to which they function. In this model, knowledge is a causal relationship in which the starting situation is associated with the final (desired) situation and the action that needs to be performed to move from the initial situation to the desired one is indicated. Each such dependency represents one rule in the agents' knowledge base. The agent's behavior, which is determined by the internal objective function, can be controlled by editing the rules in the knowledge base. Knowledge generated by various intelligent agents built based on various neurocognitive architectures can be combined as part of an intelligent agent, since the system allows recursion (nesting) of cognitive architectures and agents into each other.

The possibility of representing locative information using a multi-agent recursive cognitive architecture is based on the functional specialization of agents-neurons. Based on the hypothesis about the organization of the invariant of intelligent decision-making

[17], the following types of software agents-neurons (agneurons) are distinguished in a multi-agent architecture.

To obtain data from the onboard sensors of the robot, agneurons-sensors are introduced, Lidar, Ultrasonic and GPS agents (Fig. 1). Their main function is to receive incoming information about the environment and pass it on to the appropriate agneurons for further processing. It should be noted that the navigation sensor subsystem is not limited to these sensors and includes motor encoders and inertial sensors.

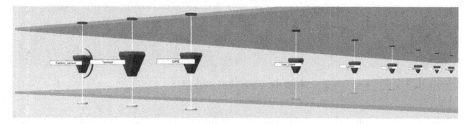

Fig. 1. Agneurons-sensors.

So, for example, data from the agneuron-sensor GPS is transmitted for processing to locative agneurons (Fig. 2), the valences of which determine contractual relations with other agents, based on the need to provide comprehensive locative information (representations of a place in space, objects located in it, and events that have occurred).

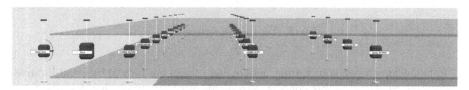

Fig. 2. Agneurons of the locative type.

The semantics of relationships between different objects is conceptualized by action agneurons (Fig. 3).

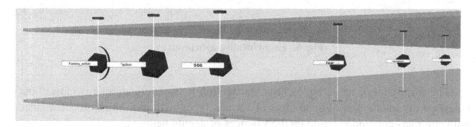

Fig. 3. Action type agneurons.

In the case of the formation of a navigation system for an autonomous robot, an agneuron of the "*locate*" action type conceptualizes the relationship between the locus and the model of the subject of communication (robot) (Fig. 4) in a multi-agent architecture.

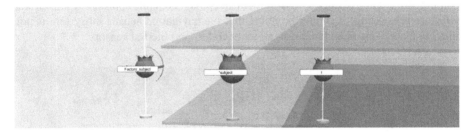

Fig. 4. Agneuron subject.

Time in the multi-agent neurocognitive architecture is represented by time-type agneurons in the Unix format (Fig. 5).

Fig. 5. Timing type agneurons.

Relationships between loci, time, action, and subject are formed by event locative agents (Fig. 6). These agents conceptualize predicative constructs that describe facts about locative information in the form "*I am located at *locus at *time*".

Fig. 6. Event locative agneurons.

The formation of an active locative connection between agneurons is carried out based on the interaction of agneurons of various types with each other in accordance with contracts concluded based on the valences of agents-neurons.

Let us now consider how locus are formed in a multi-agent neurocognitive architecture. As noted above, locus are the locations of objects in the location, or places in which any significant events occurred with the robot (or with its participation). Data on the location of objects relative to the mobile robot enters the architecture from LiDAR and ultrasonic sensors installed on the robot. The corresponding agneurons-sensors are responsible for processing this information. A conceptual object agneuron is created in the architecture (Fig. 7), information about the location of this object is stored by a locative agneuron, and information that this object is in a given place and at a given time is contained in the event agneuron *"Object is *locus at *time"*.

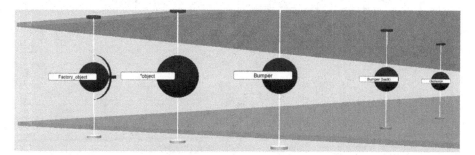

Fig. 7. Object type agneurons.

In order to find out which object is in front of it, the intelligent agent addresses the user. Figure 8 shows a functional representation of the context and content of the dialogue, in which the user explains to the intelligent agent that the object they both observe in the external environment is a *"table"* [26].

In this case, in a multi-agent neurocognitive architecture, the context of the interactive interaction of an intelligent agent with a user is registered by the following events:

$\aleph^5_{event}$: *"I see an object"* $\wedge$
$\wedge \aleph^6_{event}$: *"I see user"* $\wedge$
$\wedge \aleph^4_{event}$: $\wedge$ *"User is look at object"*
$\wedge \aleph^4_{event} \rightarrow \aleph^2_{event}$: *"That's why"* $\wedge$ $\Rightarrow$ $\aleph^5_{event} \rightarrow \aleph^8_{event}$: *"I see table"*
$\wedge \aleph^2_{event}$: *"User send a message"* $\wedge$
$\wedge \aleph^2_{event} \rightarrow \aleph^7_{event}$: *"That's why"* $\wedge$
$\wedge \aleph^7_{event}$: *"I read in chat, that it [is]table"*

Multi-agent connections are formed between events and agneurons that perform a functional representation of these events, aimed at reflecting the cause-and-effect relationships between events that describe the context of the situation, events that describe the subject (theme and rhema) of the utterance, and an event that describes the utterance itself. Such connections are hypothetically able to provide the construction of functional systems of semantic ontology, understanding and synthesis of natural language statements [26], as well as the integration of computer vision and language.

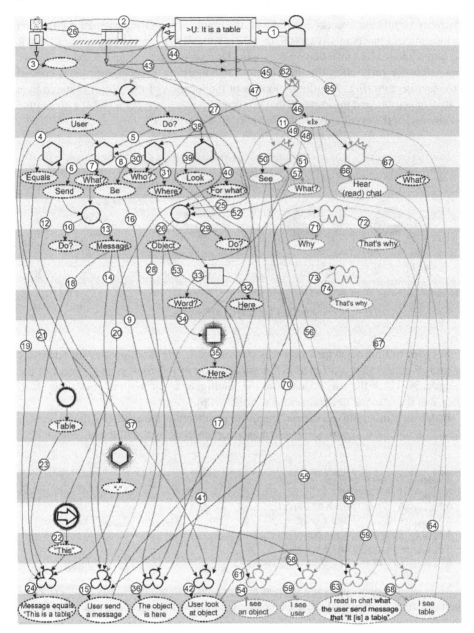

Fig. 8. Functional representation of the context and content of the dialogue in a multi-agent neurocognitive architecture.

3 Experiments

Figure 9 shows the editor of multi-agent neurocognitive architectures. Event local agents are represented, which form relations between locus, time, action, and subject. The picture shows that these agents conceptualize predicative constructions describing the facts about local information in the form of "I am at *locus in *time" and "Object is at *locus in *time". A chat window is presented in the lower left corner, in which you can see as agneurons exchange information with each other and the user.

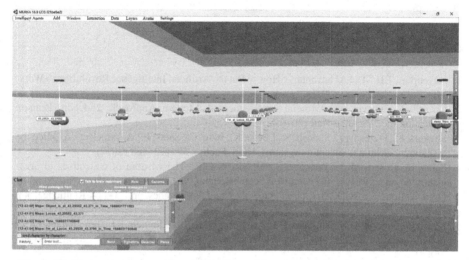

Fig. 9. Multi-agent neurocognitive architecture of the autonomous robot navigation system.

Such a multi-agent neurocognitive architecture, generating local and related software agents on demand when interacting with the environment, forms an active card containing all the local information necessary for the navigation between the loci. Information is presented in the form of interconnected predicative constructions, the elements of which are messages from neuron agents that conceptualize various parameters of locative and locus information. Such a multi-agent architecture should ensure the construction of an ontology of a map of the area and ensure the operation of the system of navigation and orientation in space for robots within the framework of the HMT.

4 Conclusion

An autonomous robot navigation system based on self-organization of distributed neurocognitive architectures has been developed.

An algorithm for the formation of contractual links between agneurons is presented, which considers the context of the dialogue situation, the content of the specific state of the "intelligent agent – environment" system, the content and form of the statement.

A multi-agent neurocognitive architecture is presented, which forms an active map containing all the locative information necessary to ensure the orientation and navigation of an autonomous robot between loci.

The use of a multi-agent architecture to provide the representation of locative information in the task of implementing an interface in a HMT will allow building an ontology responsible for representing the location of objects in the external environment, as well as providing interaction with the user in natural language, taking into account its semantics. Further development of the approach is aimed at the implementation of the natural language interface of the HMT, which is not inferior in efficiency to the interaction between people.

References

1. Davenport, T.H.: The AI advantage: How to Put the Artificial Intelligence Revolution to Work. MIT Press, Cambridge (2018)
2. Russell, S., Norvig, P.: Artificial Intelligence: A Modern Approach, 2nd edn. Pearson Education Inc., Prentice-Hall (2010)
3. Stowers, K., Oglesby, J., Sonesh, S., Leyva, K., Iwig, C., Salas, E.: A framework to guide the assessment of human–machine systems. Hum. Factors **59**, 172–188 (2017)
4. Salas, E., Rosen, M.A., Burke, C.S., Goodwin, G.F.: The wisdom of collectives in organizations: an update of the teamwork competencies. In: Team Effectiveness in Complex Organizations. Cross-Disciplinary Perspectives and Approaches, pp. 73–114. Routledge, NY (2009)
5. Klein, G., Woods, D.D., Bradshaw, J.M., Hoffman, R.R., Feltovich, P.J.: Ten challenges for making automation a "team player" in joint human-agent activity. IEEE Intell. Syst. **19**, 91–95 (2004)
6. Ososky, S., et al.: The importance of shared mental models and shared situation awareness for transforming robots from tools to teammates. Unmanned Syst. Technol. **14**(8387), 397–408 (2012)
7. Seeber, I., et al.: Machines as teammates: a research agenda on AI in team collaboration. Inf. Manage. **57**(2), 103174 (2020)
8. You, S., Robert, L.: Emotional attachment, performance, and viability in teams collaborating with embodied physical action (EPA) robots. J. Assoc. Inf. Syst. **19**(5), 377–407 (2018)
9. Lemaignan, S., Warnier, M., Sisbot, E.A., Clodic, A., Alami, R.: Artificial cognition for social human–robot interaction: an implementation. Artif. Intell. **247**, 45–69 (2017)
10. Stowers, K., Kasdaglis, N., Rupp, M.A., Newton, O.B., Chen, J.Y., Barnes, M.J.: The IMPACT of agent transparency on human performance. IEEE Trans. Hum. Mach. Syst. **50**(3), 245–253 (2020)
11. Nam, C.S., Lyons, J.B. (ed.): Trust in Human-Robot Interaction. Academic Press, London (2020)
12. Chao, C., Thomaz, A.: Timed Petri nets for fluent turn-taking over multimodal interaction resources in human-robot collaboration. Int. J. Robot. Res. **35**, 1330–1353 (2016)
13. Tellex, S., Gopalan, N., Kress-Gazit, H., Matuszek, C.: Robots that use language. Ann. Rev. Control Robot. Auton. Syst. **3**, 25–55 (2020)
14. Chen, J.Y., Lakhmani, S.G., Stowers, K., Selkowitz, A.R., Wright, J.L., Barnes, M.: Situation awareness-based agent transparency and human-autonomy teaming effectiveness. Theor. Issues Ergon. Sci. **19**, 259–282 (2018)

15. Malone, T.W., Crowston, K.: What is coordination theory and how can it help design cooperative work systems? In: Proceedings of the 1990 ACM Conference on Computer-Supported Cooperative Work, pp. 357–370. Association for Computing Machinery, NY (1990)

16. Klein, G., Feltovich, P.J., Bradshaw, J.M., Woods, D.D.: Common ground and coordination in joint activity. Organ. Simul. **53**, 139–184 (2005)

17. Nagoev, Z.V.: Intelligence, or thinking in living and artificial systems. KBNTs RAS Publishing House, Nalchik (2013)

18. Nagoev, Z., Bzhikhatlov, K.C, Nagoeva, O., Anchekov, M., Atalikov, B.: Models of orientation and navigation of autonomous household robots based on multi-agent neurocognitive architectures. In: Perspective systems and control tasks. Materials of the XVI All-Russian scientific-practical conference and the XII youth school-seminar, pp. 154–161. IP Maruk M.R., Rostov-on-Don (2021)

19. Nagoev, Z., Pshenokova, I., Gurtueva, I., Bzhikhatlov, K.: A simulation model for the cognitive function of static objects recognition based on machine-learning multi-agent architectures. In: Samsonovich, A.V. (ed.) BICA 2019. AISC, vol. 948, pp. 370–378. Springer, Cham (2020). https://doi.org/10.1007/978-3-030-25719-4_48

20. Nagoev, Z., Pshenokova, I., Nagoeva, O., Sundukov, Z.: Learning algorithm for an intelligent decision-making system based on multi-agent neurocognitive architectures. Cogn. Syst. Res. **66**, 82–88 (2021)

21. Nagoev, Z., Nagoeva, O., Gurtueva, I.: Multi-agent neurocognitive models of semantics of spatial localization of events. Cogn. Syst. Res. **59**, 91–102 (2020)

22. Nagoev, Z., Gurtueva, I., Malyshev, D., Sundukov, Z.: Multi-agent algorithm imitating formation of phonemic awareness. In: Samsonovich, A.V. (ed.) BICA 2019. AISC, vol. 948, pp. 364–369. Springer, Cham (2020). https://doi.org/10.1007/978-3-030-25719-4_47

23. Nagoev, Z., Nagoeva, O., Gurtueva, I., Denisenko, V.: Multi-agent algorithms for building semantic representations of spatial information in a framework of neurocognitive architecture. In: Samsonovich, A.V. (ed.) BICA 2019. AISC, vol. 948, pp. 379–386. Springer, Cham (2020). https://doi.org/10.1007/978-3-030-25719-4_49

24. Nagoev, Z., Nagoeva, O., Pshenokova, I., Gurtueva, I.: Multi-agent model of semantics of simple extended sentences describing static scenes. In: Ronzhin, A., Rigoll, G., Meshcheryakov, R. (eds.) ICR 2019. LNCS (LNAI), vol. 11659, pp. 245–259. Springer, Cham (2019). https://doi.org/10.1007/978-3-030-26118-4_24

25. Nagoev, Z., Lyutikova, L., Gurtueva, I.: Model for automatic speech recognition using multi-agent recursive cognitive architecture. Procedia Comput. Sci. **145**, 386–392 (2018)

26. Nagoev, Z.V., Nagoeva, O.V.: Justification of symbols and multi-agent neurocognitive models of natural language semantics. KBNTs RAS Publishing House, Nalchik (2022)

3D-CNNs-Based Touchless Human-Machine Interface

Ali Asgarov and Ali Parsayan[✉] [iD]

Process Automation Engineering Department, Baku Higher Oil School, 30, Khojaly Avenue, Baku 1025, Azerbaijan
parsayan@bhos.edu.az

Abstract. Interacting with machines via hand gestures is a common way for people to communicate with robots. Human utilize gestures in a regular talk to convey meaning and emotions to one another. Gesture-based interactions are utilized in a wide range of applied to a wide range of fields, as telephones, TVs, monitors, video games, and other electronic devices. By technological improvements, gesture recognition is now a more realistic and appealing approach in the context of human interaction. In this research, the relevant experiments are conducted using numerous types of convolutional neural networks, including the proposed customized model, to see which ones performs the best. Because of the introduction of such Microsoft Kinect sensor, increased depth and vision sensing has been widely important for several purposes. Given its ability to measure ranges to objects at a fast frame rate, these types of sensors are widely being employed for 3D acquisitions, as well as for other purposes in robotics and machine learning. This research made use of the Kinect sensor and the use of an RGB-D camera and a 3D convolution neural network, which offer a novel approach for fingertips identification and hand gesture classification in real time that is both accurate and fast (3DCNN).

Keywords: Hand Gesture Recognition · 3DCNN · HMI · HCI · Robots

1 Introduction

As information technology progresses, human desire to communicate with robots and computers in a natural way rises in importance. Because of their limited flexibility, traditional human-computer interaction input devices such as mouse, keyboards, and remote controllers are no longer natural modes of communication. This isn't a new phenomenon. They've been around for quite some time. Two of the most frequent ways for individuals to communicate with robots and computers are through voice commands and body language, both of which can be found in a wide range of applications. As a result, getting accurate results when utilizing automatic speech recognition in a noisy environment can be problematic due to the considerable variation in how people pronounce common terms. Additionally, the use of body language may be beneficial in the development of a human–computer interaction. In many circumstances, this sort of communication is more reliable than other types of communication. Hand gestures, body positioning,

A. Ronzhin et al. (Eds.): ICR 2023, LNAI 14214, pp. 70–80, 2023.
https://doi.org/10.1007/978-3-031-43111-1_7

and facial expressions are just a few instances of language to consider. Gestures with one's hands are the most effective method of communicating one's ideas and feelings. In addition, they serve as a universal language for human to communicate with. There are various ways to say "hi", such as waving your hand in front of someone's face or saying it out loud [1–3].

It is essential for people to communicate with one another via hand gestures while they are together. In communicating with individuals around us, we make hand gestures that express crucial information and ideas to them. Without making any sort of gesture or expressing anything to someone or something else with our hands, it is hard to carry on a meaningful dialogue with them. Gestures with the hands are a frequent way of transmitting information to others. According to some projections, the touchscreen on mobile phones may be phased out in the near future and replaced with hand gestures. Systems for human–computer interaction (HCI) include things like sign language recognition, robot control, virtual mouse control, medical imaging data research, and immersive gaming. Human–vehicle interaction (HVI) and immersive gaming are also included in this category. As a result, computer vision experts have been attempting to identify hand motions in video for quite some time, particularly with older, less capable cameras (RGB cameras). A huge number of persons, shifting light levels, complicated backgrounds, varying user–camera distances, fluctuating user–camera distances, and background/foreground motions during hand tracking are all examples of situations in which many existing algorithms fail. A new version of Kinect RGB-D, Microsoft's upgraded camera for gaming and other applications, has been released with a revised user interface and depth-sensing capabilities. Color and depth sensors are used to create synchronized photos with the Kinect sensor. In the beginning, users' body motions were used to communicate with video games, and Microsoft used them as an input method for its Xbox gaming device. The computer vision community has extended the use of Kinect v1's low-cost depth sensing technology well beyond the realm of gaming. The ability to interface with other devices or applications without the need to touch a controller has enabled human motion capture systems to be easily repurposed for a wide range of new applications, ranging from medical to robotics. These developments may now be of use to applications involving human motion analysis [1–3].

After being introduced to computer science in the 1990s, convolutional neural networks (CNNs) have made significant contributions to the field of human-computer interaction (HCI) [2]. With a large number of layers in CNNs, it is possible to learn features more quickly and efficiently. Data may be represented hierarchically by using deep learning frameworks, where characteristics are ordered from the lowest to the highest level, resulting in hierarchical representations of data. The ultimate goal in this research is to develop a depth video-based hand gesture interface, which is the subject of this study. In this experiment, fingertip detection and a 3D convolutional neural network are utilized to detect hand motions captured by a depth camera. Using multi-level characteristics and the right utilization of multi-level features, the network architecture under consideration may provide high-performance predictions while also exploiting multi-level characteristics. This research made use of the Kinect sensor and the use of an RGB-D camera and a 3D convolution neural network, which offer a novel approach for fingertips identification and hand gesture classification in real time that is both accurate and fast (3DCNN) [1–3].

2 Related Works

When it comes to human-to-human communication, hand gestures are extremely important [3]. This type of communication has resulted in the development of new concepts for human-computer interaction as a result of its high level of information transfer efficiency. In order for this to operate, the computer must be able to recognize the gestures made by the person who is running the machine. That is all that is necessary for the identification of hand gestures to work. When it comes to resolving these types of problems, feature extraction algorithms are the most commonly used method [2]. Using a specialized method, the hand image is matched up with a preset template image. It has been demonstrated that template matching is ineffective when dealing with a diverse range of environments, hand shapes, and actions. When it comes to classification algorithms, different feature extractors are unable to adapt to new datasets and changing scenarios effectively. Deep convolutional neural networks are excellent alternatives in these cases because of their robustness and invariance.

Deep learning techniques are becoming increasingly popular when it comes to computer vision applications. By convolutional neural networks, the parallel nature of the computations enables them to be applied elegantly to the matrix representation of data when dealing with problems that can be represented visually. When employing multicolumn deep CNNs that leverage several parallel networks [4], it has been demonstrated that the recognition rates of single networks for a variety of photo classification tasks rise by 30 to 80%. Once again, convolutional neural networks (CNNs) were used by Neverova et al. to identify between 20 different Italian sign language movements by combining RGBD data from the hand area with upper-body skeletal movement [5]. While their system, on the other hand, was intended to be used only for indoor activities, Pablo Barros and colleagues developed a Multichannel Convolutional Neural Network (MCNN) that recognizes hand gestures and extracts implicit features from the architecture itself, a process known as implicit feature extraction, from the architecture [6]. To reach their results, the researchers examined data from two existing datasets of static hand motion photos. A robot was utilized to create the first dataset in a lab environment, using four different types of hand gestures. It was done in a similar manner with the second dataset. They used a new set of data to evaluate their technique, which comprised ten distinct hand gestures performed in natural, uncontrolled environments. Hand-gesture detection in cars using RGBD data was studied by many researchers. They discovered that the best values were achieved when histogram of gradient (HOG) characteristics were combined with an SVM classifier. Molchanov et al. combined data on hand movements gleaned from depth, color, and radar sensors while simultaneously training a CNN to make use of the data. They were able to correctly identify under a variety of lighting and environmental settings [5]. As a result, the actions detailed above provided the necessary framework for our research and inspired us to keep going.

3 · Proposed Method

Figure 1 depicts a high-level representation of the proposed system. Microsoft Kinect Sensor version 2 pictures with in-depth skeleton-joint information are used to extract the hand region of interest, and a border-tracing method is used to extract and characterize the contours of hands.

Using the hand-contour coordinate model, the K-cosine algorithm detects the fingertip location, which is then translated into a gesture initialization to help identify hand movements. When a gesture is finally identified, a 3D convolutional neural network is used to do the process.

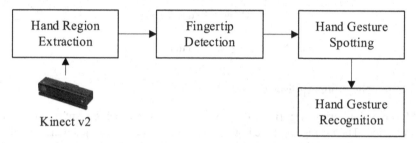

Fig. 1. The proposed system's block diagram.

3.1 Extraction of the Hand Region

The extraction procedure for the hand region is depicted in Fig. 2, and we'll go over it in more detail in the following paragraphs. The depth images of the hand region of interest and the middle of the palm that are provided by the Kinect V2 skeletal tracker are then converted to binary images. In order to extract and describe the hand outlines, a method called border tracing is utilized.

Each of the user's body parts is detected using a Microsoft Kinect V2 sensor, which uses depth pictures to map each of the learnt body parts to the depth images as the user moves. Therefore, the camera may acquire skeleton-joint information for 25 joints, such as the hip, spine, head, shoulder, hand, foot, and thumb. Kinect skeletal tracker depth images are used to accurately extract the hand region of interest (HRI) and palm center.

In order to get rid of the noise in the hand region, the Weiner filter is utilized in conjunction with morphological processing. The findings are then transferred to the binary image using the thresholds that were specified using the depth signals provided by the Kinect. The Moore–Neighbor approach may be used to produce hand contours from binary photographs of the hand regions. These hand contours can then be used to draw the hand. Utilizing this method allows for the performance of image contour extraction, also known as area extraction. As a consequence of carrying out these steps, we now have a collection of hand contour pixels. These data are used to measure the curvature of the surface.

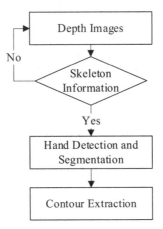

Fig. 2. Hand region extraction flowchart.

3.2 Moore–Neighbor Approach

The Moore Neighboring Algorithm (Fig. 3) is what is used to carry out the process of edge detection. The average and the highest possible value for each pixel are calculated using this procedure. The use of cellular automata [2] is a well-known method that enhances the overall quality and functionality of noisy images.

Modified Moore-Neighborhood (P) of an 8-pixel pixel, shares a vertex or edge with the other 8-pixel pixels. A white pixel will be found by P if and only if it finds one in its near surroundings. There are no white pixels in the immediate neighborhood, thus the operation continues. Setting a suitable end point is crucial when utilizing Moore-Neighbor tracing.

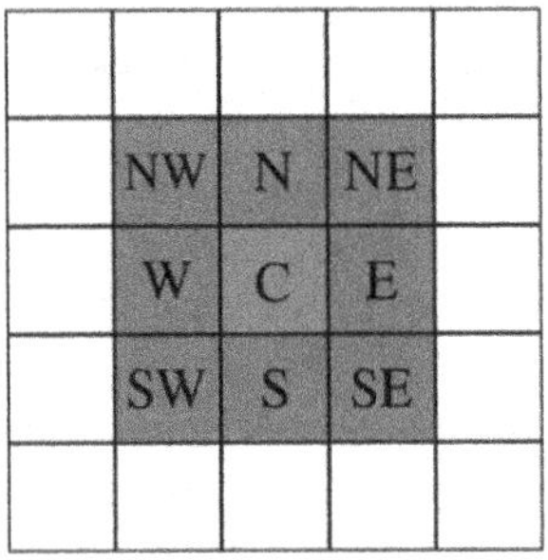

	NW	N	NE	
	W	C	E	
	SW	S	SE	

Fig. 3. The Moore Neighboring window consists of 9 cells, core cell and 8 stranding cells.

3.3 Detecting Hand Gestures Target-Person Locking

When there are a large number of people in the scene, the individual whose movements are being monitored will have control of the mouse. As can be seen in Fig. 4, the Kinect

V2 sensor was used in this research to extract 25 skeletal joints from up to six people at the same time. These joints include the head, the neck, the left and right hands, the base of the spine, and so on. Because of this, the procedure that was just detailed enables the system to locate the fingers of anywhere from one to six separate users. On the other hand, in order to control the mouse cursor, we must first determine who the intended recipient is. In order to solve this problem while hand tracking was being done, a user-locking mechanism was used.

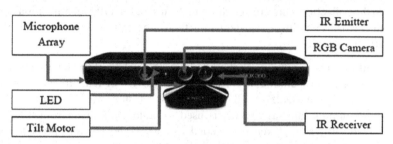

Fig. 4. Kinect Sensor.

The first algorithm presents an illustration of how to put this plan into effect. Using the Kinect skeletal tracker's head and right-hand joint coordinates, the target person is determined based on the distance between their heads and hands, as illustrated in following algorithm. Ten frames into the video, the user extends his hand over his head. However, determining the beginning and ending points of a hand gesture in real-time hand gesture detection is still difficult.

The Target Person Locking Algorithm is:

1. starts.
2. Require the User ID, the $x1$, $y1$ coordinates of the head, and the x, $y1$ coordinates of the right hand joint $(x13, y13)$.
3. Firstly, get the distance between $y1$ and $y13$ using the formula.
4. Secondly, $y13 > y1$ in 10 frames, else process target user.
5. Otherwise, redo first
6. ends, begin.

A region in which a person utilizing a Kinect device may move the mouse cursor with their hands instead of using the mouse. This idea has the benefit of being able to be carried out on a number of screen sizes and resolutions, which is a distinct advantage. A simple glimpse at a virtual screen is all that's needed to take control of the movements. At this point, the depth resolution of the Kinect V2 sensor is taken into account in order to establish the resolution of the virtual screen, which comes out to 512×424 pixels.

4   Simulations, Experimentations and Discussion of the Results

Hardware Specifications. Kinect Camera: Officially, the Xbox 360 console is referred to as Kinect (14). A partnership between Microsoft and Prime Sense led to the creation of the application in June of that year. Microsoft Windows operating system consist of this application was introduced in February 2012. Its introduction in 2009 had a significant influence on the Computer Vision and Computer Graphics fields. As a result of this Microsoft innovation, gamers may use speech and gestures to engage in a wide variety of ways in the game. Since its first release, the Kinect has grown in popularity across a variety of industries, including video games, theater, robotics, and natural interaction.

In order to verify the efficacy of the proposed method, a dataset consisting of hand gestures that had been manually categorized was developed. The hand gesture films included in the collection were created through the use of fingertip identification derived from depth videos. According to the depiction, there are 5250 videos of each move made by fifty different people.

Implementation. On a computer equipped with an Intel I7 10th Generation 10800-U Six-Core Processor operating at 2.4 GHz, 12 gigabytes of random-access memory (RAM), and a GeForce MX250 (GPU), the proposed system was constructed. Python was the programming language which is used to build the system from the ground up. There were 30 frames taken per second as part of the tracking procedure. The 3DCNN model was implemented with the help of the deep learning frameworks Keras and Scikit-learn.

Analysis of the Experiment. From the original data, 65% of it was used for training, 15% for validation, and 20% for testing in hand gesture recognition. Ensemble Decision Tree, Support Vector Machine (SVM) [7] and two-dimensional convolution neural network [8] were utilized to evaluate our proposed method for identifying hand gestures in videos (2DCNN). Convolutional neural networks (CNNs) were used in the network of the 2DCNN instead of 3DCNN, which employs 3D convolutions. 2DCNN input was similar to the standard ML model (EDT). The Scikit learn 0.20 module was used to build an SVM nonlinear multiclass approach with a kernel based on the intersection of histograms.

Evaluation Metrics. The algorithms were compared using three criteria. The accuracy rate was included to account for situations in which the number of samples in each class is exactly equal, the number of accurate predictions to the total number of input samples is known as the predictive accuracy ratio (EPR), and the training and testing times of the deep learning model which were the second and third measures. Online training with data collection was termed a scenario. For each dataset, 100 training epochs was ran with the goal of improving classification accuracy. This procedure was tested five times, and the average of the findings was used to compute the testing duration.

Discussion of the Results. The accuracy of the classification performed by 3DCNN model on both the training and validation sets is demonstrated in Fig. 5. The plots provide evidence that the model provides a satisfactory match to the issue.

By the use of prepared hand gesture dataset, the results of the proposed method were compared with the reviewed methods results which are considered to be state of the art in Table 1. In terms of accuracy rate, the overall performance of Deep Learning algorithms was superior to that of the traditional Machine Learning models. In comparison, the accuracy achieved by the Ensemble Decision Tree, SVM, and CNN models are 10%,

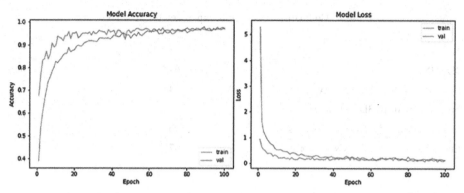

Fig. 5. Accuracy rate of the classification performed by 3DCNN model on both the training and validation sets.

20%, 27%, and 30% lower than that achieved by 3DCNN. The SVM model achieved a score of 63%, while 2DCNN model achieved 65%. On the prepared hand gesture dataset, 3DCNN network achieved superior results in terms of video classification compared to SVM, EDT (Ensemble Decision Tree), KNN and 2DCNN. It's probable that this discovery has a rational explanation, and that explanation is the flexibility of a decision boundary supplied by learning numerous frames in 3DCNN. 3DCNN took longer time to train and test than either the Ensemble Decision Tree, KNN, SVM or 2DCNN for convolutional neural networks. This fact showed that neural networks may be employed in real-time applications, since all designs were able to identify the hand motion in less than 7 s.

Table 1. Comparison of different models results.

Models	Time for Training	Time for Testing	Accuracy
Ensemble Decision Tree	25.3 m	6.4 s	83.3%
KNN	29.4 m	5.2 s	73.4%
SVM	23.5 m	5.7 s	63.4%
2DCNN	40.5 m	4.1 s	65.3%
3DCNN	97.3 m	7.3 s	93.2%

Table 2 depicts the proposed method hand motions recognition rate, which relies on ensemble learning. As a collection of 20 3DCNN models, the ensemble learning approach outperformed the single 3DCNN in video classification, with an accuracy rate of 97.4%, according to the study. The individual 3DCNN models in this dataset were shown to be considerably less accurate than the ensemble of 5 3DCNN models. But, when the number of models is raised to 10 or 20, there is no visible change. In contrast, ensemble learning necessitates a lengthy training period because of the high processing costs associated with a large number of models.

Table 2. Comparison of ensemble approach for 3DCNN.

Models	Accuracy (%)
3DCNN	93.2
Ensemble with 5 3DCNN networks	94.5
Ensemble with 10 3DCNN networks	95.6
Ensemble with 15 3DCNN networks	96.1
Ensemble with 20 3DCNN networks	97.5

Table 3 is an illustration of the confusion matrix produced by 3DCNN using an ensemble of 20 models. As it was to be expected, zooming in and zooming out (ZI) had the lowest accuracy rate, but swiping left, swiping right, and selecting "meaningless" (M) all had the highest accuracy rate. Because of the rapid hand movement, it was difficult to detect the difference between the 'drag' gesture and other motions. This was because the 'drag' gesture was quicker than other gestures, making it more difficult to differentiate between the two.

Table 3. Confusion Matrix.

Target	Selected							Acc
	S_L	S_R	S_U	S_D	Z_I	Z_O	M	
S_L	150	0	0	0	0	0	1	0.991
S_R	1	145	0	0	0	0	1	0.981
S_U	1	0	145	0	2	0	2	0.972
S_D	0	0	0	146	1	1	2	0.973
Z_I	0	0	0	0	132	15	3	0.954
Z_O	4	4	1	5	4	129	4	0.945
M	1	0	0	0	0	1	145	0.991
								0.975

5 Conclusion

In order to identify and recognize fingertip gestures, this research used a mix of a geometry algorithm and a deep learning method given in this paper. The proposed method was able to accurately predict gestures, but it also had the potential to be used in real-world contexts. Fingertip detection with better threshold segmentation using depth information and the k-cosine curvature technique is both discussed in this work in an attempt to overcome the distance restriction in gesture identification.

In addition to functioning effectively in a variety of lighting conditions and with various backdrop patterns, the suggested approach is capable of accurately detecting hand movements even at a distance of several meters, and it can even recognize the hand motions of many persons.

As the further work, the performance of the suggested method can be improved by carrying out a holistic search in an effort to optimize each of the hyperparameters individually. Also, the results of the experiments showed that this methodology is a potential method for real-time hand-gesture interfaces. Also, the proposed system can be improved to accommodate additional hand motions in the future and use it in more practical applications.

References

1. Hasan, H., Abdul-Kareem, S.: Human–computer interaction using vision-based hand gesture recognition systems: a survey. Neural Comput. Appl. **25**, 251–261 (2014)
2. Klompmaker, F., Nebe, K., Fast, A.: dSensingNI: a framework for advanced tangible interaction using a depth camera. In: Proceedings of the Sixth International Conference on Tangible, Embedded and Embodied Interaction, pp. 217–224 (2012)
3. Gallo, L., Placitelli, A.P., Ciampi, M.: Controller-free exploration of medical image data: experiencing the Kinect. In: Proceedings of the 2011 24th International Symposium on Computer-Based Medical Systems (CBMS), pp. 1–6 (2011)
4. Krejov, P., Bowden, R.: Multi-touchless: real-time fingertip detection and tracking using geodesic maxima. In: Proceeding of 10th IEEE International Conference and Workshops on Automatic Face and Gesture Recognition (FG), pp. 1–7 (2013)
5. Freeman, W.T., Roth, M.: Orientation histograms for hand gesture recognition. In: International Workshop on Automatic Face and Gesture Recognition, vol. 12, pp. 296–301 (1995)
6. Simonyan, K., Zisserman, A.: Very deep convolutional networks for large-scale image recognition. arXiv:1409.1556 (2014)
7. Fossati, A., Gall, J., Grabner, H., Ren, X., Konolige, K.: Consumer Depth Cameras for Computer Vision: Research Topics and Applications. Springer, Heidelberg (2012)
8. Dao, T.T., Tannous, H., Pouletaut, P., Gamet, D., Istrate, D., Tho, M.H.B.: Interactive and connected rehabilitation systems for e-Health. Irbm **37**(5–6), 289–296 (2016)
9. Reza, M.N., Hossain, M.S., Ahmad, M.: Real time mouse cursor control based on bare finger movement using webcam to improve HCI. In: 2015 International Conference on Electrical Engineering and Information Communication Technology (ICEEICT), pp. 1–5. IEEE (2015)
10. Pisharady, P.K., Saerbeck, M.: Recent methods and databases in vision-based hand gesture recognition: a review. Comput. Vis. Image Underst. **141**, 152–165 (2015)
11. Amin, M.A., Yan, H.: Sign language finger alphabet recognition from Gabor-PCA representation of hand gestures. In: 2007 International Conference on Machine Learning and Cybernetics, vol. 4, pp. 2218–2223. IEEE (2007)
12. Sharma, A., Mittal, A., Singh, S., Awatramani, V.: Hand gesture recognition using image processing and feature extraction techniques. Procedia Comput. Sci. **173**, 181–190 (2020)
13. Lian, S., Hu, W., Wang, K.: Automatic user state recognition for hand gesture based low-cost television control system. IEEE Trans. Consum. Electron. **60**(1), 107–115 (2014)
14. Sharp, T., et al.: Accurate, robust, and flexible real-time hand tracking. In: Proceedings of the 33rd Annual ACM Conference on Human Factors in Computing Systems, pp. 3633–3642 (2015)

15. Fossati, A., Gall, J., Grabner, H., Ren, X., Konolige, K.: Consumer Depth Cameras for Computer Vision: Research Topics and Applications. Springer, Heidelberg (2012)
16. He, K., Zhang, X., Ren, S., Sun, J.: Deep residual learning for image recognition. In: Proceedings of the IEEE Conference on Computer Vision and Pattern Recognition, pp. 770–778 (2016)
17. Bagdanov, A.D., Del Bimbo, A., Seidenari, L., Usai, L.: Real-time hand status recognition from RGB-D imagery. In: Proceedings of the 21st International Conference on Pattern Recognition (ICPR2012), pp. 2456–2459. IEEE (2012)
18. Tsai, T.H., Huang, C.C., Zhang, K.L.: Embedded virtual mouse system by using hand gesture recognition. In: 2015 IEEE International Conference on Consumer Electronics-Taiwan, pp. 352–353. IEEE (2015)
19. Wang, R.Y., Popović, J.: Real-time hand-tracking with a color glove. ACM Trans. Graph. (TOG) 28(3), 1–8 (2009)
20. Wang, P., Li, W., Ogunbona, P., Wan, J., Escalera, S.: RGB-D-based human motion recognition with deep learning: a survey. Comput. Vis. Image Underst. 171, 118–139 (2018)
21. Grif, H.-S., Farcas, C.C.: Mouse cursor control system based on hand gesture. Procedia Technol. 22, 657–661 (2016)
22. Andersen, M.R., et al.: Kinect depth sensor evaluation for computer vision applications. Aarhus University, pp. 1–37 (2012)
23. Shou, Z., Wang, D., Chang, S.-F.: Temporal action localization in untrimmed videos via multi-stage CNNs. In: Proceedings of the IEEE Conference on Computer Vision and Pattern Recognition, pp. 1049–1058 (2016)
24. Molchanov, P., Yang, X., Gupta, S., Kim, K., Tyree, S., Kautz, J.: Online detection and classification of dynamic hand gestures with recurrent 3D convolutional neural network. In: Proceedings of the IEEE Conference on Computer Vision and Pattern Recognition, pp. 4207–4215 (2016)

Development of a Mechanism for Recognizing the Emotional State Based on the Unconscious Movements of the Subject

Yaroslava Gorbunova[1,2]([✉]) [iD] and Gleb Kiselev[1,2] [iD]

[1] Artificial Intelligence Research Institute, Federal Research Center "Computer Science and Control" of Russian Academy of Sciences, 44/2, Vavilova st., 119333 Moscow, Russia
gorbunova_y_m@mail.ru
[2] Peoples' Friendship University of Russia named after Patrice Lumumba, 6, Miklukho-Maklaya st., Moscow 117198, Russia

Abstract. The task of assessing emotional state is not easy for a human and especially challenged for an automated system. It requires not only detection but also complex analysis of various factors. The effectiveness of existing algorithms based on such modalities as text, audio, video, physiological characteristics, etc., depends on the subject's race, language, and other affiliations, which makes it difficult to study in case of lack or complete absence of such data. The paper deals with the creation of a mechanism capable of detecting the emotional state of a person based on his interaction with a computer via a mouse. To solve the problem, we collected a dataset using a web application developed in the Python programming language. The application is focused on collecting data about the subject's cursor movement such as distance travelled, maximum deviation from the line that connects the start and end points of the movement, the time the subject interacted with the computer mouse during the session and the maximum speed of the cursor movement. Trained classifiers for emotion analysis based on human control of the computer mouse on the created dataset and analyzed the results.

Keywords: Emotion Analysis · Emotional Coloring · Computer Mouse · Cursor Movements · Dataset Creation · Machine Learning

1 Introduction

The task of recognizing and detecting emotions is relevant for decades. Knowledge of the emotions experienced by a subject can be useful in many fields, e.g., marketing, education, robotics, banking, advertising, and others. People's moods can be recognized through many distinctive abilities. The most common are facial expressions, gestures, voice volume and interruption, and physiological characteristics (sweating, heart rate, skin conductivity, etc.). A human is capable of recognizing emotion from a person's facial expression with a high degree of accuracy, but for an automated system, it is a highly complex task. A computer needs to take many factors into account when identifying moods, and there are other problems as well. Cultural differences are also important

A. Ronzhin et al. (Eds.): ICR 2023, LNAI 14214, pp. 81–92, 2023.
https://doi.org/10.1007/978-3-031-43111-1_8

in analysis because similar facial expressions in different cultures can sometimes mean the opposite of emotion, leading to a deliberately false assessment. Furthermore, facial expressions may not reflect a person's real feelings, or may reflect false ones. Therefore, there is a need to create a new way of identifying and analyzing emotions that can be applied to different ethnic and linguistic groups, avoiding the difficulties of existing mechanisms.

The diversity of data types is leading to new and improved analysis methods. Today, there are many approaches to detect the psycho-emotional state of a person, capable of analyzing speech recordings, digitized speech recognition results, textual data, images, and video materials. Textual information can serve as the main source of data about a person's state. The application of machine learning in text analysis leads to an accuracy of over 90% [1]. Also, high quality of emotion classification can be achieved through the study of audio signal [2, 3] and combining the modalities, audio, and video [4]. Video-based emotion analysis also makes it possible to study the relationship between cognitive function and emotion in humans, a particularly acute issue in the elderly [5]. Video streaming also makes it possible to assess the emotional state of a car driver [6], which will help to avoid accidents and keep all road users safe from dangerous situations. For more detailed research in emotion recognition, there are datasets that include several modalities at once [7], such as audio, video, oculography, speech, motion capture data, and others.

The emotions evoked in a person, intentionally or not, leave a trace in their physiology. In this way, information on afferent muscle excitation [8], skin conductance [9], functional magnetic resonance imaging (fMRI) data, respiration rate [10] can be used to determine a subject's emotional state, sadness, happiness, joy, and others.

To analyze emotional states, it is possible to use different modalities, which is a wide field for researchers.

2   The Need for a New Modality

Modalities for recognizing emotional states such as text, audio, video, or characteristics of human physiology are quite informative sources of knowledge about a subject, but each provides advantages and disadvantages in the accumulation, transformation, and processing of data.

There are more than 7000 languages in the world, many of which have dialects. However, only a seventh can be machine-processed, making it difficult to analyze the emotions of the rest of the language space. In addition, textual and audio modalities are not always available for processing, nor are video, photo and physiological characteristics. This becomes the reason for seeking out and analyzing new sources of data. One of them is unconscious actions of a subject while interacting with a computer, in particular is with a computer mouse. During this interaction, a person experiences many emotions acquired during work and from the environment, and at the same time makes hundreds of cursor movements, which can be indicative of the subject's internal state. The creation of an emotion recognition mechanism based on unconscious activity is driven by the need to monitor the emotional well-being of the population to identify problematic situations in the early stages of development. The implementation of the mechanism will solve the problem of mental ill-health of the subject (for example, emotional burnout, fatigue, depression, etc.) by identifying bad moods, irritability at the initial stage of their manifestation through computer mouse movements. However, the lack of freely available data for studying the problem entails the need to accumulate such a set. It will help to identify and assess the subject's emotions regardless of language, race or other affiliations.

A person's movements are constantly changing according to the senses they are experiencing. If we consider computer mouse movement, the subject continuously processes data about the desired hand location and its difference from the actual location, while generating the necessary motor commands to achieve the goal [11]. Neurological movement disorders, such as Parkinson's and Tourette's diseases, prove the assumption that cursor movements in a choice task are influenced by emotion [12]. Experienced arousal in online shopping influences the duration of movements and quantitative changes in computer mouse speed [13]. Decision making and change in emotion can also be encountered when using not only a computer mouse, keyboard, and other things, but also when using a smartphone. The gadget can be applied to study changes in levels of joy while interacting with it [14].

An important aspect of the analysis is to identify and define the indicators to look for. To obtain a plausible assessment of a subject's emotional state, it is necessary to understand what indicators to look for. A study of the impact of negative emotions on cursor speed and distance travelled can help in this regard [15]. Besides the distance travelled and the mouse cursor speed, the use of such spatial characteristics of the trajectory as AUC (area under the curve), and zigzag (the number of trajectory deviations from a straight line connecting the start and the end points) are considered [12].

The analysis of emotional state based on the subject's unconscious actions, such as mouse movement, interaction with a smartphone, etc., is an innovative approach for this task. The versatility of the mechanism lies in its independence from the subject's race, language, and other affiliations, which makes the modality most suitable for investigating psycho-emotional states in the absence or deficiency of such data as text, audio, video, and others. Both spatial characteristics such as distance travelled, curve deviation and temporal characteristics such as total mouse interaction time per session can be considered as properties of cursor movement for the task. This allows us to analyze how well the emotion scores are based on computer mouse activity, and to extend the dataset with additional modalities to achieve better results.

3   Creation of a Mechanism for Recognizing the Emotional State of the Subject Based on His Unconscious Actions

3.1   Designing a Mechanism for Recognizing the Emotional State of the Subject

The first step in implementing a mechanism for recognizing a person's psycho-emotional state is to design the mechanism. For successful design it is necessary to understand who will interact with the system, which blocks are needed to implement the analysis, and how the blocks will be linked together. The structure of the emotion recognition mechanism is shown in Fig. 1.

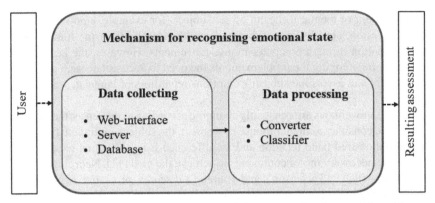

Fig. 1. Structure of the mechanism for recognizing the emotional state of the subject.

The person who will communicate directly with the system is the user who controls the mouse when performing tasks. The emotion recognition mechanism consists of two main units: data collecting and processing. Data collection for analysis in the current study is done manually, this is due to the lack of freely available datasets that provide information on human-computer interaction by controlling the mouse cursor. An algorithm for creating an in-house dataset, including the coordinates of the subject's cursor position and an estimate of his or her emotional state, developed and implemented. This mechanism will be described in more detail in Sect. 3.2. After the necessary data is received from the user, it is fed for processing to the next unit, where the estimation of the emotional state of the user interacting with the system is performed based on the spatial characteristics of the mouse cursor position and the accumulated experience of the mechanism. A detailed description of the data processing algorithm is presented in Sect. 3.2. The output of the mechanism is the classification of the user as a subject with a positive, negative, or neutral emotional state.

Based on the description of the human emotion recognition mechanism, it can be deduced that the input data for emotion analysis are the spatial characteristics of the mouse cursor position, the output data are the resulting assessment for the user. Such inputs have nothing to do with the subject's language, appearance, or other factors, confirming the universality of the emotional state analysis mechanism.

In the following chapters, the data collection and processing algorithm and the training of neural networks for classifying participants are described in detail.

3.2   Collect Spatial Characteristics of the Mouse Cursor Position and Create Own Dataset

The task of analyzing the emotional state of a user is one of the classification family, where, based on a training sample, the model identifies relationships between dependent and independent variables to enable further accurate prediction of results based on the data obtained for the first time. The classification task using information technology exists for decades, helping people to perform analysis in very different areas of life. A training dataset is a necessary part of the classification task.

The problem of emotion analysis by computer mouse movements is new and accumulating and canonizing such data is a time-consuming process. Therefore, such training sets are not publicly available, making analysis in this area difficult. To implement collection of data about a subject's cursor location during interactions with a computer, it is necessary to design and recreate a user interface that is free of distractions so that the evaluation of emotional state can be more reliable. It is also necessary to organize the data collection itself and the mechanism of interaction between the handler program and the user interface. This work is done in the data collection unit, the structure of which is shown in Fig. 2.

As a platform for research participants to interact with the interface as well as to save the coordinates of the cursor location in parallel, it is decided to create a web application, which is the block of the engine responsible for data collection. It is a structure consisting of the following elements:

1. A database into which the details of each participant are placed.
2. A server, written in the Python programming language, responsible for processing client-side requests, accumulating and transforming received data, and providing feedback.
3. Web-interface is an interface between a client (the page with which a computer user interacts) and a server, designed for the stable functioning of a web application.

The interface is written using the FastAPI web framework [16] for Python.

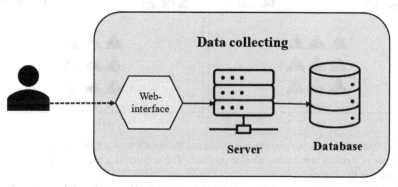

Fig. 2. Structure of the "Data collecting" block of the emotion recognition mechanism of the subject.

The participant never interacts directly with the server, it is always done by sending GET, POST and other requests going through the web interface and getting a response. These responses can be either web pages that are displayed to the user, status codes, success messages, etc.

A web application is a complex structure that combines a client and server side, as well as a web interface. First, let's look at what the client side is like. In the first step of interacting with the web application the user sees a welcome page with introductory instructions and instructions for further actions. The second page is a small survey to understand whose data will be processed in the future.

When the user completes registration in the system (by pressing the "Continue" button), a page is made available with an image that has the potential to induce a person to experience a particular emotion. These images are taken from the open affective image database OASIS [17]. There is no limit to the amount of time a participant can view the page. The participant is then asked to rate their psycho-emotional state on an emotion scale: positive, rather positive, neutral, rather negative, negative.

After viewing the affective image and self-assessment, a simple choice task (association task) [12, 18] becomes available (Fig. 3a), the meaning of which is to choose from two offered figures the one that, in the participant's opinion, is more consistent with the one given. A perfect choice is indicated by pressing the Right or Left button. An example of cursor movement during a simple choice task is Fig. 3b.

The whole test is a cycle of an affective image, a self-assessment survey and three association tasks. In total each participant completed 10 cycles, respectively viewing 10 images, completing 10 self-assessments, and solving 30 simple choice tasks. Thanks also to time recording, it can be said that, on average, it took the participants no more than 7 min to solve the complete test.

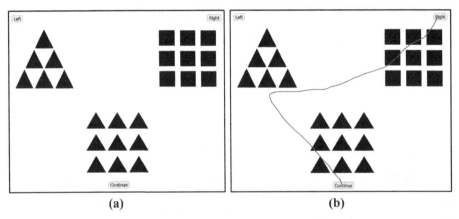

(a)   **(b)**

Fig. 3. a) Example of an association task to record the location of a subject's mouse cursor. b) An example of a solution to an association problem. The red line is a hypothetical trajectory and is not shown in the real experiment.

While the participants solve the choice tasks, each new cursor location is recorded in the background, namely the x and y coordinates. The scheme of interaction between the parties, client, and server, is shown in Fig. 4. Each time a participant moves the computer mouse, the client interface sends data such as the identification number (ID) and spatial characteristics of the cursor to the server through a POST request via the web interface. In response, the server sends a request processing report message.

In this way, the information about the movement of the cursor on each task page is sent to the server, where it is placed in the database and waits for further processing.

The next stage after the accumulation of information from the participants is its systematization and transformation into a unified data set. According to [12, 15, 18, 19], attention ceases to be directed and becomes stimulated when a person is affected

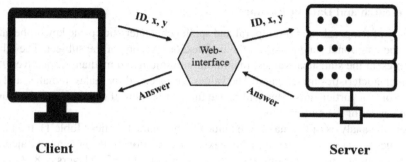

Client   **Server**

Fig. 4. Interaction between client and data collection unit server in a mechanism for analyzing emotional state based on unconscious subject movements.

by emotion, with the subject becoming more distracted by environmental stimuli. When viewed from the perspective of neuroscience, the brain's capacity for concentration is also affected by emotions, particularly negative ones. Therefore, temporal, spatio-temporal and two spatial characteristics are chosen as metrics to assess emotional state from mouse cursor movements. Temporal is the time of user's interaction with the page of the simplest choice (association) task. The spatio-temporal characteristic is the maximum speed at which the computer mouse moves. The spatial characteristics are the distance travelled by the cursor and the value of the maximum deviation from the straight line connecting the start and end points of the movement.

A program developed in Python is used to create a single dataset. The distance travelled is found by Eq. (1) as the sum of the Euclidean distance between two points, according to Eq. (2).

$$D = \sum_{i=1}^{n-1} d(a_i, a_{i+1}) \tag{1}$$

$$d(a_i, a_{i+1}) = \sqrt{\left(a_i^{(x)} - a_{i+1}^{(x)}\right)^2 + \left(a_i^{(y)} - a_{i+1}^{(y)}\right)^2} \tag{2}$$

Peak mouse speed is calculated as the difference of the Euclidean distance between points and the time it is travelled.

The maximum deviation of the cursor path from the straight line connecting the start and end points is calculated as the greatest minimum distance (perpendicular) from the point to the straight line.

After finding the four characteristics for each completed association task (assuming that the participant indicated a choice by pressing the appropriate button), all data are placed in one file, each line of which carries: id is participant number; gender is value 1 for male, 2 for female; emotion is self-rated emotional state (1-positive, 2-negative, 3-neutral); Euclidean distance - distance travelled by cursor (pixels); max straight line distance is maximum deviation of the cursor from the straight line connecting the start and end points; peak velocity is peak cursor speed (pixel/nanosecond); time is interaction time with the simplest selection task (nanoseconds). The final file contains 3139 lines of information.

3.3   Research and Data Processing

The study of temporal, spatio-temporal and spatial characteristics is the key to the analysis of the emotional state based on the unconscious actions of the subject. The tables below present the statistical values, maximum, minimum and median, respectively, for the four characteristics investigated. The values are specified for males, females, and the whole group of participants. This will reveal the correlations, if any, between the values and the gender of the participants.

From the analysis of the maximum values of the characteristics (Table 1), the maximum values for men are observed in the maximum deviation of the movement trajectory from the straight line connecting the start and end points (856.21 versus 823.48 for women), peak speed (816×10^{-6} vs. 612×10^{-6} for women), and interaction time with the simplest choice task (575.040×10^{8} vs. 382.679×10^{8} for women). The maximum value of distance travelled is observed for women (14620.5 vs. 10955.7 for men).

Table 1. Maximum values for spatial and temporal characteristics of the mouse cursor.

Characteristic	Maximum values		
	Men	Women	Shared
Distance travelled (pixels)	10955.7	14620.5	14620.5
Maximum deviation (pixels)	856.21	823.48	856.21
Peak speed (pixels/ns)	816×10^{-6}	612×10^{-6}	816×10^{-6}
Time (ns)	575.040×10^{8}	382.679×10^{8}	575.040×10^{8}

Analysis of the minimum values (Table 2) shows that the lowest values for women are observed in the maximum deviation of the trajectory from a straight line (5.87 vs. 7.26 for men), time to solve the simplest choice problem (3.671×10^{8} vs. 4.858×10^{8} for men). The minimum value of the traveled distance is observed for men (477.9 vs. 532.3 for women). The peak speed is independent of the participant's gender and amounted to 1×10^{-6}.

Table 2. Minimum values for spatial and temporal characteristics of the mouse cursor.

Characteristic	Minimum values		
	Men	Women	Shared
Distance travelled (pixels)	477.9	532.3	477.9
Maximum deviation (pixels)	7.26	5.87	5.87
Peak speed (pixels/ns)	1×10^{-6}	1×10^{-6}	1×10^{-6}
Time (ns)	4.858×10^{8}	3.671×10^{8}	3.671×10^{8}

The median peak speed values (Table 3) for males and females are closest compared to the rest of the characteristics - 5.02×10^{-6} and 5.73×10^{-6} respectively (5.28×10^{-6}

for the full group of participants). The same can be said for the association task solution time - 18.19×10^8 for men and 18.20×10^8 for women (18.19×10^8 for the full group of participants).

Table 3. Median values for spatial and temporal characteristics of the mouse cursor.

Characteristic	Median values		
	Men	Women	Shared
Distance travelled (pixels)	796.5	698.8	761.3
Maximum deviation (pixels)	134.05	89.17	115.32
Peak speed (pixels/ns)	5.02×10^{-6}	5.73×10^{-6}	5.28×10^{-6}
Time (ns)	18.19×10^8	18.20×10^8	18.19×10^8

From the analysis of the statistical characteristics, it can be concluded that the values are not strongly dependent on the gender of the participants, the observed difference in performance is not significant.

Table 4 presents the lowest and highest values of time, peak speed, spatial characteristics for the three subject states: positive, negative, neutral.

Table 4. Maximum and minimum values of characteristics for different emotional states of the subject.

Characteristic	Emotional state					
	Positive		Negative		Neutral	
	Max	Min	Max	Min	Max	Min
Distance travelled (pixels)	6838.9	538.6	10467.6	532.29	14620.5	477.9
Max. Deviation (pixels)	755.35	6.48	856.21	5.87	668.91	7.21
Peak speed ($\times 10^{-6}$ pixels/ns)	816	1	505	1	420	1

The distance travelled by the cursor reaches a maximum and a minimum when the condition is neutral. The situation is similar for the maximum deviation of the trajectory of movement from a straight line only for negative emotions. Peak speed has the highest value for a positive emotional state; the minimum is independent of the mood of the participant. The longest and shortest time to solve the simplest choice (association) task corresponds to positive emotions. The analysis shows that emotions affect subjects differently, and one cannot assess emotional state based only on the statistical characteristics of cursor movements.

Two neural networks using the Python programming language are trained to analyze emotions based on the unconscious movements of the subject, mouse movement: a multilayer perceptron using the TensorFlow library [20], and the OneVsRestClassifier from the Scikit-learn library [21]. The task of emotion recognition based on subject actions is a multi-class classification [22] because there are three classes: positive, negative, and neutral emotional states. The multi-layer perceptron (MLP) is a class of simple direct-coupled neural networks using supervised learning. The OneVsRestClassifier network is based on the principle of selecting a classifier for each class and then matching the class to others for each classifier, thus making the approach interpretive. The emotion analysis task solved using seven approaches to compare performance: in six cases, different pairs of features are taken as independent variables (two features out of four are chosen), and in the seventh case, all features are taken as independent variables. In each approach, the data set is split into a training sample and a test sample.

For MLP neural network analysis of emotion, the dependent variables (emotional state value) transformed using One-Hot coding, where the result is a binary data array whose size equals the number of features, with one in the column corresponding to the feature number and zeros in the others. The neural network consists of a normalizing layer adapted for the corresponding independent variables; two hidden full-connected layers (Dense) with 64 neurons each and a ReLU activation function [23]; an output full-connected layer (Dense) with a Softmax activation function [24] and three neurons according to the number of classes. The model trained over one hundred epochs.

To investigate the relationship between emotion and mouse movements using the OneVsRestClassifier classifier, no transformation of dependent variables is required. Reference vector classification is used in the construction of the model [25]. Table 5 summarizes the results of seven studies for each classifier.

Table 5. Training accuracy of multi-class classification models for different independent variables.

Independent variables for the dataset	Classifiers	
	MLP	OneVsRestClassifier
Euclidean distance + max straight line distance	0.4121	0.2663
Euclidean distance + peak velocity	0.4116	0.3174
Euclidean distance + time	0.4151	0.2663
max straight line distance + peak velocity	0.4087	0.3173
max straight line distance + time	0.4166	0.3174
peak velocity + time	0.4161	0.3173
All four attributes	0.4161	0.2663

From the results obtained, we can conclude that a pair of features is the maximum deviation of the movement trajectory from the straight line connecting the start and end points and the time to solve the simplest choice (association) problem is the most informative for analyzing the emotional state based on the unconscious movements of the subject, as both classifiers showed the maximum accuracy index for the pair of features. The most inefficient pair to investigate with an MLP network is the maximum deviation of the trajectory from a straight line and the peak speed, for the OneVsRestClassifier model these are three pairs: distance travelled and maximum deviation from a straight line, distance travelled and interaction time, a set of four features.

4 Conclusion

The technologies of emotion detection based on the subject's unconscious actions, computer mouse control, and interaction with a smartphone considered. The lack of freely available data for a study on this topic is revealed. A dataset containing temporal, spatial, and spatio-temporal characteristics of the cursor collected. These are the interaction time with the computer mouse during the session, the distance travelled by the cursor, its maximum deviation from the straight line connecting the start and end points of movement, and the peak speed of movement respectively. A web application in Python programming language using FastAPI web framework developed to compile the dataset. The final dataset contains 3139 lines of information. Such data helps to explore a subject's emotional state regardless of their race, language, or other affiliations.

The statistical values of the cursor characteristics, maximum, minimum and median, for men and women maximum and minimum values for each emotional state, positive, negative, neutral analyzed. From the analysis of the statistical characteristics, it is deduced the values do not depend on the gender of the participants. The MLP and OneVsRestClassifier from the TensorFlow and Scikit-learn libraries trained to identify the relationship between emotional state and cursor movement, respectively, with a 41% accuracy in determining emotional state. The results indicate there is a relationship between the emotions experienced and unconscious movements of the subject.

Acknowledgments. This study was conducted within the framework of the scientific program of the National Center for Physics and Mathematics, section №9 "Artificial intelligence and big data in technical, industrial, natural and social systems".

References

1. Sun, C., Huang, L., Qiu, X.: Utilizing BERT for Aspect-Based Sentiment Analysis via Constructing Auxiliary Sentence. CoRR, abs/1903.09588 (2019)
2. Caschera, M., Grifoni, P., Ferri, F.: Emotion classification from speech and text in videos using a multimodal approach. Multimodal Technol. Interact. **6**(4), 28 (2022)
3. Yoon, S., Byun, S., Jung, K.: Multimodal speech emotion recognition using audio and text. In: 2018 IEEE Spoken Language Technology Workshop (SLT), pp. 112–118 (2018)
4. Zhao, J., et al.: M3ED: Multi-modal multi-scene multi-label emotional dialogue database, arXiv preprint arXiv:2205.10237 (2022)
5. Fei, Z., Yang, E., Yu, L., Li, X., Zhou, H., Zhou, W.: A novel deep neural network-based emotion analysis system for automatic detection of mild cognitive impairment in the elderly. Neurocomputing **468**, 306–316 (2022)
6. Chand, H.V., Karthikeyan, J.: CNN based driver drowsiness detection system using emotion analysis. Intell. Autom. Soft Comput. **31**(2), 717–728 (2022)
7. Perepelkina, O., Kazimirova, E., Konstantinova, M.: RAMAS: Russian Multimodal Corpus of Dyadic Interaction for studying emotion recognition. PeerJ Preprints 6, e26688v1 (2018)

8. Ackerley, R., Aimonetti, J.M., Ribot-Ciscar, E.: Emotions alter muscle proprioceptive coding of movements in humans. Sci. Rep. **7**(1), 8465 (2017)

9. Troy, A.S., Shallcross, A.J., Brunner, A., Friedman, R., Jones, M.C.: Cognitive reappraisal and acceptance: effects on emotion, physiology, and perceived cognitive costs. Emotion **18**(1), 58 (2018)

10. Goldin, P., Moodie, C., Gross, J.: Acceptance versus reappraisal: behavioral, autonomic, and neural effects. Cogn. Affect. Behav. Neurosci. **19**, 927–944 (2019)

11. Smith, K.A., Morrison, S., Henderson, A.M., Erb, C.D.: Moving beyond response times with accessible measures of manual dynamics. Sci. Rep. **12**(1), 19065 (2022)

12. Yamauchi, T., Xiao, K.: Reading emotion from mouse cursor motions: affective computing approach. Cogn. Sci. **8**, 771–819 (2018)

13. Yang, L., Qin, S.: A review of emotion recognition methods from keystroke, mouse, and touchscreen dynamics. IEEE Access **9**, 162197–162213 (2021)

14. Tag, B., Sarsenbayeva, Z., Cox, A.L., Wadley, G., Goncalves, J., Kostakos, V.: Emotion trajectories in smartphone use: towards recognizing emotion regulation in-the-wild. Int. J. Hum Comput Stud. **166**, 102872 (2022)

15. Hibbeln, M., Jenkins, J.L., Schneider, C., Valacich, J.S., Weinmann, M.: How is your user feeling? Inferring emotion through human-computer interaction devices. MIS Q. **41**(1), 1–22 (2017)

16. FastAPI Documentation. https://fastapi.tiangolo.com/. Accessed 28 May 2023

17. Kurdi, B., Lozano, S., Banaji, M.: Introducing the open affective standardized image set (OASIS). Behav. Res. Methods **49**, 457–470 (2017)

18. Yamauchi, T., Leontyev, A., Razavi, M.: Assessing emotion by mouse-cursor tracking: theoretical and empirical rationales. In: 2019 8th International Conference on Affective Computing and Intelligent Interaction (ACII), pp. 89–95 (2019)

19. Ihbour, S., Anarghou, H., Boulhana, A., Najimi, M., Chigr, F.: Mental health among students with neurodevelopment disorders: case of dyslexic children and adolescents. Dement. Neuropsychologia **15**(4), 533–540 (2021)

20. How to create an MLP classifier with TensorFlow 2 and Keras. https://github.com/christianversloot/machine-learning-articles/blob/main/how-to-create-a-basic-mlp-classifier-with-the-keras-sequential-api.md. Accessed 28 May 2023

21. One-vs-the-rest (OvR) multiclass strategy. https://scikit-learn.org/stable/modules/generated/sklearn.multiclass.OneVsRestClassifier.html. Accessed 28 May 2023

22. Ghosal, D., Majumder, N., Poria, S., Chhaya, N., Gelbukh, A.: DialogueGCN: a graph convolutional neural network for emotion recognition in conversation. In: Proceedings of the 2019 Conference on Empirical Methods in Natural Language Processing and the 9th International Joint Conference on Natural Language Processing (EMNLP-IJCNLP), pp. 154–164. Association for Computational Linguistics (2019)

23. Nair, V., Hinton, G.: Rectified linear units improve restricted Boltzmann machines Vinod Nair. In: 27th International Conference on International Conference on Machine Learning, vol. 27, pp. 807–814 (2010)

24. Goodfellow, I., Bengio, Y., Courville, A.: Deep Learning. The MIT Press, Cambridge (2016)

25. Support Vector Machines. https://scikit-learn.org/stable/modules/svm.html. Accessed 28 May 2023

Development of a Device for Post-traumatic Ankle Rehabilitation

Andrey Knyazev[1]([✉]) [ID], Sergey Jatsun[1] [ID], Andrey Fedorov[1], and Jamil Safarov[2]

[1] Southwest State University, 94, 50 Let Oktyabrya st., Kursk 305040, Russia
teormeh@inbox.ru
[2] Azerbaijan Technical University, 25, Hüseyn Cavid pr., Baku AZ1073, Azerbaijan

Abstract. This article discusses a device for active-passive mechanotherapy of the ankle joint. The device is based on a controllable mobile platform equipped with force-moment sensors, on which the patient's foot is mounted by means of cuffs, and the platform rotation angles are controlled by linear motion sensors. The platform of the device is designed in such a way that the rotation axis of the platform always coincides with the centre of the ankle joint. For this purpose, a parallel kinematics mechanism is used, which is based on three linear electric drives. The control system of the device provides both active and passive movement of the platform. For realization of the control algorithm of the mobile platform movement, a mathematical model is developed, which allows establishing connections between angular motions of the mobile platform and linear drives of the parallel mechanism. Models of reaction forces of the platform support on the patient's foot during operation of the device are also described. A functional control diagram of the device is presented, and the modes of operation of the device are described.

Keywords: Ankle Mechanotherapy · Force Control Sensors · Mathematical model · Parallel Kinematics Mechanism · Functional Diagram

1 Introduction

Among injuries of lower extremities, the most widespread are those of distal part of lower leg and ankle, which, according to literature data, make up from 12.0 to 20.0% of all fractures of locomotor apparatus. In 12–39.8% of cases unsatisfactory results of treatment are observed, and the long-term disability lasts from 4 to 8 months. One of the most common injuries sustained by humans is damage to the ankle joint in sports, domestic, industrial exercises, and as a result of car accidents. Falling from heights with a landing on the feet, including parachuting, also often results in injuries to the ankle joint (AJ). Statistically, more than half of all lower limb injuries and about 40% of joint injuries are ankle injuries. We also know that 54% of ankle fractures and dislocations occur at a young age, when the ability to work is important. After an injury, there is a long process of treatment and rehabilitation, and after surgery, rehabilitation can be complicated by prolonged stiffness of the joint. In many countries, work is underway to develop devices and devices that allow for the post-traumatic rehabilitation of the

A. Ronzhin et al. (Eds.): ICR 2023, LNAI 14214, pp. 93–102, 2023.
https://doi.org/10.1007/978-3-031-43111-1_9

individual using AJ passive mechanotherapy devices. This approach makes it possible to perform foot movements according to an individual rehabilitation program (IRP) set by the doctor. The FLEX-02, A3 Ankle CPM, Kinetec Breva ankle, and ARTROMOT SP3 are widespread [1–3].

At the same time, due to the influence of indefinitely variable parameters of the AJ muscular system, it is difficult to ensure the required accuracy of the patient's foot movement along the trajectory set by the doctor, which reduces the effectiveness of the rehabilitation process. Therefore, the creation of such devices requires an in-depth study of the theory of human-device interaction, creation of man-machine interfaces, mathematical models, and control algorithms that provide the specified quality indicators. Thus, the issues of developing and creating robotic devices for post-traumatic ankle rehabilitation that provide a given movement of the foot under unpredictable changes in physiological parameters are relevant [4–6].

The aim of the study is to improve the effectiveness of the rehabilitation process with an active-passive mechanotherapy and rehabilitation device that provides a given precision through adaptive control of foot movement, taking into account the individual characteristics of the patient's AJ.

2 Tasks of Ankle Rehabilitation

The main objectives of ankle rehabilitation during the recovery period:

– reverse the processes of muscle atrophy and destructive changes in the vessels;
– return mobility to the joint;
– prevent stagnation of fluids in the reconstructed limb;
– increase the motor activity of the joint.

In the early stages of rehabilitation, it is necessary to perform simple movements of the foot in small ranges at a slow pace. Movements such as plantar flexion and dorsiflexion as well as pronation and supination. The exercises are shown in Fig. 1. Once the rehabilitator has noticed an improvement in the ankle's motor function, the range of motion can be gradually increased.

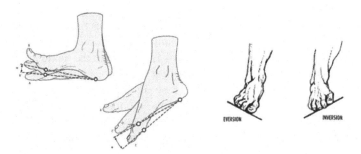

Fig. 1. Exercises for early rehabilitation.

All therapeutic and rehabilitation measures are determined by the severity of the injury as well as the individual characteristics of the patient. After the cast is removed, it is important to put stress on the ankle joint gradually. The exercises are shown in Fig. 2.

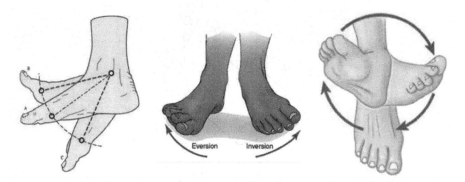

Fig. 2. Exercises for the final stage of rehabilitation.

In the final stage of recovery, you should start gradually combining these two movements by making circular movements with the foot. Also, continue to perform the operations described in the first phase, but with larger rotation angles until the ankle is able to perform the movements within the usual ranges of motion. The normal ranges of motion of the foot are shown in Fig. 3 [7, 8].

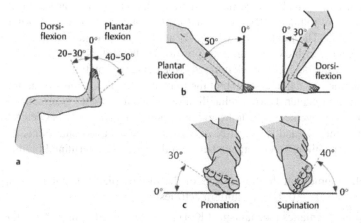

Fig. 3. Range of motion of the healthy ankle.

3   The Circuit Diagram of the Active-Passive Mechanotherapy Device

The circuit diagram of the active-passive mechanotherapy device for the ankle, shown in Fig. 4, is a parallel manipulator equipped with linear actuators [9].

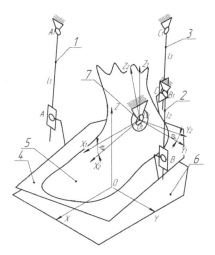

Fig. 4. Spatial kinematic diagram of the appliance.

Figure 4 shows the following designations: 1 is the linear actuator 1 (l_1); 2 is the linear actuator 2 (l_2); 3 is the linear actuator 3 (l_3); 4 is the controlled mobile platform; 5 is the patient's foot; 6 is the platform in initial position; 7 is the virtual joint.

By changing the lengths of the actuators, it is possible to change the position of the controlled mobile platform (CMP) and consequently the patient's foot. The structure of the device includes the patient's foot, mobile platform, electric actuators, power frame sensors, control system. The electric actuators of the manipulator are connected to the body by means of joints A_1, B_1, C_1. Actuators are connected to the platform by means of joints A, B, C. The joints A, B, C, A_1, B_1 are two-coordinate, while C_1 is a single-coordinate joint, capable of changing its position in the sagittal plane [10, 11].

In order for the device to work correctly, the center of rotation of the CMP "virtual joint" O_1, defined by the intersection of the joint axes (A, B, C), must be at the point O_2 of the ankle joint center. During rehabilitation measures, point O_2 remains stationary and all platform movements occur around this point. The radius vectors determining the position of points O_1 and O_2 must be equal $\bar{r}_{o1} = \bar{r}_{o2}$. At the same time, under real-world conditions, there is a tolerance between the vectors, determined by the formula: $\bar{r} = \bar{r}_{o1} - \bar{r}_{o2}$.

We will assume that the trajectories of the mobile platform points satisfying the condition $\frac{|\Delta\bar{r}|}{|\bar{r}_{O_1}|} = \varepsilon \le 0.01$, are valid trajectories.

A parallel kinematics mechanism (PKM) [12, 13] is used to implement the "virtual hinge" of the platform and ensure the intersection of the mobile platform rotation axes in the center (tibia and talus contact zone) of the AJ, based on three linear actuators.

The ankle joint is formed by the tibia and talus bones. The articular surfaces of the lower leg bones and their ankles are encompassed by the Talus block in a fork-like fashion. The ankle joint is block-shaped. In this joint, flexion (movement towards the plantar surface of the foot) and extension (movement towards the rear surface of the foot) are possible around the transverse axis that runs through the talus block. The subtalar joint is responsible for pronation (rotation of the foot with the sole turning outwards) and supination (rotation of the foot with the sole turning inwards) of the foot. The human foot moves in three planes, the rotation around the vertical axis is caused by the rotation of the lower leg, therefore when working with active-passive mechanotherapy for ankle joint device (APMAJ) you should take this fact into account and not to fix the lower leg, otherwise you can get new injuries.

4 Diagrams for Measuring Leg and Platform Interaction Forces

The principle of operation of the force meter is based on monitoring the relative movement of the upper and lower module elements of the mobile platform at four points. The device has sensors that measure the force between the patient's foot and the mobile platform at these points. In active mode the patient provides the foot movement and the APMAJ platform replicates this movement. Impedance control is used for this. The mobile platform is attached to the patient's foot via a system of elastic connections, the drive platform is equipped with angle sensors and electrically controlled actuators and ensures a defined movement of the foot. When a relative movement of one platform with respect to the other occurs, a deformation of the elastic elements of the measuring device occurs, which is registered by the movement sensor [14–16].

During operation of the device, reaction forces from the platform arise between the patient's foot and the platform. To account for these forces, it is necessary to introduce a model to describe the interactions between the foot and the platform [17].

The foot acts on the platform as a distributed load, so replace it with two concentrated forces. Assume that the foot is in contact with the platform by the heel and metatarsal bones, together they form a bony system, which is connected to the plantar side of the foot by muscular tissues. Figure 5 shows a diagram of the interaction of the foot and platform in the sagittal plane. The following symbols are included in the diagram: 1 is ankle joint; 2 is metatarsal bones; 3 is heel bone; 4 is tibia; 5 is platform; 6 is force-moment interaction sensors.

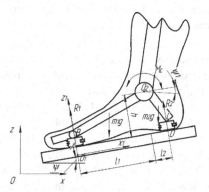

Fig. 5. Diagram of foot and platform interaction in the sagittal plane.

Let's write down the equation of moments for the patient's foot in the sagittal plane:

$$J_{bs}\ddot{\psi} = M_R + M(G) - M_C, \tag{1}$$

where: J_{bs} is the moment of inertia of the bone system;

M_R is the moment created by the support reaction forces;

$M(G)$ is the moment created by the gravity of the bone system;

M_C is the resistance moment of leg muscles.

Let's represent the muscle tissues as a Kelvin-Feugt model, with viscous and elastic components arranged in parallel. Given this, for sagittal plane, we will find forces R_1, R_2 by formulas:

$$R_1 = c_1(\psi - \psi_1) + \mu_1(\dot{\psi} - \dot{\psi}_1), \tag{2}$$

$$R_2 = c_2(\psi - \psi_1) + \mu_2(\dot{\psi} - \dot{\psi}_1), \tag{3}$$

where c is the reduced muscle stiffness coefficient;

μ is the reduced muscle viscosity coefficient;

$(\psi - \psi_1)$ is the relative strain of muscle tissues;

$(\dot{\psi} - \dot{\psi}_1)$ is the relative strain rate of the muscle tissues.

5   Functional Diagram of the Control System

The functional diagram of the APMAJ robotic device is shown in Fig. 6. The diagram consists of a hardware and software system, a physiological parameter monitoring unit, a rehabilitation program selection unit, a signal processing unit, a mobile platform, electric drives, amplifiers, a control unit, a sensor system for measuring linear and angular movements and reactions between the patient's foot and the APMAJ mobile platform in the sagittal and frontal planes [18]. The choice of rehabilitation mode determines the program of movements of the patient's foot, formalized in the form of parametric equations $\overline{\lambda}(t)^* = (\phi(t)^*, \theta(t)^*, \psi(t)^*)^T$. If the conditions are met $\overline{\lambda}(t)^* < \overline{\lambda}(t)_0^*$, where $\overline{\lambda}(t)_0^*$ is the range of permissible rotation angles. The on-board computer (signal processing unit) solves the inverse kinematics task (IKT) and determines the length change laws of the linear actuators $\overline{L}^* = (L_1^*, L_2^*, L_3^*)^T$.

Further signals are proportional $\overline{L}^* = (L_1^*, L_2^*, L_3^*)^T$ are fed to the appropriate comparison units (comparators), where they are compared with the real values $\overline{L} = (L_1, L_2, L_3)^T$. The presence of feedbacks makes it possible to determine the deviation of the real position of the platform from the set position in the form of a vector $\Delta\lambda$ and force interaction vector ΔP. The regulators receive an error value $\Delta\overline{L} = (\Delta L_1, \Delta L_2, \Delta L_3)^T$ for each controlled variable. These values are converted by the control algorithm into control voltages $\overline{U} = (U_1, U_2, U_3)^T$.

The force-moment sensing system makes it possible to evaluate changes in the reaction value over time and detect the moment of spastic effects, muscle contractures and automatically change the laws of foot movement in order to eliminate the patient's trauma and pain syndrome. In accordance with the ACS diagram, the actuators are controlled to provide the specified movement of the patient's foot. The feedback channels are the data recorded by the swing angle sensors on the respective axes, as well as the force-momentum sensor values. The LQR-optimization strategy is used to optimize the settings of the controllers to give the required quality performance of the APMAJ control

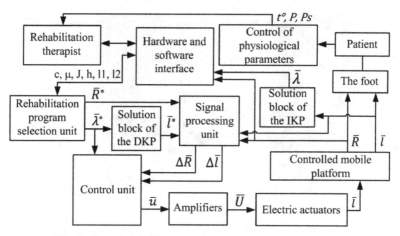

Fig. 6. Functional diagram of the APMAJ robotic appliance.

system. If an abnormal situation occurs (reaction force limits are exceeded), the ACS algorithm allows you to change the exercise pace, perform the complex movements required for safe operation of the device and stop if necessary, thus ensuring safe patient rehabilitation [19].

6   Description of the Unit's Operating Modes

The rehabilitation unit has several modes of operation. Before starting the rehabilitation procedure, the rehabilitation therapist must select the operating mode parameters, using a program on a personal computer. The operation of the device has been simulated in MATLAB/Simulink environment, information about the operation modes is presented below.

Plantar - Dorsiflexion. This robotic mode allows a rotational movement of the patient's foot in the sagittal plane. The range of rotation angle is $42° \leq \psi \leq 23°$. The results of the simulation mode are shown in Fig. 7.

Pronation - supination. This mode of operation allows a rotational movement of the patient's foot in the frontal plane. The range of rotation angle is $40° \leq \varphi \leq 40°$. The results of the simulation are shown in Fig. 8.

Any rehabilitation mode should be set according to the recommendations of the rehabilitation therapist. In this mode, the person's foot can perform both combined and circular movements of the foot. The mode chosen by the user can include changing direction, speed of movement and number of repetitions (Fig. 9).

The effectiveness of rehabilitation interventions depends largely on factors such as gender, age, duration of disability, educational level, and occupational affiliation of the patient. The Barthel and Rankin scales record the condition without offering the patient understandable benchmarks for the dynamics of the rehabilitation process, do not allow for accessible formulation of rehabilitation goals and motivation of the patient. Thus, these scales are appropriate for a screening assessment of the overall rehabilitation process. RMI, HAI and the KX test are recognized as informative techniques that

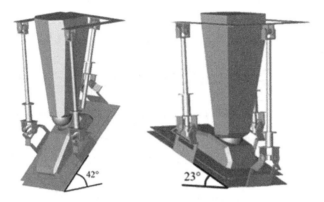

Fig. 7. Mode of operation - plantar – dorsiflexion.

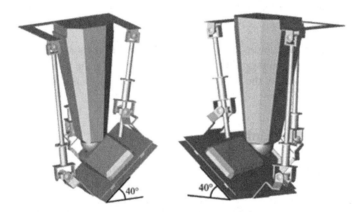

Fig. 8. Mode of operation - Pronation – supination.

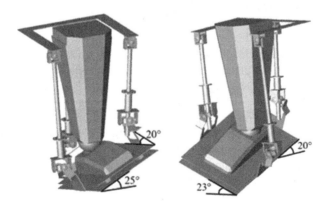

Fig. 9. User-configured operating mode.

are sensitive to changes in the patient's condition in relation to both muscle function and functioning. The clarity of objectives and graded assessment allows rehabilitation goals to be formulated in an accessible format, which increases patient motivation and satisfaction with treatment.

It is important to correctly determine the predicted end result of rehabilitation in each individual case, as this is the basis for the subsequent comprehensive assessment of the effectiveness of rehabilitation.

At the same time, objective and informative criteria for the effectiveness of medical rehabilitation in various forms of occupational diseases have not been sufficiently developed and put into practice today. Meanwhile, data from domestic and foreign sources show that the levels of rehabilitation indicators are closely interrelated with the indicators of disability, mortality, morbidity, organization and quality of medical care and are directly related to qualitative and quantitative criteria that characterize public health.

7   Conclusion

On the basis of the research carried out in the article, the following scientific and practical results have been obtained:

- Computational schemes have been given, on the basis of which mathematical models describing kinematic and dynamic interactions of the device and the patient's leg have been constructed.
- The functional diagram of the device reflecting the structure of automatic control system is given and described.
- The operating modes of the device are described.

A prototype device is under development.

Acknowledgment. The work was supported by grant of Russian Science Foundation № 22–21-00464 – "Development of models and control algorithms for biotechnical walking systems".

References

1. Pechurin, A., Fedorov, A., Jatsun, A., Jatsun, S.: Mathematical modelling of human walking in a rehabilitation exoskeleton using video gait analysis method. In: Proceedings of Southwestern State University, vol. 25, no. 3, pp. 27–40 (2022)
2. Karlov, A., Postolny, A., Fedorov, A., Jatsun, S.: Modeling an exoskeleton with a hybrid linear gravity compensator. In: Proceedings of Southwestern State University, vol. 24, no. 3, pp. 66–78 (2020)
3. Dmitriev, V., Fedorov, A.: Analysis of industrial exoskeleton qualitative performance based on a set of criteria. Issues in the methodology of natural and technical sciences: contemporary context, pp. 131–135 (2019)
4. Antipov, V., Karlov, A., Fedorov, A.: Energy distribution in the human-exoskeleton system. Issues in the methodology of natural science and engineering: contemporary context, pp. 109–112 (2019)

5. Pechurin, A.S., Jatsun, S.F., Fedorov, A.V., Jatsun, A.S.: Studying the two-legged walking system with video capture methods. In: Chugo, D., Tokhi, M.O., Silva, M.F., Nakamura, T., Goher, K. (eds.) CLAWAR 2021. LNNS, vol. 324, pp. 3–12. Springer, Cham (2022). https://doi.org/10.1007/978-3-030-86294-7_1

6. Jatsun, S., Yatsun, A., Fedorov, A., Saveleva, E.: Simulation of static walking in an exoskeleton. In: Ronzhin, A., Shishlakov, V. (eds.) Electromechanics and Robotics. SIST, vol. 232, pp. 49–60. Springer, Singapore (2022). https://doi.org/10.1007/978-981-16-2814-6_5

7. Knyazev, A., Jatsun, A., Fedorov, A.: Mathematical modeling of the biomechanical rehabilitation system of foot exoskeleton in frontal and sagittal planes. In: Ronzhin, A., Pshikhopov, V. (eds) Frontiers in Robotics and Electromechanics. Smart Innovation, Systems and Technologies, vol. 329, pp. 19–32. Springer, Cham (2023). https://doi.org/10.1007/978-981-19-7685-8_2

8. Knyazev, A., Yatsun, S., Fedorov, A.: Control of a Device for mechanotherapy of the ankle joint. Biomed. Eng. **56**, 392–396 (2023)

9. Knyazev, A., Jatsun, S., Fedorov, A.: Algorithm of personalized adjustment of the active-passive mechanotherapy device for the ankle joint. In: International Conference on Industrial Engineering, Applications and Manufacturing, pp. 661–666 (2023)

10. Hassan, M., Khajepour, A.: Optimization of actuator forces in cable-based parallel manipulators using convex analysis. IEEE Trans. Rob. **24**, 736–740 (2008)

11. Alvarez-Perez, G., Garcia-Murillo, A., Jesús Cervantes-Sánchez, J.: Robot-assisted ankle rehabilitation: a review, disability and rehabilitation. Assist Technol. **15**(4), 3e94-408 (2020)

12. Antonellis, P., Galle, S., Clercq, D., Malcolm, P.: Altering gait variability with an ankle exoskeleton. PLoS One **13**(10), 0205088 (2018)

13. Jamwal, P., Hussain, S., Xie, S.: Restage design analysis and multicriteria optimization of a parallel ankle rehabilitation robot using genetic algorithm. IEEE Trans. Autom. Sci. Eng. **12**(4), 1433–1446 (2014)

14. Tsoi, H., Xie, Q.: Design and control of a parallel robot for ankle rehabiltation. In: 15th international conference on mechatronics and machine vision in practice, pp. 515–520 (2008)

15. Vallés, M., Cazalilla, J., Valera, Á.: A 3-PRS parallel manipulator for ankle rehabilitation: towards a low-cost robotic rehabilitation. Robotica **35**, 1939–1957 (2017)

16. Zeng, X., Zhu, G., Zhang, M.: Reviewing clinical effectiveness of active training strategies of platform-based ankle rehabilitation robots. Healthcare Eng. **2018**, 1–12 (2018)

17. Zhang, M., McDaid, A., Veale, A.: Adaptive robot with trajectory tracking control of a parallel ankle rehabilitation joint-space force distribution. IEEE Access **7**, 812–820 (2019)

18. Shevko, D.: Adaptive management in the conditions of undefinition. Sci. Rev. Tech. Sci. **2**, 75–77 (2017)

19. Yatsun, A., Karlov, A., Malchikov, A., Jatsun, S.: Investigation of the dynamical characteristics of the lower-limbs exoskeleton actuators. In: MATEC Web of Conferences. EDP Sciences, vol. 161, pp. 3–8 (2018)

Evaluation of EEG Data for Zonal Affiliation of Brain Waves by Leads in a Robot Control Task

Daniyar Wolf⬤, Yaroslav Turovsky ⬤, Anastasia Iskhakova$^{(\boxtimes)}$ ⬤,
and Roman Meshcheryakov ⬤

V.A. Trapeznikov Institute of Control Sciences of Russian Academy of Sciences, 65,
Profsoyuznaya Street, Moscow 117997, Russia
shumskaya.ao@gmail.com

Abstract. The task of creating a neural interface for controlling a robotic system by means of an oculographic interface and bioelectric signals, is considered. The article highlights the results of scientific experimental research aimed at the evaluation of the representativeness of bioelectrical signals obtained by electroencephalography (EEG). The basic hypothesis is formulated and tested with the help of artificial neural network technology. The authors consider an experiment on the formation of steady-state visually evoked potentials in a group of people with the subsequent creation of an applied database. They describe an original approach for extracting representative features from the EEG signal. With the help of deep machine learning technology the representativeness of the data under study is evaluated. The main conclusions are formulated and the hypothesis that each brain lead reproduces unique waves which are characteristic of each brain zone is confirmed. The proposed model of a symmetric multilayer multi-adaptive direct propagation neuron can find its application in solving problems related to the processing of EEG signals. Based on the results of this study, the authors suggest that data on the bioelectrical activity of the brain can be uniquely identified, and thus used as control signals for various robotic devices.

Keywords: Robot Control · Brain-Computer Interface · Bioelectrical Signals · Electroencephalography · Steady-State Visual Evoked Potentials · Machine Learning

1 Introduction

The development of modern interdisciplinary approaches at the junction of information technology and physiology has led in recent decades to the appearance of a large number of human-computer communication devices. Managing robotic systems poses new challenges, including the development and improvement of control methods. For example, controlling copter movement using bioelectric operator signals. In addition to the movement of robotic systems, such interfaces can be applied to a wide range of tasks related to the rehabilitation of patients with neurological and traumatological

A. Ronzhin et al. (Eds.): ICR 2023, LNAI 14214, pp. 103–115, 2023.
https://doi.org/10.1007/978-3-031-43111-1_10

profiles, and improvement of control of various devices: from a personal computer to aviation systems. That is, in this case, the benefits to humans are multifaceted - both a new level of control, combining the benefits of the human brain, and helping humans themselves to analyze and interpret their brain signals in cases of rehabilitation. The most common tasks currently being solved are improving their hardware, developing new algorithms for processing received signals and transforming them into commands to effector devices, and searching for new physiological phenomena that can be used as the basis for commands transmitted through new interfaces.

The relevance of developments in the field of systems that could help to organize interaction between a human being and external devices through brain signals or brain–computer interface (BCI) is confirmed by the fact that at the moment there is already a number of studies dedicated to this topic. One of the studies in 2020 was conducted by Dalin Yang, Trung-Hau Nguyen, and Wan-Young Chung of Busan National University in South Korea. Their work aimed to create their own neurocomputer interface. The researchers proposed a simplified synchronized hybrid system for multiple command control of electroencephalograph signals in the motor cortex. The proposed system can issue 38 control commands, for which the user only needs to focus on the stimulus and blink his eyes [1].

Another study was conducted by researchers at the National Chin-Yi University of Technology in Taiwan. In their research paper, they draw attention to the significance of BCI for people suffering from motor neuron disease (MND) who are unable to move independently. The paper mainly proposed a brain-computer interface (BCI) based on a wireless electroencephalogram and DC motor drive circuit to control electric wheelchairs via Bluetooth interface for paralyzed patients [2].

S. Rihana, P. Damien, T. Moujaess aimed their work at detecting eye blink signals from electroencephalography (EEG) signals. The researchers collected data, described methods used for pre-processing of EEG signals and also for the classification of eye blink signals using a probabilistic neural network as a binary classifier. Their ultimate goal was to apply the resulting database to a neurorehabilitation application for patients with movement disorders [3].

One of the ambitious projects in this direction is the Neuralink project by Elon Musk, as a result of which a neuro-technology capable of connecting the human brain with a computer is to be created. As of today, Neuralink presents a miniature chip with a diameter of about 23 mm and a height of 8 mm. The chip can have a maximum of 1024 connections to the brain, flexible filaments for invasive connection of chips to the brain, efficient algorithms for signal processing, and immediately a robotic surgeon to perform invasive procedures of filament implantation [4].

Despite significant scientific advances in technological development, the human brain remains the most powerful, unique and fastest computing system. In this regard, developments and research allowing a human being to interact directly with technology excluding any physiological activity (as BCI) are becoming more and more widespread and relevant.

Nevertheless, in the above-mentioned works, the topics of obtaining and preparing statistical information, as well as their theoretical evaluation, are poorly covered. Undoubtedly, the use of hybrid technologies (elements and technologies of "artificial intelligence") to obtain scientific and engineering results is currently the current world practice.

The main hypothesis of this study is that, supposedly, during successive cycles of formation of steady-state visually evoked potentials (SSVEP), the brain reproduces unique waves consisting in changes of frequency-time characteristics of registered signals, typical for each head zone (leads). In other words, presumably, it is possible to identify with a certain degree of probability a particular EEG signal belongs to which brain lead.

However, before making this kind of estimation, it is necessary to perform some transformations of the collected EEG data. Thus, this study is aimed at obtaining informative features from the EEG signals with their subsequent machine classification. The authors in the article [5] evaluated for brain fatigue during sessions of the SSVEP. The statistical conclusions that were obtained as a result of this experiment served as a reason to continue research in this direction.

Thus, it is necessary to conduct a study to confirm the hypothesis that the waves recorded by the electroencephalograph sensors from the head leads are subject to grouping and can be applied in machine learning tasks, and subsequent machine classification in various scientific and engineering tasks. And, as a consequence, the results of this study will advance research into the identification of EEG signals of the human brain. The task of controlling robots without using physical influence on the device – with the use of human brain signals (as if thoughts) can be solved using the data from this study.

2 Collecting and Preparing Statistical Data

EEG-type bio-signals are difficult to interpret and use directly in the control task. In order to formalize and further standardize in the solution of this problem, an experiment was conducted. The scheme of interaction looks quite ordinary (Fig. 1). But an important component is a block BCI, which is the intellectual part of the processing of complex formalized signal of the person to the formal signal to the device. To improve the efficiency and quality of interpretation of human control signals, it is necessary to study the signals, to try to identify them, to select the best attributes for their recognition. By doing so, the BCI unit will become progressively more effective.

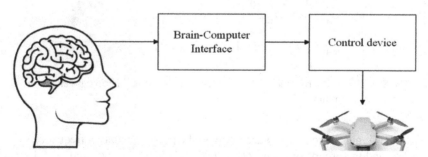

Fig. 1. Scheme of human-robot interaction via BCI.

The aim was to test the previously presented hypothesis, whether the signal could be claimed to have been caused by one or another zone of the brain.

For the study, we created a database with EEG SSVEPs obtained from SSVEP sessions from 30 subjects of both sexes aged from 17 to 23 (12 women and 18 men) with no neurological or psychiatric pathologies. Before the experiment, the participants did not take any psychotropic drugs and had normal or corrected to normal vision. The electroencephalogram data were recorded using Neuron-Spectr-4VP device (Neurosoft, Russia) at $O1$, $O2$, Oz, $P3$, $P4$ and Pz leads with a sampling frequency of 5000 Hz, with the cutoff filter on and with the high and low frequencies filter off. Photostimulation was performed at frequencies 1, 8, and 14 Hz. The duration of each SSVEP session was 15 s.

Based on the available input dataset, the dynamics of frequency-time characteristics of SSVEP was determined. When the retina is excited by flashes of frequency ranging from 3.5 to 75 Hz, the brain generates electrical activity with the frequency of flashes [6–10].

After data accumulation, the electroencephalograms were filtered by a Sixth Order Butterworth Low Pass Filter with 2 (low cut) to 35 (high cut) Hz bandwidth (Fig. 2).

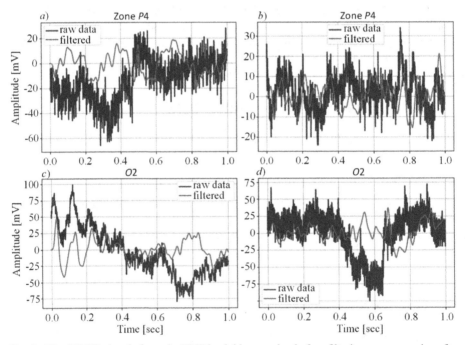

Fig. 2. The SSVEP signals from the "P4" lead: blue graph – before filtering; green graph – after filtering (Color figure online).

Next, the signals were grouped according to the photostimulation frequencies (1, 8, and 14 Hz) and the groups of leads "$O1$", "$O2$", "Oz", "$P3$", "$P4$", and "Pz" for each subject. Given the sampling rate, three data matrices were obtained after grouping:

$N = 30 \times M = 75000 \times V = 6$ elements, where:

N is the ordinal number of the subject;

M is the number of samples in the signal;

V is the number of signals in the group for each subject (also let this value denote the set consisting of {"O1", "O2", "Oz", "P3", "P4", "Pz"}).

If only the first and the last 25000 signs are selected, two matrices could be obtained containing information about the signals for the first and the last 5 s.

However, this approach of data preparation for both machine learning and machine classification produces a very large vector of informative features – M, and a very small vector with the samples for each signal (examples) – N.

At a minimum, the high dimensionality of the features is associated with very high computational costs, and to a greater extent, a large number of trainable parameters can lead to a complex classification model, which will have a high variance and will not allow to qualitatively identify the desired features.

It is not difficult to see that there are sufficiently large sets on M for set V. To reduce the dimensionality of V, we performed resampling of each signal in groups up to $M = 25,000$ while maintaining the data structure.

Data augmentation was accomplished by "splitting" the feature M into windows of 1260 counts in increments of 625 counts, giving a total of 1140 samples for each lead.

As a result of the above work, applied data were obtained which is a structured record of the electrical activity of the human brain as a result of the experiment with SSVEP (Fig. 3).

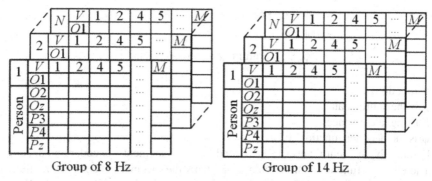

Fig. 3. The structure of the EEG input data with SSVEP for each subject in the frequency groups of 8 and 14 Hz. Similarly for 1 Hz.

A number of studies [11–14] noted the individual psychophysical and psychoemotional features of each subject – there is no guarantee that the signs are unambiguously separable in time for the entire group of subjects. To solve this problem, we applied deep machine learning for the further machine classification based on classical methods [15].

3 Obtaining Representative Features

To integrate the elements of the artificial neural network (ANN), a specialized computer program was developed [16]. Taking into account the obtained data structure, a special autoencoder for EEG coding was developed.

An autoencoder (AE) is a kind of artificial neural network the purpose of which is to restore input information (data) at the output. AE performs only two tasks: 1) compression of the input data into a representation of the hidden space (or latent vector), also known as the information bottleneck; 2) recovery of the output data based on the resulting representation. The autoencoding process itself is an unsupervised machine learning algorithm since the feature extraction algorithm is determined by deep machine learning.

The concept of information bottleneck (IB) was introduced by Tishby et al. [17]. This notion was introduced together with the hypothesis that IB can extract relevant information by compressing the amount of information that passes through the entire neural network using previously learned input data compression.

Traditionally, AE has been used in dimensionality reduction tasks to study informative features. And, only relatively recently, AE models with hidden parameters which use the concept of prior and posterior distribution, such as variational AE, began to be used to build generative models that can generate new data. This is accomplished by compressing information in an information bottleneck such that only important attributes are extracted from the entire data set, and these extracted attributes (representations) can be used to generate new data.

From a formal point of view, the mathematical model of AE can be expressed as follows:

$$\phi : \chi \rightarrow F$$
$$\psi : F \rightarrow \chi \tag{1}$$
$$\phi, \psi = \operatorname*{argmin}_{\phi, \psi} \| \chi - (\phi \circ \psi)\chi \|^2,$$

coder function;

χ is the source data;

F is the latent space;

ψ is the decoder function.

Essentially, the neural network is divided into two segments: encoder and decoder.

The encoder function (1), denoted as ϕ, maps the original data χ into the hidden space F which is present in IB. The decoder function, denoted as ψ, maps the hidden space F into the IB at the output. The output in this case coincides with the input function. Thus, the original image is reconstructed after some generalized nonlinear compression.

The coding network can be represented by a standard neural network function gated through the activation function, where z is the latent dimensionality:

$$z = \sigma(Wx + b). \tag{2}$$

Similarly, the decoding network can be represented in the same way but with different weight and offset $- b$, and with potentially used activation functions:

$$x' = \sigma'(W'x + b'). \tag{3}$$

Using (2) and (3), the loss function will take the form:

$$(x, x') = \| x - x' \|^2 = \| x - \sigma'(W'(\sigma(Wx + b)) + b') \|^2. \tag{4}$$

The loss function (4) is used to train the neural network using the standard backpropagation procedure.

Since the input and output are the same data, and as already indicated above, the AE machine learning algorithm is unsupervised, the AE deep machine learning process is self-supervised learning. The goal of self-supervised learning for AE is to select encoder and decoder functions such that the IB dimensionality is minimal to encode the input signal but sufficient to recover it at the output.

If the number of perceptrons in the IB layer is small enough, the ability to reconstruct the input information on the output will be limited and very different from the original (high losses). If too many perceptrons are used, it makes no sense to use compression at all. AE can start the task of reconstructing the original signal (a negative effect in the current study) without extracting useful information about the data distribution, if

1. the dimensionality of the hidden representation is the same as the dimensionality of the input;
2. the dimensionality of the hidden representation is greater than the dimensionality of the input;
3. a too large amount of data is provided for AE.

In these cases, even a linear encoder and a linear decoder simply copy the input data to the output without learning anything useful about the distribution.

Summarizing the theoretical aspects outlined above, we can conclude that in an AE network functionally the left part is the encoding part and the right part is the decoding part. Ideally, any AE architecture can be organized by setting the IB dimensions based on the complexity of the simulated distribution.

Therefore, the goal of deep machine learning of the AE is not to copy the input data at the output of the neural network but to train AE to reconstruct the input data so that the informative bottleneck highlights (as if it recognizes) only useful information.

Today, the application of AE is actively popularized in the tasks of image reconstruction and basic coloring, data compression, conversion of grayscale images into color images, creation of images with higher resolution, etc. The problem, however, is that the various AE models work only with data that is similar to the data on which they have been trained – applied data.

The final implementation of the model of the obtained AE – "encoder-decoder" – is a symmetric multilayer multi-adaptive forward propagation neuron [18–20]. The encoder can map attributes with a dimension of 1260 elements into attributes with a dimension of 24 elements. However, this dimensionality was not obtained at once. The relevance of the received features was also estimated by means of a deep neural network in the decoder part which allows one to reconstruct the original signal (Fig. 4).

Figure 4 shows the final AE network consisting of 9 layers, of which 7 layers with perceptrons are hidden (hidden1 – hidden7). The layers are reduced to the 4th hidden layer (5th layer for the whole network) and also increase towards the output layer, forming symmetric neural network architecture. Except for the 5th output layer IB, each output of the inner layers is provided by the activation function – Relu. It is worth noting that if a linear activation function is applied in each layer, then the hidden parameters present in IB correspond directly to the main components from PCA (principal components approach).

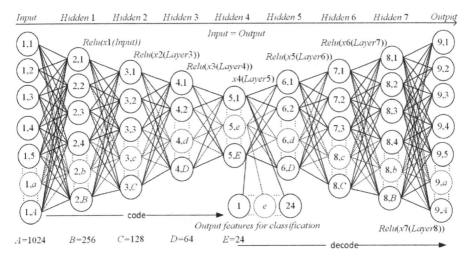

Fig. 4. Graph of the symmetric multilayer multi-adaptive forward propagation neuron providing functions of the encoder and the decoder.

AE training was reproduced until the AE was incomplete. Based on the results of each cycle of deep learning, the representation of the hidden space was evaluated by learning the informative features in the direction of decreasing IB size.

As a result of each deep learning cycle of the network, a periodic test data run of $N = 582 \times M = 1260 \times V = 6$ was performed. The coding results were then subjected to machine classification. The input dimensionality of the machine classification data was as follows: $N = 582 \times M = p \times V = 6$, where p is the empirically chosen unknown value [21].

4   Evaluation of the Representativeness of the EEG Data

Before performing machine classification the neural network was evaluated for the presence of significant features in the resulting data set. A random forest – an ensemble technique – was used to evaluate significant features [20–23]. By applying the random forest we were able to estimate the importance of the features as an average reduction in "contamination" [23, 24] calculated from all decision trees in the forest. This allowed us to make no assumptions about whether or not the data obtained were linearly separable.

By training a forest of 500 trees on the resulting dataset, 24 features were obtained in order of their relative importance (Fig. 5).

Histograms A, B in Fig. 5 show the distributions of features according to their importance. Histogram A shows the significance of features x7 and x16 for stimulation at 8 Hz, and histogram B shows x12 and x13 as significant features.

Certainly, the features x22, x9, x6, x14, x0, and x18 for histogram A are also significant. The same can be said for features x11, x0, x7, x14, x15, x18, x16, as well as x23 of histogram B. However, machine evaluations were made based on the first two significant ones.

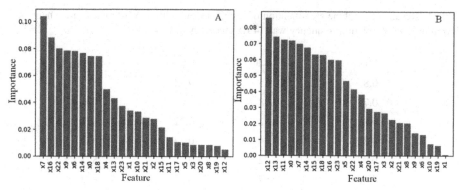

Fig. 5. Histograms of the relative importance of the features in the dataset for the leads: A) $O2$; B) $P4$.

The k-nearest neighbor algorithm [25] was used for machine classification. For the tests, 873 non-training samples were used (cross-validation of 20% of the training sample). The results of the machine classification for the test sample are shown in Tables 1 and 2.

Table 1. Results of the machine classification of encoded EEGs with SSVEP using the k-nearest neighbor algorithm. The stimulation frequency was 8 Hz (accuracy of 88%).

Leads	Precision	Recall	F1-score	Support
$O1$	0.88	0.97	0.92	873
$O2$	0.90	0.57	0.70	873
Oz	0.92	0.84	0.88	873
$P3$	0.75	0.94	0.83	873
$P4$	0.98	0.99	0.99	873
Pz	0.91	0.97	0.94	873

Tables 1 and 2 contain estimates of the classifier's ability to distinguish encoded EEG signals from one another (distinguish zonal leads). This is indicated quantitatively by the evaluation precision. The evaluation recall demonstrates the quality of the classifier algorithm to detect a series of corresponding coded EEG with SSVEP in general. The characteristic f1-score confirms the necessary medium-harmonic balance between the precision and recall evaluations, especially since the classes are almost balanced. The parameter support indicates the number of test samples.

The reliability of the obtained results of machine classification can be estimated by the Confusion matrices shown in Fig. 6.

In Fig. 7 we can observe the borders and clusters within them which correspond to the six leads: $O1$, $O2$, Oz, $P3$, $P4$ и Pz. We can also observe that the hidden space contains "gaps"; this is equivalent to missing data in the teacher-trained task because AE was not

Table 2. Results of machine classification of encoded EEG with SSVEP by k-nearest neighbor algorithm. The stimulation frequency was 14 Hz (accuracy of 80%).

Leads	Precision	Recall	F1-score	Support
O1	0.82	0.85	0.84	873
O2	0.72	0.68	0.70	873
Oz	0.82	0.82	0.82	873
P3	0.80	0.86	0.83	873
P4	0.97	0.92	0.94	873
Pz	0.68	0.67	0.67	873

8 Hz stimulation

True labels		O1	O2	Oz	P3	P2	Pz
	O1	848	0	25	0	0	0
	O2	28	497	31	225	5	87
	Oz	82	4	737	49	1	0
	P3	0	38	12	822	0	1
	P2	0	3	0	0	870	0
	Pz	3	10	0	5	9	846
		O1	O2	Oz	P3	P2	Pz
		Predicted labels					

14 Hz stimulation

True labels		O1	O2	Oz	P3	P2	Pz
	O1	744	2	125	0	2	0
	O2	0	596	1	72	16	188
	Oz	151	0	713	0	9	0
	P3	0	28	0	754	1	90
	P2	12	17	34	7	803	0
	Pz	0	180	0	111	0	582
		O1	O2	Oz	P3	P2	Pz
		Predicted labels					

Fig. 6. Confusion matrices on leads O1, O2, Oz, P3, P4 and Pz.

trained on these features of the hidden space. Another problem is the separability of the gaps; some leads are well separated but there are also areas where there are "embeddings" of some features into others, which makes it difficult to separate the unique features of these leads.

Nevertheless, we can conclude that the obtained features have a good enough separability, and therefore can be applied in further machine learning for the task of EEG signals classification.

Based on the results of this study we can conclude that each brain lead reproduces unique waves specific to each area of the head. Moreover, the results of the experimental study show that there is a certain generalization of signals by their leads in a part of samples from the general population of statistical data from the subjects.

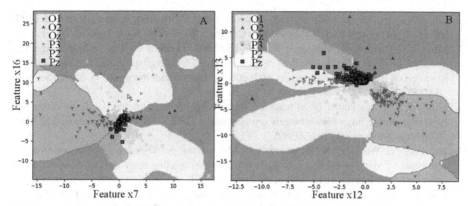

Fig. 7. Borders of the solutions for leads O1, O2, Oz, P3, P4 and Pz obtained on the basis of the signs under study: A) for significant signs x7 and x16 (stimulation with 8 Hz); B) for significant signs x12 and x13 (stimulation with 14 Hz).

5 Conclusion

Statistical information was collected to confirm the main hypothesis. Obtaining statistical data was achieved by creating technical conditions and organizational arrangements for a scientific experiment with a group of 30 subjects of both sexes. The experiment was provided with specialized medical measuring equipment of high-resolution – electroencephalograph.

The achievability of the set task and the obtaining of 85% of the expected results were based on the preliminary estimation of relevance and representativeness of the received data as a result of an experiment on the gathering of bioelectrical activity of a brain, where the frequency-time response was taken as the sets of primary features. Thus, the representativeness of the experimental data was evaluated before proceeding to deep machine learning and the machine classification task.

The proposed model of symmetric multilayer multi-adaptive forward propagation neuron which provides encoder and decoder functions can find its application in solving problems related to EEG signal processing.

Based on the results of this study, the authors suggest that the data on the bioelectrical activity of the brain recorded by EEG can be represented as a multidimensional random variable, where the center position is also the mathematical expectation of its projections on the axes of the principal components.

Acknowledgements. The study was financially supported by the Russian Science Foundation under scientific project No. 23-19-00664.

References

1. Yang, D., Nguyen, T.H., Chung, W.Y.: A bipolar-channel hybrid brain-computer interface system for home automation control utilizing steady-state visually evoked potential and eye-blink signals. Sensors (Basel) **20**(19), 5474 (2020). https://doi.org/10.3390/s20195474.

2. Lin, J.-S., Yang, W.-C.: Wireless brain-computer interface for electric wheelchairs with EEG and eye-blinking signals. Int. J. Innovative Comput., Inf. Control **8**, 6011–6024 (2012)
3. Rihana, S., Damien, P., Moujaess, T.: EEG-Eye blink detection system for brain computer interface. In: Pons, J.L., Torricelli, D., Pajaro, M. (eds.) Converging Clinical and Engineering Research on Neurorehabilitation, pp. 603–608. Springer, Heidelberg (2013). https://doi.org/10.1007/978-3-642-34546-3_98
4. Musk, E.: An integrated brain-machine interface platform with thousands of channels. BioRxiv preprint, https://www.biorxiv.org/content/10.1101/703801v4. Last accessed 31 May 2023. https://doi.org/10.1101/703801
5. Turovsky, Y., Wolf, D., Meshcheryakov, R., Iskhakova, A.: Dynamics of frequency characteristics of visually evoked potentials of electroencephalography during the work with brain-computer interfaces. In: Mahadeva Prasanna, S.R., Alexey Karpov, K., Samudravijaya, S.S., Agrawal, (eds.) Speech and Computer: 24th International Conference, SPECOM 2022, Gurugram, India, November 14–16, 2022, Proceedings, pp. 676–687. Springer International Publishing, Cham (2022). https://doi.org/10.1007/978-3-031-20980-2_57
6. Tao, T., Yi, X., Xiaorong, G., Shangkai, G.: Chirp-modulated visual evoked potential as a generalization of steady state visual evoked potential. J. Neural Eng. **9**(1), 016008 (2011). https://doi.org/10.1088/1741-2560/9/1/016008
7. Kwak, N.-S., Müller, K.-R., Lee, S.-W.: Toward exoskeleton control based on steady state visual evoked potentials. In: 2014 International Winter Workshop on Brain-Computer Interface (BCI 2014), pp. 1–2. Gangwon, Korea (2014). https://doi.org/10.1109/iww-BCI.2014.6782571
8. Balnytė, R., Uloziene, I., Rastenytė, D., Vaitkus, A., Malcienė, L., Laučkaitė, K.: Diagnostic value of conventional visual evoked potentials applied to patients with multiple sclerosis. Medicina **47**(5), 263–269 (2011)
9. Markand, Omkar N.: Visual evoked potentials. In: Clinical Evoked Potentials, pp. 83–137. Springer, Cham (2020). https://doi.org/10.1007/978-3-030-36955-2_3
10. Chaudhary, U., Birbaumer, N., Curado, M.R.: Brain-machine interface (BMI) in paralysis. Ann. Phys. Rehabil. Med. **58**(1), 9–13 (2015). https://doi.org/10.1016/j.rehab.2014.11.002
11. Aminoff, M., Goodin, D.: Visual evoked potentials. J. Clin. Neurophysiol.: Official Publ. Am. Electroencephalographic Soc. **11**, 493–499 (1994). https://doi.org/10.1097/00004691-199409000-00004
12. Taylor, M., McCulloch, D.: Visual evoked potentials in infants and children. J. Clin. Neurophysiol.: Official Publ. American Electroencephalographic Soc. **9**, 357–372 (1992). https://doi.org/10.1097/00004691-199207010-00004
13. Liasis, A.: Visual evoked potentials. Acta Ophthalmol. 94 (2016). https://doi.org/10.1111/j.1755-3768.2016.0215
14. Carter, J.: Visual evoked potentials. Clinical Neurophysiology, 311–322 (2011). https://doi.org/10.1093/med/9780195385113.003.0022
15. Kwak, N.-S., Müller, K.-R., Lee, S.-W.: A convolutional neural network for steady state visual evoked potential classification under ambulatory environment. PLoS ONE **12**(2), 1–20 (2017). https://doi.org/10.1371/journal.pone.0172578
16. Wolf, D.A., Turovsky, Y.A., Meshcheryakov, R.V., Iskhakov, A.Y., Iskhakova, A.O.: EEG signal auto encoder, computer software, https://www1.fips.ru/iiss/document.xhtml?faces-redirect=true&id=d4eb144baee4f995556af206cde9da36. Last accessed 31 May 2023. (In Russ.)
17. Naftali, T., Pereira, F.C., Bialek, W.: The information bottleneck method. In: Proceedings of the 37th Allerton Conference on Communication, Control and Computation, https://www.researchgate.net/publication/2844514_The_Information_Bottleneck_Method. Last accessed 31 May 2023

18. Nguyen, H., Bottone, S., Kim, K., Chiang, M., Poor, H.V.: Adversarial Neural Networks for Error Correcting Codes (preprint), https://www.researchgate.net/publication/357267696_Adversarial_Neural_Networks_for_Error_Correcting_Codes. Last accessed 31 May 2023

19. Kose, U., Deperlioglu, O., Alzubi, J., Patrut, B.: Diagnosing parkinson by using deep autoencoder neural network. In: Deep Learning for Medical Decision Support Systems. SCI, vol. 909, pp. 73–93. Springer, Singapore (2021). https://doi.org/10.1007/978-981-15-6325-6_5

20. Mirjalili, V., Raschka, S., Namboodiri, A., Ross, A.: Semi-adversarial networks: convolutional autoencoders for imparting privacy to face images. In: 2018 International Conference on Biometrics (ICB), pp. 82–89. IEEE, Gold Coast, QLD, Australia (2018). https://doi.org/10.1109/ICB2018.2018.00023

21. Meshcheryakov, R.V., Wolf, D.A., Turovsky, Y.A.: An autocoder of the electrical activity of the human brain. Bulletin of the South Ural State University, Series Mathematics. Mechanics. Physics 15(1), 34–42 (2023). https://doi.org/10.14529/mmph230104. (In Russ.)

22. Bicego, M., Escolano, F.: On learning random forests for random forest-clustering. In: 2020 25th International Conference on Pattern Recognition (ICPR), pp. 3451–3458. IEEE, Milan, Italy (2021). https://doi.org/10.1109/ICPR48806.2021.9412014

23. Olson, M.: Essays on Random Forest Ensembles, https://repository.upenn.edu/ dissertations/AAI10786136/. Last accessed 31 May 2023

24. Nayyar, A., Mahapatra, B.: Effective classification and handling of incoming data packets in mobile Ad Hoc networks (MANETs) using random forest ensemble technique (RF/ET). In: Sharma, N., Chakrabarti, A., Balas, V.E. (eds.) Data Management, Analytics and Innovation. AISC, vol. 1016, pp. 431–444. Springer, Singapore (2020). https://doi.org/10.1007/978-981-13-9364-8_31

25. Fahim, A.: K and starting means for k-means algorithm. J. Comput. Sci. 55, 101445 (2021). https://doi.org/10.1016/j.jocs.2021.101445

Comparison of ROS Local Planners for a Holonomic Robot in Gazebo Simulator

Artem Apurin[1]([⊠]) [iD], Bulat Abbyasov[1] [iD], Edgar A. Martínez-García[2] [iD],
and Evgeni Magid[1,3] [iD]

[1] Intelligent Robotics Department, Institute of Information Technology and Intelligent Systems,
Kazan Federal University, 35, Kremlyovskaya street, Kazan 420111, Russia
`aaa@it.kfu.ru`
[2] Institute of Engineering and Technology, Department of Industrial Engineering and
Manufacturing, Autonomous University of Ciudad Juarez, Manuel Díaz H. No. 518-B Zona
Pronaf Condominio, Chihuahua, 32315 Cd Juárez, Mexico
[3] Tikhonov Moscow Institute of Electronics and Mathematics, HSE University, 34, Tallinn
street, Moscow 123458, Russia

Abstract. A safe robot navigation in a dynamic environment is an essential part
of an autonomous exploration path planning. A path planning part of a navigation
involves global and local planners. While a global planner finds an optimal path
with a prior knowledge of an environment and static obstacles, a local planner
recalculates the path to avoid dynamic obstacles. The main goal of a local planning is adjusting an initial plan produced by a global planner in an online fashion.
It is a crucial step to ensure a robot operation in dynamic environments because in
real world scenarios an environment usually contains people and thus, a dynamic
obstacles avoidance must respond quickly and recalculate an actual route. Holonomic robotic platforms are robotic vehicles that use omni-wheels to move in any
direction, at any angle, without an additional rotation. These robotic platforms are
ideal for working zones with a limited space access. This paper provides a comparison of ROS local planners that support omni-wheel mobile robots: Trajectory
Rollout, DWA, EBand, and TEB. The algorithms were compared using a path
length, a travelling time and a number of obstacle collisions. Gazebo simulator
was used for modeling virtual scenes with dynamic obstacles.

Keywords: Mobile Robot · Mecanum Wheel · Local Planner · ROS · Gazebo

1 Introduction

Nowadays, mobile robotics provides new opportunities for developing novel robotic systems. A wide range of wheels of various sizes, different design types and materials used
allow to integrate mobile robotic platforms into many areas of a human life. Common
mobile robot applications include industrial automation [1], transportation [2], medical
care [3], emergency rescue operations [4], and other areas. Mobile robots are featured
by different motion systems.

© The Author(s), under exclusive license to Springer Nature Switzerland AG 2023
A. Ronzhin et al. (Eds.): ICR 2023, LNAI 14214, pp. 116–126, 2023.
https://doi.org/10.1007/978-3-031-43111-1_11

There are two different types of mobile robots drive systems: a holonomic and a non-holonomic. For a wheeled robot, a non-holonomic drive system is a robot configuration limited by a number of wheels or their orientation. Holonomic drive systems have more than two degrees of freedom, which provide more freedom and flexibility of motion. The main benefit of a holonomic drive system is an ability to travel in any desired direction at any specified orientation without additional rotations with regard to Z-axis (yaw) of a series of intermediate motions (e.g., a typical car parking procedure). To perform such locomotion a robotic platform uses a special design of wheels called mecanum or omnidirectional [5]. Omnidirectional wheels increase a robot mobility and are used in tasks where a high maneuverability is required. Omnidirectional robotic platforms are ideal for working zones with a limited space access and cluttered environments, e.g., for scheduling pick-up and delivery tasks in hospitals [6].

Performing safe robot navigation is a general issue faced by a robot operating in a real environment [7]. Real world environments usually contain people and other dynamic obstacles. A real-time path planning is an essential part of an autonomous exploration. An obstacle avoidance capability used by a path planning approach must detect obstacles quickly and replan an actual route [8]. A path planning part of a robot navigation involves global and local planners [9]. While a global planner finds an optimal path with a prior knowledge of an environment and static obstacles, a local planner recalculates the path to avoid dynamic obstacles. The main goal of a local planning approach is adjusting a plan produced by a global planner in an online fashion.

This paper presents a comparison of ROS local planners supporting a holonomic drive system: Trajectory Rollout [10], DWA [11], EBand [12] and TEB [13]. These local planner algorithms were selected because they are most popular for ROS environment, easily pluggable and support a holonomic motion. The main contribution of the paper is a benchmark to discover the most suitable ROS local planner for a holonomic system used within a dynamic environment. Virtual experiments were conducted in Gazebo simulator [14] using static and dynamic obstacles.

2 System Setup

2.1 Mecanum Wheel Robot

A virtual model of a modular multifunctional robotic omni-wheeled mobile platform ArtBul [15] was used for experiments. Mecanum wheel models were created in Blender software [16]. To reduce complex collision calculations and increase a real time factor (RTF), low-poly models were used for a roller collision part. A 3D model of the mecanum wheel is shown in Fig. 1. Each roller has its own joint and can be freely rotated along the Z-axis of its frame.

A ROS plugin was developed to control the robot in Gazebo simulation [17] by publishing messages with linear velocities along the X and Y axes and an angular velocity along the Z-axis to a robot command topic. To detect collisions *gazebo_ros_bumper* plugin [18] was used. The mobile platform with a laser range finder (LRF) and an enabled bumper plugin is depicted in Fig. 2.

Fig. 1. 3D model of a mecanum wheel in Gazebo: a red, green and blue arrows' set denotes a coordinate frame of each roller.

Fig. 2. ArtBul mobile robot in Gazebo: blue rays visualize LRF beams.

2.2 Virtual Environments

Simulation provides a significant support in early stage testing. A 3D modeling can be used to produce a necessary 3D digital representation of real objects with a varying difficulty. Modern modeling tools are often used for designing virtual environments [19]. Testing local planners requires a special navigation map called an occupancy grid map (OGM). The OGM is a 2D binary map that consists of cells. The OGM encodes occupancy data where white pixels represent free cells, black pixels are occupied cells and gray pixels are not yet explored. In our test cases, OGMs should not contain any information about obstacles because a goal of a local planner is a real-time path planning processing.

Two different virtual worlds in Gazebo were created to benchmark ROS local planner algorithms. The first world had $20 \times 6 \times 3$ m dimensions and contained static obstacles (Fig. 3, top). An OGM of the first virtual environment is shown in Fig. 3, bottom. The second world of $10 \times 10 \times 3$ m dimensions contained a single dynamic obstacle – a cube with a 1 m length side (Fig. 4). We created two motion patterns that the cube uses while moving: along X-axis (Fig. 4, left top) and Y-axis (Fig. 4, left bottom). An OGM of the second virtual world is shown in Fig. 4, right.

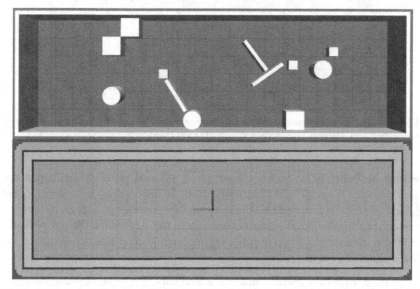

Fig. 3. A 3D virtual environment filled with static obstacles: cubes of varying sizes, cuboids and cylinders (top). The corresponding 2D OGM with static obstacles excluded (bottom).

3   ROS Local Planners

A motion control plays an important role in an autonomous navigation. ROS local planners use sensory information to perceive a current robot state and generates feasible trajectories that the robot is allowed to follow. Avoiding any dynamic or static obstacles that may (or may not) be included in a given global map is a responsibility of a ROS local planner. ROS local planners use sensory data from various sensors such as LRF sensors or ultrasound sensors, and various devices to plan an optimal trajectory [20].

All local planners use the same values for coinciding parameters and the same global and local costmap configurations. For all local planners limitations were set as follows: a linear acceleration was limited to 2.5 m/s^2, an angular acceleration to 3.2 rad/s^2, a linear speed to 0.5 m/s, and an angular speed to 1 rad/s. A controller tolerance in yaw/rotation (*yaw_goal_tolerance*) was set as 0.05 rad, a controller tolerance in the X and Y distance (*xy_goal_tolerance*) as 0.1 m.

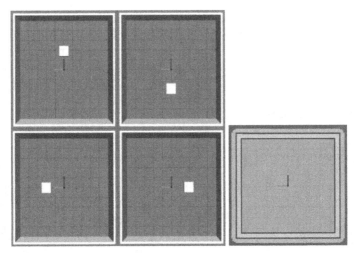

Fig. 4. (Left) 3D virtual environment with a dynamic obstacle: a cube moves along X-axis (top) and Y-axis (bottom). (Right) The corresponding 2D OGM with static obstacles excluded.

Trajectory Rollout. ROS package *base_local_planner* provides implementations of the Dynamic Window and Trajectory Rollout approaches to a local control. *Base_local_planner* is a basic ROS local planner that provides an application programming interface for other local planners. In order to use Algorithm Trajectory Rollout, the parameter *dwa* should be set to *false*. For mecanum wheel robots *holonomic_robot* parameter should be set to *true*.

DWA. ROS package *dwa_local_planner* is a modular DWA implementation with more flexible y-axis variables for holonomic robots than *base_local_planner*'s DWA. DWA discretely samples a robot's control space, performs a forward simulation for each sample, evaluates and filters each trajectory in the local costmap and finally selects a highest-scoring trajectory.

Eband. ROS package *eband_local_planner* implements the Elastic Band (EBand) method. An elastic band is a deformable collision free path generated by a global path incorporating information about obstacles proximity. A main drawback of *eband_local_planner* is that the ROS-based method implementation does not support an obstacle avoidance for moving obstacles.

TEB. ROS package *teb_local_planner* implements the Timed-Elastic-Band (TEB) method for an online trajectory optimization. A difference between TEB and EBand is that a local trajectory is optimized not by external forces, but by applying a cost function. For a holonomic robot *min_turning_radius* parameter should be set to 0 and *weight_kinematics_nh* parameter to 1.

4   Performance Comparison

Three experiments with different scenarios were conducted to identify a most suitable local planner for a mecanum wheeled robot. In the first experiment, a starting position of the robot was set to $(0; -8)$ and a goal was set to $(0; 8)$. A 2D occupancy grid map did not contain static obstacles. Next, several static obstacles were added to the world after a global map had been built. In the second experiment, the robot started at $(-3.5; 0)$ and targeted to $(3.5; 0)$. A cube with sides of 1 m moved linearly without an acceleration along a trajectory from point $(2; 0)$ to point $(-2; 0)$ and backwards, with 0.4 m/s linear velocity. In the third experiment, the cube moved from $(0; 2)$ to $(0; -2)$ and backwards. A reference trajectory depicted in Fig. 5 represents a suggested optimal path. Distance-optimal robot trajectories in the world with static objects are shown in Fig. 6.

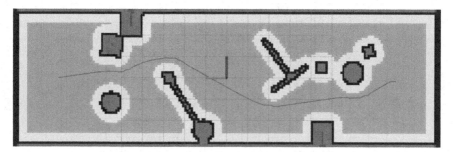

Fig. 5. Distance optimal robot trajectory.

Experiments showed that the Trajectory local planner never generated linear velocities along the Y-axis, and the omnidirectional robot moved as a differential wheeled robot with any planner settings. The Eband local planner trajectory was the smoothest, but this planner cannot handle dynamic obstacles and does not perform an online trajectory replanning. The drawbacks of the Eband are that the algorithm uses a global costmap updated dynamically, does not publish a response after reaching a target point and a task execution time is unmeasurable.

Table 1 demonstrates experimental results of local planners evaluated in the first world. Max T, Min T and Avg T stand for a maximum, minimum and average task execution time, respectively. Max D, Min D and Avg D denote a maximum, minimum and average path length, respectively. Success (Suc) column depicts how many times the robot reached the goal without obstacle collisions. Success with collision (SwC) column depicts how many times the robot reached the goal with at least one obstacle collision. Failed (F) column depicts how many times the robot failed to reach the goal. The TEB local planner showed the lowest minimum time and the lowest average time to complete the task. In one case, the robot with the TEB collided with an obstacle because the TEB heavily loaded the PC system and a frequency of publishing velocities to a command topic decreased. The DWA achieved the lowest minimum and the lowest average path length.

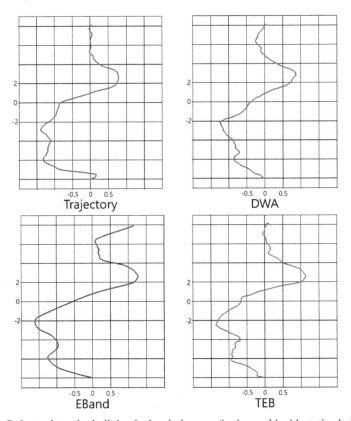

Fig. 6. Robot trajectories built by the local planners (in the world with static obstacles).

Table 1. ROS local planners' evaluation results (in the world with static obstacles).

Planner	Max T	Min T	Avg T	Max D	Min D	Avg D	Suc	SwC	F
Trajectory	188.6	64.8	100.9	23.2	17.9	19.6	50	0	0
DWA	67.1	39.6	43	18.9	17.2	17.7	50	0	0
EBand	-	-	-	19.2	18.1	18.9	50	0	0
TEB	91.6	32.4	38.3	43.4	17.9	19	49	1	0

In the experiment with the moving along the X-axis cube, all planners generated approximately the same trajectory (Fig. 7). Table 2 demonstrates experiments results of the local planners evaluated in the second world with the dynamic obstacle (a pattern of motion along X-axis). In this case, the TEB also showed the lowest minimum and the lowest average time required for a successful task completion. The Trajectory local planner showed the worst result within 50 experiments with only 7 successful and 15 (completely) failed. The EBand was successful in all 50 cases.

Table 2. ROS local planners evaluation results (the pattern of motion along X-axis).

Planner	Max T	Min T	Avg T	Max D	Min D	Avg D	Suc	SwC	F
Trajectory	222.5	23.4	40.8	15.4	2.7	8.6	7	28	15
DWA	41.2	18.6	22.1	13.3	1.7	8	24	23	3
EBand	-	-	-	9	8.3	8.6	50	0	0
TEB	31.41	16.2	20.8	16.9	8.5	11	47	2	1

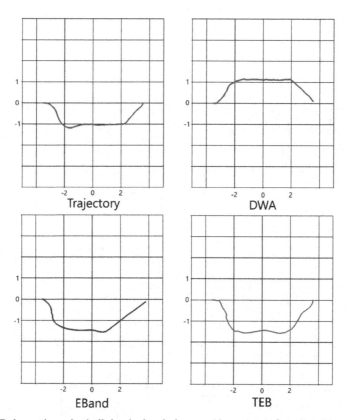

Fig. 7. Robot trajectories built by the local planners (the pattern of motion along X-axis).

In the case of the moving along the Y-axis cube, the DWA and the Trajectory Rollout showed a similar behavior (Fig. 8). When the cube appeared in the local costmap, the robot stopped and attempted to select an optimal movement trajectory. When the cube left the local costmap, the robot moved forward. The Eband and the TEB rebuilt the trajectory and continued the motion.

Table 3 demonstrates experimental results of the local planners evaluated in the second world with a dynamic obstacle (a pattern of motion along Y-axis). The TEB generated a maximum robot velocity. This method demonstrated the minimum task execution time and the least number of collisions with the obstacle. The worst result was shown by the DWA, which completely failed the task in 32 cases out of 50.

Table 3. ROS local planners evaluation results (the pattern of motion along Y-axis).

Planner	Max T	Min T	Avg T	Max D	Min D	Avg D	Suc	SwC	F
Trajectory	75	15.6	30.1	8.9	4.1	6.7	21	9	20
DWA	78	17.2	32.4	14.4	3.4	6.3	7	11	32
EBand	-	-	-	60	19.6	56.5	22	1	27
TEB	21.4	15	17.3	11	5.8	9	30	19	1

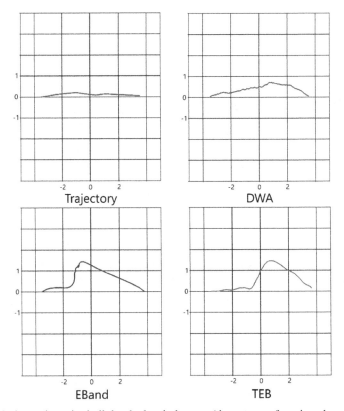

Fig. 8. Robot trajectories built by the local planners (the pattern of motion along Y-axis).

5   Conclusion

This paper presented a comparison of ROS local planners for mecanum wheeled robots (Trajectory Rollout, DWA, EBand, and TEB) and provided a benchmark that allowed to experimentally determine a recommended ROS local planner for a wheeled holonomic system. Virtual experiments were conducted in Gazebo simulator, which was used for modeling virtual environments with static and dynamic obstacles. Three types of virtual environments were employed with 50 virtual experiments within each environment. The algorithms were compared using a path length, a travelling time and a number of obstacle collisions.

The virtual experiments showed that the Trajectory Rollout local planner did not generate linear velocities along the Y-axis in all configurations; this planner demonstrated the worst task execution time and the longest trajectory path lengths. The DWA local planner handled static obstacles effectively, but performed poorly with dynamic obstacles. The EBand local planner did not rebuild a local motion trajectory when it worked on a non-renewable costmap of an explored environment; therefore, the use of this planner is possible only when a global costmap is dynamically updated, in which case the robot's trajectory will be rebuilt by a global planner. The TEB local planner achieved a significantly better performance in terms of a task execution time and showed the least number of obstacle collisions. Therefore, the TEB local planner could be recommended for dynamic scenes since it demonstrated the best results within a dynamic environment.

Acknowledgements. The reported study was funded by the Russian Science Foundation (RSF) and the Cabinet of Ministers of the Republic of Tatarstan according to the research project No. 22-21-20033.

References

1. Koubaa, A., et al.: Introduction to mobile robot path planning. In: Robot Path Planning and Cooperation. SCI, vol. 772, pp. 3–12. Springer, Cham (2018). https://doi.org/10.1007/978-3-319-77042-0_1
2. Gul, F., Rahiman, W., Nazli Alhady, S.S.: A comprehensive study for robot navigation techniques. Cogent Eng. **6**(1), 1–25 (2019)
3. Hai, N.D.X., Nam, L.H.T., Thinh, N.T.: Remote healthcare for the elderly, patients by tele-presence robot. In: 2019 International Conference on System Science and Engineering (ICSSE), pp. 506–510 (2019)
4. Murphy, R.R.: Humans and robots in off-normal applications and emergencies. In: Chen, J. (ed.) Advances in Human Factors in Robots and Unmanned Systems: Proceedings of the AHFE 2019 International Conference on Human Factors in Robots and Unmanned Systems, July 24–28, 2019, Washington D.C., USA, pp. 171–180. Springer International Publishing, Cham (2020). https://doi.org/10.1007/978-3-030-20467-9_16
5. Taheri, H., Zhao, C.X.: Omnidirectional mobile robots, mechanisms and navigation approaches. Mech. Mach. Theor. **153**, 103958 (2020)
6. Safin, R., Lavrenov, R., Hsia, K.H., Maslak, E., Schiefermeier-Mach, N., Magid, E.: Modelling a turtlebot3 based delivery system for a smart hospital in gazebo. In: 2021 International Siberian Conference on Control and Communications (SIBCON), pp. 1–6 (2021)
7. Pimentel, F., Aquino, P.: Performance evaluation of ROS local trajectory planning algorithms to social navigation. In: 2019 Latin American Robotics Symposium (LARS), 2019 Brazilian Symposium on Robotics (SBR) and 2019 Workshop on Robotics in Education (WRE), pp. 156–161 (2019)

8. Vagale, A., Oucheikh, R., Bye, R.T., Osen, O.L., Fossen, T.I.: Path planning and collision avoidance for autonomous surface vehicles I: a review. J. Marine Sci. Technol. **26**(4), 1292–1306 (2021). https://doi.org/10.1007/s00773-020-00787-6

9. Cybulski, B., Wegierska, A., Granosik, G.: Accuracy comparison of navigation local planners on ROS-based mobile robot. In: 2019 12th International Workshop on Robot Motion and Control (RoMoCo), pp. 104–111 (2019)

10. Gerkey, B. P., Konolige, K.: Planning and control in unstructured terrain. In: ICRA Workshop on Path Planning on Costmaps (2008)

11. Fox, D., Burgard, W., Thrun, S.: The dynamic window approach to collision avoidance. IEEE Robot. Autom. Mag. **4**(1), 23–33 (1997)

12. Gehrig, S.K., Stein, F.J.: Elastic bands to enhance vehicle following. In: 2001 IEEE Intelligent Transportation Systems, pp. 597–602 (2001)

13. Keller, M., Hoffmann, F., Hass, C., Bertram, T., Seewald, A.: Planning of optimal collision avoidance trajectories with timed elastic bands. IFAC Proc. Volum. **47**(3), 9822–9827 (2014)

14. Koenig, N., Howard, A.: Design and use paradigms for gazebo, an open-source multi-robot simulator. In: 2004 IEEE/RSJ International Conference on Intelligent Robots and Systems (IROS), pp. 2149–2154 (2004)

15. Apurin, A., et al.: LIRS-ArtBul: design, modelling and construction of an omnidirectional chassis for a modular multipurpose robotic platform. In: Interactive Collaborative Robotics: 7th International Conference (ICR 2022), pp. 16–18 (2022)

16. Gschwandtner, M., Kwitt, R., Uhl, A., Pree, W.: BlenSor: blender sensor simulation toolbox. In: Bebis, G., et al. (eds.) Advances in Visual Computing: 7th International Symposium, ISVC 2011, Las Vegas, NV, USA, September 26-28, 2011. Proceedings, Part II, pp. 199–208. Springer Berlin Heidelberg, Berlin, Heidelberg (2011). https://doi.org/10.1007/978-3-642-24031-7_20

17. Apurin, A., Abbyasov, B., Dobrokvashina, A., Bai, Y., Svinin, M., Magid, E.: Omniwheel chassis' model and plugin for gazebo simulator. Proc. Int. Conf. Artif. Life Robot. **28**, 170–173 (2023). https://doi.org/10.5954/ICAROB.2023.OS6-7

18. Takaya, K., Asai, T., Kroumov, V., Smarandache, F.: Simulation environment for mobile robots testing using ROS and Gazebo. In: 2016 20th International Conference on System Theory, Control and Computing (ICSTCC), pp. 96–101 (2016)

19. Iskhakova, A., Abbyasov, B., Mironchuk, T., Tsoy, T., Svinin, M., Magid, E.: LIRS-MazeGen: an easy-to-use blender extension for modeling maze-like environments for gazebo simulator. In: Ronzhin, A., Pshikhopov, V. (eds.) Frontiers in Robotics and Electromechanics, pp. 147–161. Springer Nature Singapore, Singapore (2023). https://doi.org/10.1007/978-981-19-7685-8_10

20. Valera, Á., Valero, F., Vallés, M., Besa, A., Mata, V., Llopis-Albert, C.: Navigation of autonomous light vehicles using an optimal trajectory planning algorithm. Sustainability **13**(3), 1233 (2021)

Movement Along the Trajectory of a Home Quadruped Robot

Dmitry Dobrynin$^{(\boxtimes)}$ (iD)

Federal Research Center "Computer Science and Control" of Russian Academy of Sciences,
44/2, Vavilova Street, 119333 Moscow, Russia
rabota51@mail.ru

Abstract. Home walking robots imitating pets have a high appeal due to increased maneuverability in a cramped home environment. Planning the movements of a home robot is an important component of the control system of a quadruped walking robot. The article deals with the problem of following the trajectory of a walking robot, which relates to motion planning. The article presents a model of a robot and a mathematical model of its legs. Two methods of approximation of the trajectory of motion are proposed in the article are piecewise linear approximation and approximation by arcs of a circle. The use of piecewise linear approximation makes it possible to solve the problem using simple robot movements. The use of approximation by arcs of a circle allows you to build a universal gait for a walking robot. The simulation of robot movements using two types of approximations is carried out. The article presents experimental modeling data. It is shown that the average speed of a walking robot with piecewise linear approximation is significantly lower than the speed of the robot moving in a straight line. The article presents the conclusions drawn from the results of experiments.

Keywords: Quadruped Robot · Motion Planning · Walking Robot

1 Introduction

Walking robots are currently an important area of research in the field of robotics. An attractive feature of walking robots is the ability to adapt to difficult terrain. For example, home walking robots have more maneuverability than wheeled robots. An important area of research in the development of walking robots is the planning of robot movement in a complex environment. Choosing a suitable trajectory planning algorithm helps to ensure safe and efficient point-to-point navigation, and the optimal algorithm depends on the geometry of the robot, as well as computational constraints. Some algorithms consider the robot as a point object, the structure of which is not important for solving the problem. Other algorithms take into account the peculiarities of robot movement, including static holonomic and dynamic non-holonomic-bounded systems. An overview of planning methods is given in [1, 2].

Movement along the trajectory of a walking robot can be attributed to the task of planning robot movements. Motion planning is aimed at generating interactive trajectories in the workspace when robots interact with a dynamic environment, therefore, when planning movement, it is necessary to take into account the peculiarities of kinetics, speed and posture of robots and dynamic objects nearby. At this level of motion planning, the robot body and its individual parts move relative to surrounding objects. In this case, the robot cannot be considered as a point object, since the size of the individual parts of the robot greatly affects the nature of movement as a whole. An overview of motion planning methods is given in [3].

Research in the field of four-legged robots has been actively going on since the 1980s. Initially, gaits based on the kinematic model of the robot's leg were used, similar to the gaits of insects and animals [4]. Matsuoka [5] proposed a CPG method to simulate rhythmic movement. CPG-based gait control uses a simplified single-layer feedback model. This method is widely used by many researchers [6–8]. CPG allows you to generate periodic gaits using a small number of parameters.

Modern research in the field of walking robots is aimed at solving the problems of moving through difficult terrain [9–11]. With this method of movement, the robot must choose a fulcrum for each step-in order to optimally solve the problems of patency and stability. Such a robot gait is called a free gait. McGee and Frank [12] were engaged in the analysis of free gait when studying the movement of a robot over difficult terrain. To calculate a free gait, various methods are used is optimization of the center of gravity position to ensure a given stability [13], training of multilayer neural networks [14], etc. A good overview of some methods can be found in [15].

Free gait involves calculating each step of the robot, which requires a lot of computing power [16]. Home robots usually do not have powerful computers on board, so they need methods of movement that have low computational complexity. It is possible to combine the robot's gaits, depending on the terrain on which the robot moves [17].

In this paper, we propose two ways to approximate the trajectory of the robot is straight lines and circular arcs. The approximation of the circle arcs allows you to build a universal gait for a home robot that requires small computing resources.

2   Model of Home Robot

A home walking robot is similar to a dog (Fig. 1a). The robot has four legs of a simple design. Each leg can move with three degrees of freedom. The robot leg (Fig. 1b) has three drives M1, M2 and M3, which allow you to move the touch point of the foot in three dimensions. The touch point can move in some area relative to the robot body, as shown in Fig. 1a. The dimensions of this area are determined by the geometric parameters of the robot leg and the height of the robot body relative to the surface. The lower the robot body is located to the surface, the larger the area of possible movements of the touch point.

In Fig. 2 presents a mathematical model of a walking robot's leg. The initial parameters for calculating the angles of the drives θ_1, θ_2 and θ_3 are the coordinates of the fulcrum (X, Y, Z) with respect to the beginning of the leg. The calculation of the drive angles is similar to the equations presented in [18].

To simplify the calculations, we will assume that the robot body retains a horizontal position during movement. Since the home robot must move on flat surfaces, this

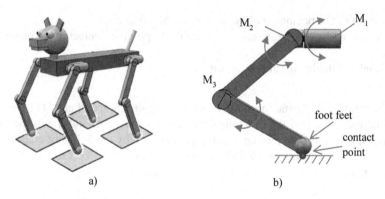

Fig. 1. a) Robot model; b) Model of robot's leg.

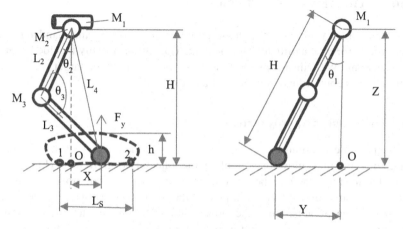

Fig. 2. Mathematical model of robot's leg.

assumption is quite justified.

$$\theta_1(Y, Z) = arc\,tg\frac{Y}{Z},$$

$$\theta_2(X, H) = \arccos\frac{L_2^2 + L_4^2 - L_3^2}{2L_2L_4} - \arcsin\frac{X}{L_4},$$

$$\theta_3(X, H) = \arccos\frac{L_2^2 + L_3^2 - L_4^2}{2L_2L_3},$$

$$L_4 = \sqrt{X^2 + H^2}, \quad H = \sqrt{Z^2 + Y^2}.$$

$$(1)$$

Here L_2 and L_3 are the lengths of the robot leg links,

M_1, M_2 and M_3 are the robot leg drives,
O is projection of the beginning of the foot on the support surface,
X and Y are the displacement of the point of contact of the foot from the projection of the beginning of the foot in the plane of the support surface,

Z is the height of the beginning of the foot from the surface,
H is the distance from the beginning of the leg to the point of contact in the plane of the leg,
h is the height of the leg lift above the surface,
Ls is step length.

The stability of the home robot can be ensured by the choice of gait [18]. The robot will be statically stable if the horizontal projection of its center of gravity lies inside the reference polygon. The reference polygon is formed by the points of contact of the robot's legs with the reference surface. When performing the steps, the support phase and the leg transfer phase are selected in such a way that the stability condition is always met.

3 Movement Along the Trajectory

The movement of a walking robot along the trajectory is one of the mandatory tasks when moving a robot in a difficult environment. Trajectories usually include linear and rounded sections. We will use two options: approximation of the target trajectory by straight lines and approximation by arcs of a circle.

3.1 Piecewise Linear Approximation

One of the possible solutions is piecewise linear approximation of a given trajectory. In this case, the robot must move in steps along the trajectory of movement (Fig. 3a).

Note that for this type of robot movement, two types of robot movement are necessary: moving straight and turning in place. Due to the fact that the turn requires the robot to stop, the general nature of the movement turns out to be intermittent. Consider the movement of the robot from point A to point C (Fig. 3a). At point A, the robot turns, then moves in a straight line to point B. After stopping, a turn is made, and then moving to point C.

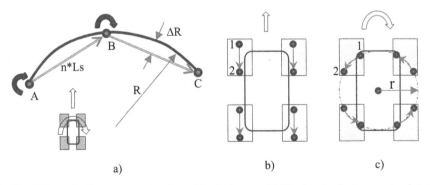

Fig. 3. a) Piecewise linear approximation of the trajectory; b) Moving the foot support points for linear movement; c) Moving the support points of the legs when turning.

The length of the robot's elementary movement is a multiple of the robot's step Ls. Equation (2) shows that the positioning error of the robot relative to the trajectory ΔR is smaller the larger the turning radius R. As the step length Ls decreases, the error ΔR also decreases:

$$\frac{\Delta R}{R} = 1 - \sqrt{1 - \left(\frac{nL_s}{2R}\right)^2} \tag{2}$$

To move in a straight line, the robot can use different types of gaits [18]. The point of contact of the robot's foot with the surface thus performs a rectilinear movement relative to the robot body (Fig. 3b). Point 1 corresponds to the beginning of the reference phase (Fig. 2). Point 2 corresponds to the end of the reference phase. The length of the leg movement from point 1 to point 2 is equal to the step of the robot Ls. The trajectories of the reference points of all robot legs are the same.

The rotation of the robot body by a certain angle is carried out in steps (Fig. 3c). In this case, the trajectories of the reference points of the robot's legs lie on a circle of radius r. As can be seen from Fig. 3c, the trajectories of the reference points of the robot's legs are different and represent the arcs of a circle with a common center.

The advantages of piecewise linear movement along the trajectory include the simplicity of implementation, since the individual movements of the walking robot are simple.

The disadvantage of piecewise linear movement along the trajectory is the low speed of movement. Stopping the robot to make a turn does not allow you to develop a high speed of movement. The accuracy of the trajectory repetition can be adjusted by changing the value of the robot's step length Ls.

3.2   Gait with Variable Turning Radius (VTR Gate)

To improve the nature of the robot's movement along the trajectory, it is necessary to move the walking robot along the arc of a circle. From Fig. 3c, it can be seen that if the center of rotation is moved outside the body, then the nature of the movement of the support points of the legs becomes similar to the case of rectilinear movement.

The design of the robot's leg has three degrees of freedom, so it is possible to realize a circular trajectory of movement of the support points of the legs. The limitations in this case are the size of the leg movement area and compliance with the stability criteria of the robot.

Let's define such a gait as a VTR gate is a gait with a variable turning radius. This gait is periodic and has versatility.

In Fig. 4a shows the principle of moving the robot around a circle with a radius of Rc. Each leg of the robot moves in such a way that the trajectory of its reference point (from 1 to 2) lies on a circle. The centers of all circles must match. The angular velocity of the movement of the reference points on the surface must also be the same. Under these conditions, the center of the robot will move in a circle around the common center C_0 with an angular velocity ω.

Note that each leg of the robot requires its own trajectory of movement of the reference point. When moving, the robot must rearrange its legs in accordance with the

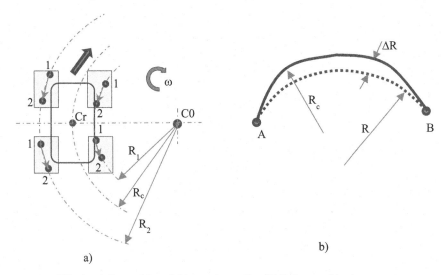

Fig. 4. a) Gate with variable turning radius; b) Robot positioning error.

selected type of gait. The reference points for the legs external to the center of the circumference move at high speeds.

As the radius of the circle increases, the trajectories of the reference points increasingly approach straight lines. In the extreme case, when the radius of the circle is infinite, the trajectories of the reference points are straight lines. This case corresponds to the movement of the robot in a straight line.

By changing the position of the center of the circle, you can change the orientation of the robot body during movement.

The positioning error of the robot (Fig. 4b) in this case depends on the difference between the radius of rotation of the robot and the target trajectory. The mismatch of the centers of rotation also increases this error.

VTR gate replaces several types of movements of a walking robot is movement in a straight line, rotation, and sideways movement. Note that when moving the pivot point back, such a gait can provide lateral movement of the robot body. When moving by a walking robot using the VTR gate, there is no need to stop for turning. Therefore, the speed of movement of the walking robot will be higher than when using piecewise linear movement.

4   Experiments

For experimental verification, a robotic simulator was used (Fig. 5). The robot moved in a circle using two types of approximations are piecewise linear and VTR gate. The diameter of the circle = 280 cm, the linear speed of the robot was 10 and 20 cm/s. The robot's step length is 5 cm.

When using piecewise linear approximation, the robot performed one or more steps in a straight line, then stopped and made a turn. The rotation was performed by rotating

Fig. 5. Robot on the test polygon.

the robot body when all the legs of the robot were in the reference phase [18]. The turn execution time is about 2 s.

When using the VTR gate, the robot moved along a circle of constant radius. Correction of the position of the center of the circle and the turning radius was not carried out.

When moving the robot around the polygon, the average deviation of the robot from the specified trajectory and the average speed of movement were estimated. The results of the experiments are shown in Table 1.

Table 1. Experimental results on the test polygon.

V linear, cm/s	Piecewise linear approximation				VTR gate	
	n*Ls	ΔR, cm calculated	ΔR, cm measured	V avg cm/s	ΔR, cm measured	V avg cm/s
10	5	0.022	4	1.9	8.5	9.2
	10	0.09	5.5	3.3		
	15	0.2	7	4.3		
20	5	0.022	6.5	2.2	12.5	18.1
	10	0.09	8.5	3.9		
	15	0.2	10.5	5.5		

Let us analyze the experimental results for the case of piecewise linear approximation. For a low speed of movement of the robot (10 cm/s) with a small step, the highest accuracy of movement is achieved (deviation of about 2 cm). Note that the measured deviation (ΔR measured) is much larger than the calculated deviation (ΔR calculated), which was calculated by the formula (2). This is due to the fact that instabilities during the execution of the robot step greatly affect the accuracy of movement.

The average speed of movement when using linear approximation is lower than the possible speed of movement in a straight line. This is due to the fact that the robot stops to perform a turn. At the same time, considerable time is spent, which reduces the average speed. As the length of the linear segments of the path increases, the average speed also increases.

With an increase in the speed of movement up to 20 cm/s, an increase in the error of movement is observed. The instability of the robot's step performance increases with increasing speed, so the movement error also increases. The average speed is also increasing but remains quite low compared to the linear speed.

When using VTR gate, the average speed of movement is significantly higher than when using linear approximation. This is because the robot does not waste time stopping to turn on the spot. The average speed is slightly lower than the linear travel speed. The speed of movement of the legs external to the center of the circle is equal to the linear speed. The speed of the other parts of the robot is lower because they are closer to the center of rotation (Fig. 4a).

The accuracy of robot movement when using VTR gate is slightly lower than with piecewise linear approximation. During the movement, the trajectory correction was not carried out, so errors in the execution of steps accumulated.

It should be noted that in order of magnitude of the displacement error for the considered cases of piecewise linear displacement and VTR gate approximately coincide. To accurately track the trajectory, it is necessary to adjust the direction of movement of the walking robot depending on its deviation from the target trajectory. The difficulty in this case lies in the discrete nature of the steps and the complex control of the robot's walking process.

5   Conclusion

Moving a walking robot along a trajectory is a more difficult task than for wheeled robots. The robot's steps are discrete and must be synchronized with each other in time. Note that for walking robots, movement planning and step execution are closely related, since when walking, the robot moves relative to the objects surrounding it. Known ways of moving along the path are the approximation of the trajectory by simple curves along which the robot can move. The article considers two types of approximation are piecewise linear approximation and approximation by arcs of a circle. The proposed methods of trajectory approximation allow solving the problem of movement along the trajectory for home quadruped robot.

Approximation of the trajectory using rectilinear sections and turns allows you to solve the problem with fairly simple robot movements. The disadvantage of this representation is the intermittent movement of the robot, which reduces the average speed of movement. Approximation of the trajectory using arcs of circles allows you to build a universal gait for a walking robot (VTR gate). Such a gait can replace the rectilinear movement of the robot and turns on the spot. The calculation of the trajectories of the reference points of the robot's legs for this gait is more complex than for rectilinear gaits. The average speed of movement is slightly lower than for rectilinear movement and significantly higher than for piecewise linear approximation. Experiments have shown that when performing the movement of a walking robot using VPN gate, errors accumulate that occur when performing individual steps. To increase the accuracy of movement, it is necessary to adjust the position of the center of rotation and the radius of rotation.

Note that to move a home robot in a home environment, high accuracy of movement is not required. It is enough that the robot does not touch obstacles and confidently passes difficult sections of the path. It should be noted that improving the accuracy of moving a walking robot is a separate difficult task and deserves separate consideration.

The proposed methods of trajectory approximation for a home robot have a small computational complexity. This reduces the requirements for the necessary computing power for the control system of a home walking robot.

References

1. Karur, K., Sharma, N., Dharmatti, C., Siegel, J.E.: A survey of path planning algorithms for mobile robots. Vehicles 3(3), 448–468 (2021)
2. Jogeshwar, B.K., Lochan, K.: Algorithms for path planning on mobile robots. IFAC-PapersOnLine 55(1), 94–100 (2022)
3. Zhou, C., Huang, B., Fränti, P.: A review of motion planning algorithms for intelligent robots. J. Intell. Manuf. 33(2), 387–424 (2022)
4. De Santos, P.G., Garcia, E., Estremera, J.: Quadrupedal locomotion: an introduction to the control of four-legged robots, vol. 1. Springer, London (2006)
5. Matsuoka, K.: Mechanisms of frequency and pattern control in the neural rhythm generators. Biol. Cybern. 56(5–6), 345–353 (1987)
6. Shao, J., Ren, D., Gao, B.: Recent advances on gait control strategies for hydraulic quadruped robot. Recent Patents Mech. Eng. 11(1), 15–23 (2018)
7. Ijspeert, A.J.: Central pattern generators for locomotion control in animals and robots: a review. Neural Netw. 21(4), 642–653 (2008)
8. Barron-Zambrano, J.H., Torres-Huitzil, C., Girau, B.: Hardware implementation of a CPG-based locomotion control for quadruped robots. In: Diamantaras, K., Duch, W., Iliadis, L.S. (eds.) ICANN 2010. LNCS, vol. 6353, pp. 276–285. Springer, Heidelberg (2010). https://doi.org/10.1007/978-3-642-15822-3_35
9. Kim, H., Won, D., Kwon, O., Kim, T.J., Kim, S.S., Park, S.: Foot trajectory generation of hydraulic quadruped robots on uneven terrain. IFAC Proc. Vol. 41(2), 3021–3026 (2008)
10. Adak, O.K., Erbatur, K.: Bound gait reference generation of a quadruped robot via contact force planning. Int. J. Mech. Eng. Robot. Res. 11(3), 129–137 (2022)
11. Xu, X., Yang, Y., Pan, S.: Motion planning for mobile robots. In: Róka, R. (ed.) Advanced Path Planning for Mobile Entities. InTech (2018). https://doi.org/10.5772/intechopen.76895
12. McGhee, R.B., Frank, A.A.: On the stability properties of quadruped creeping gaits. Math. Biosci. 3, 331–351 (1968)
13. Estremera, J., de Santos, P.G.: Free gaits for quadruped robots over irregular terrain. Int. J. Robot. Res. 21(2), 115–130 (2002)
14. Yamamoto, H., Kim, S., Ishii, Y., Ikemoto, Y.: Generalization of movements in quadruped robot locomotion by learning specialized motion data. Robomech. J. 7, 1–14 (2020)
15. He, J., Shao, J., Sun, G., Shao, X.: Survey of quadruped robots coping strategies in complex situations. Electronics 8(12), 1414 (2019)

16. Shao, Y., Jin, Y., Liu, X., He, W., Wang, H., Yang, W.: Learning free gait transition for quadruped robots via phase-guided controller. IEEE Robot. Autom. Lett. **7**(2), 1230–1237 (2021)
17. Gehring, C., Coros, S., Hutter, M., Bloesch, M., Hoepflinger, M.A., Siegwart, R.: Control of dynamic gaits for a quadrupedal robot. In: 2013 IEEE International Conference on Robotics and automation, pp. 3287–3292. IEEE (2013)
18. Dobrynin, D.: Gait synthesis of a home quadruped robot. In: International Conference on Interactive Collaborative Robotics, vol. 13719, pp. 179–188. Springer International Publishing, Cham (2022). https://doi.org/10.1007/978-3-031-23609-9_16

Study of Path Planning Methods
in Two-Dimensional Mapped Environments

Nizar Hamdan, Viacheslav Pshikhopov⬥, Mikhail Medvedev, Dimitry Brosalin,
Maria Vasileva, and Boris Gurenko(✉)⬥

Joint Stock Company "Scientific-Design Bureau of Robotics and Control Systems", 154,
Socialist St, Taganrog, Rostov Region 347900, Russia
boris.gurenko@gmail.com

Abstract. The article studies the problem of path planning in two-dimensional
environments. The review and analysis of known planning algorithms are carried
out. This article is devoted to the development of a modified rapidly growing
random trees algorithm (RRT) and the study of its effectiveness in comparison
with known methods. The presented modified RRT algorithm checks the path
to some area near the specified node while planning the path to a new potential
node of the tree, which reduces the constructed nodes of the tree. The developed
algorithm is compared with the original RRT algorithm. The comparison criteria
are the path calculation time, the amount of memory required, the path length,
and the percentage of situations in which the trajectory to the target point was
successfully found. Next, the developed algorithm is compared with the planning
algorithms of other classes. The study uses representative samples of numerical
experiments and various environments that differ in the density of obstacles and the
presence of mazes. A study of planning algorithms using the results of experiments
on a ground-based wheeled robot has also been conducted.

Keywords: Path Planning · Two-dimensional Environment · Random Tree
Method · Optimization of Planning Algorithms · Comparative Analysis

1 Introduction

Today, mobile robots have reached a level of development that allows them to be used
autonomously. In this regard, the problem of optimal path planning in real-time is of
importance. Path planning is a complex task that does not have a universal solution.
Hence, the development and modification of various algorithms used in path planning,
applicable and optimal for various conditions, is needed. In general, the task of path
planning consists in calculating the sequence of states of a moving object that ensures
its transfer from the initial state to the target state. Note that the transition from the
initial state to the target can usually be done in several ways. In this regard, additional
requirements are imposed on how the transition to the target state will be carried out.
As a rule, the requirements for the optimal existential feasibility of the movement path
are imposed. The requirements of existential feasibility include, for example, that the

A. Ronzhin et al. (Eds.): ICR 2023, LNAI 14214, pp. 137–150, 2023.
https://doi.org/10.1007/978-3-031-43111-1_13

requirement to go to the target point at a specified time and with limited control actions, including the absence of any collisions in the optimal trajectory and this means reducing or maximizing the quality criterion, for example, travel time, route length, energy expended, etc. Thus, the planning algorithm is understood as a set of rules which calculates the state of a moving object for each planning moment. As a result of the action of the planning algorithm, a set of states is formed at the output, which can be converted into a set of agent's actions. According to [1], the trajectory planning of a moving object can be represented in general terms as the sequential execution of actions, including calculating the trajectory without collisions, smoothing the trajectory considering the characteristics of the object, and calculating control actions. Most often, the path is planned in the configuration space [1]. The main advantage of solving the path planning problem in configuration space is that this method reduces the calculations of a solid body to the calculations of a material point, which greatly simplifies the process [2]. For a moving object in two-dimensional Euclidean space, all configurations can be described by a vector (x, y, j), where x, y are the linear coordinates of the object, and j is the orientation angle. Space configurations are divided into subgroups {"Free"}, {"Obstacles"} and {"Unknown"}.

2   Overview of Motion Planning Methods

Today, methods based on cellular decomposition are often used, which use the division of the map into cells. In the case of representing the configuration space in the lattice form, popular planning methods are Dijkstra's algorithm and A* and D* based on it [3, 4]. Algorithm A* is a development of Dijkstra's algorithm. In A*, the computational complexity is reduced due to the heuristic function of estimating the cost of the path. At the same time, this algorithm requires a lot amount of memory usage, and its computational complexity increases significantly as the number of cells on the map increases. In this regard, there are quite many modifications of the A* algorithm that are aimed at reducing these disadvantages [5–8].

The D* algorithm [4] is optimized for path planning in a dynamic environment, when information is updated during the robot's movement. Note that the considered methods of path planning, as a rule, do not give smooth trajectories. In this regard, they are supplemented by various algorithms for smoothing the path [9]. Smooth movement paths are provided when using the artificial potential fields method for planning [10, 11]. Due to its simplicity, high computational efficiency and the indicated possibility of obtaining smooth trajectories of motion, the method of potential fields has become widely used [12, 13]. However, there are a few problems, which include local minimalism, the complexity of considering the dynamics of a moving body, and the reasonable selection of repulsive and attractive forces [14]. In this regard, potential fields are often used as a part of complex planning algorithms [15].

Planning methods using intelligent technologies, especially learning systems, have recently become popular [16, 17]. The advantage of neural network planning methods is their high adaptability to uncertain dynamic environments. The main disadvantage of planning systems is the high requirements for onboard computing systems [12].

Algorithms based on representing states in graph form are widely used. These include a planning algorithm for building a vision graph [18], Voronoi diagrams [19], rapidly-growing random trees [20], and probabilistic road maps [21].

The main limitation of the visibility graph construction algorithm is its high computational complexity, which is estimated as $O(n^2 log(n))$, where n is the number of nodes in [22], the problem of USV path planning in the waters of the coast of South Korea was considered. Due to many islands, the graph contains 54625 vertices. In this regard, the direct construction of the visibility graph is impractical. Therefore, in the article, adaptive meshing is first applied using the quadrant tree (quadtree) technology. Next, Dijkstra's algorithm finds a path on the quadtree and builds a visibility graph using the obtained path points.

The Voronoi diagram is a section of a plane with n centers in a set of convex polyhedrons such that any point within the polyhedron is closer to its center than the other centers [19]. This property allows you to plan the path farthest from obstacles if the centers of the latter act as points for the Voronoi diagram. The computational complexity of constructing a Voronoi diagram is estimated as $O(n \cdot log(n))$[12]. The main disadvantages of the Voronoi diagram method are its low computational efficiency, which requires the use of additional algorithms and map processing.

The probabilistic road map method [23] is used to solve problems of local and global planning. Due to high computational costs, the main efforts of researchers are aimed at improving the efficiency of the roadmap method, especially for narrow environments [24, 25]. The main role here is played by the method of generating new potential nodes of the graph. For example, in [24], a path planning method was proposed that uses a random roadmap algorithm. A new procedure for generating nodes in a limited area has been developed, and its effectiveness is shown in comparison with the original method of a randomized road map in a confined space. The paper [25] also studies the problem of enhancing the roadmap method in narrow spaces. For this, virtual fields are used that define the spaces in which potential new nodes of the roadmap are generated. Numerical experiments have been carried out, confirming the reduction of the time required to build a trajectory in a roadmap manner in bottlenecks. Thus, the roadmap method is common in path planning, but its computational efficiency is reduced in labyrinths, corridors, passages, and other bottlenecks.

The method of rapidly growing random trees (RRT - rapidly random trees) is more computationally efficient than the probabilistic road maps method. However, the main limitations of this method for use in dynamic environments are low convergence with an optimal solution and high memory usage requirements. For this reason, an increase in computational efficiency will expand the scope of the application of the method of RRT. The problem of applying the RRT algorithm under conditions of partial uncertainty is considered in [26], where it is proposed to divide the area of operation into separate regions. The RRT algorithm is used to find paths between regions. Path planning within local areas is performed by a simple algorithm using straight line segments. The uncertainty of the map is considered by introducing the probability that the map cell is occupied by an obstacle. The main result presented in this paper is a method that ensures the achievement of the target point with a probability of at least a certain value

p_{min}. The main disadvantage of this method is a significant increase in computational complexity with an increase in the value of p_{min}.

The problem of reducing computational complexity and required memory was also considered in [26]. The work [26] combines the RRT algorithm and artificial potential fields (the P-RRT* method). In this method, a random tree is generated in the direction of reducing the potential repulsion field, which makes it possible to increase the rate of convergence to the optimal path. The computational complexity of the method remains very high; moreover, the methods of [26] give non-smooth paths.

In [27], an improved version of the RRT* algorithm [28] was used. The bidirectional growth of a random tree is used in the RRT algorithm to increase the rate of convergence to the optimal solution. The main results of [27] indicate that bidirectional random search in combination with potential fields reduces the number of iterations to find the shortest path. In addition, these algorithms allow moving in narrow corridors without falling into local minima. To reduce the amount of memory required trees are computed sequentially by time, which increases the time complexity.

In [29], is used a two-stage path planning procedure in a dynamic environment. The global planner computes the initial path of the first approximation using the RRT algorithm. Next, a dynamic planner is applied, which changes the position of the path nodes using repulsive and inertial forces. The prediction procedure is used to calculate moving obstacles. In this work, is used a heuristic optimization function, the choice of which depends on various requirements and limitations. The main problem of the method is the rational choice of this function.

In [10], a two-stage planning algorithm is proposed, in which virtual obstacles are added to the map to consider the dynamic limitations of the mobile robot, blocking impossible sections of motion [30]. A modified version of the RRT algorithm, the MPN-RRT algorithm, is used as a global planning algorithm. This algorithm, unlike the original version, uses several parent nodes, which reduces the length of the planned path compared to the original version of RRT with a single node. To solve the problem of slow convergence of algorithms based on random search and path smoothing, the RRT algorithm is supplemented with a local optimization algorithm. The RRT algorithm searches for a global path, which is smoothed and optimized by the iterative local algorithm proposed in [31].

In this article, the task is to develop a modified RRT algorithm that is more efficient in terms of computation time than the original RRT algorithm. The task is also to conduct a study of the proposed algorithm in comparison with the original RRT method and other methods of path planning.

3   Mathematical Description of the Robot Movement and the Environment

In the general case, the robot model can be represented by kinematics and dynamics equations of a rigid body and actuators [32]. For a ground-based wheeled robot mathematical model can be represented as [9, 12, 15]:

$$\dot{x} = (\omega_l + \omega_r) r \cos \phi, \ \dot{y} = (\omega_l + \omega_r) r \sin \phi, \tag{1}$$

$$\dot{\phi} = (\omega_l - \omega_2)\frac{r}{l}, \tag{2}$$

$$\dot{\omega}_l = k_1 u_l, \quad \dot{\omega}_r = k_2 u_r, \tag{3}$$

where (x, y) are linear coordinates of the robot; φ is the robot orientation angle; $\omega_{l,r}$ are the angular velocity of the left and right wheels; u_l, u_r are control actions; r is the radius of the wheels; l is the distance between the wheels; k_1, k_2 are the constant coefficients.

The operating environment of the robot is shown in Fig. 1.

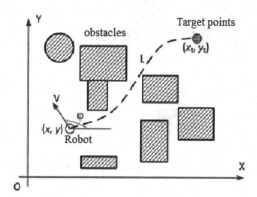

Fig. 1. The operating environment of the robot.

The robot with coordinates (x, y) is indicated in Fig. 1 with an unshaded circle. The target with coordinates (x_t, y_t) is represented as a double hatched circle. Obstacles are shown as shaded boxes and circles. Individual obstacles can form complex configurations, dead ends roads, walls, labyrinths, etc. Since obstacles can form random configurations, then it does not make much difference in the shape of individual obstacles. For this reason, both shapes will be used below – rectangles and circles.

The path appears as a dotted line. The task is to plan the collision-free path L in such a way that:

- for a given computation time t_p, the path length L is minimized;
- when the condition $L \leq L_{allowed}$ is met, the computation time does not exceed the specified value $t_{allowed}$.

The RRT algorithm is adopted as the basic algorithm, which allows the bypass the problem of local minima, can be used in uncertain conditions, but as mentioned earlier, requires a long computation time.

4   Modified Rapidly-Growing Random Trees Algorithm

To increase the efficiency of the RRT algorithm, the following heuristics methods are used to compensate for the existing disadvantages. This optimization is achieved through the following principles:

- instead of checking the free path from the current node to the target node, it checks whether there is a path from the current node to an obstacle-free region around the target node, as shown in Fig. 2;
- instead of checking the free path from the potential node to the parent node, the presence of a path from the current potential node to the free node is checked from the obstacles in the area around this parent node.

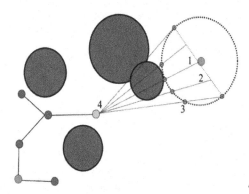

Fig. 2. Checking the path in the area near the target point.

Figure 3 shows a block diagram of the modified algorithm. The main part of the RRT algorithm has remained unchanged. The difference between RRT algorithm and the proposed algorithm is the additional verification. Before forming a new node, it is checked that there is a free direct path from the current node 4 in Fig. 2 to target node 1. If the straight path is crossed by obstacles, the free area around the target node is calculated. A diameter is built through the center of the free zone, straight lines are generated on it with a given step expand from the current node. Nodes are initialized at the intersection of lines with the boundaries of the free region. It checks for a free direct path from the current node to the node on the boundary of the free zone. If a free direct path from the current node was found, then a direct path is laid. Further, if the path is found then algorithm completes the execution, otherwise, the algorithm continues to build the graph according to the original method. Similarly, the free path from the newly generated node to the parent node is checked the same way.

Thus, the application of the proposed heuristic method expands the list of adjustable parameters of the planning algorithm. In the implemented classical algorithm, the following are configured: the size of the rand_area region, in which a random point is selected in the configuration space; the maximum distance expand_dist that a tree branch can grow from the parent node towards an arbitrary point in space; The target_sample_rate probability that the path target node is chosen as the point towards which the tree branch grows; the maximum number of max_iter attempts to build a new tree node. If this number is exceeded, the algorithm terminates.

Since checking the path to a given area introduces additional computational costs, it is not performed every step. In this regard, an additional configurable parameter is a frequency of checking the presence of a path to the free zone boundary around the target

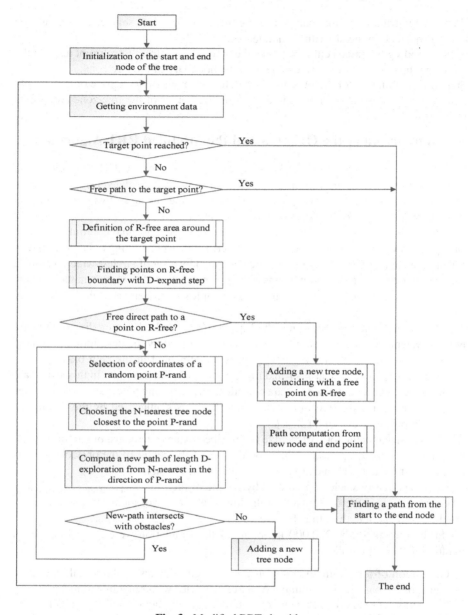

Fig. 3. Modified RRT algorithm.

point *straight_path_to_area_check*. Determination of the presence of a direct path from the current node to the boundary of the free zone around the target point or the generated new node is performed according to the following algorithm:

Step 1. Calculation of the radius of the free zone around the target point or the new generated node: R_{free} – equal to the distance to the boundary of the nearest obstacle.

Step 2. Segmentation of the diameter of the free zone d_{free} into segments with the step d_{expand} specified in the algorithm parameters.

Step 3. Finding the intersection points of the straight lines from the current node to the points on the diameter of the free zone with the boundary of the free zone.

Step 4. Determination of the presence of a collision-free path along one of the straight lines going from the current node to a point on the border of the free zone around the target point.

5 Comparison of the Original and the Modified RRT Algorithm

A comparative modeling of two methods was carried out: the original RRT algorithm and the modified algorithm shown in Fig. 3. The algorithms were modeled using the Python 3.9 programming language. The simulation was performed using software simulation in the PyCharm integrated development environment.

The simulated environment is represented as a two-dimensional coordinate grid, at each point of which a robot can be located, described by a positioning point (x, y) and an orientation angle φ (Fig. 1). Obstacles are described by a set of circles, which include a safety buffer zone. Single action means a change in the state of the agent, namely one or more of its coordinates (x, y). The modeling complex is implemented in the PyCharm environment.

The moving object is represented by Eqs. (1), (2) and (3). The modeling of the navigation system and vision system blocks are implemented by the description presented in [32]. The calculation of the global path is implemented in the path planning system, where both the classical RRT and the modified version proposed in this article are implemented. The actuator sensors are considered as ideal, and the actuators themselves are proportional inertia–free links. The controller was synthesized by the method of positional trajectory control [12, 32].

Each obstacle in the form of a circle is described by an ordered list of the form (x_{obst}, y_{obst}, r_{obst}), where x_{obst}, y_{obst} are the coordinates of the center of the obstacle, r_{obst} is the radius of the danger zone around the center of the obstacle.

A rectangular obstacle is described by a tuple of the form (x_{obst}, y_{obst}, a_{obst}, b_{obst}), where x_{obst}, y_{obst} – the coordinates of the lower left corner of the obstacle, a_{obst}, b_{obst} are the width and length of the obstacle.

In the present study, 270,000 iterations of the simulation were carried out. Each iteration includes the following steps:

1. Generation of a random situation on the map: coordinates of the initial and target points of the path, a given number N_{obst} of obstacles with random parameters.
2. Simulation of the robot's movement on the map using the original RRT algorithm.
3. Simulation of the robot's movement on the map using the modified RRT algorithm.
4. Fixing the performance indicators of the original and modified RRT algorithms. The indicators include algorithm running time (t_{RRT}, t_{new_RRT}); the amount of memory required (m_{RRT}, m_{new_RRT}); the length of the resulting path (l_{RRT}, l_{new_RRT}); the frequency of successful goal achievement without collisions (f_{RRT}, f_{new_RRT}).

A series of launches was performed on maps of different dimensions $map_{dim} = $ [50:50, 500:500, 5000:5000], with a different number of obstacles $map_{obst} = $ [10, 30, 50], with different positions of the starting and target points.

The simulation results are represented in Tables 1, 2. Examples of the operation of the classical and modified RRT algorithms are shown in Figs. 4 and 5. The following designations are used in the tables: t_{av} – the average running time, m_{av} – the average amount of used memory, l_{av} – the average path length, i_n – the percentage of unsuccessful iterations of modeling, i_{max} – the maximum number of iterations, map_{dim} – the map dimension.

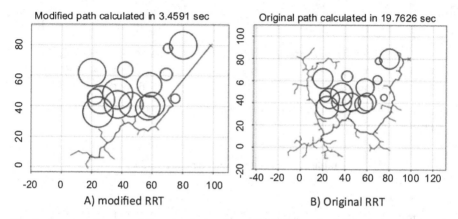

Fig. 4. An example of modeling classical and modified RRT methods for constructing a path.

According to the data presented in Table 1, using of the modified RRT algorithm with an increased number of obstacles allowed to reduce the computation time iby17.4–46.8%, reduce the amount of memory used by 45.6–86.0%, and reduce the path length by 3.0–13.5%. In addition, the original RRT method failed to find the path, depending on the size of the map and the maximum number of iterations, in 0.13–11.7% of cases. At the same time, the modified RRT algorithm did not find the path in 0–1.7% of cases. A total of 90000 experiments were performed using the parameters described above.

Analyzing to the data presented in Table 2, we determine that using of the modified method, with the number of obstacles 50, allowed to reduce the computation time by 14.3–47.3%, reduce the amount of memory used by 29.8–80.2%, and reduce the path length by 1.9–8.9%. In addition, the original RRT method failed to find the path, depending on the size of the map and the maximum number of iterations, in 6.9–88.7% of cases. At the same time, the modified RRT algorithm did not find the path in 0.2–4.6% of cases.

Note that as the number of obstacles and the dimension of the map increase, the effect of the heuristics used in this article is decreases a little. So, from Figs. 6 and 7 it can be seen that on a map with a dimension of 5000 × 5000 with the number of obstacles equal to 50, the modified RRT algorithm loses in time to the classical algorithm if the maximum number of iterations is more than 1000. Due to the fact that on a large map with many obstacles, it becomes increasingly difficult to determine the direct path from the current point to a given area

Table 3 shows the success percentage of the modified algorithm according to all criteria for all 270,000 experiments conducted.

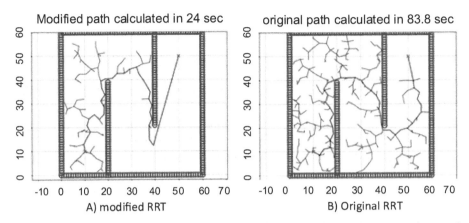

Fig. 5. An example of modeling the classical and modified RRT methods for constructing a path in the presence of two walls.

Table 1. Simulation results for $N_{obst} = 30$.

i_{max}	Method	t_{av}, second			l_{av}, unit		
	map$_{dim}$	50	500	5000	50	500	5000
700	RRT	0.0097	0.0266	0.0591	338108	1709574	2760827
	M-RRT	0.0051	0.0141	0.0400	326533	1565291	2387731
1500	RRT	0.015	0.0474	0.1374	399790	2930239	11103805
	M-RRT	0.008	0.0309	0.1135	385079	2745523	10001515
3000	RRT	0.0190	0.1124	0.2827	413072	3305314	29437582
	M-RRT	0.0104	0.0619	0.2288	400049	3106780	27433970
i_{max}	Method	m_{av}, byte			i_n, %		
	map$_{dim}$	50	500	5000	50	500	5000
700	RRT	1224.01	2502.32	3475.78	11.7%	43.22%	84.54%
	M-RRT	636.28	713.05	488.05	1.69%	1.52%	0.13%
1500	RRT	1541.64	3455.61	6107.81	3.05%	18.16%	57.96%
	M-RRT	816.14	1229.59	1238.44	0.4%	1.41%	0.6%
3000	RRT	1679.25	5821.56	6905.18	0.74%	11.76%	17.52%
	M-RRT	914.10	2105.76	2254.93	0.08%	0.93%	1.25%

Table 2. Simulation results for $N_{obst} = 50$.

i_{max}	Method	t_{av}, second			l_{av}, unit		
	map$_{dim}$	50	500	5000	50	500	5000
700	RRT	0.0133	0.0326	0.0772	222692	570338	1826683
	M-RRT	0.0088	0.0172	0.0652	216445	519433	1608241
1500	RRT	0.0268	0.0666	0.1600	345404	1370839	6354044
	M-RRT	0.0188	0.0486	0.1866	338594	1288650	5814408
3000	RRT	0.0463	0.1328	0.2980	427098	2317289	14420732
	M-RRT	0.0336	0.1062	0.4708	419115	2198826	13550898
i_{max}	Method	m_{av}, byte			i_n, %		
	map$_{dim}$	50	500	5000	50	500	5000
700	RRT	1073.89	2456.67	3095.97	35.96%	74.55%	88.73%
	M-RRT	679.88	691.59	612.80	4.63%	1.14%	0.2%
1500	RRT	1625.69	3733.38	5158.43	16.82%	53.0%	72.33%
	M-RRT	1089.77	1463.61	1390.18	3.14%	3.0%	1.29%
3000	RRT	2174.86	5289.81	7529.37	6.94%	33.07%	51.21%
	M-RRT	1526.72	2466.74	2863.20	1.11%	3.53%	2.67%

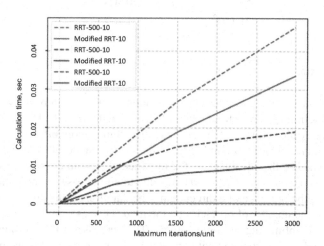

Fig. 6. Graph of the change in the path search time on the map 50×50.

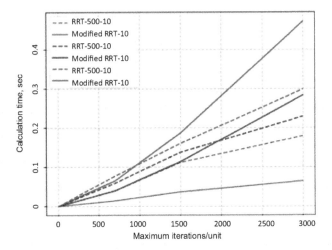

Fig. 7. Graph of the change in the path search time on the map 5000 × 5000.

Table 3. Simulation results grouped by the size of the environment.

Map dimensions	t_{av}, second	m_{av}, byte	l_{av}, unit
50 × 50	55,48%	54,67%	8,03%
500 × 500	53,06%	70,56%	9,56%
5000 × 5000	21,16%	81,46%	11,27%

6 Conclusion

An analysis of the results of a series of experiments allows us to draw a few conclusions in order to determine in which situations the use of the modified RRT algorithm is effective, and in which situations the original algorithm is more effective.

With the increase in the complexity of the environment and the increase in the number of obstacles, the advantage of the modified algorithm decreases (but remains) in terms of $t_{average}$, $m_{average}$, $l_{average}$. This is due to an increase in computational costs for determining the presence of a direct path - the duration of this procedure is directly proportional to the number of obstacles on the map. This disadvantage can be partially compensated by optimizing of computations. The decrease in the advantage value in terms of m_{av} and l_{av} is associated with an increase in the number of maneuvers that the agent must perform when going around many obstacles. Many obstacles on the map reduces the number of sections in which the modified algorithm outstands the original one.

As the dimensions of the environment increase, the advantage of the modified algorithm in terms of t_{av} decreases but remains. The advantage of m_{av} and l_{av} increases. The change in the advantage is associated with an increase in the number of iterations of tree growth performed by the algorithm; respectively, the modified algorithm performs more computations that are heuristic and spends more time on them.

Using the modified algorithm increases the percentage of the probability of finding a solution within the specified requirements for the allowed number of i_{max} (Tree growth iterations). Among all the experiments, the modified algorithm did not find a solution in 1.07% of the cases; meanwhile the original algorithm solution did not find a solution in 30.13% of the cases.

Thus, the modified algorithm showed an advantage:

in cases of environment without obstacles;
in cases where there is a limit on the maximum number of iterations;
in cases where the memory space allowed for storing the computation tree is limited.

The disadvantages of the algorithm include the dependence of temporal computational efficiency on the environment dimension for medium and high obstacle density maps.

Acknowledgements. The work was supported by the grant of the Russian Science Foundation No. 22-29-00533, carried out in JSC "Scientific Design Bureau of Robotics and Control Systems".

References

1. LaValle, S.: Planning Algorithms, pp.1–842. Cambridge University Press (2006)
2. Lozano-Perez, T.: Spatial planning: a configuration space approach. IEEE Trans. Comput. **32**(2), 108–120 (1983)
3. Hart, P.E., Nilsson, N.J., Raphael, B.A.: Formal basis for the heuristic determination of minimum cost paths. IEEE Trans. Syst. Sci. Cybern. **2**, 100–107 (1968)
4. Stentz, A.: Optimal and efficient path planning for partially known environments. In: Intelligent Unmanned Ground Vehicles, pp. 203–220. Springer, Boston, MA, USA (1997)
5. Wang, Q., Hao, Y., Chen, F.: Deepening the IDA* algorithm for knowledge graph reasoning through neural network architecture. Neurocomputing **429**, 101–109 (2021)
6. Zhou, R., Hansen, E.A.: Memory-bounded {A*} graph search. In: The Florida AI Research Society Conference – FLAIRS, pp. 203–209 (2002)
7. Holte, R., Perez, M., Zimmer, R., MacDonald, A.: Hierarchical A*: searching abstraction hierarchies efficiently. Proc. Thirteenth Natl. Conf. Artif. Intell. **1**, 530–535 (1996)
8. Liu, B., Xiao, X., Stone, P.: A lifelong learning approach to mobile robot navigation. IEEE Robot. Autom. Lett. **6**(2), 1090–1096 (2021)
9. Pshikhopov, V., Medvedev, M., Kostukov, V., Houssein, F., Kadim, A.: Algorithms for trajectory planning in a two-dimensional environment with obstacles. Inf. Autom. **21**(3), 459–492 (2022)
10. Khatib, O.: Real-time obstacles avoidance for manipulators and mobile robots. Int. J. Robot. Res. **5**(2), 90–98 (1986)
11. Platonov, A., Karpov, I., Kirilchenko, A.: The method of potentials in the laying of the route. M.: Preprint of the Institute of Applied Mathematics of the USSR Academy of Sciences 27 (1974)
12. Pshikhopov, V.: In: Beloglazov, D., et al.: (eds.) Path Planning for Vehicles Operating in Uncertain 2D Environments, Elsevier, Butterworth-Heinemann, ISBN: 9780128123058, 312 (2017)

13. Filimonov, A., Filimonov, N.: Issues of motion control of mobile robots by the method of potential guidance. Mekhatronika, Avtomatizatsiya, Upravlenie **20**(11), 677–685 (2019)
14. Pshikhopov, V., Medvedev, M.: Group control of the movement of mobile robots in an uncertain environment using unstable regimes. Proc. SPIIRAN **60**, 39–63 (2018)
15. Malone, N., Chiang, H.-T., Lesser, K., Oishi, M., Tapia, L.: Hybrid dynamic moving obstacle avoidance using a stochastic reachable set-based potential field. IEEE Trans. Rob. **33**(5), 1124–1138 (2017)
16. Gaiduk, A., Martyanov, O., Medvedev, M., Pshikhopov, V., Hamdan, N., Farkhud, A.: Neural network control system for a group of robots in an unidentified two-dimensional environment. Mechatron., Autom., Control **21**(8), 470–479 (2020)
17. Wang, Y., Cheng, L., Hou, Z.-G., Yu, J., Tan, M.: Optimal formation of multirobot systems based on a recurrent neural network. IEEE Trans. Neural Netw. Learn. Syst. **27**(2), 322–333 (2016)
18. De Berg, M., Cheong, O., Van Kreveld, M., Overmars, M.: Computational Geometry: Algorithms and Applications, 3rd edn. Springer-Verlag (2008)
19. Guibas, L.J., Knuth, D.E., Sharir, M.: Randomized incremental construction of delaunay and voronoi diagrams. Algorithmica **7**(1), 381–413 (1992)
20. LaValle, S.M., Kuffner, J.J.: Rapidly exploring random trees: progress and prospects. In: Workshop on the Algorithmic Foundations of Robotics, pp. 293–308 (2000)
21. Kedem, K., Sharir, M.: An efficient motion planning algorithm for a convex rigid polygonal object in 2-dimensional polygonal space. Discrete Comput. Geom. **5**(1), 43–75 (1990)
22. Lee, W., Choi, G.-H., Kim, T.-W.: Visibility graph-based path-planning algorithm with quadtree representation. Appl. Ocean Res. **117**, 102887 (2021)
23. Kavraki, L.E., Svestka, P., Latombe, J.C., Overmars, M.H.: Probabilistic roadmaps for path planning in high-dimensional configuration spaces. IEEE Trans. Robot. Autom. **12**(4), 566–580 (1996)
24. Kamil, A.R.M., Shithil, S.M., Ismail, Z.H., Mahmud, M.S.A., Faudzi, A.A.M.: Path planning based on inflated medial axis and probabilistic roadmap for duct environment. Lecture Notes in Electrical Engineering 834 (2022)
25. Chen, G., Luo, N., Liu, D., Zhao, Z., Liang, Ch.: Path planning for manipulators based on an improved probabilistic roadmap method. Rob. Computer-Integrated Manuf. **72**, 102196 (2021)
26. Qureshi, A., Ayaz, Y.: Potential functions-based sampling heuristic for optimal path planning. Auton. Robot **40**, 1079–1093 (2016)
27. Karaman, S., Frazzoli, E.: Sampling-based algorithms for optimal motion planning. Int. J. Robot. Res. **30**(7), 846–894 (2011)
28. Chen, L., Shan, Y., Tian, W., Li, B., Cao, D.: A fast and efficient double-tree RRT∗-like sampling-based planner applying on mobile robotic systems. IEEE/ASME Trans. Mechatron. **23**(6), 2568–2578 (2018)
29. Wang, J., Meng, M.Q.-H., Khatib, O.: EB-RRT: optimal motion planning for mobile robots. IEEE Trans. Autom. Sci. Eng. **17**(4), 2063–2073 (2020)
30. Medvedev, M., Pshikhopov, V., Gurenko, B., Hamdan, N.: Path planning method for a mobile robot with maneuver restrictions. In: Proceedings of the International Conference on Electrical, Computer, Communications and Mechatronics Engineering (ICECCME) (2021)
31. Kostjukov, V., Medvedev, M., Pshikhopov, V.: Method for optimizing of mobile robot trajectory in repeller sources field. Inf. Autom. **20**(3), 690–726 (2021)
32. Pshikhopov, V., Medvedev, M.: Multi-loop adaptive control of mobile objects in solving trajectory tracking tasks. Autom. Remote Control **81**(11), 2078–2093 (2020)

DHC-R: Evaluating "Distributed Heuristic Communication" and Improving Robustness for Learnable Decentralized PO-MAPF

Vladislav Savinov[1]([⊠]) [iD] and Konstantin Yakovlev[2] [iD]

[1] St Petersburg State University, 7-9, Universitetskaya Emb., St. Petersburg 199034, Russia
vlad.al.savinov@gmail.com
[2] Federal Research Center "Computer Science and Control" of the Russian Academy of Sciences, 44/2, Vavilova street, Moscow 119333, Russia

Abstract. Multi-agent pathfinding (MAPF) is a problem of coordinating the movements of multiple agents operating a shared environment that has numerous industrial and research applications. In many practical cases the agents (robots) have limited visibility of the environment and must rely on local observations to make decisions. This scenario, known as partially observable MAPF (PO-MAPF), can be solved through decentralized approaches. In recent years, several learnable algorithms have been proposed for solving PO-MAPF. However, their performance is oftentimes not validated out-of-distribution (OOD), and the code is often not properly open-sourced. In this study, we conduct a comprehensive empirical evaluation of one of the state-of-the-art decentralized PO-MAPF algorithms, Distributed Heuristic Communication (DHC), Ma, Z., Luo, Y., Ma, H.: Distributed heuristic multi-agent path finding with communication. In: 2021 International Conference on Robotics and Automation (ICRA), pp. 8699–8705. IEEE, Xi'an, China (2021), which incorporates communication between agents. Our experiments reveal that the performance of DHC deteriorates when agents encounter complete packet loss during communication. To address this issue, we propose a novel algorithm called DHC-R that employs a similar architecture to the original DHC but introduces randomness into the graph neural network-based communication block, preventing the passage of some data packets during training. Empirical evaluation confirms that DHC-R outperforms DHC in scenarios with packet loss. Open-sourced model weights and the codebase are provided: https://github.com/acforvs/dhc-robust-mapf.

Keywords: PO-MAPF · Reinforcement Learning · Generalization · Out-of-distribution · AI safety

1 Introduction

Multi-agent pathfinding (MAPF) is a problem of coordinating the movements of multiple agents to achieve a common goal in a shared environment. One of the most challenging scenarios in MAPF arises when agents cannot observe the entire environment in

© The Author(s), under exclusive license to Springer Nature Switzerland AG 2023
A. Ronzhin et al. (Eds.): ICR 2023, LNAI 14214, pp. 151–163, 2023.
https://doi.org/10.1007/978-3-031-43111-1_14

which they operate and must make decisions based on partial observations. In such cases, communication with a central controller might also be restricted, and each agent might plan its movements in a decentralized manner. This scenario, known as partially observable multi-agent pathfinding (PO-MAPF, see Fig. 1), poses a complex challenge as agents must cooperate without explicit coordination. Addressing this challenging task has traditionally relied on classical computer science or heuristic algorithms. However, with the increasing availability of data and advancements in computational capabilities, researchers have begun exploring learnable algorithms for these problems. Reinforcement learning (RL), in particular, has emerged as a promising tool for addressing these challenges.

Fig. 1. Example of a single PO-MAPF scenario; image from [1].

Previous learnable decentralized algorithms did not provide thorough empirical evaluation of algorithms and failed to consider important real-world scenarios, such as a complete packet loss in communication-based algorithms. This work is aimed at closing this gap. Our main contributions are:

1. We extend the empirical evaluation for one of the state-of-the-art learnable decentralized PO-MAPF algorithms, DHC [2], and benchmark it out-of-distribution. We provide empirical evaluation for this algorithm in scenarios where a complete packet loss occurs.
2. We introduce a novel algorithm, DHC-R, built upon the DHC architecture, that handles the scenario of a complete packet loss significantly better than the original algorithm.
3. We fully open source the code base and set up programming instruments for easy development and experiments.

2   Background

The problem of multi-agent pathfinding (MAPF) consists of the computation of collision-free paths for a group of agents from their location to an assigned target. The elements of a classical MAPF problem are as follows:

1. An undirected graph $G = (V, E)$.
2. A set of N agents; each agent i is associated with its starting point $s_i \in V$ and the unique target point $g_i \in V$.

It is assumed that the time is discrete, and that each agent can perform one action at each timestep. *Path*, or *plan*, for the i-th agent is a sequence of vertexes $v_0, v_1, \ldots, v_N$: $v_j \in V; v_0 = s_i, v_N = g_i$. The vertex v_j is a result of a taken action (usually wait or move) from the previous vertex v_{j-1}, e.g., for every $j \geq 1$ either $v_j = v_{j-1}$ or $(v_{j-1}, v_j) \in E$, meaning that two consecutive vertexes in a path are either adjacent or identical. The *collision* between two agents occurs when one of the following transpires:

1. At timestamp t two agents end up being in the same vertex $s \in V$. This can happen if they either came from different vertexes to s or one of the agents stayed in place, and the other moved to s at timestamp t.
2. Two agents, being located at $s_1 \in V$ and $s_2 \in V$ at timestamp $t - 1$ changed their positions to s_2 and s_1 correspondingly at t.

The *solution* for the MAPF problem is a set of N collision-free paths, one for each agent.

In the partially observable setting, agents do not receive the full graph as an input. Instead, at each timestamp, they can observe only the part of the environment, called *field of view* or *FOV*. In the example shown in the Fig. 1, FOV is represented by a small square window around the agent. The PO-MAPF problem can be formulated as a Markov decision process (MDP) and described by a 7-tuple $(N, S, \{A_i\}, \{O_i\}, \{R_i\}, P, \gamma)$, where N is a number of agents, S is a set of states, A_i is a set of actions allowed for agent i, O_i is a set of observations for agent i, P is the dynamics of the MDP, $R_i : S \times A \to \mathbb{R}$ is a reward function for the i-th agents and γ is a discount rate, $0 < \gamma < 1$. Dynamics of the MDP $P(s', \vec{o}|s, \vec{a})$ outputs the probability of moving to the state s' from s and receiving an observation $\vec{o}$ for it by selecting an action $\vec{a}$. A reward function for the i-th agent outputs a numerical signal for the action that was taken from a given state. Discount rate determines how much the future rewards are important to the current state. In a finite MDP, A_i, O_i and S are finite sets. A *policy* maps each state s in the state space to a probability $\pi(a|s)$ for each action a in the action space. The *solution* to the PO-MAPF problem for each agent is a policy that maximizes the sum of discounted with the rate γ rewards.

In this manuscript, we consider PO-MAPF problem to be located on a 2D map, called a *grid*, which consists of *empty* cells where agents can be located and *blocked* cells occupied by obstacles. In our setting, each agent can undertake 1 out of 5 available actions: move left, right, up or down, or stay still. Collisions which were described above are also not allowed. The goal of each agent is to reach the *target*. In this work, a policy is a neural network that receives an encoded state/observation from the environment and outputs $\pi(a \mid s)$. To evaluate a policy once it is found, several metrics are usually utilized:

1. *Collective success rate (CSR)*: The percentage of tasks that were fully solved, meaning that each agent successfully reached its corresponding goal. The higher, the better.
2. *Individual success rate (ISR)*: The percentage of agents that arrived at their goals. The higher, the better.

During test invocation, these metrics are usually averaged across different runs.

Reinforcement learning [3] is learning from interactions with an environment to maximize a numerical signal, called reward. In general, there are two types of tasks in RL: episodic and continuing tasks. In episodic ones, the agent's interactions with the environments break into subsequences called episodes. Each episode ends in a terminal state, which is a special state that resets the agent's state to one of the starting states. In continuing tasks, there are no terminal states, and the agents interacts with the environment forever. The goal of a reinforcement learning agent is to maximize the expected *return* after timestep t which can be defined as follows:

$$G_t = \sum_{k=1}^{\infty} \gamma^k r_{t+k+1}.$$

In the equation above, r_i is the reward received at timestep i. If the task is episodic with the terminal state at timestamp T, all $r_{T+1}, r_{T+2}, \ldots$ are zeroed. A policy $\pi : S \times A \rightarrow [0, 1]$ is a mapping from states to actions; $\pi(a \mid s)$ is the probability of choosing the action a in s. The *value function* of a state s under policy π, $V_\pi(s)$, is the expected return that the agent receives starting at state s and following the given policy π. $V_\pi(s)$ can be formally defined as follows:

$$V_\pi(s) = \mathrm{E}[G_t | S_t = s] = \mathrm{E}\left[\sum_{k=0}^{\infty} \gamma^k r_{t+k+1} | S_t = s\right].$$

The *state-action value function* $Q_\pi(s, a)$ outputs the expected return when following the policy π starting at s and taking the action a as the initial action.

$$Q_\pi(s, a) = \mathrm{E}[G_t | S_t = s, A_t = a] = \mathrm{E}\left[\sum_{k=0}^{\infty} \gamma^k r_{t+k+1} | S_t = s, A_t = a\right].$$

In addition, an advantage function is usually defined as the different between the Q-function and a V-function:

$$A_\pi(s, a) = Q_\pi(s, a) - V_\pi(s).$$

In the past, numerous methods have been suggested to find the optimal policy that maximizes the sum of discounted rewards. While these methods are beyond the scope of this study, one commonly used approach is to approximate or precisely calculate the Q-function. In this work, we adopt this approach and train a neural network to approximate the Q-function that can be then written as $Q(s, a, \theta)$. Once the network is trained, agents can utilize it to select the action with the highest expected return.

3   Related Work

Heuristic Algorithms. In a single agent setting, the goal is to find the optimal path from a starting point to a finishing point. The standard approach is to use the A* [4] algorithm. This algorithm uses a heuristic function to estimate the distance from the current location of the agent to its goal and guide the algorithm towards the optimal solution. Although A* can find the optimal solution, it may not be suitable for real-world usage due to its time complexity. There are many other single-agent algorithms, but since they are not our main focus in this work, we will not be investigating them further. For multi-agent scenarios, there exist several methods that extend the A* algorithm. As a basic modification, one could run A* in a joint space of actions. However, this would result in an exponential growth of the number of vertexes in a graph, and the algorithm would take a long time to output a solution for a large number of agents. Further modifications include LRA* [5], M* [6] or OdRM* [7] that plan each agent independently but transfer the planning to a higher dimensional space once the collision occurs. Other techniques, including Conflict Based Search (CBS)-based [8–11] algorithms were also introduced for this problem. In addition, reduction-based algorithms [12, 13] that reduce the MAPF problem to a SAT problem were suggested. Although these algorithms may provide optimal solutions, they are not polynomial and can take a long time to converge. In situations where optimality is not guaranteed, conflicts can arise during plan execution, and agents may need to communicate with a central controller for replanning. This may result in frequent calls to the global expert, causing agents to wait for a response and remain idle.

Learning-based Algorithms. In response to the challenges outlined above, researchers have proposed several non-heuristic methods for MAPF. Among these, RL approaches have been particularly appealing [2, 14, 15]. While some RL-based methods may still rely on a central planner, they use it not as a sole point of coordination, but as an expert to guide learning during training. The expert generates trajectories, and agents try to replicate them. These algorithms typically use imitation learning (IL) and can be executed in a decentralized manner. They can also accommodate partially observable maps. For instance, in [16], a switch determines whether the next stage will be RL- or IL-based. During the IL phase, the central planner generates new trajectories that the agent can follow using behavioral cloning. During the RL stage, agents regress on generated trajectories to learn. However, IL builds upon the idea that experts generate trajectories of good quality. This is not the only problem with the described approach. First, the experts themselves may be too complex and time-consuming to run, making it impractical to use them for training. Additionally, while regressing on expert demonstrations, the model may not learn how to efficiently deviate from them even if doing so would be beneficial [2].

Recently, there has been growing interest in communication-based algorithms that leverage the exchange of packets between agents to improve coordination. Early works in this area used a collective reward to guide agent behavior, but later approaches employed individual rewards, enabling decentralized execution. All these methods have been trained in a centralized manner. More recent works have explored decentralized training methods as well. For example, in [17], agents form clusters based on learned priorities, and communication occurs only within clusters. Central agents receive and aggregate data packets from others, then transmit the results back to their clusters. The development of graph neural networks (GNNs) has led to recent works leveraging this powerful architecture for the MAPF problem. One early work is [18], which combines imitation learning with communication using CBS as a central planner. However, it is worth noting that the number of works that utilize communication and decentralized training together remains limited. For instance, in [2], agents receive information from all neighbors and consider packets only from the two closest ones. Another study [19] adopts a similar architecture but employs a request-reply mechanism instead of broadcasting, allowing only the most crucial agents to exchange information.

4   Method

The objective of this work is to address a scenario where communication-based algorithms are unable to utilize inter-agent communication during inference, which can occur in real-world situations due to technical issues. To accomplish this, we propose a novel algorithm called DHC-R, which builds upon DHC [2]. Additionally, our aim is to validate the original DHC algorithm [2] across various settings to expand upon previous empirical evaluations. To begin, we thoroughly reproduce the DHC algorithm and refer to this reproduced version as DHC-paper. Building upon the reproduced version, we then train our algorithm, DHC-R. In this section, we provide a detailed description of the architecture of the original DHC algorithm, along with implementation details that were not explicitly covered in the original paper.

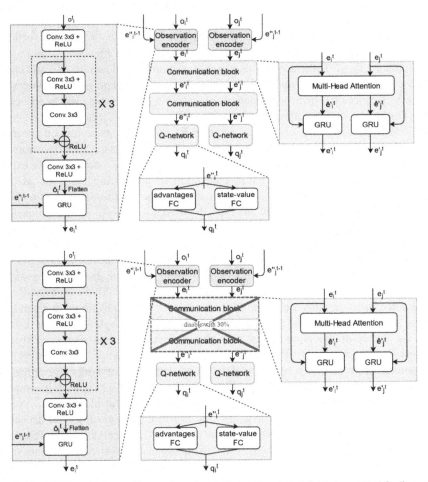

Fig. 2. Up: DHC architecture (image from "Distributed Heuristic Multi-Agent Pathfinding with Communication"). Down: DHC-R architecture.

The code that was used for evaluations can be found here [20].

4.1 Architecture

The original DHC algorithm has an architecture which consists of three main components (Fig. 2, above):

1. *Observation encoder* receives stacked matrixes that represent a single observation of an agent and outputs an embedding.
2. *Communication block* is an attention-based neural network that outputs an embedding that incorporates information from the two nearest neighbors, if any. Each agent sends the result of its observation encoder to every other agent inside its FOV. When messages are received by an agent, only those from the two nearest neighbors are selected for further processing. Then, the selected observations are passed through two communication blocks consisting of a multi-head attention and a GRU.
3. *Q-network* consists of two heads, the advantage and state-value, and combines their outputs to approximate the value of the Q-function. The final encoding is passed through the Q-network, which calculates the value $V(s)$ and a vector of advantages $\{A(s, a_i)\}_i$ for every action a_i. These values are then summed to obtain a vector $\{Q(s, a_i)\}_i$.

DHC-R. The robust version of DHC follows the same architecture as the original DHC but introduces randomness in the communication block. During training, there is a 30% chance of disabling the communication block, simulating communication failure scenarios. We propose this algorithm due to the anticipated poor performance of classical DHC in adversarial scenarios, particularly in cases involving communication loss. The architecture of DHC-R is depicted in Fig. 2 at the bottom.

4.2 Observations

Observations are represented by a $6 \times N \times N$ tensor, with $N \times N$ being the FOV of the agent. The tensor uses six channels to encode the following information:

1. *Binary mask encoding agents inside the FOV:* a value of 1 represents the position of an agent, while 0 denotes an empty position.
2. *Binary mask encoding obstacles inside the FOV:* a value of 1 represents an obstacle, while 0 marks an empty cell.
3. *Four heuristic channels:* a representation of the potential direction an agent should take to get closer to its target.

Each heuristic channel indicates whether an agent gets closer to its goal by taking a certain action. Refer to Fig. 3 for an example. Heuristic channels are necessary as the agents do not rely on imitation learning and need to acquire navigation skills. These channels provide agents with information about the location of the goal which helps them to navigate towards it.

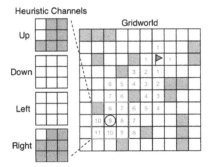

Fig. 3. Heuristic channel; image from "Distributed Heuristic Multi-Agent Path Finding with Communication".

4.3 Training

In the original paper, the DHC algorithm was trained on maps with randomly generated obstacles. To train DHC-R, we utilize the same type of maps, which we will refer to as random maps. We generate them and corresponding scenarios using the GenerateRandomScen procedure, presented in Fig. 4 (algorithm 1). In comparison to the original implementation, we speed up the GenerateRandomScen procedure by up to 400 times for large map instances. It is guaranteed that each agent can reach its end point when no other agents are present when the described algorithm is applied.

Algorithm 1 GenerateRandomScen: Generating Random Maps and Scenarios

---

1: **Input:** size of map M, density of obstacles p, number of agents N
2: **Output:** Map and N pairs of start and end points for each agent
3: **procedure** GENERATE_RANDOM_MAPS_AND_SCENARIOS(M, p, N)
4:     **Create** an empty map Map of size $M \times M$
5:     **Add** obstacles to the Map with probability p
6:     **Partition** the Map into individual connected components
7:     $start\_end\_pairs \leftarrow \emptyset$
8:     **for** $i \leftarrow 1$ to N **do**
9:         **if** no connected component with ≥ 2 nodes **then**
10:             **Output** GENERATE_RANDOM_MAPS_AND_SCENARIOS(M, p, N)
11:         **end if**
12:         $component \leftarrow$ select a random component with ≥ 2 nodes from the list of connected components
13:         Select two random cells $start$ and end inside $component$
14:         $start\_end\_pairs$.append(($start$, end))
15:         **Remove** $start$ and end from $component$
16:     **end for**
17:     **Output** Map, $start\_end\_pairs$
18: **end procedure**

Fig. 4. GenerateRandomScen algorithm.

However, authors do not validate that each end goal can be reached from the starting point when other agents are present, and we employ the same strategy. If the target becomes unreachable for one of the agents, the experimental results of different algorithms would be equally impacted since the test set is generated beforehand. The loss function is a multi-step TD error:

$$L(\theta) = Huber(G_t - Q(s_t, a_t, \theta), \kappa),$$

where G_t is the total return of an agent; $G_t = r_t + r_{t+1}\gamma + \ldots + \gamma^n Q(s_{t+n}, a_{t+n}, \overline{\theta}), \overline{\theta}$ represents the parameters of a target network and *Huber* is the Huber loss. The authors employ curriculum learning to handle tasks with complex configurations on large maps with many agents. They start by training a single agent on a 10×10 map to learn how to navigate and reach goals in small-sized environments using generated trajectories. The policy is trained from a single-agent perspective, treating other agents as part of the environment. During training, 16 actors are set up on the CPU, and a single learner is set up on the GPU. The actors generate episodes with a copy of the global network, which are collected into a shared prioritized replay buffer. An ε-greedy exploration strategy is used during training, where each actor chooses a random action with a probability ranging from 0.0008 to 0.4, with actor i having a probability of $0.4^{1 + \frac{7i}{num\_actors - 1}}$. During inference, the action with the maximum Q-value is selected. To implement curriculum learning, a list of settings in the form of (map size, number of agents) is initialized with (10, 1). As actors interact with the environment, they store useful information obtained from the environment in the local buffer. Every 400 steps, the collected transitions are added to the global prioritized buffer. Every 10 seconds, statistics are calculated for each setting based on the information in the global buffer. If the success rate for a specific configuration exceeds 90%, the list of settings is extended with two additional configurations: one with the same number of agents but a larger map (10 cells added to each dimension), and the other with the same map size but one additional agent added. The training stops either when the maximum possible configuration is reached and successfully solved, which is determined by a CSR exceeding 90% of the last 200 runs, or when 600.000 training steps have been completed. We train each algorithm on a single A100 GPU, and the training takes around 3–4 full days.

5   Empirical Evaluation

Adaptability to unfamiliar environments is a critical factor for running the algorithm in the real world. This section aims to assess the algorithm's generalizability on non-randomly structured maps. For this study, we select multi-agent scenarios from the MovingAI collection [21], which includes maps with different structures and characteristics.

Specifically, we choose four maps: lak303d.map, den520d, Berlin_1_256.map and ht_chantry.map (displayed in Fig. 5). The MovingAI website offers various scenarios for each map, where each scenario consists of a series of rows representing the start and goal positions for a single agent. Typically, these scenarios are used to evaluate single-agent performance. To generate test sets for multi-agent pathfinding problems with N agents, we select consecutive batches of N rows from each scenario, as illustrated in Fig. 6. During the experiments, we set the maximum episode length to 1024 steps. As

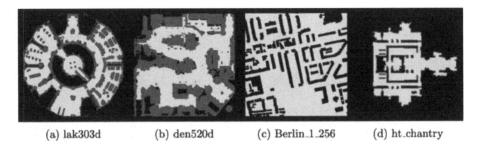

(a) lak303d   (b) den520d   (c) Berlin_1_256   (d) ht_chantry

Fig. 5. MovingAI maps used for evaluation.

	ID	Map	W	H	X0	Y0	X1	Y1	Dist
	25	den520d.map	256	256	146	105	104	158	101.0832611
Test 1	85	den520d.map	256	256	124	13	8	214	343.3502883
	31	den520d.map	256	256	97	52	206	82	125.5685424
	46	den520d.map	256	256	109	46	198	169	185.6396102
	20	den520d.map	256	256	150	30	197	84	81.66904755
Test 2	84	den520d.map	256	256	14	213	105	41	339.0660171
	18	den520d.map	256	256	193	85	186	148	72.28427124
	53	den520d.map	256	256	241	199	208	37	214.9238815
	13	den520d.map	256	256	124	56	157	53	54.97056274
	26	den520d.map	256	256	73	58	148	100	104.0121933

Fig. 6. Creating a multi-agent scenario using the.scen file from MovingAI.

shown in Fig. 7, the value of ISR consistently exceeded 90%. However, while most agents individually achieved their goals, the collective metric on this set of experiments was significantly worse (Fig. 7, left) than on random maps (results for random maps were reported in the original DHC [2] paper and were replicated by us prior to the start of OOD testing). These results suggest that communication can sometimes mislead an agent and negatively affect cooperation.

In real-world scenarios, however, perfect communication between agents cannot always be guaranteed. Weather conditions, deceptive agents in the environment, or the malfunction of an agent can result in the loss of data packets. As communication is the primary tool for cooperation in this algorithm, the loss of packets can potentially impact the performance of the system. To analyze the impact of packet loss on the performance of the algorithm, we evaluate two different algorithms, DHC-R and DHC-paper, on randomly generated maps with varying obstacle densities, where message passing was not allowed at all.

We generate a set of 200 tests on an $M \times M$ random map with density p using the procedure GenerateRandomScen explained in detail in Fig. 4. In each test, agents act in parallel by choosing one of five allowed actions: move left, right, up, down, or stay. Upon reaching the goal, an agent remains stationary and does not receive a new target. Note that an agent can still communicate with other agents to coordinate movements, such as stepping aside to allow another agent to pass. Execution stops either when all agents have reached their respective targets or upon reaching a terminal episode, which is set to 256. We report an average metric across all 200 runs. Charts depicting the collective success

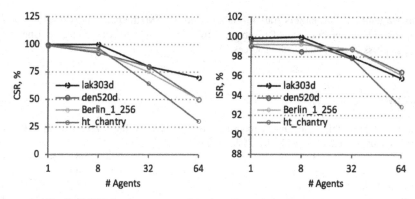

Fig. 7. DHC. Performance on MovingAI maps. Left: CSR; right: ISR.

rates for each agent in scenarios with obstacle densities of 0.1 are presented in Fig. 7 (right). As evident from the results, DHC-R demonstrates significant improvement over DHC on small random maps with a density of 0.1, as observed by the 20% (absolute) increase in performance (Fig. 8).

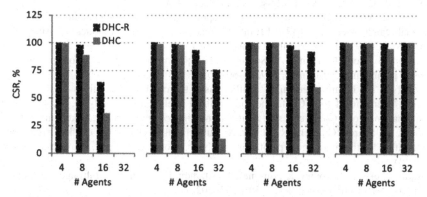

Fig. 8. DHC-R vs. DHC-paper, CSR, random square maps (10, 20, 30, 40). Density 0.1.

6 Conclusion

In this paper, we have studied the problem of partially observable multi-agent pathfinding and extensively analyzed the existing DHC [2] algorithm in various scenarios. The paper's original experimental setup was replicated and extended, and novel experiments on MovingAI maps and custom maps were conducted to test agent performance. Furthermore, this study introduced a new experiment testing the performance of the algorithm under complete packet loss, revealing a significant drop in performance. We suggested a modification to the algorithm, named DHC-R, to mitigate these issues and improve the algorithm's performance under these conditions and open sourced our implementation (including model weights).

Acknowledgement. The authors gratefully acknowledge the Mathematics and Computer Science Department of St. Petersburg State University, with special thanks to Aleksandr Avdiushenko for providing access to computational resources.

References

1. Partially-Observable Grid Environment for Multiple Agents: https://github.com/AIRI-Instit ute/pogema. Last accessed 11 May 2023
2. Ma, Z., Luo, Y., Ma, H.: Distributed heuristic multi-agent path finding with communication. In: 2021 International Conference on Robotics and Automation (ICRA), pp. 8699–8705. IEEE, Xi'an, China (2021)
3. Sutton, R.S., Barto, A.G.: Reinforcement Learning: An Introduction. MIT Press, Cambridge, MA, USA (1998)
4. Zelinsky, A.: A mobile robot exploration algorithm. IEEE Trans. Robot. Autom. **8**(6), 707–717 (1992)
5. Hart, P.E., Nilsson, N.J., Raphael, B.: A formal basis for the heuristic determination of minimum cost paths. IEEE Trans. Syst. Sci. Cybern. **4**(2), 100–107 (1968)
6. Wagner, G., Choset, H.: M*: A complete multirobot path planning algorithm with performance bounds. In: 2011 IEEE/RSJ International Conference on Intelligent Robots and Systems, pp. 3260–3267. IEEE, San Francisco, CA, USA (2011)
7. Ferner, C., Wagner, G., Choset, H.: ODrM* optimal multirobot path planning in low dimensional search spaces. In: 2013 IEEE International Conference on Robotics and Automation, pp. 3854–3859. IEEE, Karlsruhe, Germany (2013)
8. Sharon, G., Stern, R., Felner, A., Sturtevant, N.R.: Conflict-based search for optimal multi-agent pathfinding. Artif. Intell. **219**, 40–66 (2015)
9. Boyarski. E.: Iterative-deepening conflict-based search. In: Proceedings of the Twenty-Ninth International Joint Conference on Artificial Intelligence (IJCAI-20), pp. 4084–4090. International Joint Conferences on Artificial Intelligence Organization, Yokohama (2020)
10. Barer, M., Sharon, G., Stern, R., Felner, A.: Suboptimal variants of the conflict-based search algorithm for the multi-agent pathfinding problem. Front. Artif. Intell. Appl. **263**, 961–962 (2014)
11. Andreychuk, A., Yakovlev, K., Surynek, P., Atzmon, D., Stern, R.: Multi-agent pathfinding with continuous time. Artif. Intell. **305**, 103 (2022)
12. Surynek, P., Felner, A., Stern, R., Boyarski, E.: Efficient SAT approach to multi-agent path finding under the sum of costs objective. In: Proceedings of the Twenty-Second European Conference on Artificial Intelligence, pp. 810–818. IOS Press, The Hague, The Netherlands (2016)
13. Lam, E., Le Bodic, P., Harabor, D.D., Stuckey, P.J.: Branch-and-cut-and-price for multi-agent pathfinding. In: Proceedings of the Twenty-Eighth International Joint Conference on Artificial Intelligence (IJCAI-19), pp. 1289–1296. International Joint Conferences on Artificial Intelligence Organization, Macao, China (2019)
14. Yakovlev, K.S., Andreychuk, A.A., Skrynnik, A.A., Panov, A.I.: Planning and learning in multi-agent path finding. Dokl. Math. **106**(1), 79–84 (2022)
15. Sunehag, P.: Value-decomposition networks for cooperative multi-agent learning. In: Proceedings of the 17th International Conference on Autonomous Agents and Multi-Agent Systems, pp. 2085–2087. International Foundation for Autonomous Agents and Multiagent Systems, Stockholm, Sweden (2018)
16. Sartoretti, G.: PRIMAL: pathfinding via reinforcement and imitation multi-agent learning. IEEE Robot. Autom. Lett. **4**(3), 2378–2385 (2019)

17. Li, W., Chen, H., Jin, B., Tan, W., Zha, H., Wang, X.: Multi-Agent Path Finding with Prioritized Communication Learning. In: 2022 International Conference on Robotics and Automation (ICRA), pp. 10695–10701. Philadelphia, PA, USA (2022)
18. Li, Q., Gama, F., Ribeiro, A., Prorok, A.: Graph Neural Networks for Decentralized Path Planning. In: Proceedings of the 19th International Conference on Autonomous Agents and Multi-Agent Systems, pp. 1901–1903. International Foundation for Autonomous Agents and Multiagent Systems, Auckland, New Zealand (2020)
19. Ma, Z., Luo, Y., Pan, J.: Learning selective communication for multi-agent path finding. IEEE Robot. Autom. Lett. **7**(2), 1455–1462 (2022)
20. Learnable Decentralized MAPF using reinforcement learning with local communication. https://github.com/acforvs/dhc-robust-mapf. Last accessed 11 May 2023
21. Stern, R., et al., Multi-agent pathfinding: definitions, variants, and benchmarks. In: Symposium on Combinatorial Search (SoCS), pp. 151–158 (2019)

Ground Mobile Robot Localization Algorithm Based on Semantic Information from the Urban Environment

Artur Podtikhov[(✉)] and Anton Saveliev

St. Petersburg Federal Research Center of the Russian Academy of Sciences (SPC RAS), 39, 14th Line, St. Petersburg 199178, Russia
apodtikhov@gmail.com

Abstract. This paper presents the SLAM algorithm, which use the semantic information extracted from the urban environment to increase the accuracy of ego-vehicle localization in ORB-SLAM2 system. For this purpose, a semantic segmentation module is added to the standard algorithm to assign an object on each frame to one of a given set of classes. The CARLA Simulator was used as a simulation environment, which generates a photorealistic urban environment with the ability to run an arbitrary number of active elements in it, which usually make localization difficult, causing interference with the system. Based on the environment, a training dataset for semantic segmentation was collected. The training dataset consists of 3,696 pairs of city images and corresponding segmentation masks in which each pixel corresponds to one of 23 semantic labels. Using this dataset, the DeepLabV3+ segmentation model was trained with mean per-class IoU metric equals to 81.48%. By using semantic information to filter potentially dynamic objects and matching key points, we were able to increase the localization accuracy relative to the base algorithm by an average of 23% and build a semantic map of the environment.

Keywords: SLAM · ORB-SLAM2 · DEEPLAB · CARLA · Robot

1 Introduction

Simultaneous Localization and Mapping (SLAM) is a technique used in mobile autonomous vehicles to build a map of an unknown environment or to update a map of a known environment while simultaneously keeping track of agent's location and the traveled path within it. In general terms, the control scheme of a modern mobile robot moving in a known environment can be represented in the following chain of actions: obtaining information about the world around; determining one's own position on a predetermined map; traffic planning with regard to the environment; control over the implementation of planned actions and transmission of control signals to actuators (motors, wheels and other manipulators). However, if the environment is not known in advance, then first you need to build a map of the area. Traditional mapping algorithms require an estimate of the robot's position, while accurate localization requires a previously known map. That is why SLAM methods can be called complex, because they are aimed at solving two mutually dependent tasks: localization and map construction.

© The Author(s), under exclusive license to Springer Nature Switzerland AG 2023
A. Ronzhin et al. (Eds.): ICR 2023, LNAI 14214, pp. 164–174, 2023.
https://doi.org/10.1007/978-3-031-43111-1_15

This approach was first proposed at the IEEE Conference on Robotics and Automation in San Francisco in 1985 [1]. Then, and over the next few years, it was solved using various active sensors, such as a laser range finder, lidar or sonar, to determine the position of landmarks in space. SLAM is a cornerstone for autonomous navigation tasks in unknown environment, its applications are found in unmanned vehicles [2, 3], aircraft [4], underwater vehicles [5], virtual reality [6], in space exploration, for example, the surface map of Mars was constructed using SLAM methods [7].

The relevance of solving the problem of simultaneous localization and mapping is due to the fact that maps commonly used for agent navigation mainly reflect the type of space fixed at the time of their construction, and it is not at all necessary that the type of space will be the same at the time the maps are used. At the same time, the complexity of the technical process of determining the current location with the simultaneous construction of an accurate map is due to the low accuracy of the instruments involved in the process of calculating the current location.

Recently, visual SLAM methods, which are based on information from cameras, have become very popular, since cameras are cheaper to purchase and operate, while they can provide more information about the world around the robot. For instance, only cameras can transmit color, therefore, in unmanned vehicles they are used. Although the use of cameras increases the complexity and resource intensity of the algorithms, since they do not allow you to directly calculate the distance to the object of interest.

Most visual SLAM methods rely solely on geometric information, building a map of the unknown terrain in dense/semi-dense (DTAM [8], LSD-SLAM [9]) or keypoint-based (PTAM [10], ORB-SLAM [11]) point clouds. Such maps are homogeneous: the dots on them indicate only the presence or absence of an obstacle and do not carry any additional information. At the same time, visual SLAM works with camera images – a rich source of additional information. Often, when working with images, not the points themselves are used, but the objects they form, for example, various algorithms for analyzing biomedical images are based on this approach. Such enlarged objects are usually obtained using object detection methods, and if more accurate prediction of the boundaries of objects is necessary, using segmentation methods. Simultaneous localization and mapping methods that use this approach to working with images from cameras are grouped under the name Semantic SLAM.

All semantic SLAM methods can be divided into 2 broad categories according to the type of problem being solved: improving map representation [12–17] and improving localization [18–24]. The purpose of using methods that improve the presentation of a map is to add an additional "semantic" layer to it, so that points on it are distinguishable from each other and belong to a certain class. Such map representations can be useful in navigation, often in articles the following example is given: semantic information provides an ideal level of abstraction for a robot to understand and execute human commands (e.g., "bring me a cup of coffee", "leave the house through the red door") and provide people with models of the environment that are easy to understand. In turn, methods aimed at improving localization consider segmentation not as a goal, but as a tool that helps to take into account additional non-geometric information during localization. Such methods, for instance, include filtering moving objects and localization or mapping solely on the basis of those objects that a priori cannot change their location in the world, thus helping the robot to localize in the so-called "dynamic" environments.

This paper presents a new method of semantic SLAM, which uses one of the most stable and accurate algorithms ORB-SLAM2 [25] as a basic algorithm for localization and map building. But it also considers semantic information using the DeepLabV3+ [26] model for semantic segmentation in order to: (a) build meaningful maps, where each point is associated with the class of the object to which it belongs, and (b) use semantic information to increase localization accuracy (by excluding potentially dynamic scene objects and building associations between points from different frames).

2 Description of the Training Data Collection Methodology for Semantic Segmentation

To collect a dataset for training the segmentation network, a high-quality map "Town10HD" from the CARLA Simulator [15] was used, which is an urban area with various infrastructure facilities. On this map, software developers pre-set a list of locations in which it is recommended to spawn cars in order for them to appear on the road directed towards traffic (Fig. 1).

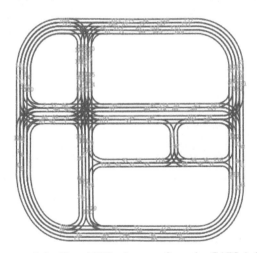

Fig. 1. Schematic image of the Town10HD city map from the CARLA Simulator. The points where the training images from the camera were collected are marked in orange (Color figure online).

The recommended points for car spawn were used to collect a dataset of camera images and corresponding ground-truth segmentation masks according to the following algorithm:

1. The car was spawned at a given point (X_i, Y_i, Z_i), parallel to the ground surface with a rotation angle relative to the perpendicular to the surface equal to 0.

2. On the hood of the car, 2 pseudo-cameras were spawned: standard RGB and segmentation, both with a resolution of 800 × 600 pixels.
3. The car (with the cameras) turned through an angle of 15°.
4. The images received from the cameras were recorded and saved to disk.
5. Steps 3–4 were repeated until the car made a complete turn.
6. The car and both cameras were destroyed.
7. The transition to the next spawn point and, respectively, to point 1 was performed.

Thus, 3,696 pairs of images with segmentation masks were collected from the 154 recommended vehicle spawn points. Figure 2 shows an example of an image obtained with an RGB camera mounted on a car hood (left) and its corresponding ground-truth segmentation mask (right), in which each pixel belongs to one of the given classes. In total, CARLA provides a segmentation map for 23 classes, which are listed in Table 1.

A random subset of images of 80% of the original data set was used for training, with the remaining 20% exclusively for validating the results.

Fig. 2. An example of an RGB camera image (left) and a ground-truth semantic segmentation mask (left) from the training dataset.

3 Segmentation Model

DeepLabV3+ was used as the segmentation model, with the resnext50_32x4d encoder [27] pre-trained on the ImageNet dataset [28]. A small number of augmentations were used: random cropping the image to a size of 512 × 512 pixels, horizontal flipping (with probability 0.5), adding normally distributed noise (with probability 0.2), and performing a random four-point perspective (with probability 0.5). The loss function chosen was FocalLoss [29] since the class distribution in the dataset is highly irregular. Optimization was performed using AdamW optimizer [30]. The training batch size was set to 6 and the learning rate was set to 1e-4.

The table shows that for large objects the segmentation accuracy is quite high, while for objects with a small area (such as traffic lights, road signs and poles) it is less. However, the obtained distribution of accuracy for different classes is consistent with the distribution of accuracy of the best segmentation models of the CityScapes benchmark, so this distribution can be associated with the limitations of modern semantic segmentation architectures.

Table 1. Metrics reflecting the quality of segmentation on the validation dataset. The MISSING label marks classes that do not exist in the Town10HD map.

ID	Class label	Per-class IoU	Per-class Accuracy	ID	Class label	Per-class IoU	Per-class Accuracy
0	Unlabeled	SKIP	SKIP	12	TrafficSign	69.65%	76.47%
1	Building	95.05%	97.66%	13	Sky	93.70%	96.20%
2	Fence	32.83%	42.83%	14	Ground	94.17%	97.62%
3	Other	84.67%	89.02%	15	Bridge	MISSING	MISSING
4	Pedestrian	MISSING	MISSING	16	RailTrack	98.10%	98.97%
5	Pole	58.49%	66.19%	17	GuardRail	MISSING	MISSING
6	RoadLine	84.98%	89.98%	18	TrafficLight	78.44%	87.59%
7	Road	98.65%	99.47%	19	Static	81.89%	90.01%
8	SideWalk	97.01%	98.43%	20	Dynamic	79.31%	89.68%
9	Vegetation	84.76%	93.74%	21	Water	63.54%	74.03%
10	Vehicles	90.62%	95.70%	22	Terrain	79.56%	85.09%
11	Wall	82.62%	87.96%				

4   The Algorithm Developed

As previously mentioned, the ORB-SLAM2 algorithm was chosen as the base algorithm for simultaneous localization and mapping. Interaction with the CARLA simulation environment was performed using the ros_bridge package which allows to receive sensor and odometry information from the simulator and publish them to ROS topics.

Figure 3 shows a generalized architecture of the proposed algorithm. The architecture is almost the same as that of ORB-SLAM2, except for the new block responsible for semantic segmentation included in the Tracking thread. The rest of the changes are internal and adjust some functions, which will be described below.

Semantic Segmentation Block. In order to integrate the image segmentation model into the system, it was converted from the PyTorch format to TorchScript, after which it became possible to use it in scripts written in C++. The resulting model is initialized by the GPU in the Tracking module and applied after each new frame is received, thus, at the start of the algorithm, there is not only the image itself, but also a segmentation mask that matches each pixel of the image with a semantic class.

Extract ORB Block. Since storing a full segmentation mask for each frame requires a significant amount of RAM, the corresponding semantic information is stored only for selected key points. For this purpose, at the moment of extracting key points and ORB descriptors, semantic information is added to these key points, indicating that the point belongs to one of the 23 classes, after which the rest of the mask is removed.

New Points Creation Block. When a map point is created, semantic information is also added to it, with each point storing a list of all predicted semantic classes, when it is seen from different angles, at the current moment its class is the class it takes most often. This approach reduces the segmentation error and eliminates outliers. Also, a map point is considered inactive and does not participate in further calculations if it belongs to one of the potentially dynamic (or low-informative) classes (Unlabeled, Other, Pedestrians, Vehicles, Sky, Dynamic).

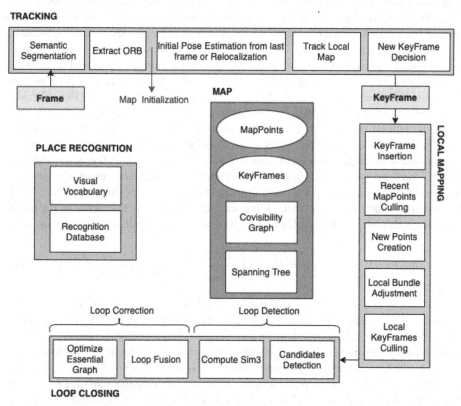

Fig. 3. Generalized architecture of ORB-SLAM2, to which a semantic segmentation block has been added, which is triggered on receipt of each new frame.

Key Point Association. The keypoint (or map points and keypoints) association algorithm is one of the central algorithms of ORB-SLAM2, since it is used in almost all submodules. In the original algorithm, the association is performed solely based on the calculation of the distance between the two ORB descriptors. To account for semantic information, a penalty factor equal to 0.5 * current distance is added to this distance.

5 Results Analysis

To evaluate the quality of localization, 3 experiments were conducted in a simulation environment, lasting from 1 to 3 min, sensor information and ground-truth odometry were stored at a frequency of 20 frames per second. Simulations were run from various recommended vehicle spawn points, in addition, except ego-vehicle, 20 cars with a built-in autopilot and 10 pedestrians were also generated in the environment. After that, ORB-SLAM2 model and the developed modification were launched separately. Having ground-truth and predicted odometry, it is impossible to compare them directly, because when using a monocular camera, it is possible to restore the world coordinates of a map point with an accuracy to scale constant. The Horn algorithm [31] was used to estimate the scale constant and alignment of coordinate systems. For each simulation, it shows the ground-truth trajectory of the car (blue), the trajectory obtained using the ORB-SLAM2 algorithm (orange) and the trajectory obtained using the developed algorithm (green). From the motion trajectories it is difficult to draw conclusions about the increase in localization accuracy, therefore, plots of localization errors are also attached (Fig. 4). The reconstructed trajectories for all simulations are shown in Fig. 5. The horizontal axis denotes the frame number, the vertical axis denotes the distance between the ground-truth position of the vehicle at a given time and the predicted position. Comparison of localization accuracy over the entire route was performed using the metric of the mean percentage absolute error in the Cartesian coordinate system, calculated by the formula:

$$MAPE([x, y], [\hat{x} + \hat{y}]) = MEAN\left(\frac{100\%}{n_{samples}} \sum \frac{[|x_i - \hat{x}_i|, [y_i - \hat{y}_i]]}{[|x_i|, |x_i|]}\right). \quad (1)$$

The results of comparing the quality of localization are in Table 2. It can be seen that the proposed algorithm performs slightly better than the basic algorithm in determining the location of the vehicle, while from the reconstructed trajectories (Fig. 5) it can be concluded that the predictions change slightly, mainly due to reducing the probability of wrong key points matching. At the same time, if it is strictly forbidden to assign points corresponding to different semantic classes, it fails to initialize the map (due to the fact that the number of matches falls below the threshold value), therefore, to further improve the approach, it is necessary to improve the quality of semantic segmentation.

A side effect of our work is the construction of a semantic map of the environment; after a complete route around of the city, the map of the area looks like Fig. 6. It can be concluded that the algorithm for determining key points basically extracts points from buildings (white color on the map), road markings (purple) and trees (green).

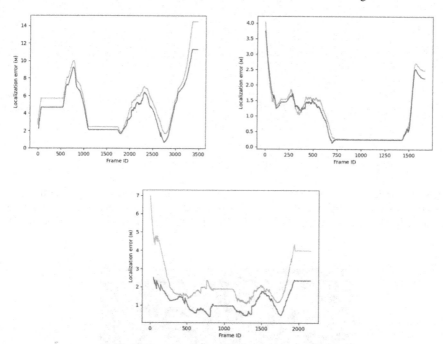

Fig. 4. Plots for estimating position errors for each frame (in meters). Green colors indicate the errors of the implemented algorithm, orange is ORB-SLAM2 (Color figure online).

Table 2. Localization accuracy in different simulations. The table shows the duration of the route, it's length (in simulator units) and the mean absolute percentage error of estimating the ego vehicle location by the base and developed implementation. The last column displays the % change in the localization error of the developed algorithm relative to the base one.

No.	Duration (s)	Length (m)	ORB-SLAM2	Developed Algorithm	Relative change in localization error
1	172.8	610	25.85%	21.7%	−16.05%
2	83.2	241.7	1.10%	1.02%	−7.27%
3	105.6	456.36	7.83%	4.22%	−46.1%

Fig. 5. The trajectory of the car. The ground-truth trajectory is shown in blue, the trajectory predicted by the ORB-SLAM2 algorithm in orange, and the trajectory predicted by developed algorithm in green. The order of the images corresponds to the sequence numbers of the simulations in Table 2.

Fig. 6. Semantic map of the city Town10HD in the form of a point cloud, obtained after simulating the movement of a car throughout the city. Different colors indicate urban infrastructure objects belonging to different classes (Color figure online).

6   Conclusion

In this paper, we proposed an algorithm for simultaneous localization and mapping, taking into account semantic information about the objects of the urban environment. The proposed approach excludes potentially dynamic objects from the consideration of the algorithm and improves the matching of key points. The developed algorithm has demonstrated a 23% increase in localization accuracy on mean absolute percentage error relative to the basic algorithm, at the same time, it requires more computing resources to apply the segmentation model. The quality of the current segmentation model does not allow to completely eliminate the comparison of key points assigned to different semantic classes, so further development of the algorithm should be aimed at increasing the segmentation accuracy and increasing the number of semantic classes under consideration.

References

1. Chatila, R., Laumond, J.: Position referencing and consistent world modeling for mobile robots. In: Proceedings. International Conference on Robotics and Automation, vol. 2, pp. 138–145. IEEE (1985)
2. Henning, L., Andreas, G., Bernd, K.: Visual slam for autonomous ground vehicles. In: IEEE International Conference on Robotics and Automation, Shanghai, pp. 1732–1737, China (2011)
3. Qin, T., Chen, T., Chen, Y., Su, Q.: Avp-slam: semantic visual mapping and localization for autonomous vehicles in the parking lot. In: 2020 IEEE/RSJ International Conference on Intelligent Robots and Systems (IROS), pp. 5939– 5945. IEEE (2020)
4. Milford, M.J., Schill, F., Corke, P., Mahony, R., Wyeth, G.: Aerial slam with a single camera using visual expectation. In: 2011 IEEE international conference on robotics and automation, pp. 2506–2512. IEEE (2011)
5. Ribas, D., Ridao, P., Tardo´s, J.D., Neira, J.: Underwater slam in man-made structured environments. J. Field Robot. 25(11–12), 898–921 (2008)
6. Jinyu, L., Bangbang, Y., Danpeng, C., Nan, W., Guofeng, Z., Hujun, B.: Survey and evaluation of monocular visual-inertial slam algorithms for augmented reality. Virtual Reality Intell. Hardware 1(4), 386–410 (2019)
7. Zheng, B., Zhang, Z.: An improved EKF-SLAM for mars surface exploration. Int. J. Aerosp. Eng. **2019**, 1–9 (2019)
8. Newcombe, R.A., Lovegrove, S.J., Davison, A.J.: Dtam: Dense tracking and mapping in real-time. In: 2011 International Conference on Computer Vision, pp. 2320–2327. IEEE (2011)
9. Engel, J., Scho¨ps, T., Cremers, D.: Lsd-slam: Large-scale direct monocular slam. In: Computer Vision–ECCV 2014: 13th European Conference, Zurich, Switzerland, 6–12 Sep 2014, Proceedings, Part II 13, pp. 834–849. Springer (2014)
10. Klein, G., Murray, D.: Parallel tracking and mapping for small AR workspaces. In: 2007 6th IEEE and ACM International Symposium on Mixed and Augmented Reality, pp. 225–234. IEEE (2007)
11. Mur-Artal, R., Montiel, J.M.M., Tardos, J.D.: Orb-slam: a versatile and accurate monocular slam system. IEEE Trans. Rob. 31(5), 1147–1163 (2015)
12. Dub´e, R., Cramariuc, A., Dugas, D., Nieto, J., Siegwart, R., Cadena, C.: Segmap: 3d segment mapping using data-driven descriptors, arXiv preprint arXiv:1804.09557 (2018)
13. Hermans, A., Floros, G., Leibe, B.: Dense 3d semantic mapping of indoor scenes from rgb-d images. In: 2014 IEEE International Conference on Robotics and Automation (ICRA), pp. 2631–2638. IEEE (2014)
14. McCormac, J., Handa, A., Davison, A., Leutenegger, S.: Semantic fusion: dense 3d semantic mapping with convolutional neural networks. In: 2017 IEEE International Conference on Robotics and automation (ICRA), pp. 4628–4635. IEEE (2017)
15. Rosinol, A., Abate, M., Chang, Y., Carlone, L.: Kimera: an open-source library for real-time metric-semantic localization and mapping. In: 2020 IEEE International Conference on Robotics and Automation (ICRA), pp. 1689–1696. IEEE (2020)
16. Salas-Moreno, R.F., Newcombe, R.A., Strasdat, H., Kelly, P.H., Davison, A.J.: Slam++: simultaneous localisation and mapping at the level of objects. In: Proceedings of the IEEE Conference on Computer Vision and Pattern Recognition, pp. 1352–1359 (2013)
17. Stückler, J., Behnke, S.: Multi-resolution surfel maps for efficient dense 3d modeling and tracking. J. Vis. Commun. Image Represent. 25(1), 137–147 (2014)
18. Bowman, S.L., Atanasov, N., Daniilidis, K., Pappas, G.J.: Probabilistic data association for semantic slam. In: International Conference on Robotics and Automation (ICRA), pp. 1722–1729. IEEE (2017)

19. Fuentes, O., Savage, J., Contreras, L.: A SLAM system based on Hidden Markov Models. Inform. Autom. **21**(1), 181–212 (2022). https://doi.org/10.15622/ia.2022.21.7

20. Mahamudul Hashan, A., Md Rakib Ul Islam, R., Avinash, K.: Apple leaf disease classification using image dataset: a multilayer convolutional neural network approach. Inform. Autom. **21**(4), 710–728 (2022). https://doi.org/10.15622/ia.21.4.3

21. Ganti, P., Waslander, S.L.: Network uncertainty informed semantic feature selection for visual slam. In: 2019 16th Conference on Computer and Robot Vision (CRV), pp. 121–128. IEEE (2019)

22. Gawel, A., Del Don, C., Siegwart, R., Nieto, J., Cadena, C.: X-view: graph-based semantic multi-view localization. IEEE Robot. Autom. Lett. **3**(3), 1687–1694 (2018)

23. Lianos, K.N., Schonberger, J.L., Pollefeys, M., Sattler, T.: Vso: Visual semantic odometry. In: Proceedings of the European Conference on Computer Vision (ECCV), pp. 234–250 (2018)

24. Stenborg, E., Toft, C., Hammarstrand, L.: Long-term visual localization using semantically segmented images. In: 2018 IEEE International Conference on Robotics and Automation (ICRA), pp. 6484–6490. IEEE (2018)

25. Mur-Artal, R., Tardo´s, J.D.: ORB-SLAM2: an open-source SLAM system for monocular, stereo, and RGB-D cameras. IEEE Trans. Robot. **33**(5), 1255–1262 (2017)

26. Chen, L.C., Zhu, Y., Papandreou, G., Schroff, F., Adam, H.: Encoder-decoder with atrous separable convolution for semantic image segmentation. In: Proceedings of the European Conference on Computer Vision (ECCV), pp. 801–818 (2018)

27. Xie, S., Girshick, R., Doll´ar, P., Tu, Z., He, K.: Aggregated residual transformations for deep neural networks. In: Proceedings of the IEEE conference on computer vision and pattern recognition, pp. 1492–1500 (2017)

28. Deng, J., Dong, W., Socher, R., Li, L.J., Li, K., Fei-Fei, L.: Imagenet: a large-scale hierarchical image database. In: Conference on Computer Vision and Pattern Recognition, pp. 248–255. IEEE (2009)

29. Lin, T.Y., Goyal, P., Girshick, R., He, K., Dolla´r, P.: Focal loss for dense object detection. In: Proceedings of the IEEE International Conference on Computer Vision, pp. 2980–2988 (2017)

30. Reddi, S.J., Kale, S., Kumar, S.: On the convergence of a dam and beyond, arXiv preprint arXiv:1904.09237 (2019)

31. Horn, B.K.: Closed-form solution of absolute orientation using unit quaternions. Josa a **4**(4), 629–642 (1987)

Remote Control Robotic System
for the Perimeter Security

Azad Bayramov[1]([⊠]) [iD] and Samir Suleymanov[2] [iD]

[1] Institute of Control Systems, 68, B. Vahabzadeh street, Baku AZ1141, Azerbaijan
azad.bayramov@yahoo.com
[2] Institute of Geology and Geophysics, 119, H. Javid avenue, Baku AZ1073, Azerbaijan

Abstract. The the results of the development, preparation and preliminary laboratory and field tests of the robotic security system along the perimeter of any object remotely controlled by radio waves have been presented in paper. Radio signals are coded using a cryptographic method. The robotic system consists of a remote control and controlled units (blocks) that can perform various functions to protect the perimeter of the selected zone. The principle of operation and the structure of the robotic security system are presented. To ensure safety, the blocks are controlled by coded signals. The working principle, management, operation rules, management and telemetry of the security system were explained. Cryptographic coding based on the Neyman algorithm was used to encrypt the telemetry of the security system. The robotic security system can be used for the protection of territory, borders or objects, including for military purposes. Such control can be carried out around the clock, in any weather, at any area and distance. The working principle and management of the protection system are given in the paper.

Keywords: Security System · Robotic · Remotely Controlled · Coded Signals · Control Block · Sensor Block

1 Introduction

Effective control of unauthorized access to any territory, or crossing the borders, or the perimeter of any object is one of the urgent problems in industry, in the military field, in the border service and many others. The most effective method is an automated control, which is carried out remotely. Such control can be carried out around the clock, in any weather, at any area and distance. Here the human factor plays a minimal role, so the probability of error is minimized here. A number of the scientific works (for example, [1–4]) is devoted this problem. In particular, in the work [3] it was analyzed a perimeter defense problem in which a single turret, having a finite range and service time, is tasked to defend a perimeter against at most N intruders that arrive in the environment. An offline as well as an online version of this setup was considered. In the offline setup in which N intruders have already arrived in the environment, it was established that the problem is equivalent to solving a Travelling Repairperson Problem with Time Windows.

This paper presents the developed unified automated robotic system for remote control of a given territory and access protection. Seismic sensors, acoustic sensors, fuses, video observation blocks, etc. can serve as remote sensor units that are activated by coded radio signals. The advantage of this system is that it is controlled by coded signals, the frequency and control protocol of which are set by the developers, so this system is safe and not available to a third party.

2   Principle of Operation of the Security System

The common functional block diagram of the system is shown in Fig. 1.

Here: RC – Remote Control, SB – sensors blocks, 1 – device programmer (operating mode selection block), 2 – signal encryption block, 3 – antennas and feeders, 4 – signal decoding block, 5 – start relay, 6 – functional sensors.

The operating modes of the secutity system are selected through the programmer located in the control panel. These modes are activation of one or all sensor blocks and their sequence. The sequence of:

$$f_c(S, \Delta t) = S_1(t_1) + S_2(t_2) + S_3(t_3) + S_4(t_4) + \ldots + S_n(t_n), \tag{1}$$

signals are generated in this block and is passed to the encryption block and encrypted there.

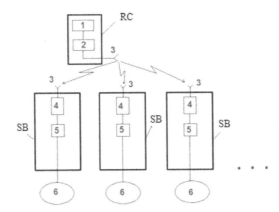

Fig. 1. The common functional block diagram of a remotely controlled radio system.

Encryption occurs due to the change of the time sequence of signals. This sequence can be represented as a function as follows:

$$f_c(S, \Delta t) = S_4(t_4) + S_1(t_1) + S_3(t_3) + S_2(t_2) + \ldots = \sum f_k(S_k, t_k).$$

The signals through the feeder antenna, are spread into space and received by the antennas of the sensor blocks located at a certain distance. Electromagnetic signals in sensor blocks are decoded through selection:

$$f_{dc}(S, \Delta t) = \sum f_k(S_k, t_k) = S_1(t_1) + S_2(t_2) + S_3(t_3) + S_4(t_4) + \ldots + S_n(t_n). \tag{2}$$

If the $f_{dc}(S,t)$ function does not coincide with the $f_c(S,t)$ function,

$$f_{dc}(S, t) \neq f_c(S, t),$$

that is, the time sequence is violated, then the sensor block is activated.
If the $f_{dc}(S,t)$ function coincide with the $f_c(S,t)$ function,

$$f_{dc}(S, t) = f_c(S, t),$$

then, then the received signals affect the electric relay, the sensor block is activated through the electric relay. After that, the sensor block records the variouse change in the environment at a certain distance.

The encryption code is based on Neyman's algorithm [5, 6].

3   Choosing the Encryption Algorithm of the Security System

In order to choose the encryption algorithm to be used in the created cryptosystem, first of all, it is necessary to pay attention to the following features of the algorithms [5, 6]:

- Crypto durability. The algorithm must be carefully analyzed by the world cryptographic community for a long time (at least five years) and be considered cryptographically robust against various types of attacks;
- The length of the key. The key used in the encryption algorithm must be at least 256 bits for symmetric encryption algorithms and at least 2048 bits for open key algorithms. This is intended to make it impossible to open the code directly by brute force (strong force) in the 21st century;
- Encryption speed. Therefore, the data encryption speed for the selected algorithm should be very high to avoid interruptions in data transfer.
- Resourcefulness. The algorithm must be optimized for implementation in hardware implementation. The amount of RAM and the performance of the microprocessor needed should be within the limits of general purpose microcontrollers.
- The system encryption algorithm was selected from the following group of algorithms:

Des, Aes, Cast, Rc4, Verman.

All of the above algorithms meet the requirements of different levels for them. For the implementation of the algorithm, operations on large numbers (increase in degree) are needed, for the fast execution of which it is necessary to use special microcircuits in the project. Public key algorithms cannot be used due to their low speed. It is best not to use stream ciphers. They are useful for encrypting the flow of information, for example, information packages in computer networks, or conversations on a telephone line.

Also, the "disposable notepad scheme" is popular in Vernam's cipher cryptography. The solution is the symmetric encryption system, which was invented in 1917 by AT&T employees Major Joseph Moborn and Vernam Gilbert. Vernam's cipher is the most secure available cryptosystem. Taking these into account, it was accepted to use the Vernam encryption algorithm in radio control of security system.

Now let's give detailed information about the encryption process and the password itself. Since this cipher was invented for computer systems, it should be noted that it is based on binary arithmetic.

The radio security robotic system consists of 10 radio block detectors and 1 control panel. After the radio block detectors are activated, the keys for each radio block detectors are selected from the random number machine block of the control panel, sent to the block detectors and written to the control panel memory accordingly.

Random keys are 32 bytes long. During operation, the command sent by the remote control to the selected radio block detectors is encrypted with the key stored in the memory for that radio block detectors. Vernam encryption is based on the absolute summation logical operation of addition by module 2.

In Bull's algebra, the absolute addition operation 2 is a function of two variables (the operands of the operations or the arguments of the function). The summation of the result is calculated according to the truth Table (see Table 1).

Table 1. Truth table {\displaystyle true > false}.

a	b	a b
0	0	0
0	1	1
1	0	1
1	1	0

10010111 11101001 xxxxxxxx 10010111 (the start-command for the selected radio block detectors).

01100110 10111100 xxxxxxxx 00011010 (the key for selected radio block detectors).

11110001 01010101 xxxxxxxx 10001101 (the result of a logical operation between an address and a key).

11110001 01010101 xxxxxxxx 10001101 (adopted command).

01100110 10111100 xxxxxxxx 00011010 (the key for the selected radio block detector).

10010111 11101001 xxxxxxxx 10010111 (the result of a logical operation between the received command and the key, or the command to start for the selected radio block detectors).

Thus, the encryption of signals prevents the security system from being activated by the outside on purpose or by accident.

4 Structure of the Security System

The main tasks of the security system:

- activation of sensor blocks through an electric relay in the front line and areas close to it, in the radius of visual distances;
- control of 10 sensor blocks with one controller.

The security system is managed by one operator.

The security system is made according to the modular principle and consists of a control unit (block) (remote control), 10 sensor units (blocks), antennas and special narrow iron plates for burying in the ground. The tactical and technical indicators of the security system are given in Table 2.

Working conditions, ambient temperature: $-20° \div +50°$.

The security system complies with the IP67 protection class against dust and moisture. This means that the equipment is completely protected from dust and solid bodies with dimensions of at least 1.0 mm; has protection against water ingress into the shell when immersed at a certain depth and time, and is regulated by IEC 60529 (DIN 40050, GOST 14254) standards [7].

The sensor blocks are controlled by coded one-way radio signals during operation mode and two-way radio signals during control mode.

The coding scheme used completely excludes arbitrary (without operator permission) activation.

Table 2. Tactical and technical indicators of the security system.

No.	Indicators	Quantification of the indicators
1	Control radius (with direct view)	2 km
2	Standby time	> 6 months
3	Duration of operation in activation mode	72 h
4	Activation period	3 s
5	Weight of device (with case)	5 kg
6	Mass of 1 sensor block	280 gr
7	The mass of the control panel	500 gr
8	Overall dimensions of the device	$45 \times 50 \times 20$ cm
9	Power supply	3,7V Li – battery
10	Power of the radio transmitter	1 W
11	Retention period: in stock - field conditions -	10 years 2 years

Assignment of commands coming from the control unit (block):

- putting the security system into working condition;
- disable the security system;
- activate the sensor blocks or neutralize (deactivate) the sensor blocks in the active state;

– check the current state of each sensor block individually.

Remote control of the sensor blocks with a remote control should take place either in individual mode, or in group mode, all of them are activated by command.

In operation mode, the control unit (remote control) sends a coded radio signal that is unique to each sensor block or group of sensor blocks. First of all, the security system is designed for the use of special-purpose army engineers.

The security system is programmed to work in the following modes:

Commands
In command mode, the controlling remote control unit transmits a specific command to the selected sensor unit. It is planned to send the commans to several sensor blocks.
Checking
This mode allows checking the current status of the sensor block selected through the "TEST status" command. This command responds to putting the sensor unit in the ready working state, removing it from the ready working state, checking the state or neutralizing the sensor unit.
Bring to Ready Working Condition
The ready working state is created after the "Connect" command is issued. This command is intended to load the firing capacitor.
Remove from Ready Worker State
Unloading from the ready worker state occurs after issuing the "Open" command. This command discharges the firing capacitor.
Neutralization
By pressing the "Neutralization" button, the sensor block is neutralized. At this time, the relay is disconnected from the sensor block.
Start Operating Mode
The "Run" command must be transmitted after the "Connect" command. The "Start" command can be sent to each sensor block or to all sensor blocks.

5   Description of the Security Robotic System

The control unit of the security system is powered by a 7.4V Li-battery. The battery is located in a waterproof compartment. The display of the control unit is permanently connected.

The main components of the security system are located in a hard case. Between the components is filled with foam. Cases for automobile, aviation, etc. transport is possible. The control unit of the security system concentrates all the elements of the control for processing. The command of the security system is carried out by radio communication. There are two "Encoding" buttons in the control block, through which various commands are selected from the menu.

A LED type indicator is placed on the cover of the security system, which shows the connection of the food. There is also a pin on the cap, which, in "Neutralization" mode, protrudes 10 mm above the cap for better control of the situation.

The power button and remote protection button are located at the bottom of the security system. In two-way radio communication mode, when a request is received

Fig. 2. The security robotic system in the suitcase.

from the control unit, the protection can send information about the current state of the system. General view of security robotic system in the suitcase shown in Fig. 2.

Figure 3 shows two versions of the remote control for securiry robotic system: mini (pocket version) and stationary.

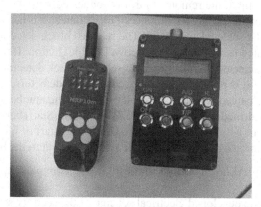

Fig. 3. Two versions of the remote control for securiry robotic system: mini (pocket version) and stationary.

Figure 4 shows the developed topology diagram of the security robotic system. A two-layer board was used to create the topological scheme.

6 Security Robotic System Operation

6.1 Preparation for Operation

1. Remove the control block unit and the power source (battery) from the suitcase. Placing the battery in the lower part of the control block unit.
2. Remove the protective cap and insert the antenna into the antenna junction located on the front side of the control block unit.

Fig. 4. Topology diagram of the security robotic system on two-layer board.

6.2 Operation Algorithm

Connect. The connection is made within 1 s by pressing the "ON" button. The connection is observed by the reflection of information on the display. Each time the control block unit is connected, the battery voltage is measured, and if the voltage is lower than normal, the display shows "LOW BAT" (in percent). At this time, it is necessary to feed the battery.

Command Selected. First, the remote control is connected with the "On" button. By " +", "−" (up, down) buttons using the number of block detector is hanged (from 1 to 10). The display shows the selected command. The selected block detector launcher can be activated or deactivated using the "A/D" (Active/Disable) button. If the "A/D" button is pressed on with the selected number, then the selected block detector number is shown on the display, and if it is necessary to select other block detectors, the numbers of the block detectors are changed with the " +" and "−" keys. The number of block detectors to be used can be confirmed by pressing the "T/P" (Confirm/Start) button after activating (or deactivating) them with the "A/D" button. Confirmed start of block detectors need to press the "T/P" button again to transmit the start command to the block detector.

By selecting the "ALL" button on the display, the command applies to all block detectors.

Figure 5 shows the developed electrical scheme of the security system.

Developed topological scheme of security robotic system telemetry, that is, remote control with electromagnetic waves shown in the Fig. 6.

Figure 7 shows the schematic diagram of security sistem telemetry.

7   Results of Laboratory and Field Tests of Security System

The tests were carried out in laboratory and field conditions with 2 different remote controls from the initial test. 1 control panel is designed for every 10 seismic sensor blocks. At first, the MRP-10M type control panel was used. After preliminary tests in laboratory conditions, the field tests were conducted in open air conditions and the results of the tests were as follows.

The field tests were conducted at a distance of 300–1200 m. At a distance of 300–1000 m, both on the ground and at a height of 1 m, the system worked perfectly normally.

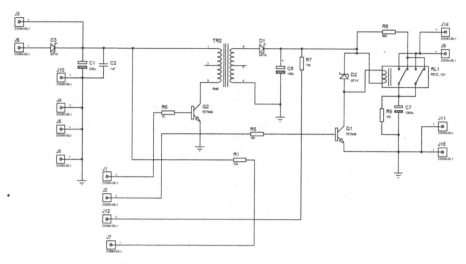

Fig. 5. Security robotic sistem electrical circuit.

Fig. 6. Topological scheme of security robotic system telemetry.

At 1200 m, 1 m above the ground surface, the data sent was not received. Later, the tests were conducted using the MRP-10 m control panel. These tests were carried out at distances of 200–400 m. The tests were successful both on the ground surface and at a height of 1 m above the ground surface. Tests were conducted in different weather conditions. Weather conditions did not adversely affect the tests.

A total of 100 field tests were conducted. The tests showed positive results. During the tests, there was no violation of the working mode of the protection system and it showed 100% reliability.

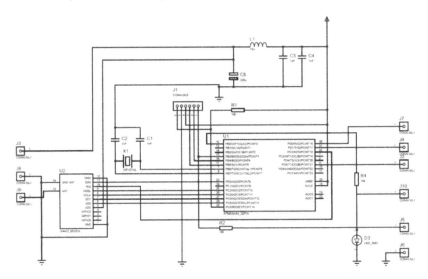

Fig. 7. Security sistem telemetry electrical diagram.

8   Conclusion

Thus, the paper shows the results of the development, preparation and preliminary laboratory and field tests of the security system working in the telemetry mode. The working principle, management, operation rules, management and telemetry of the security system were explained. Cryptographic coding based on the Neyman algorithm was used to encrypt the telemetry of the security system. During 100 laboratory and field tests of the security robotic system, no violations of the system's operation mode were observed.

References

1. Vorona, V., Tixonov, V.: Control Systems and Access Control. Goryachiya Liniya-Telekom, Moscow (2010). (In Russ)
2. Hashimov, E., Bayramov, A., Abdullayev, F., Suleymanov, S., Nazarov, M.: Analysis of systems that detonate mines from a distance. In: Proceeding of "Defence and Srcurity" Scientific-practical Conference, p. 24. Bilik Fondu, Baku (2017)
3. Bajaj, S., Bopardikar, S.D., Von Moll, A., Torng, E., Casbeer, D.W.: Perimeter Defense using a Turret with Finite Range and Service Times. arXiv preprint arXiv:2302.02186 (2023)
4. Guerrero-Bonilla, L., Nieto-Granda, C., Egerstedt, M.: Robust perimeter defense using control barrier functions. In: 2021 International Symposium on Multi-Robot and Multi-Agent Systems (MRS), pp. 164–172 (2021)
5. Standard, D.E.: Federal information processing standards publication 46. National Bureau of Standards, US Department of Commerce 23, 1–18 (1977)
6. GOST 28147-89: Information development systems. Cryptographic protection. Cryptographic transformation algorithm (1989) (in Russian)
7. International Electrotechnical Commission. IEC 60529: degrees of protection provided by enclosures (IP code). National Electrical Manufacturers Association, Rosslyn, VA, USA (2004)

Development of a Robot for Agricultural Field Scouting

Olga Mitrofanova[1,2(✉)] ⓘ, Ivan Blekanov[1] ⓘ, Danila Sevostyanov[1] ⓘ, Jia Zhang[1] ⓘ, and Evgenii Mitrofanov[1,2] ⓘ

[1] St. Petersburg State University, 7-9 Universitetskaya Emb., St. Petersburg 199034, Russia
o.a.mitrofanova@spbu.ru
[2] Agrophysical Research Institute, 14, Grazhdansky Pr., St. Petersburg 195220, Russia

Abstract. Since agricultural environments are mostly in unstructured feature information, in order to facilitate agricultural robots to better adapt to environmental change problems in agricultural environments, this paper proposes a robot system architecture for agricultural fields scouting. The article proposes: 1) the analysis of some existing field agricultural robots; 2) a novel approach that first constructs a map using the Rtabmap SLAM technique and second employs a particle filter-based Monte Carlo method to estimate the robot's position post-hoc with a loopback detection process; 3) the pipeline of robot works (which is developing), including its architecture, taking into account selected hardware and software components. Firstly, the hardware architecture of the robot and its required sensors are considered, then the AMCL route planning algorithm is applied. The depth camera+lidar+RTK approach is used for the robot's map construction, the simulation model of robot route planning by ROS, the robot design by SolidWorks, and finally the required sensors and hardware structure parts are analyzed and summarized. Based on the considered project, it is planned to create a field agricultural scouting robot, which will become part of the implementation of a digital twin in crop production.

Keywords: Agricultural Scouting Robots · Route Planning · Sensors · Smart Agriculture · Digital Twin · Crop Production

1 Introduction

Smart agriculture will critically combine technologies such as computer vision and multi-sensor fusion to provide effective and efficient agricultural services. Smart agriculture can utilize a wide range of advanced technologies such as artificial intelligence, the Internet of Things and robotics. In smart agriculture, the "eyes" of agricultural robots (i.e., depth cameras) are used to identify and understand the soil or vegetation in a farm field in order to obtain valuable information to accomplish manually predetermined tasks and purposes. The aggravation of the food crisis in the world determines the urgent need for the development of this industry, including in the field of modern technologies and artificial intelligence.

A. Ronzhin et al. (Eds.): ICR 2023, LNAI 14214, pp. 185–196, 2023.
https://doi.org/10.1007/978-3-031-43111-1_17

Against the backdrop of the departure of leading international companies in the field of computerization and electronation of agriculture, the issue of replacing developments with domestic ones is in the first place. Indeed, without the constant improvement of agricultural technologies, it is impossible to ensure the stable development of the industry.

One of the main challenges of our country is the digitalization of the crop industry, the transition to resource-saving and environmentally friendly agricultural technologies. In this regard, a team based on two organizations (AFI and St. Petersburg State University) as the main direction of research work has chosen a set of tasks in the field of so-called smart-farming, which covers various scale levels (small farm, large agricultural fields, region, etc.), concentrating on automatic driving equipment, collecting and analyzing data using robotic systems, predicting yields and improving the efficiency of existing field processing systems.

Robotic unmanned technologies have proven themselves well in solving the problems of smart agriculture, many processes can be automated in greenhouses [1], as well as in orchards [2]. In recent years, the development of field robots for agroscouting [3], which allow us to automate problems related to monitoring the state of soil and crops, has also become promising. So, for example, the problem of detecting and recognizing pests in an agricultural field [4] or weeds [5] is solved. However, most of these developments are aimed at application for crops such as maize [6], vineyard [7], strawberry [8], etc. There is a need to create a field agro-robot for scouting on grain crops, which would take into account the physiological characteristics of the culture.

Currently, in the agricultural environment, most agricultural sites are in an unstructured and uncertain working environment. The growing environment of crops not only depends on the terrain conditions, but is also directly affected by seasonal and weather conditions. In open agricultural environments, there are various disturbing factors, such as light, overlap, and occlusion, which make target identification difficult; in agricultural environments, there are variations in scale and perspective as well as various noises and errors that lead to inaccurate 3D reconstruction; in agricultural environments, there are semantic and functional differences with blurred and uncertain boundaries that lead to incomplete semantic separation. These are the difficulties and challenges faced by the adaptation of agricultural robot environments. Agricultural robots need to make appropriate and timely adaptations to different working conditions to ensure successful work. Agricultural robots work with crops. The spatial shape of crops varies as they grow. Agricultural robots must be able to adapt to the different spatial shapes of the crops while ensuring that the critical physiological parts of the crops are not damaged.

Since the SLAM problem in smart agriculture has high academic value and broad application prospects, it has become a very active research area in academia. For navigation and crop scouting of maize fields in agricultural fields, Schmitz A [4] et al. developed an RGV vehicle that uses low-cost ultrasonic sensors to detect the location of maize rows. [9] developed a small autonomous field inspection vehicle that uses cameras and GPS for localization to identify field contours and crop types. The end of the crop rows were detected by threshold segmentation of photos of the crop and a straight line from the center of the crop rows was used for localization. Pak J [10] analyzed and compared Dijkstra's algorithm, A* algorithm and RRT algorithm and finally A* algorithm was used for greenhouse localization. Piersthal [11] proposed the Graph-SLAM method for accurate localization of forest vehicles in a forest environment using 3D LiDAR and stereo cameras. Therefore, graph search-based trajectory planning methods, such as Dijkstra's algorithm and A* algorithm, use analytical methods for discretization to guarantee the existence of feasible solutions. However, it is difficult to apply them to trajectory planning in multidimensional space due to the large computational effort. The trajectory planning method based on random sampling probability, which only requires the positions of computer robots to collide, can effectively solve the trajectory planning problem in multidimensional space and complex constraints. Moreover, its effectiveness is related to the collision detection module, and its performance in the low-dimensional case needs to be improved. In addition, most researchers' SLAM-based studies are mostly used indoors, while there is less literature on SLAM studies in outdoor agricultural scenarios, which are highly influenced by ambient light.

In this study, we propose a novel approach that first constructs a map using the Rtabmap SLAM technique and second employs a particle filter-based Monte Carlo method to estimate the robot's position post-hoc with a loopback detection process. This approach allows for fast and accurate robot localization in outdoor agricultural scenarios. The innovation of this paper is that using LIDAR + RTK for SLAM map construction and navigation is difficult to guarantee high accuracy in large agricultural environments, so based on the above navigation and positioning algorithm, the feature data collected by vision is added to the SLAM algorithm as crop feature correction data to correct the map construction error and improve the real-time accuracy of navigation and positioning.

The objective of our research is to bridge the gap between the robotic technologies applying and optimization of precision farming agrotechnological processes for grain crops.

2 Movement Organization

2.1 Precise Positioning with RTK

To ensure accurate positioning, the GPS RTK (Real-Time Kinematic) system, model RTK Emlid REACH RS2+, was chosen. This model allows you to receive the following signals: GPS/QZSS L1C/A, L2C – GLONASS L1OF, L2OF – BeiDou B1I, B2I – Galileo E1-B/C, E5b – SBAS L1C/A and others.

The essence of this complex is to install a rover (AVG) on a robot, which, in turn, communicates with a base installed at a distance of up to 8 km. Hours of operation, depending from the regime, starts from 16 h. Thus, this kit is excellent for positioning the robot in the agricultural field.

Processing of the signals received by the base takes place in the open-source program RTKLib, which is free and offers the following set of functions:

- support for various GNSS positioning modes, in real time and for post-processing;
- support for standard and precise positioning algorithms;
- support for various RTK complexes;
- support of communication protocols Serial, TCP/IP, NTRIP, FTP/HTTP.

2.2 Building a Map in an Unknown Area

When the robot first passes through the field, the map of the area and the route are not predetermined. To build a map and determine routes, it is proposed to use SLAM methods in conjunction with the Percipio RGBD camera.

The essence of the method is to calculate the location estimate x_t of the agent and the environment map m_t from a series of observations z_t over discrete time with a sampling step t. The goal of the problem is to compute $(m_{t,t}|z_t)$.

To build a map, the SLAM Rtabmap method is used – this is a method based on finding and matching the visual data of the sensors (In this case, the RGBD vision sensor FS830-HD has two main infrared cameras, a color camera and a fill light system. (An active binocular vision technique is used)). The benefits of using this camera, due to the fact that in strong natural light, the laser scatter in the structured light camera is susceptible to great interference, therefore, in outdoor conditions and can only be used indoors; and none of the ordinary binocular stereo vision cameras are suitable for use in dim environments or where features are not obvious. It can also play the role of image optimization by adjusting the brightness of the optical enhancement system or the exposure parameters of the image sensor according to the needs of the specific working environment light.

The environment sensing component contains lidar, imu inertial measurement unit. LIDAR, as an important environment sensing sensor, can collect the outline of the surrounding obstacles in the current environment. Imu can quickly obtain the angle, angular velocity and acceleration of the angle change of the current environment and other information. LIDAR scans the surrounding 360-degree environment by rotation, and the acquired environmental data can be used by slam algorithm to quickly construct a map of the mobile robot's environment and reflect the robot's current position change by this map.

The method of constructing a map using depth cameras is initially capable of scanning volumetric space. In this case, the algorithm will map the projections of all objects that it scans during the movement of the robot. As a result, the resulting map will be less visual, but more complete and secure for the robot to move around. Moreover, the robot's path planner will build its route at once, taking into account all the objects; while when using a map built using lidar, the robot will first drive up to an obstacle not fixed by this same lidar, then recognize it with the help of a camera, and only after that, rebuild its route [12, 13].

Rtabmap SLAM builds not only a 2D map, but also creates a database of visual images. Thus, Rtabmap searches for global matches in visual images, while the compiled room map can be used by lidar to locally adjust the location of the robot in space.

In an agricultural environment, the robot needs to achieve all inspection tasks through autonomous navigation. The key to navigation is robot positioning and path planning, which are based on ROS move_base and amcl. Among them, move_base provides the main operation and interaction interface for robot navigation. Meanwhile, in order to ensure the accuracy of the robot's navigation path, the robot also needs to estimate its own location through amcl implementation. In the ROS-based robot navigation, the robot only needs to publish the necessary sensor information and the target location for navigation. Real-time obstacle avoidance of the robot is achieved by collecting information from

LiDAR/Laser_scan and publishing odometer information nav_msgs/Odometry and the corresponding TF transformations.

AMCL Monte Carlo Positioning. In the process of outdoor farming operations, it is necessary to ensure that the robot accurately reaches each instrument monitoring station, which requires the robot to realize the autonomous positioning function. Autonomous positioning of mobile robots means that the robot can project its own position in the map in any situation, which is mainly divided into two parts: global positioning and local positioning [14]. The robot determines its position relative to the environment based on the given environment map, based on the perception of the environment and its own motion, and its positioning model is schematically shown in Fig. 1.

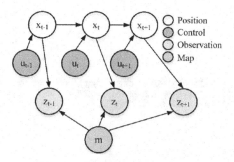

Fig. 1. Autonomous positioning model of mobile robot.

KLD Sampling. The size N of the sample set used to represent the confidence level is an important parameter for the efficiency of particle filtering. In order to avoid scattering due to Monte Carlo localization sampling consumption, a sufficiently large sample set must be chosen to achieve accurate global localization and position tracking of the robot. In the early stages of localization, a sufficiently large number of particle sets is needed to accurately represent the state confidence of the robot. Using KLD sampling in amcl localization, for each particle filtering iteration, the number of samples is determined with probability $1 - \delta$. That is, the number of particles required is determined based on statistical bounds on the quality of the sampled approximation such that the error between the true posterior and the sampling-based approximation is less than ε. The number of particles required for sampling is given in the algorithm. The more dispersed the particles are, the larger the value of k and the larger the M_χ, the larger the number of particles sampled. In robot navigation, the initial poses of the robot are unknown, and the initial confidence $bel(x_0)$ is used to reflect the initial positional information of the robot, initialized by a uniform distribution over the space of all free poses on the map as follows:

$$bel(x_0) = \frac{1}{|X|}, \tag{1}$$

where: $|X|$ - the volume of all positional spaces in the map. Simulation tests are performed in ros, as shown in the Fig. 2.

In the initial state of the robot, the robot's position in the map is unknown, and the particles are uniformly distributed in the map in terms of their poses. As the robot moves and the robot's state is estimated based on the odometer input and the LIDAR observations, the confidence in the robot's position increases and the particles tend to converge.

It should be noted that it is additionally planned to provide for the option of loading a ready-made polygon map of an agricultural field in the kml format. In this case, the construction of the route is simplified.

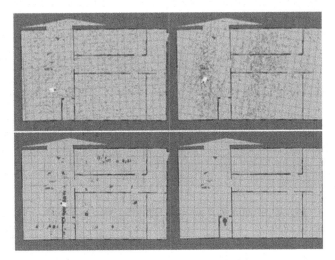

Fig. 2. Amcl positioning.

2.3 Obstacle Avoidance

Avoiding obstacles encountered in an agricultural field is proposed to be carried out using 2D LiDAR – a type of sensor that uses laser beams to measure distances and create accurate maps of the environment. The principle of operation of LiDAR is to emit laser beams and measure the time required for the light to reflect back to the sensor, which allows you to calculate the distance to the object, as well as its geometric characteristics. LiDAR "LSLIDAR N10P" is used for this purpose.

The difference between 2D and 3D sensors is the level of detail that can be captured and the types of information that can be extracted from the data.

Two-dimensional LiDAR, as the name implies, collects information in two dimensions, on a plane in front of it, the general principle of operation of such a sensor is shown in Fig. 3 [15].

To implement obstacle avoidance, the sensor must be installed at the bottom of the robotic complex in order to collect information about obstacles as fully as possible [16].

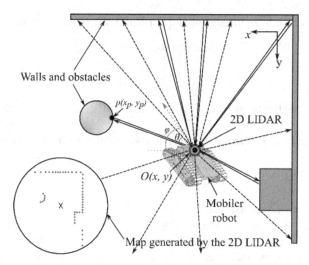

Fig. 3. How 2D LiDAR Works to Avoid Obstacles.

The algorithm used in our work is designed to be used on computers with limited computing capabilities, in other words, we can process data directly on the processor that controls the robot.

The pseudocode of the algorithm used is shown in Table 1.

Table 1. Algorithm of cluster contouring.

	Input: Set of clusters B Output: Set of obstacles O
1	$O \leftarrow \emptyset$;
2	for $i = 1, 2, \ldots, c\, do :$
3	$O_i \leftarrow \emptyset$;
4	for $j = 1, 2, \ldots, (|B_i| - a)do :$
5	$s \leftarrow \left[\left(\overline{\theta}^{(j-1)}, d_{min}^{(j-1)} \right), \left(\overline{\theta}^{(j)}, d_{min}^{(j)} \right) \right]$;
6	add s to the set O_i;
7	$s \leftarrow \left[\left(\overline{\theta}^{(j-1)}, d_{max}^{(j-1)} \right), \left(\overline{\theta}^{(j)}, d_{max}^{(j)} \right) \right]$;
8	Add s to the set O_i;
9	Add O_i to the set O;
10	end
11	end

The data received from the sensor is described in the polar coordinate system:

$$\theta = (\theta_1, \theta_2, \ldots, \theta_n), \tag{2}$$

$$d = (d_1, d_2, \ldots, d_n), \tag{3}$$

where θ is the vector of angles, d is the vector of distances, n is the number of measurements.

This data can be converted to a Cartesian coordinate system as follows:

$$\begin{cases} x_i = d_i \cos \theta_i \\ y_i = d_i \sin \theta_i \end{cases}, \quad i \in [1, n]. \tag{4}$$

Thus, points x_i, y_i are obtained by scanning relative to the position of the robot.

Also, the necessary data for the developed algorithm is the robot displacement vector $S = (S_x, S_y, S_\varphi)$ from the previous scan by the LiDAR sensor to the current one. The value of this displacement vector may have an error (as a rule, it is impossible to accurately calculate the distance traveled by the robot) [17].

3 Pipeline of Robot Works

3.1 Robot Concept

While doing research, we focused, among other things, on reducing the price of a robotic complex.

Many parts are made in-house using machine tools or a 3D printer. Figure 4 shows a preliminary diagram of a robot with caterpillars and movement sensors.

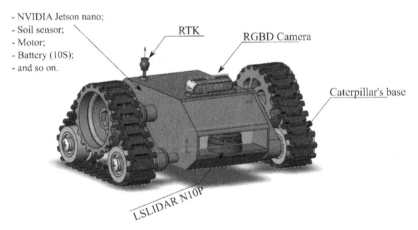

Fig. 4. Preliminary scheme of the robot.

As we can see from the figure, the robot uses a caterpillar's base, the sensors are mounted on the outer parts of the robot, the motors and the control board are hidden inside the body.

3.2   Choice of Components

The choice of components for the robotic complex was carried out with a focus on price and availability.

Next, the advantages and disadvantages of control panels and chassis will be considered. Table 2 shows the set of components for the robot.

Table 2. Comparison of the cost of RTK complexes.

Name	Quantity	Price per piece, rubles
Wheel with motor OR	4	7703,57
Rubber caterpillar	1	13744,84
Raspberry Pi 4	1	16115,46
OR		
Nvidia Jetson Nano	1	20490,98
Soil sensor	1	15067,50
Wiring	5 m	1000

Table 2 shows only those components that we do not have in stock. The rest of the components are available. These are components such as:

- an electric motor for moving the robot with the option of using caterpillars;
- rechargeable batteries for powering the robotic complex;
- 2D lidar for avoiding obstacles;
- RGBD camera to implement computer vision;
- RTK module for precise positioning.

The body and fasteners of the robot will be made using a 3D printer.

Our team is more inclined to use a robot with a caterpillar, since movement on such base is easier than on wheels, it is cheaper and it is easier to implement turning mechanisms.

Choosing a control panel is an important step in robot design. We agreed on the choice of Nvidia Jetson Nano, as it outperforms its competitors in key indicators (for example, Raspberry Pi4). The Nvidia Jetson Nano has a faster modern CPU, expandable RAM up to 8 GB, and more ports for connecting and testing possible sensors.

In conclusion, we tend to use the Nvidia Jetson Nano, since there are a sufficient number of inputs/outputs, the board is completely complete, the power allows us to do the processes we need.

3.3   Pipeline of Our Model

Figure 5 shows the pipeline of actions of our robot. It begins with the release of the robot on the field. After that, you can conditionally divide the actions of the robot into collecting data on the field itself and data on movement. The collection and processing of movement data is carried out in real time on the control panel of the robot, and is also collected on the server for subsequent construction of a field map.

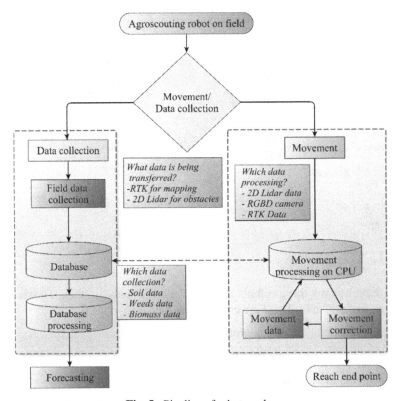

Fig. 5. Pipeline of robot works.

The architecture pipeline consists of the following main modules:

- After launching the robot in the field, we separate 2 aspects of its work: movement and data collection.
- While moving, the robot moves across the field and collects data (marked as Movement Data). It collects information about obstacles using 2D Lidar and RGBD cameras, tracking GPS coordinates, collecting data for terrain mapping using the RTK complex.
- On the Movement Processing on CPU block, all the data collected about the movement is processed in real time to optimize the movement.
- In the Movement correction block, the processed data is used to change the robot's movement, if necessary.
- Data Collection block. This block deals with the data that the robot collects directly for future analysis, such as plant health data, soil data, etc.

- The Field data collection block describes directly the collection of field data, on the basis of which yield analysis, analysis of plant diseases, etc. will subsequently be carried out.
- The collected data on plants are transferred to a common database (Data Base block), in which information will be collected and analyzed in the future.
- The Database Processing block is directly responsible for processing the collected data: analyzing the results, comparing with past results, and predicting yields. The collected field data on plants and soil are transferred to a single service for further processing, including by artificial intelligence methods, and the output of analysis results for decision-making in various problems: yield forecasting, determining the required doses of fertilizers for application, biomass forecasting, etc.
- In the end, all collected data is used to further combine with data from other sources (drone, underground sensor), which are used to forecasting the yield of the field.

4 Conclusion

An increasingly actual and perspective direction is the creation of field agricultural scouting robots that allow real-time collection and processing of heterogeneous big data to solve a large number 'of management tasks: from yields forecasting to building a map of fertilizer doses for applying specialized precision machines. The paper proposes a project of such robot. It is planned to use it for research problems on grain crops and potatoes. It will allow us to quickly collect various information about crops and soil (optical, agrochemical, agrophysical indicators, etc.) for further analysis. In fact, the considered task is one of the first stages of creating a digital twin for crop production. A digital twin is, in fact, a digital analogue of a real object, reflecting its state and behavior in virtual space over time. The use of digital twins in the future will allow agricultural producers to manage agro-technological operations remotely based on digital information in real time, to model the consequences of management actions based on real data [18, 19]. It is assumed that the data collected by the robot and the unmanned aerial system will be automatically processed in a web service, after which the system will issue a result with management decisions, for example, a map with fertilizer doses, which will be loaded into the tractor's on-board computer for automatic differential application to the field [20].

References

1. Gao, J., et al.: Development and evaluation of a pneumatic finger-like end-effector for cherry tomato harvesting robot in greenhouse. Comput. Electron. Agric. **197**, 106879 (2022)
2. Wakchaure, M., Patle, B.K., Mahindrakar, A.K.: Application of AI techniques and robotics in agriculture: a review. Artif. Intell. Sci. **3**, 100057 (2023)
3. Yamasaki, Y., Morie, M., Noguchi, N.: Development of a high-accuracy autonomous sensing system for a field scouting robot. Comput. Electron. Agric. **193**, 106630 (2022)
4. Schmitz, A., Badgujar, C., Mansur, H., Flippo, D., McCornack, B., Sharda, A.: Design of a reconfigurable crop scouting vehicle for row crop navigation: a proof-of-concept study. Sensors **22**, 6203 (2022)

5. Pradel, M., de Fays, M., Seguineau, C.: Comparative life cycle assessment of intra-row and inter-row weeding practices using autonomous robot systems in French vineyards. Sci. Total Environ. **838**(3), 156441 (2022)
6. Manish, R., Lin, Y.C., Ravi, R., Hasheminasab, S.M., Zhou, T., Habib, A.: Development of a miniaturized mobile mapping system for in-row, under-canopy phenotyping. Remot. Sens. **13**(2), 276 (2021)
7. Longo, D., Pennisi, A., Bonsignore, R., Muscato, G., Schillaci, G.: A multifunctional tracked vehicle able to operate in vineyards using GPS and laser range-finder technology. In: International Conference Ragusa SHWA2010-September 16–18 2010 Ragusa Ibla Campus-Italy "Work safety and risk prevention in agro-food and forest systems (2010)
8. Ge, Y., Xiong, Y., Tenorio, G.L., From, P.J.: Fruit localization and environment perception for strawberry harvesting robots. IEEE Access **7**, 147642–147652 (2019)
9. Bengochea-Guevara, J.M., Conesa-Muñoz, J., Andújar, D., et al.: Merge fuzzy visual servoing and GPS-based planning to obtain a proper navigation behavior for a small crop-inspection robot. Sensors **16**(3), 276 (2016)
10. Pak, J., Kim, J., Park, Y., et al.: Field evaluation of path-planning algorithms for autonomous mobile robot in smart farms. IEEE Access **10**, 60253–60266 (2022)
11. Pierzchała, M., Giguère, P., Astrup, R.: Mapping forests using an unmanned ground vehicle with 3D LiDAR and graph-SLAM. Comput. Electron. Agric. **145**, 217–225 (2018)
12. Labbé, M., Michaud, F.: RTAB-Map as an open-source lidar and visual simultaneous localization and mapping library for large-scale and long-term online operation. J. Field Robot. **35**, 416–446 (2019)
13. Silva, B.M.F.D., Xavier, R.S., Gonçalves, L.M.G.: Mapping and Navigation for Indoor Robots under ROS: An Experimental Analysis. Preprints.org. 2019070035 (2019)
14. Al-Turjman, F.: A novel approach for drones positioning in mission critical applications. Transactions on Emerging Telecommunications Technologies **33**(1), e3603 (2022)
15. Bouazizi, M., Mora, A.L., Ohtsuki, T.: A 2D-Lidar-equipped unmanned robot-based approach for indoor human activity detection. Sensors **23**(5), 2534 (2023)
16. Baek, S., Lee, T.-K., Se-Young, O., Ju, K.: Integrated on-line localization, mapping and coverage algorithm of unknown environments for robotic vacuum cleaners based on minimal sensing. Adv. Robot. **25**, 16511673 (2011)
17. Mochurad, L., Hladun, Y., Tkachenko, R.: An obstacle-finding approach for autonomous mobile robots using 2D LiDAR data. Big Data Cogn. Comput. **7**, 43 (2023)
18. Dyck, G., Hawley, E., Hildebrand, K., Paliwal, J.: Digital Twins: a novel traceability concept for post-harvest handling. Smart Agr. Technol. **3**, 100079 (2023)
19. Purcell, W., Neubauer, T.: Digital twins in agriculture: a state-of-the-art review. Smart Agr. Technol. **3**, 100094 (2023)
20. Mitrofanova, O., Yakushev, V., Zakharova, E., Terleev, V.: An alternative approach to managing the nitrogen content of cereal crops. Smart Innov. Syst. Technol. **247**, 481–491 (2022)

Optimization of the Placement of Measurement Points and Control of the Power of Moving Sources in Rod Heating

Kamil Aida-Zade$^{(\boxtimes)}$ ⓘ and Vugar Hashimov ⓘ

Institute of Control Systems of the Ministry of Science and Education of Republic of Azerbaijan, 68, B. Vahabzadeh street, Baku AZ1141, Azerbaijan
kamil_aydazade@rambler.ru

Abstract. The problem of synthesis of power control of point-wise heat sources of heating of a rod moving along the rod by given trajectories and optimization of the placements of temperature measurement points is considered. To form the current power values of each of the heat sources, it is proposed to use the formula of their linear dependence on the temperature of the rod at the measured points. In general, the original optimal control problem is reduced to finding a finite-dimensional vector of feedback parameters and coordinates of measurement points that optimize the given objective functional. Regarding the feedback parameters and the coordinates of the measurement points, the necessary conditions for the optimality of the functional of the problem are formulated, containing formulas for the components of the gradient of the objective functional. The obtained formulas make it possible to use effective numerical first-order optimization methods for solving the problem. The results of numerical experiments obtained on initial test data are presented, and the analysis of the results is carried out. In particular, the influence of the temperature measurement errors at the measurement points on the quality of process control, namely on the value of the objective functional is analyzed.

Keywords: Rod Heating · Feedback Control · Moving Sources · Feedback Parameters · Temperature Measurement Points

1 Introduction

The problem of optimal synthesis of control of the process of heating a rod by lumped sources moving along given trajectories and rules is considered. The current values of the power of the sources are assigned depending on the measured values of the temperature of the rod at the points where the measuring devices are installed.

The problem under consideration belongs to the class of problems of optimal control of objects with distributed parameters [1–6]. Various formulations of problems of control of lumped sources in distributed systems were studied by Butkovsky A.G. and his students [7, 8]. In contrast to the control problems for systems with lumped parameters [9, 10], the control problems for systems with distributed parameters, especially

A. Ronzhin et al. (Eds.): ICR 2023, LNAI 14214, pp. 197–207, 2023.
https://doi.org/10.1007/978-3-031-43111-1_18

with feedback, have been studied much less [4, 11–14]. Numerical methods for solving problems of optimal control of objects with distributed parameters with feedback are even less developed.

In this paper, main goal is firstly, an approach is proposed for building a control system with feedback, objects with distributed parameters, and secondly, the problem of optimizing the locations of control points used for feedback is posed and solved.

Formulas for the components of the gradient of the objective functional with respect to the feedback parameters are obtained, which made it possible to use well-known effective numerical first-order optimization methods to solve the problem of control synthesis. The results of computer experiments obtained by solving the test problem are presented.

The results of the work can be used in systems for automatic control and regulation of lumped sources for various objects described by some other types of initial-boundary-value problems.

2 Formulation of the Problem

The problem of control of the heating of the rod, described by the equation:

$$u_t(x, t) = a^2 u_{xx}(x, t) - \lambda_0 [u(x, t) - \theta] + \sum_{i=1}^{N_s} q_i(t)\delta(x - z_i(t)), \tag{1}$$
$$x \in (0, l), t \in (0, T],$$

with initial and boundary conditions:

$$u(x, 0) = b(x) = b = \text{const} \in \text{B}, \tag{2}$$

$$u_x(0, t) = \lambda_1(u(0, t) - \theta), u_x(l, t) = -\lambda_2(u(l, t) - \theta), t \in (0, T]. \tag{3}$$

Here: $u(x, t)$ is temperature of the rod at the point $x \in [0, l]$ at the time t; a, λ_0, λ_1 and λ_2 are given parameters of the heating process; θ is ambient temperature; $\delta(\cdot)$ is the Dirac delta function.

The heating of the rod is carried out by N_s lumped sources moving along given trajectories with controlled powers determined by piecewise continuous functions $q_i(t)$, $i = 1, 2, \ldots, N_s$ such that:

$$Q = \left\{ \underline{q_i} \leq q_i(t) \leq \overline{q_i}, i = 1, 2, \ldots, N_s, t \in [0, T] \right\}, \tag{4}$$

where $\underline{q_i}, \overline{q_i}, i = 1, 2, \ldots, N_s$ are given. The given continuous functions $z_i(t) \in [0, l]$ determine the coordinates of the location on the rod of the i th source at the time t, $i = 1, 2, \ldots, N_s$.

The solution of the initial-boundary-value problem (1)–(3) is understood in the generalized sense [1, 6, 12], i.e. for an arbitrary function such that:

$$\psi(x, T) = 0, x \in [0, l],$$
$$\psi_x(0, t) = \lambda_1 \psi(0, t), \psi_x(l, t) = -\lambda_2 \psi(l, t), t \in [0, T),$$

we have:

$$\int_0^T \int_0^l u(x,t)\left(-\psi_t(x,t) - a^2\psi_{xx}(x,t) + \lambda_0\psi(x,t)\right)dxdt$$

$$= \sum_{i=1}^{N_s}\int_0^T q_i(t)\psi(z_i(t),t)dt + \int_0^l \psi(0,t)b(x)dx + \lambda_0\int_0^T\int_0^l \psi(x,t)\theta dxdt$$

$$+\lambda_1\theta\int_0^T\psi(0,t)dt + \lambda_2\theta\int_0^T\psi(l,t)dt, \, x \in (0,l), t \in [0,T).$$

In [1, 12], the existence and uniqueness of a generalized solution of the considered initial-boundary-value problem (1)–(3) were proved for arbitrary admissible functions $q_i(t)$, $i = 1, 2, \ldots, N_s$.

It is assumed that the initial temperature in (2) is the same at all points of the rod, but it is not exactly specified, and belongs to a given set $B \subset R$ with a known density function $\rho_B(b)$:

$$\rho_B(b) \geq 0, b \in B, \int_B \rho_B(b)db = 1.$$

The ambient temperature involved in (1), (3) does not change during heating, and its possible values are distributed over a set $\Theta \subset R$ with a known density function $\rho_\Theta(\theta)$ $\rho_\Theta(\theta)$ such that:

$$\rho_\Theta(\theta) \geq 0, \theta \in \Theta, \int_\Theta \rho_\Theta(\theta)d\theta = 1.$$

The above problem of optimal control is consists of finding admissible values of source powers $q = q(t) = (q_1(t), q_2(t), \ldots, q_{N_s}(t)) \in Q$, delivering to minimum on average over all possible values $b \in B$ of the initial states of the rod and the ambient temperature values $\theta \in \Theta$ of the following objective functional:

$$\mathcal{I}(q) = \int_B \int_\Theta I(\vartheta; b, \theta)\rho_B(b)\rho_\Theta(\theta)d\theta db, \tag{5}$$

$$I(q; b, \theta) = \int_0^l \mu(x)[u(x,T) - U(x)]^2dx + \varepsilon\|q(t) - \hat{q}\|^2_{L_2^{N_s}[0,T]}. \tag{6}$$

Here: $u(x,t) = u(x,t; q, b, \theta)$ is the solution of the initial-boundary-value problem (1)–(3) with the initial condition $b \in B$, the ambiant temperature of the $\theta \in \Theta$ and at admissible values of the source powers $q(t) \in Q$; $U(x)$ is the given temperature distribution of the rod, which is desirable to achieve at the end of the heating process; $\mu(x) \geq 0$, $x \in [0,l]$ is a given weight function; $\varepsilon > 0$, $\hat{q}$ are the given regularization parameters of the problem functional [6].

Now suppose that at given N_o points of the rod $\xi_j \in [0,l]$, $j = 1, 2, \ldots, N_o$, the temperature values are measured at these points continuously during its heating:

$$\breve{u}_j(t) = u(\xi_j, t), t \in [0,T], \xi_j \in [0,l], j = 1, 2, \ldots, N_o. \tag{7}$$

The measured values are used to assign the current values of the power sources $q_i(t)$, $i = 1, 2, \ldots, N_s$ according to the following linear dependence on the measured temperature values:

$$q_i(t) = \sum_{j=1}^{N_o} \alpha_i^j [u(\xi_j, t) - \beta_i^j], \tag{8}$$

where α_i^j, β_i^j, ξ_j are feedback parameters, $i = 1, 2, \ldots, N_s$, $j = 1, 2, \ldots, N_o$ [13, 14].

In (8), the value in square brackets determines the deviation of the temperature measurement at the jth measurement point from the nominal value β_i^j relative to the ith source at the jth measurement point. α_i^j is the corresponding gain factor. The nominal values are largely determined by the values of the given function $U(x)$ at the measurement points $x = \xi_j$, $j = 1, 2, \ldots, N_o$.

Substituting expressions for powers with continuous feedback (8) into Eq. (1), we obtain:

$$u_t(x, t) = a^2 u_{xx}(x, t) - \lambda_0 [u(x, t) - \theta]$$
$$+ \sum_{i=1}^{N_s} \sum_{j=1}^{N_o} \alpha_i^j [u(\xi_j, t) - \beta_i^j] \delta(x - z_i(t)), x \in (0, l), t \in (0, T]. \tag{9}$$

Equations (9) belong to the class of loaded equations due to the participation of the values of the searched function $u(x, t)$ in them at the measurement points ξ_j [15]. For the corresponding initial-boundary-value problems, in [16–18] the conditions for the existence and uniqueness of their solution were studied, and numerical methods for their solution were proposed and studied.

In general, in the problem considered below, it is required to determine the feedback parameters $\alpha = \left((\alpha_i^j) \right) = \left(\alpha_1^1, \alpha_1^2, \ldots, \alpha_1^{N_o}, \ldots, \alpha_{N_s}^1, \alpha_{N_s}^2, \ldots, \alpha_{N_s}^{N_o}, \right)$, $\beta = \left((\beta_i^j) \right) = \left(\beta_1^1, \beta_1^2, \ldots, \beta_1^{N_o}, \ldots, \beta_{N_s}^1, \beta_{N_s}^2, \ldots, \beta_{N_s}^{N_o}, \right)$, $\xi = (\xi_j) = (\xi_1, \xi_2, \ldots, \xi_{N_o})$, $i = 1, 2, \ldots, N_s$, $j = 1, 2, \ldots, N_o$, taking into account restrictions (4) on the power of the sources, under which the objective functional will take the minimum possible value. Denote by the parameter vector $y = \left(\alpha_i^j, \beta_i^j, \xi_j \right) \in \mathbb{R}^n$, $n = N_o(2N_s + 1)$ optimized in the problem, which consists of: $N_o N_s$ parameters α_i^j, $N_o N_s$ parameters β_i^j and N_o parameters ξ_j. The objective functional (5), (6) of the problem under consideration is finally written as follows:

$$\mathcal{I}(y) = \int_B \int_\Theta I(y; b, \theta) \rho_B(b) \rho_\Theta(\theta) d\theta db, \tag{10}$$

$$I(y; b, \theta) = \int_0^l \mu(x) [u(x, T) - U(x)]^2 dx + \varepsilon \|y - \hat{y}\|_{\mathbb{R}^n}^2. \tag{11}$$

Here: $u(x, t) = u(x, t; y, b, \theta)$ is the solution of the initial-boundary-value value problem with respect to Eq. (9) with optimized parameters $y = \left(\alpha_i^j, \beta_i^j, \xi_j \right)$, initial condition $u(x, 0) = b$ and ambient temperature θ.

Restrictions (4) on the power of sources when using dependence (7) for feedback will turn into the following joint restrictions on the optimized parameters y and temperature at the measurement points $\xi_j \in [0, l], j = 1, 2, \ldots, N_o$.

$$\underline{q_i} \le \sum_{j=1}^{N_o} \alpha_i^j [u(\xi_j, t) - \beta_i^j] \le \overline{q_i}, \quad i = 1, 2, \ldots, N_s, \quad t \in [0, T]. \quad (12)$$

which we denote and write in the following equivalent form:

$$g_i(t; y) = |g_i^0(t; y)| - \frac{\overline{q_i} - \underline{q_i}}{2} \le 0, i = 1, 2, \ldots, N_s, t \in [0, T].$$

$$g_i^0(t; y) = \frac{\overline{q_i} + \underline{q_i}}{2} - \sum_{j=1}^{N_o} \alpha_i^j [u(\xi_j, t) - \beta_i^j]. \quad (13)$$

Problem (9), (2)–(4), (10), (11) considered below is a problem of parametric optimal control of objects with distributed parameters with feedback. The finite-dimensional vector $y = \left(\alpha_i^j, \beta_i^j, \xi_j \right) \in R^n$ is optimized. The features of the problem are: the loaded differential equation; participation in the equation Dirac δ-functions; the value of the objective functional is determined not by one solution of the initial-boundary-value problem, but by a bunch of solutions, provided that the initial condition and the ambient temperature of the take not one value, but a set of values, respectively, from the sets B and Θ; comparatively not very large for problems of synthesis of control systems with distributed parameters, the dimension of the resulting finite-dimensional optimization problem, determined by the double product of the number of sources and measurement points.

3 Approach and Formulas for the Numerical Solution of the Problem

By direct verification according to the definition of the convexity of the functional, it is easy to show that the objective functional of the original optimal control problem (1)–(6) without feedback is convex in $q(t)$. It is easy to show that the functional of the considered control problem (10), (11) with continuous feedback (8) is not convex in terms of the optimized feedback parameters y. The admissible range of parameters y defined by inequalities (12) is also not convex, which follows from the obvious, in the general case, non-linearity of the dependence of the solution of the initial-boundary-value $u(x, t; y, b, \theta)$ on the parameters $y = (\alpha, \beta, \xi)$, which implies the non-convexity of the considered problem of optimizing feedback parameters (8) as a whole. Nevertheless, the formulas obtained below for the components of the functional gradient can be used to numerically determine the locally optimal values of the feedback parameters or to locally refine any of their values given by an expert. It is clear that to find the optimal values of the parameters, known methods of global optimization can be used together with methods of local improvement of the values of parameters by first-order optimization methods using the approach to the numerical solution proposed below and the obtained formulas for calculating the gradient of the objective functional of the control problem by the feedback parameters.

For the numerical solution of problem (1)–(6), namely, finding the local minimum of the objective functional (10), (11), it is proposed to use the external penalty method to take into account constraints (13) [6]. Considering the possible multi-extremality of the problem due to its non-convexity, the above approach can be used to solve the problem using, for example, the "multistart" method, which uses various randomly selected starting points for the optimized parameter vector using algorithms for parallelizing the computational process.

We choose the penalty functional with respect to functional (10), (11) in the following form:

$$\mathcal{I}_\mathcal{R}(y) = \int_B \int_\Theta I(y; b, \theta)\rho_B(b)\rho_\Theta(\theta)d\theta db, \tag{14}$$

$$I_\mathcal{R}(y; b, \theta) = \int_0^l \mu(x)[u(x, T; y, b, \theta) - U(x)]^2 dx + \varepsilon \|y - \hat{y}\|_{\mathbb{R}^n}^2 + \mathcal{R}G(y),$$
$$G(y) = \sum_{i=1}^{N_s} \int_0^T [g_i^+(t; y)]^2 dt. \tag{15}$$

Here $\mathcal{R}$ is the penalty coefficient tending to $+\infty$, the function $g_i^+(t; y) = 0$, if $g_i^+(t; y) \le 0$, and $g_i^+(t; y) = g_i(t; y)$, if $g^i(t; y) > 0$.

We have the following theorem.

Theorem. The objective functional $\mathcal{I}_\mathcal{R}(y)$ of the problem (9), (2)–(4), (14), (15) for each given penalty coefficient $\mathcal{R}$ and continuous feedback (8) is differentiable with respect to the synthesized parameters $y = (\alpha, \beta, \xi)$ and the components of its gradient are determined by the formulas:

$$\frac{\partial \mathcal{I}_\mathcal{R}(y)}{\partial \alpha_i^j} = \int_B \int_\Theta \left\{ -\int_0^T \left(\psi(z_i(t), t) + 2\mathcal{R}g_i^+(t; y)\text{sgn}\left(g_i^0(t; y)\right) \right)\left[u(\xi_j, t) - \beta_i^j\right]dt \right.$$
$$\left. +2\left(\alpha_i^j - \hat{\alpha}_i^j\right) \right\} \rho_B(b)\rho_\Theta(\theta)d\theta db, \tag{16}$$

$$\frac{\partial \mathcal{I}_\mathcal{R}(y)}{\partial \beta_i^j} = \int_B \int_\Theta \left\{ \int_0^T \left(\alpha_i^j \psi(z_i(t), t) - 2\mathcal{R}g_i^+(t; y)\text{sgn}(g_i^0(t; y)) \right)dt + 2\left(\beta_i^j - \hat{\beta}_i^j\right) \right\}$$
$$\times \rho_B(b)\rho_\Theta(\theta)d\theta db, \tag{17}$$

$$\frac{\partial \mathcal{I}_\mathcal{R}(y)}{\partial \xi_j} = \int_B \int_\Theta \left\{ -\sum_{i=1}^{N_s} \int_0^T \left(\alpha_i^j \psi(z_i(t), t) + 2\mathcal{R}g_i^+(t; y)\text{sgn}(g_i^0(t; y)) \right)u_x(\xi_j, t)dt + \frac{\partial \mathcal{I}_\mathcal{R}(y)}{\partial \xi_j} \right.$$
$$= \int_B \int_\Theta \left\{ -\sum_{i=1}^{N_s} \int_0^T \left(\alpha_i^j \psi(z_i(t), t) + 2\mathcal{R}g_i^+(t; y)\text{sgn}(g_i^0(t; y)) \right)u_x(\xi_j, t)dt \right.$$
$$\left. +2\left(\xi_j - \hat{\xi}_j\right) \right\} \rho_B(b)\rho_\Theta(\theta)d\theta db,. \tag{18}$$

where $i = 1, 2, \ldots, N_s, j = 1, 2, \ldots, N_o$, $\psi(x, t) = \psi(x, t; y, b, \theta, \mathcal{R})$ with the current vector of parameters y, admissible initial condition $b \in B$, ambient temperature $\theta \in \Theta$ and penalty coefficient $\mathcal{R}$ is the solution of the following conjugate-boundary-value problem:

$$\psi_t(x, t) = -a^2 \psi_{xx}(x, t) + \lambda_0 \psi(x, t) - \sum_{j=1}^{N_o} \delta(x - \xi_j)$$
$$\times \sum_{i=1}^{N_c} \left(\alpha_i^j \psi(z_i(t), t) + 2\mathcal{R}g_i^+(t; y)\text{sgn}(g_i^0(t; y)) \right), x \in (0, l), t \in [0, T), \tag{19}$$

$$\psi(x, T) = -2\mu(x)(u(x, T) - U(x)), x \in [0, l], \tag{20}$$

$$\psi_x(0, t) = \lambda_1 \psi(0, t), \psi_x(l, t) = -\lambda_2 \psi(l, t), t \in [0, T]. \tag{21}$$

4 Numerical Experiments

The solution of the problem under consideration was carried out with the following values of the data involved in its formulation:

$$a = 1, l = 1, T = 1, \lambda_0 = 0.01, \lambda_1 = 0.001, N_s = 2, N_o = 4,$$
$$\mu(x) \equiv 1, U(x) = 10, x \in [0; 1], \underline{q_i} = -1, \overline{q_i} = 14, i = 1, 2,$$
$$B = [0.1; 0.2; 0.3], \rho_B(b) = 1/3, \Theta = [0.2; 0.3; 0.4], \rho_\Theta(\theta) = 1/3,$$
$$z_1(t) = 0.05 + 0.9\left(\sin^2(\pi t)\right), z_2(t) = 0.75 - 0.6\left(\sin^2(\pi t)\right), t \in (0; 1].$$

The penalty coefficient successively, starting from $\mathcal{R} = 5$, increased by 5 times for three times. The dimension of the vector of synthesized parameters y in this case is equal to $N_o(2N_s + 1) = 20$. The setsB, Θ and the corresponding integrals in the objective functional were discretized uniformly by three points. To approximate the Dirac δ-function, we used, as is easy to see, an everywhere smooth (differentiable) function:

$$\delta_\sigma(x; \check{z}) = \begin{cases} 0 & |x - \check{z}| > \sigma, \\ \frac{1}{2\sigma}\left[1 + \cos\left(\frac{x-\check{z}}{\sigma}\pi\right)\right], & |x - \check{z}| \leq \sigma. \end{cases}$$

In this case, for an arbitrary value σ,

$$\int_{\check{z}-\sigma}^{\check{z}+\sigma} \delta_\sigma(x; \check{z})dx = 1.$$

The value of σ was set equal to $3h_x$, where h_x is the step of the grid approximation of the segment $x \in [0; 1][0; 1]$, which was varied during numerical experiments. Such an approximation of the Dirac δ-function smoothes the dependence $\psi(x, t)$ of the solution of the conjugate-boundary-value problem (19)–(21), and hence the gradient of the objective functional (16)–(18), on the optimized coordinates of the location of the measurement points $\xi_j, j = 1, 2, \ldots, N_o$, which are the arguments δ-functions [7, 19].

An iterative procedure for minimizing the penalty functional by the gradient descent method for a given penalty coefficient $\mathcal{R}$ was built using the formula:

$$y^{k+1} = y^k - \alpha_k \text{grad}_y \mathcal{I}_\mathcal{R}(y^k), \quad k = 0, 1, \ldots,$$
$$\alpha_k = \arg\min_{\alpha \geq 0} \mathcal{I}_\mathcal{R}\left(y^k - \alpha \text{grad}_y \mathcal{I}_\mathcal{R}(y^k)\right), \tag{22}$$

with a stop criterion on argument increment $\|y^{k+1} - y^k\|_{R^{20}} \leq 0.0001$.

Table 1. Problem solutions obtained for two initial values y_1^0 and y_2^0.

	y^0			$\mathcal{I}_{\mathcal{R}}\left(y^0\right)$	y^*			$\mathcal{I}_{\mathcal{R}}(y^*)$	M^{it}
1	−0.1058	−0.2652	0.0194	5.0693	0.0147	−0.4523	0.0210	0.0002	45
	−0.4408	−0.0272	−0.312		−0.8643	0.4891	−0.7126		
	−0.2752	−0.2143	12.000		−0.5668	−0.4421	12.243		
	12.000	12.000	12.000		12.582	12.167	12.928		
	12.000	12.000	12.000		11.973	13.072	12.939		
	12.000	0.2537	0.5671		12.811	0.1564	0.4584		
	0.9244	0.7963			0.6272	0.8956			
2	−0.3542	−0.3123	−0.3460	2.7898	−0.2220	0.1870	−0.2608	0.0003	82
	−0.6856	−0.3571	−0.2619		−0.9727	−0.6362	0.3212		
	−0.2635	−0.4339	12.044		−0.2897	−0.6535	12.499		
	12.026	12.041	12.185		12.202	12.530	13.167		
	12.047	12.005	12.006		13.073	12.243	12.737		
	12.079	0.9283	0.3178		13.151	0.9067	0.2764		
	0.7433	0.3249			0.8592	0.0500			

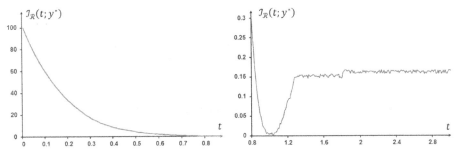

Fig. 1. Graphs of the function $\mathcal{I}_{\mathcal{R}}\left(t; y^*\right)$: the values of the objective functional calculated for y_1^* for the process time t.

One-dimensional minimization with respect to α in (22) was carried out using the golden section method. The implicit scheme of the grid method [20] was used to solve the direct and conjugate boundary-value problems, and the methods proposed in [17, 18] was used to take into account the loading of differential equations.

The regularization parameters ε and $\hat{y}$ at each value of the penalty coefficient $\mathcal{R}$ changed according to the algorithm proposed in [6], namely, ε decreased by a factor of 5, starting from $\varepsilon = 0.05$, and $\hat{y}$ at the beginning for each $\mathcal{R}$ were chosen to be zero, and then were equated y^* found in the previous step.

Table 1 shows the results of solving the problem obtained for two initial values $y^0 \in R^{20}$ of the iterative process (22). It can be seen from the table that the corresponding values of the parameters α, β and ξ obtained in this case differ significantly, but the values of the functional $\mathcal{I}_R(y)$ are quite small, and the number of iterations M^{it} differs little. Here it is possible that the objective functional is either multi-extremal or has a strong ravine structure.

On Fig. 1a, b shows the graphs of the function $\mathcal{I}_R(t; y^*)$ of the value of the objective functional, calculated with $y^* = y_1^*$ for the end time of the process t. The time $t = T = 1$ corresponds to the time interval $[0;1]$ for which the source synthesis problem was solved. Next, for $t > 1$, the process of heating the rod was observed using the synthesized vector of parameters y_1^*. Due to the relatively large values of $\mathcal{I}_R(t; y^*)$ at $t > 0.8$, its graph is divided into two using different scales along the ordinate axis. Figure 1.b shows that the heating control process at $t > 1.8$ has stabilized. This means that the value of the functional at $t > 1.8$, which characterizes the deviation of the current temperature state on the entire rod from the desired desired temperature $U(x) = 10$, $x \in [0; 1]$, is small, and therefore the heating control process has switched to the regularization process with feedback.

Figure 2 shows the results of calculating the temperature of the rod at $t = T = 1$ using the optimal feedback parameters given in the first row of Table 1 in the presence of noise in measurements (7). Noisy measurements $\hat{u}(\xi_j, t)$, $j = 1, 2, \ldots, N_o$, were determined by the formula:

$$\hat{u}(\xi_j, t) = u(\eta_j, t)[1 + \xi_j(t)\chi], j = 1, 2, \ldots, N_o, t \in [0, T],$$

where $\xi_j(t)$ are uniformly distributed over a function whose random values for each $t \in [0; T]$ were generated using the RAND program; χ noise level: $\chi = 0$ corresponds to no noise, $\chi = 0.01$ corresponds to 1% noise, $\chi = 0.03$ to 3% noise.

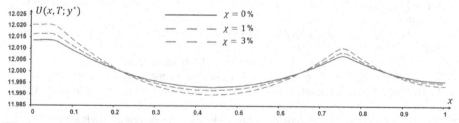

Fig. 2. Calculated rod temperature for $T = 1$ for the optimal feedback parameters shown in the first line of Table 1 under measurement noise $\chi = 0$ (1), $\chi = 0.01$ (2), $\chi = 0.03$ (3).

As can be seen from Fig. 2, the order of magnitude of the deviation from the desired state of the rod at $T = 1$ is quite consistent with the noise level, and the process of heating with feedback can be considered quite stable.

5 Conclusion

The paper proposes an approach to solving the problem of feedback control of the power of point sources of heating of a rod moving according to given rules and trajectories. In the problem to be optimized is also the location of the points of the current state of the process. To form the current values of the powers of each of the sources, it is proposed to use for them the formula of a linear dependence on the measured values of the temperature of the rod at the measured points. Thus, the original optimal control problem is reduced to finding a finite-dimensional vector of feedback parameters and placement of measuring points that optimize the given objective functional.

Formulas are obtained for the gradient components with respect to the parameters to be optimized, which allow efficient first-order optimization methods to be used for the numerical solution of the problem. The results of numerical experiments obtained on test initial data and their analysis are presented. In particular, an analysis was made of the influence of the temperature measurement error at measurement points on the quality of process control, namely, on the value of the objective functional.

The approach presented in the paper and the scheme for obtaining formulas can be extended to many other problems of optimal control of lumped sources in systems with distributed parameters, which are described by other types of initial-boundary-value problems, including those with a higher dimension of the spatial variable. The proposed approach can be easily generalized to the problems of controlling two-dimensional and three-dimensional technological processes arising in metallurgy, economics and other areas. The analogues obtained above those given in the article have no fundamental differences and are associated only with technical difficulties.

References

1. Lions, J.L., Lelong, P.: Contrôle optimal de systèmes gouvernés par des équations aux dérivées partielles (1968)
2. Deineka, V.S., Sergienko, I.V.: Optimal Control of Inhomogeneous Distributed Systems. Naukova Dumka, Kiev (2003)
3. Ray, W.H.: Advanced Process Control. McGraw-Hill Book Company (1981)
4. Egorov, A.I.: Principles of the Control Theory, p. 504. Fizmatlit (2004). (In Russ.)
5. Sirazetdinov, T.K.: Optimization of systems with distributed parameters. (No title) (1977). (In Russ.)
6. Vasil'ev, F.P.: Optimization Methods. Faktorial Press, Moscow (2002). (In Russ.)
7. Butkovskiy, A.G.: Methods of Control of Distributed Parameter Systems. Nauka, Moscow (1984). (In Russ.)
8. Butkovskiy, A.G., Pustylnikov, L.M.: The Theory of Mobile Control of Systems With Distributed Parameters. M. Nauka (1980). (In Russ.)
9. Utkin, V.I.: Sliding Conditions in Optimization and Control Problems. Nauka, Moscow (1981). (In Russ.)
10. Polyak, B.T., Khlebnikov, M.V., Rapoport, L.B.: Mathematical Theory of Automatic Control, p. 500. M. LENAND (2019). (In Russ.)
11. Sergienko, I.V., Deineka, V.S.: Optimal Control of Distributed Systems with Conjugation Conditions, vol. 75. Springer Science & Business Media (2005)

12. Lions, J.-L., Magenes E.: Problemes Aux Limites Non Homogenes at Application, vol. 1. Paris (1968)
13. Guliyev, S.Z.: Synthesis of zonal controls for a problem of heating with delay under nonseparated boundary conditions. Cybern. Syst. Anal. **54**(1), 110–121 (2018)
14. Aida-zade, K.R., Abdullaev, V.M.: Optimizing placement of the control points at synthesis of the heating process control. Autom. Remote. Control. **78**(9), 1585–1599 (2017)
15. Nakhushev, A.M.: Loaded Equations and their Application. Nauka, Moscow (2012). (In Russ.)
16. Alikhanov, A.A., Berezgov, A.M., Shkhanukov-Lafishev, M.X.: Boundary value problems for certain classes of loaded differential equations and solving them by finite difference methods. Comput. Math. Math. Phys. **48**(9), 1581–1590 (2008)
17. Abdullaev, V.M., Aida-Zade, K.R.: Optimization of loading places and load response functions for stationary systems. Comput. Math. Math. Phys. **57**(4), 634–644 (2017)
18. Aida-zade, K.R.: An approach for solving nonlinearly loaded problems for linear ordinary differential equations. Proc. Instit. Math. Mech. Natl. Acad. Sci. Azerbaijan **44**(2), 338–350 (2018)
19. Aida-zade, K.R., Bagirov, A.G.: On the problem of spacing of oil wells and control of their production rates. Autom. Remote. Control. **67**(1), 44–53 (2006)
20. Samarsky, A. A.: Theory of Difference Schemes. PML (1989). (In Russ.)

Design of Hybrid Control System for Nonaffine Plants

Anatoly Gaiduk⑩, Viacheslav Pshikhopov⑩, Mikhail Medvedev$^{(\boxtimes)}$ ⑩,
Vladislav Gissov, Ali Kabalan, and Evgeny Kosenko⑩

Southern Federal University, 105/42, Bolshaya Sadovaya St, Rostov-On-Don 344006, Russia
medvmihal@sfedu.ru

Abstract. The purpose of this article is to develop a design method that ensures the stability of the zero-equilibrium position of a closed nonaffine control system in a certain area. The objects described by a nonlinear system of differential equations with one control and one output are considered. A constraint is introduced, which consists in the differentiability of the right-hand sides of differential equations with respect to all state variables. The task of designing control in the form of a function of the setting action, state variables and control values at previous points in time is set. This problem is solved using a quasilinear model of the control object. In the quasilinear model, matrices and vectors are functions of the variables of the state of the control object. The control is found using an algebraic polynomial matrix method. This article presents the expressions for calculating the control in accordance with the polynomial-matrix method. Based on the given coefficients of the desired polynomial, as a result of solving an algebraic system of equations, coefficients are found that are a function of control and state variables. The fulfillment of the controllability condition guarantees the existence of a solution of the specified algebraic system.

Keywords: Nonlinear System · Nonaffine Control Plant · Quasilinear Model · Polynomial Matrix Method · Controllability Condition · Static Error

1 Introduction

Nonlinear control plants are characterized by a wide variety of nonlinear characteristics. In particular, this leads to one of the difficult tasks of control theory – designing the control systems for nonaffine control objects [1–4]. In the equations of such objects, control enters nonlinearly, and the influence of the control action on the derivatives of the state variables of the plant is not additive. Such plants include underwater vehicles, surface vessels, aircraft, mobile robots, etc. [2, 4, 5].

Various approaches are used to design the control systems for nonaffine objects. Most often, these include a block approach with discontinuous controls [2], systems with sliding modes [3], the maximum principle, leading to a program piecewise constant control or optimal control in terms of speed [6, 7].

The article [2] considers the problem of designing a control for nonaffine plants under the uncertainty of mathematical models describing them. It is noted that the solution of

A. Ronzhin et al. (Eds.): ICR 2023, LNAI 14214, pp. 208–220, 2023.
https://doi.org/10.1007/978-3-031-43111-1_19

this problem by the methods of structural synthesis [8] or backstepping [9] leads to complex expressions for the obtained controls. In this regard, the paper [2] proposes a method based on sliding modes [10–12] that makes it possible to obtain a control with a simpler structure. In the article [12], the calculation expressions for the control calculated from the output are obtained, and the boundedness of the error and state variables is shown. A significant disadvantage of systems with a variable structure is the need for high-frequency switching of drives in saturation modes. Such modes require the use of special drives and can be difficult to implement, because the switching frequency in such systems is limited by the inertial properties of the drives.

In [6, 7], a method for controlling plants with a block structure [11] is proposed, for which, based on the maximum principle [13, 14], a piecewise constant control is obtained, which is then approximated by a continuous function close to it. This allows maintaining the robustness of the system and avoiding the use of sliding modes. In [6, 7], the controllability and stability conditions were also obtained in the form of inequalities corresponding to [15]. However, in [6, 7] the question of the influence of the approximation of the "signum" function by a continuous function on the degree of optimality of the resulting system is not studied. The control is obtained in a continuous form and its implementation in digital form is not considered.

In this article, to solve the problem of designing control systems for nonaffine plants, it is proposed to apply an algebraic polynomial-matrix design method based on quasi-linear models [16]. These models are easily constructed by an analytical or numerical method [17], if the nonlinearities of the plant are differentiable, and make it possible to find a control that ensures stability, the required speed, and other indicators of the quality of the control process. It will be shown below that this control is easily implemented using digital automation tools, without loss of accuracy and quality of the nonlinear control system. As a result, a hybrid control system is formed, which includes a continuous nonaffine control plant and a discrete control device.

2 Formulation of the Problem

Let a nonlinear nonaffine plant with one control and one controlled variable be described by a differential equation of the form:

$$\dot{x} = \zeta(x, u, f). \tag{1}$$

where $x = [x_1 \, x_2 \ldots x_n]$ is the n-vector of state variables; $\zeta(x,u,f)$ is the nonlinear n-vector function, differentiable with respect to all variables x_i, $i = 1, 2, \ldots, n$, as well as with respect to u and f, and $\zeta(0,0,0) = 0$; u is the control; f is the external disturbance; y is the controlled variable; $\psi(x)$ is the scalar function, also differentiable in all variables x_i; the state vector x is assumed to be measurable; and $\mathbf{0}$ is the null n-vector.

The task is to determine the control as a function of the setting action $g = g(t)$, the state vector x and, possibly, the control. This control should ensure the stability of the system; zero value of static error $\varepsilon(t) = g(t)\text{-}y(t)$ at $t \to \infty$. The duration of the transient process t_{pp} according to the setting effect $g(t) = g_0 1(t)$ under zero initial conditions should not exceed the specified value of t_{pp}^*. Here g_0 is the value at which the control module $u = u(x)$ does not exceed the allowable values.

Note that since the control plant is nonlinear, it is impossible to specify in advance the possibility of ensuring the stability of the position $x = 0$ of the control system as a whole or in some area of its state space, since this significantly depends on the properties of nonlinearities from Eq. (1) of each specific object [16, 17].

3 Solution of the Problem

Since the vector function $\zeta(x,u,f)$ is differentiable, moreover, $\zeta(0,0,0) = 0$ Eqs. (1) can be represented by the following quasilinear model:

$$\dot{x} = A(x)x + b(x, u)u + b_f(x, u, f)f, \qquad y = c^T(x)x, \qquad (2)$$

where:

$$A(x) = \begin{bmatrix} a_{11}(x) \ a_{12}(x) \ \ldots \ a_{1n}(x) \\ a_{21}(x) \ a_{22}(x) \ \ldots \ a_{2n}(x) \\ \ldots \quad \ldots \quad \ldots \quad \ldots \\ a_{n1}(x) \ a_{n2}(x) \ \ldots \ a_{nn}(x) \end{bmatrix}, , b(x, u) = \begin{bmatrix} b_1(x, u) \\ b_2(x, u) \\ \ldots \\ b_n(x, u) \end{bmatrix}$$

$$b_f(x, u, f) = \begin{bmatrix} b_{1f}(x, u, f) \\ b_{2f}(x, u, f) \\ \ldots \\ b_{nf}(x, u, f) \end{bmatrix}, c^T(x) = [c_1(x), c_2(x), \ldots, c_n(x)], \qquad (3)$$

The functional coefficients in (2) and (3) when obtained by the analytical method [17, 18] are determined by the expressions:

$$a_{ij}(x) = \int_0^1 \zeta'_{ij}(x_1, \ldots, x_{j-1}, \theta x_j, \mathbf{0}_{n-j}, 0, 0)d, \theta, \cdot b_i(x, u) = \int_0^1 \zeta'_{iu}(x, \theta u, 0)d\theta,$$

$$b_{1f}(x, u, f) = \int_0^1 \zeta'_{if}(x, u, \theta f)d\theta, \cdot c_j(x) = \int_0^1 (\psi'_j x_1, \ldots, x_{j-1}, \theta x_j, \mathbf{0}_{n-j})d\theta,$$

$$(4)$$

where $\zeta_{ij}'(x, u, f) = \partial \zeta_i(x, u, f)/\partial x$; $\zeta_{iu}'(x, u, f) = \partial \zeta_i(x, u, f)/\partial u$; $\zeta_{if}'(x, u, f) = \partial \zeta_i(x, u, f)/\partial f$; $\psi_j'(x) = \partial \psi_i(x)/\partial x \cdot \psi_{j}'(x) = \partial \psi_j(x)/\partial x$; and 0n-j is the sequence 0, ..., 0, containing $n - j$ zeros.

We emphasize that the quasilinear model (2) – (4) describes the nonlinear plant (1) exactly, i.e. with the preservation of all its nonlinear features. Expressions for determining the coefficients from the expressions (2) and (3) by the numerical method can be found in [17]; however, in this case, the model (2) – (3) becomes discrete-continuous and describes the nonlinear plant (1) approximately. In the expressions (2) – (3), the nonaffinity in control of the considered object (1) is manifested in the fact that the input vector $b(x,u)$ depends on the control u.

As can be seen, the Eqs. (2) are similar in form to the equations of one-dimensional linear control plants [19], except that the matrix and vectors in these equations are nonlinear functions of plant variables, which is why they were called a quasilinear model [20, 21].

Note that for $f = f(t) = 0$ and $\partial^2 \zeta_{iu}(x, u)/\partial u^2 = 0$ vector $b(x)$, as well as the matrix $A(x)$, depend only on the state vector. In the Western literature, such models (2) are called state-dependent coefficient (SDC) [22, 23], while the method of constructing the matrix $A(x)$ and vector $b(x)$ is usually not covered in such works.

As in the linear case, the design problem here has a solution if the quasilinear model (2) satisfies the controllability condition, which has the form:

$$|\det U(x, u)| \geq \zeta_1 > 0, \quad x \in U, \quad u \in I_u, \tag{5}$$

where $\zeta_1 > 0$ is some not too small number; Ω_U is some region of the state space R^n, which includes the point $x = \mathbf{0}$, and in which the condition (5) is satisfied; I_u is the interval of allowable control values u; and the functional matrix of controllability $U(x,u)$ $U(x, u)$ is determined by the expression

$$U(x, u) = \left[b(x, u) A(x) b(x, u) \ldots A^{n-1}(x) b(x, u) \right]. \tag{6}$$

The design of a control system for a nonaffine plant (1) based on a quasilinear model (2) – (4) under condition (5) is conveniently carried out using the algebraic polynomial-matrix method [16], in which the control law is sought in the form:

$$u = u(x) = h_0 g - h^T(x)x = h_0 g - [h_1(x)x_1 + h_2(x)x_2 + \ldots + h_n(x)x_n]. \tag{7}$$

i.e. in the form of influence and state control [24].

To derive the calculated relations in this case, we substitute the control (7) into the first Eq. (2), taking into account the second Eq. (2), and present similar terms; as a result we get:

$$\dot{x} = D(x)x + b(x, u)h_0 g + b_f(x, u, f)f, \, y = c^T(x)x, \tag{8}$$

where:

$$D(x) = A(x) - b(x, u)h^T(x). \tag{9}$$

The characteristic polynomial $D(p,x) = \det[pE - D(x)]$ of the matrix $D(x)$ (9) by formula (A.25) from [25] can be represented as

$$D(p, x) = A(p, x) + \sum_{i=1}^{n} h_i(x)V_i(p, x, u), A(p, x) = \det\left[pE - A(x)\right]. \tag{10}$$

where:

$$V_i(p, x, u) = e_i\left(adj\left[pE - A(x)\right]\right)b(x, u) = \sum_{i=0}^{n-1} v_{ij}(x, u)p^j, i = \overline{1, n}, \tag{11}$$

e_i is the i-th row of the identity $n \times n$-matrix E. The dependence of the coefficients $v_{ij}(x,u)$ of polynomials (11) on the control u is also a consequence of the nonaffinity in control of the plant (1).

Note. The matrix $D(x)$ (9) is included in the equation of the quasilinear model (8) of the closed system (1), (7), but for brevity, we will call it the system matrix.

In accordance with the algebraic polynomial-matrix method, the functional polynomial $D(p,x)$ in the first expression (10) is replaced by the Hurwitz polynomial $D^*(p)$, which has constant, real and different roots, i.e. λ_j^*, i.e.

$$D^*(p) = \prod_{j=1}^{n} \left(p - \lambda_j^*\right) = p^n + \delta_{n-1}^* p^{n-1} + \ldots + \delta_1^* p + \delta_0^*, \tag{12}$$

where: $\lambda_j^* < -\zeta_2 < 0;\ \left|\lambda_j^* - \lambda_l^*\right| > \zeta_3, j \neq l, j,l = 1,2,\ldots,n, \zeta_2 > 0, \zeta_3 > 0$ [18, 20].

Having performed the indicated replacement in the equality (10) and moving the polynomial $A(p,x)$ to its left side, we obtain a polynomial equation with respect to the coefficients $h_i(x)$ from the expression (7):

$$\sum_{i=1}^{n} h_i(x)V_i(p, x, u) = R(p, x), \tag{13}$$

$$R(p, x) = D^*(p) - A(p, x) = \sum_{j=0}^{n-1} \rho_j(x)p^j. \tag{14}$$

It is advisable to obtain the solution of the polynomial Eq. (13) by passing to the equivalent system of algebraic equations [16, 20], which in this case has the form:

$$\begin{bmatrix} v_{1,0} & v_{2,0} & \ldots & v_{n,0} \\ v_{1,1} & v_{2,1} & \ldots & v_{n,1} \\ \ldots & \ldots & \ldots & \ldots \\ v_{1,n-1} & v_{2,n-1} & \ldots & v_{n,n-1} \end{bmatrix} \begin{bmatrix} h_1 \\ h_2 \\ \ldots \\ h_n \end{bmatrix} = \begin{bmatrix} \rho_0 \\ \rho_1 \\ \ldots \\ \rho_{n-1} \end{bmatrix}. \tag{15}$$

Note that many coefficients in system (15) in this case are functions of the vector x and control u, but for brevity, the arguments of these coefficients in (15) are omitted. We also emphasize that the existence of a solution to system (15) is guaranteed by the fulfillment of the controllability condition (5).

The solution of system (15) is determined by the vector of coefficients from (7):

$$h(x, u) = [h_1(x, u)\ h_2(x, u)\ \ldots\ h_n(x, u)], \tag{16}$$

which in the case of a nonaffine plant can be functions not only of the vector x, but also of the control u. Therefore, the system matrix can also depend on the control, i.e. in the general case, it has the form $D(p,x,u)$. Nevertheless, its characteristic polynomial $D(p,x,u)$ is equal to the polynomial $D^*(p)$ (12), i.e. the roots of the polynomial $D(p,x,u)$ are constant, distinct, real, and negative. Therefore, it follows from the theorem proved in [21] that there is some neighborhood $\Omega_0 \in \Omega_u$ of the equilibrium position of system (8) n, which the following condition is satisfied:

$$\lim_{t \to \infty} x(t, x_0) = 0, \forall x_0 \subset \Omega_0, x \in \Omega_x. \tag{17}$$

Here $x(t, x_0)$ is the solution of the free system (8), i.e. at $g(t) = f(t) = 0$; x_0 is the vector of initial conditions for this solution.

It follows from condition (17) and Eq. (8) that in the steady state at $f(t) = 0$ and $g(t) = g_0 1(t)$ the following equality takes place:

$$0 \stackrel{\circ}{=} D\left(x^\circ, u_g^\circ\right)x^\circ + b\left(x^\circ, u_g^\circ\right)h_0 g_0. \tag{18}$$

From here, taking into account the second equality (8) and determining the deviation of the system $\varepsilon = g - y$, we derive the following expressions:

$$x^\circ = -D^{-1}\left(x^\circ, u_g^\circ\right)b\left(x^\circ, u_g^\circ\right)h_0 g_0, \quad y^\circ = -c^T D^{-1}\left(x^\circ, u_g^\circ\right)b\left(x^\circ, u_g^\circ\right)h_0 g_0,$$

$$\varepsilon^\circ = \left[1 + c^T(x^\circ)D^{-1}\left(x^\circ, u_g^\circ\right)b\left(x^\circ, u_g^\circ\right)h_0\right]g_0. \tag{19}$$

In equalities (18), (19) x^0, y^0, ε^0 are the steady-state values of the corresponding variables. From (19) it follows that the steady value of the controlled variable of the nonlinear system (8) may have a non-zero value, and its error ε^0 can be provided equal to zero, if only the following condition is met:

$$1 + c^T(x)D^{(-1)}(x)b(x, u) \neq 0. \tag{20}$$

When condition (20) is met, to ensure the zero value of the static error for the setting action $g(t) = g_0 1(t)$, the coefficient h_0 from the expression (7) should be equal to:

$$h_0(x, u) = -1/c^T(x)D^{-1}(x, u)b(x, u). \tag{21}$$

The fulfillment of condition $\varepsilon^0 = 0$ n determining the coefficient $h_0(x,u)$ by equality (21) is due, first of all, to the fact that for all x and u the matrix $D(x,u)$ (9) has an inverse, and secondly, due to condition (16) in the steady state $x(t) \to x^0$, and $u(t) \to u^0$, respectively.

The condition (20) and equality (21) can be simplified if we take into account that $D^{-1}(x,u) = [\text{adj}D(x,u)]/\text{det}D(x,u)$. When designing nonlinear Hurwitz systems by the algebraic polynomial-matrix method, for all values of the vector $x = x(t)$ and control $u(t)$ the condition $D(p,x,u) = \det[pE - D(x,u)] = D^*(p)$ is satisfied. Therefore, considering equality (12) and the properties of the determinant, we have the equality $\text{det}D(x,u) = D(p,x,u)_{p=0} = (-1)^n \delta_0^*$. Therefore, the denominator in equality (21) can be represented as: $(-1)^n c^T(x)[\text{adj}D(x,u)]b(x,u)/\delta_0^*$. . On the other hand, according to (9), $D(x,u) = A(x) - b(x,u) h^T(x,u)$, therefore, in accordance the with expression (A.26) from [25],

$$\left[\text{adj}D(x, u)\right]b(x, u) = \left\{\text{adj}\left[A(x) - b(x, u)h^T(x, u)\right]\right\}b(x, u) =$$

$$= \left[\text{adj}A(x)\right]b(x, u). \tag{22}$$

Here, adj denotes the adjoint matrix [26].

From the foregoing and relations (21), (22) it follows that the equality $\varepsilon^0 = 0$ at $g(t) = g_0 1(t)$ can be ensured if only:

$$h_0(x, u) = (-1)^{n+1}\delta_0^*/\gamma(x, u), \gamma(x, u) \neq 0, x \in \Omega_x, u \in I_u, \tag{23}$$

$$\gamma(x, u) = c^T(x)\big[\mathrm{adj}A(x)\big]b(x, u). \tag{24}$$

In the case of linear plants described by a system of equations $x = Ax + \dot{b}u;\ y = c^T x$, the value $\gamma = (-1)^{(n-1)}K_{ob}\,\mathrm{det}A$, where K_{ob} is the transmission coefficient of the channel $u \to y$. Obviously in the nonlinear case $\gamma(x,u)$ has the same meaning, but in this case, it is a nonlinear function.

Assuming condition $\gamma(x,u) \neq 0$ to be satisfied and substituting the obtained coefficients (16) and (23) into expression (7), we obtain a continuous control:

$$u = \frac{(-1)^{n+1}\delta_0^*}{\gamma(x, u)}g - h^T(x, u)x,\ \gamma(x, u) \neq 0,\ x \in \Omega_x,\ u \in I_u, \tag{25}$$

As a continuous control, (25), of course, is physically unrealizable. However, if on the left side of this expression the control $u = u(x(t))$ is replaced by the control u_k, $k = 1, 2, 3, \ldots$, then with a sufficiently small T, with virtually no loss of quality, the vector $x(t)$ and control $u(x)$ on the right sides of the above expressions can be replaced by x_k and u_{k-1}, respectively, assuming $u_0 = u(0) = 0$. In particular, the expression (25) in this case will have the form:

$$u_k = \frac{(-1)^{n+1}\delta_0^*}{\gamma(x_k, u_{k-1})}g_{k-1} - h^T(x_k, u_{k-1})x_k,\ \gamma(x_k, u_{k-1}) \neq 0,\ x_k \in \Omega_x,\ u_k \in I_u, \tag{26}$$

where, with accordance to (24),

$$\gamma(x_k, u_{k-1}) = c^T(x_k)\big[\mathrm{adj}A(x_k)\big]b(x_k, u_{k-1}),\ k = 1, 2, 3, \ldots \tag{27}$$

The discrete control, defined by expressions (26), (27), is obviously physically realizable by some digital control device. In this case, the resulting nonlinear control system (1), (26), (27) is practically continuous, since rather small values of the sampling period T are usually required, which are typical for solving non-rigid differential equations on a computer using standard programs.

It follows from the above expressions that the main feature of the he nonaffine systems (8) synthesized by the algebraic polynomial-matrix method based on the approach proposed here is the constancy of the coefficients of the Hurwitz characteristic polynomial $D(p,x,u)$ of the system matrix $D(x,u)$ (9). As noted above, for the stability of the equilibrium position of such nonlinear systems at $x(t,x_0) \in \Omega_u$, $u \in I_u$, $x_0 \subset \Omega_0 \in \Omega_u$ $\in R^n$ it is sufficient that all the roots of the indicated Hurwitz polynomial be real and different.

Let us show the effectiveness of the proposed approach using a numerical example.

4   Example of Control Design and Simulation Results

Let's design a control system for the direction of movement (course) of a surface vessel moving at a constant longitudinal speed. To change the course of the vessel, a hydrodynamic steering element is used [2]. The process of controlling the direction of movement of the vessel is described by the equations:

$$\dot{x}_1 = x_1,\ \dot{x}_2 = u + u^3,\ y = x_1 + 0.5x_2^3, \tag{28}$$

where x_1, x_2 are the state variables, u is the control, and y is the controlled variable (vessel's course). In this case, if $g = g_0 1(t)$ then the condition $\varepsilon^0 = g_0 - y^0 = 0$ must be satisfied, and the duration of transient processes when changing course should not exceed 2 s.

Solution. This plant is nonaffine, since the control enters its equations in a nonlinear way, so we will use the proposed method. First, the quasilinear model (2), (3) of the plant (28) is found:

$$\dot{x} = \begin{bmatrix} 0 & 1 \\ 0 & 0 \end{bmatrix} x + \begin{bmatrix} 0 \\ 1 + u^2 \end{bmatrix}, y = \begin{bmatrix} 1 & 0.5x \end{bmatrix} x, \tag{29}$$

where $x = [x_1 \ x_2]^T$ and the controllability of the system (29) is checked under the conditions (5), (6):

$$\det U = \det \begin{bmatrix} 0 & 1 + u^2 \\ 1 + u^2 & 0 \end{bmatrix} = -(1 + u^2)^2,$$

It follows from this that the controllability condition (5) is obviously satisfied in the entire space R^n, i.e. the area $\in \Omega_u = R^2$. It follows that the designed nonlinear system will have one equilibrium position $x = 0$, i.e. instead of the words "the equilibrium position of the system is stable or unstable" one can simply say "the system is stable or unstable". By (10), (11) and (29) we determine the polynomials:

$$A(p) = \det \begin{bmatrix} p & -1 \\ 0 & p \end{bmatrix} = p^2,$$

$$[adj(pE - A)]b(u) = \begin{bmatrix} p & -1 \\ 0 & p \end{bmatrix} \begin{bmatrix} 0 \\ 1 + u^2 \end{bmatrix} = \begin{bmatrix} 1 + u^2 \\ (1 + u^2)p \end{bmatrix},$$

$$V_1(u) = \begin{bmatrix} 1 & 0 \end{bmatrix} \begin{bmatrix} 1 + u^2 \\ (1 + u^2)p \end{bmatrix} = 1 + u^2,$$

$$V_2(u) = \begin{bmatrix} 0 & 1 \end{bmatrix} \begin{bmatrix} 1 + u^2 \\ (1 + u^2)p \end{bmatrix} = (1 + u^2)p, \tag{30}$$

and the value

$$\gamma(x, u) = \begin{bmatrix} 1 & 0.5x_2^2 \end{bmatrix} \begin{bmatrix} 0 & -1 \\ 0 & 0 \end{bmatrix} \begin{bmatrix} 0 \\ 1 + u^2 \end{bmatrix} = -(1 + u^2). \tag{31}$$

As can be seen, the value $(x, u) \neq 0$ for all x and u. Therefore, the design problem has a solution. In this case $n = 2$, therefore, in accordance with (7), the continuous control has the form:

$$u(x) = h_0 g - [h_1 x_1 + h_2 x_2]. \tag{32}$$

To determine its coefficients, a second-order Hurwitz polynomial $D^*(p) = p^2 + \delta_1^* p + \delta_0^*$ is formed, the roots of which satisfy conditions (12), and the difference $R(p) =$

$p^2 + \delta_1 p + \delta_0 - p^2 = \delta_1 p + \delta_0$ is found from (14). Based on the coefficients of polynomials (30) and $R(p)$, the system (15) is formed:

$$\begin{bmatrix} 1 + u^2 & 0 \\ 0 & 1 + u^2 \end{bmatrix} \begin{bmatrix} h_1 \\ h_2 \end{bmatrix} = \begin{bmatrix} \delta_0^* \\ \delta_1^* \end{bmatrix}.$$

The solution of this system leads to the expressions: $h_1(u) = \delta_0^*/(1 + u^2)$, $h_2(u) = \delta_1^*/(1 + u^2)$. . The expression (23) determines the coefficient $h_0(x, u) = \delta_0^*/(1 + u^2)$, which allows using (32) to write down the continuous control $u(x) = (\delta_0^* g - \delta_0^* x_1 - \delta_1^* x_2)/(1 + u^2)$. This expression, taking into account the definition of $\varepsilon = g$-y and the second equality (28) $y = x_1 + 0.5x_2^3$, can be represented as follows:

$$u(x) = \left[\delta_0^* + \left(0.5\delta_0^* x_2^2 - \delta_1^* \right) x_2 \right] / \left(1 + u^2 \right).$$

In this case, the implemented discrete control is described by the expression:

$$u_k = \frac{\left[\delta_0^* \varepsilon k + \left(0.5\delta_0^* x_{2,k}^2 - \delta_1^* \right) x_{2,k} \right]}{\left(1 + u_{k-1}^2 \right)}, k = 1, 2, 3, \ldots . \tag{33}$$

where $\varepsilon_k = g_k - y_k$. Let's pay attention to the fact that the system was designed with the symbolic coefficients δ_j^*. This makes it possible to study the dependence of the properties of control systems designed using the algebraic polynomial-matrix method, including non-affine plants, both on the sampling period T and on the values of the roots of the characteristic polynomial $D(p,x,u)$ of the system matrix $D(x,u)$ by simulation.

In this case, to determine the coefficients δ_j^* we use a correlation that connects the moduli of the real roots δ_j^* of the Hurwitz characteristic polynomial $D(p,x,u)$ of the system matrix with the desired duration of the transient processes t_{pp}^* of the synthesized system:

$$\min \left| \lambda_j^* \right| \geq (5 \div 7)/t_{tr}^*, \tag{34}$$

which often used in the synthesis of linear control systems. For a given $t_{pp}^* = 2$ s from (33) it follows: $\min \left| \lambda_j^* \right| \geq (5 \div 7)/2 = 2.5 \div 3.5$. The values of the roots adopted for modeling and the coefficients corresponding to them are given in Table 1.

Table 1. The values of the roots adopted for modeling

Variant	λ_1^*	λ_2^*	δ_0^*	δ_1^*
1	−0.6	−2	1.2	2.6
2	−1.5	−3	4.5	4.5
3	−3	−6	18	9

The simulation was carried out in MATLAB under various initial conditions $x_0 = [0\ 0]^T$; $x_0 = [2\ \text{-}1]^T$; $x_0 = [\text{-}2\ 3]^T$, setting step action $g = g_0 1(t)$ at $g_0 = 0,1,5$ and sampling period $T \in [0.001; 0.02; 0.05]$ s. Some simulation results are presented in Figs. 1–3.

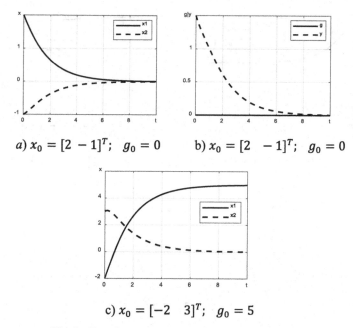

a) $x_0 = [2 \ -1]^T; \quad g_0 = 0$ b) $x_0 = [2 \ -1]^T; \quad g_0 = 0$

c) $x_0 = [-2 \ 3]^T; \quad g_0 = 5$

Fig. 1. Transient processes at small modules of roots.

Figure 1 shows transient processes for the first version of the roots of the polynomial $D(p,x,u)$ and $T = 0.05$ s. The state variables of the system also have a damping character for other values of the vector of initial conditions x_0 and period T.

As can be seen, in this case the nonaffine system is stable for all values of T, up to $T = 0.05$ s. The steady value of the controlled variable y is exactly equal to the setting value. This follows from Fig. 1c, since at $x_2 = 0$ this variable is in accordance with the second Eq. (28) $y = x_1$.

With an increase in the modules of the roots of the polynomial $D(p,x,u)$, the stability margin of the designed system decreases. On Fig. 2. Transient processes are shown for the second variant of the values of the roots of the polynomial $D(p,x,u)$ given in Table 1, as well as for different values of the vector x_0 and period T.

As seen in Fig. 2, in this case the designed system remains stable only at $T \leq 0.02$. In a stable system, the system error ε^0 at $g = g_0 1(t)$ is also equal to zero, i.e. $\varepsilon^0 = 0$. Based on the graphs shown in Fig. 1 and Fig. 2, we can conclude that the duration of transient processes t_{pp} of stable nonaffine systems designed on the basis of the proposed approach, in the first approximation, corresponds to dependence (33). Indeed, according to this relation, in the first variant of the roots $t_{pp} = 3/0.6 = 5$ s, and in the second $t_{pp} = 3/1.5 = 2$ c. These values obviously correspond to the duration of transient processes, the graphs of which are shown in Fig. 1(a, b, c), Fig. 2a, and Fig. 2c.

The conclusion that with an increase in the modules of the roots of the polynomial $D(p,x,u)$ the stability margin of the system decreases is confirmed by the transient processes obtained with the third variant of the roots of the polynomial $D(p,x,u)$, shown in

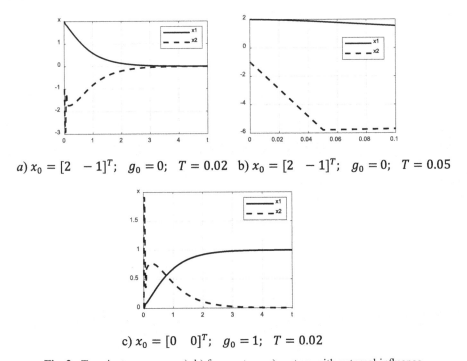

$a)\ x_0 = [2\ \ -1]^T;\ \ g_0 = 0;\ \ T = 0.02$ $b)\ x_0 = [2\ \ -1]^T;\ \ g_0 = 0;\ \ T = 0.05$

$c)\ x_0 = [0\ \ 0]^T;\ \ g_0 = 1;\ \ T = 0.02$

Fig. 2. Transient processes: $a)$, b) free system; c) system with external influence.

Table 1. The corresponding graphs for $x_{10} = -2$, $x_{20} = 1$, $g_0 = 0$ and $T = 0.001\ s$ are shown in Fig. 3.

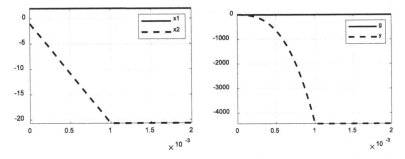

Fig. 3. Transient processes at "large modules" of roots of the polynomial $D(p,x)$.

Based on the simulation results obtained, the following conclusions can be drawn. The roots of the characteristic polynomial of the system matrix have the greatest influence on the stability of the designed nonaffine system. The smaller the modules of the roots of this polynomial, the greater the allowable sampling period.

5   Conclusion

The proposed approach makes it possible to obtain stable Hurwitz control systems for nonaffine plants using the algebraic polynomial-matrix method for sufficiently small periods of discretization of the variables of the control plant and small modules of the roots of the characteristic polynomial of the matrix of a closed system in its quasilinear model. The area of attraction of the equilibrium position of a closed system is determined by the area of the state space of the plant, in which the condition of controllability of the quasilinear model of the plant is satisfied. In this case, the control is formed by the computing device on the basis of previous control values, as well as discrete values of the measured variables of the object and the setting action.

The proposed approach can be applied in design of control systems for nonaffine objects for various purposes. In the future, it is proposed to extend the obtained results to the case of incomplete information about the state variables of control plants and plants with external disturbances.

Acknowledgements. This work has been supported by the grant of the Southern Federal University No. SP02/S4_0708Prioritet_06.

References

1. Zhang, J., Zhu, Q., Wu, X., Li, Y.: A generalized indirect adaptive neural networks back-stepping control procedure for a class of non-affine nonlinear systems with pure-feedback prototype. Neurocomputing **121**(9), 131–139 (2013)
2. Pshikhopov, V.Kh., Medvedev, M.Yu., Gaiduk, A.R., Fedorenko, R.V., Krukhmalev, V.A., Gurenko, B.V.: Position-Trajectory Control System for Unmanned Robotic Airship. In: The 19th World Congress the International Federation of Automatic Control, pp. 8953–8958. IFAC Proceeding, Cape Town, South Africa (2014)
3. Zhou, J., Li, X.: Finite-Time Mode Control Design for Unknown Nonaffine Pure-Feedback Systems. Mathematical Problems in Engineering (2015)
4. Liu, Y.-J., Wang, W.: Adaptive fuzzy control for a class of uncertain nonaffine nonlinear systems. Inf. Sci. **177**(18), 3901–3917 (2007)
5. Pshikhopov, V., Medvedev, M., Kostjukov, V., Houssein, F., Kadhim, A.: Trajectory planning algorithms in two-dimensional environment with obstacles. Info. Autom. **21**(3), 459–492 (2022)
6. Pshikhopov, V., Medvedev, M.: Multi-loop adaptive control of mobile objects in solving trajectory tracking tasks. Autom. Remote. Control. **81**(11), 2078–2093 (2020)
7. Pshikhopov, V., Medvedev, M.: Block design of robust control for a class of dynamic systems by direct lyapunov method. J. Mechan. Eng. Autom. **2**, 154–162 (2012)
8. Pshikhopov, V., Medvedev, M., Kupovikh G., Shibanov V.: Position control of mobile robots with multi-contour adaptation. In: Proc. of 18th IEEE International Conference on Autonomous Robot Systems and Competitions (ICARSC). Torres Vedras, Portugal (2018)
9. Kristic, M., Kanellakopoulos, I., Kokoyovic, P.V.: Nonlinear and Adaptive Control Design. Wiley, New York (1995)
10. Petrov, B.N., Emel'yanov, S.V., Utkin, V.I.: Principles for the construction of invariant automatic-control systems with variable structure. Soviet Physics Doklady **154**(6), 1294–1296 (1964)

11. Krasnova, S.A., Utkin, V.A., Miheev, Y.: Cascade design of state observers. Autom. Remote. Control. **62**(2), 207–226 (2001)
12. Druzhinina, M.V., Nikiforov, V.O., Fradkov, A.L.: Methods of nonlinear adaptive control with respect to output. Autom. Remote. Control. **57**(2), 153–176 (1996)
13. Pontryagin, L.S., Boltyansky, V.G., Gamkrelidze, R.V., Mikchenko, E.F.: Mathematical theory of the optimal processes. Fizmatgiz, Moscow (1961)
14. Boltjansky, V.G.: Mathematical methods of the optimal control. Nauka, Moscow (1969)
15. Pyatnickiy, E.S.: Controllability of lagrange systems with limited controls. Autom. Remote. Control. **12**, 29–37 (1996)
16. Gaiduk, A.R.: Towards design of quasilinear Gurvits control systems. SPIIRAN Proceedings **18**(3), 678–705 (2019)
17. Gaiduk, A.R.: Numerical design method of quasilinear models for nonlinear objects. Mekhatronika, Avtomatizatsiya, Upravlenie. **22**(6), 283–290 (2021)
18. Gaiduk, A.R.: Nonlinear control systems design by transformation method. Mekhatronika, Avtomatizatsiya, Upravlenie **19**(12), 755–761 (2018)
19. Gupta, S.C., Hasdorff, L.: Fundamentals of automatic control. NY Wiley (1970)
20. Gaiduk, A.R.: A polynomial design for nonlinear control systems. Autom. Remote. Control. **64**(10), 1638–1642 (2003)
21. Gaiduk, A.R.: Analytical synthesis of controls for nonlinear objects of a certain class. Autom. Remote. Control. **54**(2), 227–237 (1993)
22. Çimen, T.: State-Dependent Riccati Equation (SDRE) Control: A Survey. In: Proceedings of the 17th World Congress of the International Federation of Automatic Control, pp. 3761–3775 (2008)
23. Lin, L.-G., Vandewalle, J., Liang, Y.-W.: Analytical representation of the state-dependent coefficients in the SDRE/SDDRE scheme for multivariable systems. Automatica **59**, 106–111 (2015)
24. Levine, W.S.: The Control Handbook: Control System Fundamentals, 2nd ed., CRC Press (2011)
25. Gantmakher, F.R.: Theory of Matrices. Nauka, Moscow (1988)

Sliding-Mode Control of Phase Shift for Two-Rotor Vibration Setup

Nikolay Kuznetsov[1,2] , Boris Andrievsky[1,2] , Iuliia Zaitceva[1,2,3(✉)],
and Elizaveta Akimova[1]

[1] Department of Applied Cybernetics, Faculty of Mathematics and Mechanics, St. Petersburg State University, 28, Universitetsky Pr., Stary Peterhof, St. Petersburg 198504, Russia
julia.zaytsev@gmail.com

[2] Institute for Problems in Mechanical Engineering of Russian Academy of Sciences, 61, Bol'Shoy Prospect V.O., St. Petersburg 199178, Russia

[3] Department of Automatic Control Systems, St. Petersburg, Electrotechnical University "LETI", 5, Professora Popova St., St. Petersburg 197376, Russia

Abstract. This paper successfully developed and studied a phase shift control system for a two-rotor vibration mechatronic setup, aiming to maintain the desired revolving speed of the rotors. The sliding mode motion was achieved by utilizing a relay controller in the phase loop, while PI controllers were employed in the velocity control loops. Through numerical study and simulations using the parameters of the Mechatronic Vibration Setup SV-2M, the effectiveness of the proposed velocity and phase shift control laws was demonstrated. The possibility of sliding mode occurrence in the phase shift loop was examined through analytical and numerical analysis, confirming its presence. The relationship between the relative degree of the transfer function of the plant and the possibility of the occurrence of a sliding mode is analyzed based on the locus of a perturbed relay system approach. Simulation results indicated that sliding mode motion appeared after a finite transient time and showcased the dynamical properties of the closed-loop system. In conclusion, the findings of this study validate the efficacy of the phase shift control system in achieving the desired rotor speed and demonstrate the feasibility of implementing sliding mode motion in the mechatronic setup.

Keywords: Phase Shift Control · Two-Rotor Vibration Mechatronic Setup · Induction Motor · Sliding Mode Motion · Relay Control · PI Control

1 Introduction

Vibration technologies are applied in various industries and manufacturing sectors, including ore enrichment, metallurgy, mechanical engineering, chemical industries, production of construction materials, grinding, fine grinding, or surface treatment of various parts. The concept of the feedback control for system performance improvement with the help of a controller is fairly easy to implement as long as it is possible to obtain a satisfactory description of the model systems, there is no influence of nonlinearities or the dimension of space is low states [1–7]. When designing a control system for a vibratory machine (VM), all these factors are present [8–15]. In addition, design parameters can vary. In this case, the use of machine learning has greatly simplified to achieve the set control goals.

For a vibration machine, both classical control tasks such as start-up, regulation, and tracking, as well as specific tasks related to vibrations, such as passing through resonance speed, synchronization of vibrators, and modification of attractors, are relevant [4, 16, 17]. The start-up of vibration machine electric drives can be achieved in various ways, providing energy savings and reducing the power of electric motors. The output to the desired rotational speed of the motors can pass through the electromechanical resonance point (the Sommerfeld effect), the overcoming of which is a non-trivial task [8, 11]. In [8], it is shown how the resonant frequencies and oscillation modes change when the center of mass of the technological load is shifted. An algorithm based on the velocity gradient method for overcoming the resonant frequency was proposed in [11].

The main operating modes and control of a vibration system are start-up, passage through resonance, and synchronization. In this case, the movement of the vibration system in the vertical plane is considered, and deviations from planar parallel motion are neglected. To perform operations such as screening, crushing, and vibratory conveying of bulk materials to increase productivity, the synchronous rotation mode of the vibrators is used. The synchronous mode of operation, in the form of self-synchronization that occurs naturally, was discovered and studied by I.I. Blekhman [16, 17]. The conditions for stable operation in the mode of multiple synchronizations, based on the mass ratio and arrangement of rotors, were obtained in the works of I.I. Blekhman, N.P. Yaroshevich, and others. However, adherence to these conditions does not always guarantee stable operation of the vibrators in the multiple synchronization modes, so the development of new algorithmic approaches to solving this problem is a relevant task.

The artificial mode of multiple synchronizations is implemented by different (multiple) rotational frequencies of the rotors, forming complex shapes and heterogeneous trajectory fields of the points on the vibrator [18]. This effect expands the technological possibilities of using vibration machines for performing challenging transportation tasks, such as the movement of dusty, wet, and sticky loads, as well as simultaneous screening and separation of bulk materials. Asymmetry of vibrations at multiple rotor speeds creates and enhances vibratory conveying with increased productivity. In [19], a criterion is derived for achieving multi-frequency synchronization and the ratio of the phase difference between exciters based on the approximate equation of motion of the system drive to improve the loosening of granular material. An analysis of the stability of synchronous operation was also carried out in [20], where a fuzzy PID controller was used. It was shown in [21] that the use of sliding control significantly improves the state of synchronization of the vibrating screen, which makes it possible to qualitatively separate cuttings from drilling fluid.

Thus, the digitalization of manufacturing technology is a necessary step towards the transition to smart factories, which will subsequently increase productivity, and efficiency of use, and have a positive effect on the environment and the conservation of natural resources. To do this, this article continues the development and research of the phase shift control system of the two-rotor vibration mechatronic setup, maintaining the desired revolving speed of the rotors. The sliding mode motion is ensured using the relay controller in the phase loop, whereas the PI controllers are employed in the velocity control loops. Parameters of the Mechatronic Vibration Setup SV-2M of the Institute for Problems in Mechanical Engineering of RAS (IPME RAS) are taken for numerical study and simulations.

The remainder of the paper is organized as follows. A description of the laboratory setup SV-2M is given in Sect. 2. Section 3 represents the proposed velocity and the phase shift control laws. Studying the possibility of sliding mode occurrence for the proposed control law is given in Sect. 4 both analytically and numerically. The simulation results are presented in Sect. 5. Section 6 summarizes the results obtained and outlines the intentions for future work.

2 Servo System Model of Two-Rotor Vibration Setup

A vibration complex SV-2M is a nonlinear electromechanical system equipped by two induction motors (IM) with unbalanced rotors. The system operates in two modes: self-synchronization of the vibrators and controlled synchronization mode [22, 23]. All devices of the complex are interconnected into a closed-loop system in which mechanical processes and control processes take place.

The dynamics model mechanical part of setup SV-2M can be derived from [24], based on the standard Lagrange formalism. But in [24] is assumed that the control actions are input torques. However, the torques cannot be either directly controlled by the outer equipment or even measured for the existing setup. For certain conditions that are supposed for the present study it is reasonable to use the simplified model, which reflects the motor gains and the principal time constants with a suitable precision, employing an approach of [6, 10, 23, 25], where it was obtained for the SV-2M that at low frequencies (down to 5 Hz), the significant impact of the gravitational ("pendular") torque to the motor rotation is observed, which cannot be ignored for controller design [5, 24], but at medium and high-frequency ranges (5 – 20 Hz), the so-called "averaging property", when the fast oscillating components are averaged and for revolving rotors only the "slow" motions can be taken into account [26, 27]. Besides, since the induction motors have their local feedback controllers, the dynamics of the drive systems, including the induction motor and the frequency converter with the feedback local controller can be approximately described by the second-order transfer function from the control signal to angular velocity ω [28–30] as follows:

$$W_d(s) = \frac{\omega}{u} = \frac{b_0}{a_0 s^2 + a_1 s + 1} = \frac{k_d}{T^2 s^2 + 2\xi T s + 1}, \qquad (1)$$

where b_0, a_0, a_1 stand for the drive model parameters, where $b_0 = k_d$ corresponds to the drive system static gain; $T = (a_0)^{1/2}$ is the time constant; $\xi = a_1(2T)^{-1}$ denotes the damping ratio; $s \in C$ stands for the Laplace transform variable.

Identification of motor model parameters was performed in [6, 15] based on the standard non-recursive least-square estimation (LSE) method [31], see details and results in [15].

3   Robust Phase-Shift Control Algorithm

Based on the approach of [15] and the speed-gradient (SG) method of [32, 33], let us use the following control law for control of rotation speed and the phase shift between the rotors for the two-rotor vibration setup:

$$e_{\omega l} = \omega_l^* - \omega_l, \; e_{\omega r} = \omega_r^* - \omega_r, \tag{2}$$

$$\dot{\delta}_{\omega l} = e_{\omega l}, \; u_{\omega l} = k_{I\omega l}\delta_{\omega l} + k_{P\omega l}e_{\omega l}, \tag{3}$$

$$\dot{\delta}_{\omega r} = e_{\omega r}, \; u_{\omega r} = k_{I\omega r}\delta_{\omega r} + k_{P\omega r}e_{\omega r}, \tag{4}$$

$$\Delta\omega = \omega_l - \omega_r, \tag{5}$$

$$u_l = sat_0^{u_{max}}\left(u_{\omega l} - u_\psi\right), \; u_r = sat_0^{u_{max}}\left(u_{\omega r} - u_\psi\right), \tag{6}$$

where u_ψ is the "phase-loop" control signal, produced by the following separate algorithm:

$$\psi = \varphi_r - \varphi_l, \; e_\psi = \psi^* - \psi, \tag{7}$$

$$\sigma = e_\psi + \tau_M \Delta\omega, \tag{8}$$

$$\dot{v} = \gamma_1 sign(\sigma), \tag{9}$$

$$u_\psi = -sat_{\bar{u}_\psi}(v + \gamma sign(\sigma)\sqrt{|\sigma|}, \tag{10}$$

where τ_M is the reference model time constant; k_I and k_p are the rotation frequency controller gains; ω^* denotes the desired rotation frequency, while ψ^* stands for the desired phase shift; γ is the relay controller parameter (the relay "shelf" level).

The objective is to determine the existence and time of appearance of the sliding mode (SM) in the closed-loop system (1)-(10), considering the presence of two control channels, each involving servo-drives described by (1) with different parameters. The linear time-invariant (LTI) single-input-single-output (SISO) systems controlled using the relay algorithm [32–35]:

$$\dot{x}(t) = Ax(t) + Bu(t),$$

$$y(t) = GCx(t), \tag{11}$$

$$u = -\gamma sign(\sigma(t))$$

where $x(t) \in R^n$, $u(t) \in R^n$, $\sigma(t) = GCx(t) \in R^1$ it was proved that a SM occurs on the surface $\sigma(t) = 0$, if transfer function $W(s) = GC(sI-A)^{-1}B = N(s)/D(s)$ of $D(s)$ (12)

from control input u to measured output σ is a strictly minimal phase (SMP), i.e. if $N(s)$ is the Hurwitz polynomial, the $W(s)$ relative degree is ρ, defined as $\rho = degD(s) - degN(s)$ is equal to 1, and $\gamma > 0$ is sufficiently large (with respect to a given region of initial conditions $x(0)$). Then for (12) the auxiliary control goal $\lim\limits_{t \to \infty} \sigma(t) = 0$ is achieved.

The algorithm represented by (7)-(10) is referred to as the Implicit Reference Model (IRM) algorithm [32, 33, 35]. In the case under consideration, this mentioned model is expressed by the identity $\sigma(t) = 0$, and the applied control law, according to the SG method, ensures the decrease in $|\sigma(t)|$. The equivalence $\sigma(t) = 0$ means fulfillment of equation:

$$\tau_M \dot{\psi}(t) + \psi(t) = \psi^*(t), \tag{12}$$

which can be called "the reference equation" by the analogy with the habitual reference model in Model Reference Adaptive Control (MRAC), as presented by [36].

4 Exploring Sliding Mode Potential

4.1 Analytical Study

Firstly, let us check the SMP property for the system with control input u_ψ as in (6) and output σ, given by (9). To represent the system model in the state-space LTI form under the assumption that the saturations are not active, introduce drives state vectors $x_l = [\varphi_l, \omega_l, \varepsilon_l]^T \in R^3$, $x_r = [\varphi_r, \omega_l, \varepsilon_l]^T \in R^3$, where $\varphi_l, \omega_l, \varepsilon_l$ denote rotation angles, angular velocities, and accelerations of the left (l) and right (r) rotors respectively; variables $u_{l,r}$ are taken as drive inputs u, and vectors $\varphi_{l,r}, \omega_{l,r} \in R^2$ as drives outputs y. Evidently, the state-space representation of transfer function (1) leads to the following triples (A, B, C) in the state-space form:

$$A_{d,l} = \begin{bmatrix} 0 & 1 & 0 \\ 0 & 0 & 1 \\ 0 & -1/a_{0,l} & -a_{1,l}/a_{0,l} \end{bmatrix}, B_{d,l} = \begin{bmatrix} 0 \\ 0 \\ b_{0,l}/a_{0,l} \end{bmatrix}, C_{d,l} = \begin{bmatrix} 1 & 0 & 0 \\ 0 & 1 & 0 \end{bmatrix}, \tag{13}$$

Similar (13) expressions have matrices for the right drive. Then the transfer functions for the left and right drives from $u_{l,r}$ to $y_{l,r}$ are

$$W_{dl}(s) = C_{dl}(sI_2 - A_{dl})^{-1}B_{dl}, W_{dr}(s) = C_{dr}(sI_2 - A_{dr})^{-1}B_{dr}, \tag{14}$$

respectively.

Now let us consider the PI-controllers (2)-(4). To this end, let us introduce the controller gain matrices (row-vectors) $G = [1, \tau_M] \in R^{1 \times 2}$ and $K = [k_I, k_P] \in R^{1 \times 2}$. This leads to the following block matrices in the state-space form for the system with input u_ψ and output σ, defined as in (7)-(9):

$$A = \begin{bmatrix} A_{d,l} - B_{d,l}KC_{d,l} & 0_{3,3} \\ 0_{3,3} & A_{d,r} - B_{d,r}KC_{d,r} \end{bmatrix}, B = \begin{bmatrix} B_{d,l} \\ -B_{d,r} \end{bmatrix}, \tag{15}$$

$$C = \begin{bmatrix} 1 & 0 & 0 & -1 & 0 & 0 \\ 0 & 1 & 0 & 0 & -1 & 0 \end{bmatrix}. \tag{16}$$

Substituting the matrices from (15) to (18) one gets the system matrices in the following expanded form:

$$A = \begin{bmatrix} 0 & 1 & 0 & 0 & 0 & 0 \\ 0 & 0 & 1 & 0 & 0 & 0 \\ -\frac{b_{0,1}k_I}{a_{0,1}} & -\frac{1+b_{0,1}k_P}{a_{0,1}} & -\frac{a_{1,1}}{a_{0,1}} & 0 & 0 & 0 \\ 0 & 0 & 0 & 0 & 1 & 0 \\ 0 & 0 & 0 & 0 & 0 & 1 \\ 0 & 0 & 0 & -\frac{b_{0,r}k_I}{a_{0,r}} & -\frac{1+b_{0,1}k_P}{a_{0,r}} & -\frac{a_{1,r}}{a_{0,r}} \end{bmatrix}, \quad (17)$$

$$B = \begin{bmatrix} 0 & 0 & \frac{b_{0,1}}{a_{0,1}} & 0 & 0 & -\frac{b_{0,r}}{a_{0,r}} \end{bmatrix}, C = \begin{bmatrix} 1 & 0 & 0 & -1 & 0 & 0 \\ 0 & 1 & 0 & 0 & -1 & 0 \end{bmatrix}. \quad (18)$$

The state-space system representation with matrices (18), (19) gives the following transfer function from input u_ψ to output σ

$$W_{u_\psi}^\sigma(s) = GC(sI_6 - A)^{-1}B \equiv \frac{N_{u_\psi}^\sigma(s)}{D_{u_\psi}^\sigma(s)}, \quad (19)$$

where
$N_{u_\psi}^\sigma(s) = \tau_M\left(a_{0,1}b_{0,r} + a_{0,r}b_{0,1}\right)s^4 + (a_{0,1}b_{0,r} + a_{0,r}b_{0,1} + \tau_M(a_{1,1}b_{0,r} + a_{1,r}b_{1,1}))s^3 + (a_{1,1}b_{0,r} + a_{1,r}b_{1,1} + \tau_M(a_{0,1}b_{0,r} + 2b_{0,1}b_{0,r}k_P))s^2 + (b_{0,1} + b_{0,r} + 2b_{0,1}b_{0,r}k_P + 2b_{0,1}b_{0,r}k_I\tau_M)s + 2b_{0,1}b_{0,r}k_I, D_{u_\psi}^\sigma(s) = a_{0,1}a_{0,r}s^6 + (a_{0,1}a_{1,r} + a_{1,1}a_{0,r})s^5 + \left(a_{1,1}a_{1,r} + a_{0,1}(b_{0,r}k_P + 1) + (a_{0,r}(b_{0,1}k_P + 1))s^4 + (a_{1,1}(b_{0,r}k_P + 1) + (a_{1,r}(b_{0,1}k_P + 1) + a_{0,1}b_{0,r}k_I + +(a_{0,r}b_{0,1}k_I)s^3 + (b_{0,1}k_P + 1) + a_{1,1}b_{0,r}k_I + a_{1,1}b_{0,1}k_I)s^2 + (b_{0,1}k_I(b_{0,r}k_P + 1) + +b_{0,r}k_I(b_{0,1}k_P + 1))s + b_{0,1}b_{0,r}k_I^2)$

The transfer function of the system under consideration is not SMP since its relative degree of ρ is equal to 2. However, under some conditions, [33, 37–43], this restriction can be relaxed, and the case $\rho = 2$ ensures achievement of the auxiliary control goal $\lim_{t\to\infty} \sigma(t) = 0$ if γ is sufficiently large.

In [33, 38] a significant contribution by introducing the concept of passifiability is made, which involves achieving passification via feedback for systems related to a specific output, even if it differs from the controlled output [35].

Results of [38] made a significant contribution by introducing the concept of passifiability [33, 38], which involves achieving passification via feedback for systems related to a specific output, even if it differs from the controlled output. This concept is known as extended passifiability (EP). Fradkov not only established the necessary and sufficient conditions for EP of LTI systems through linear output feedback but also demonstrated the connection between these results and high-gain stabilization, providing a framework for passifying systems by utilizing feedback control techniques, focusing on outputs that may not be directly controlled. By expanding the notion of passifiability to include such outputs, the concept of EP broadens the scope of control possibilities. In [38], the following closed-loop system model is considered

$$\dot{x}(t) = Ax(t) + Bu(t), y(t) = Cx(t), \quad (20)$$

$$u(t) = -Ky_1(t) + Lv(t), \tag{21}$$

where $x \in R^n$, $u \in R^m$, $y \in R^1$, and A, B, C are matrices of corresponding sizes, $y_1 = C_1 x \in R^{l_1}$ denotes the second output, $v \in R^m$ is a new input, $L \in m \times m$ is a real matrix, and $detL \neq 0$. Hereafter the case of $m = l = l_1 = 1$ is taken for brevity. For system (20), (21) the following notations are introduced [37]: $D(s) = det(sI_n - A) \equiv s^n + d_{n-1}s^{n-1} + \ldots + d_0$, $W(s) = C(sI_n - A)^{-1}B \equiv N(s)/D(s)$, $W_1(s) = C_1(sI_n - A)^{-1}B \equiv N_1(s)/D(s)$, $\Psi(s) = B_1(s)/B(s)$. Introduce the following F-property [36]: system (21), (22) is said to possess the $D(i\omega)$ F-property if either $(Re\Psi(i\omega) = 0)$ for all ω and $Re\left(\frac{D(i\omega)}{N(i\omega)}\right) > 0$ for $Re\Psi(i\omega) = 0)$ or $(Re\Psi(i\omega) \leq 0$ for all ω and $Re\left(\frac{D(i\omega)}{N(i\omega)}\right) < 0$ for $Re\Psi(i\omega) = 0$, $i \in C)$, denotes the imaginary unit, $i^2 = -1$.

As stated in [38], if polynomial (s) is Hurwitz of degree $n - 1$, $degN_1(s) = n - 2$, the system possesses F-property and $d_{n-1} \neq 0$, then system (20) is strictly passifiable by output feedback (21). To find the necessary and sufficient conditions for the feasibility of high gain passification, the following Theorem is proved:

Theorem 1 [38]. System (22) is strictly passifiable by output feedback (23) with all sufficiently large K if and only if polynomial $N(s)$ is Hurwitz of degree $n - 1$ and either *(A)* $degN_1(s) = n - 1$, and the system possesses F-property, or *(B)* $degN_1(s) = n - 2$, the system possesses F-property and $d_{n-1} \neq 0$.

Variant B of Theorem 1 gives the high-gain stabilizability condition for the relative degree $\rho = 2$ case of interest and, consequently, opens, in principle, an opportunity for the stable sliding-mode relay control as $\rho = 2$. The corresponding algebraic conditions in the terms of $N(s)$, $D(s)$ coefficients are given in [33].

Frequency conditions for the existence of an SM, obtained based on the describing functions (DF) method, are given in [37, 39]. [37] analyzed the relationship between the relative degree of a plant's transfer function and the possibility of SM occurrence in relay systems using the locus of a perturbed relay system (LPRS) approach. The LPRS is defined in [41] as a characteristic of the response of a linear part to an unequally spaced pulse control of variable frequency in a closed loop. Based on the LPRS concept, [37, 42] shows that if $\rho = 1$ or $\rho = 2$, and the LPRS will not have intersection points with the real axis except for the origin the ideal SM occurs. In this case, the frequency of chattering is infinity, and the equivalent gain becomes infinity too. Namely, the following Theorem was proved.

Theorem 2 [39]. If the transfer function (s) is a quotient of two polynomials (s) and (s) of degrees m and n, respectively, with non-negative coefficients, then for the existence of ideal SM, it is necessary that the relative degree $\rho = n - m$ of (s) be one or two. If $\rho = 1$, then a conventional ideal SM can occur; if $\rho = 2$, then the so-called asymptotic second-order SM can occur.

As stated in [39], Theorem 2 does not provide a sufficient condition, as a periodic motion of a finite frequency can exist even if the relative degree is one or two [37]. In [37], an example is demonstrated showing that if the LPRS intersects the real axis from below, returns then to the lower half-plane, and finally approaches the origin of the coordinates from below having the real axis as an asymptote, the SM appears in some vicinity of the quiescent state. In this case, the SM appears only if initial conditions are sufficiently small.

4.2 Numerical Study

Let us analyze the system properties numerically for the specific values of the system model parameters, taken from [15]: $b_{0,l} = 0.0042s^{-1}$, $a_{0,l} = 0.1187s^2$, $a_{l,l} = 0.8110$ s, $b_{0,r} = 0.0043s^{-1}$, $a_{0,r} = 0.1185s^2$, $a_{l,r} = 1.2195$ s, $\tau_M = 1$ s, $k_I = 240$ s, $k_P = 1680$, $\omega^* = 40$ rad/s for both drives; the natural bounds of control signals saturation are $u_{max} = 40000$ in (6).

To start with, consider the Proportional (P) control law as

$$u_\psi(t) = -\gamma\sigma(t), \tag{22}$$

where $\gamma > 0$ denotes the controller gain. Then the LTI closed-loop system (20), (22) dynamics are described by the following equation

$$\left(D^\sigma_{u_\psi}(p) + \gamma N^\sigma_{u_\psi}(p)\right)\sigma(t) = 0, \tag{23}$$

where $p = d/dt$ denotes the time derivation operator.

Transfer function (19) of the open-loop system has the following distributions of poles s_P and zeros s_Z: $s_P = \{-508 \pm 650i, -335 \pm 747i, -0128, -0127\}$, $s_Z = \{-421 \pm 706i, -10, -0127\}$, in Fig. 1 (left plot). For $\gamma = 2600$, characteristic polynomial of closed-loop system (19), (22) has the following roots: $s_D = \{-383 \pm 152i, -428 \pm 71i, -0783, -0127\}$. Figure 1 illustrates the positions of zeros and poles for (19), (23) and the corresponding root locus for γ values ranging from 1 to 2600. The plots clearly indicate that as γ increases, four poles s_D of the closed-loop LTI system converge towards the open-loop system zeros s_Z, while the remaining two poles move towards infinity in modulus, aligned parallel to the imaginary axis in the left-hand complex plane.

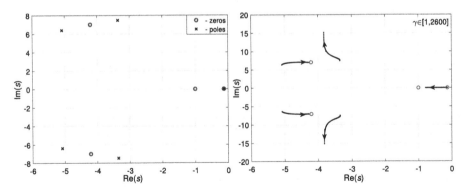

Fig. 1. Zeros and poles positions for (19), (22) (left plot); root locus for (19), (22) (right plot), $\gamma \in [1, 2600]$.

To further analyze the open-loop system (19) and (24) with $\gamma = 2600$, Fig. 2 presents the Bode diagram and Nyquist chart. These results affirm the asymptotic stability of the closed-loop system (19) and (24) for all $\gamma > 0$. Additionally, as follows from the DF method and the abovementioned results of [35, 39], the presence of the sliding mode (SM) in the closed-loop system with the relay controller

$$u_\psi = -\gamma \, sign(\sigma), \quad \gamma > 0, \tag{24}$$

is also ensured.

To confirm the conclusion made, let us simulate the complete system, including the plant model (19), tracking the reference action by the drives' angular velocities and the relay law of phase shift control. The overall control law is (2)-(11). The "square-root" term in (10), inspired by the super-twisting method of [42, 43].

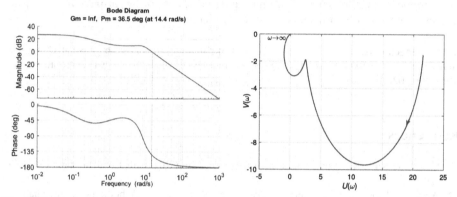

Fig. 2. Bode diagram (left plot) and Nyquist chart (right plot) for open-loop system (19), (22), $\gamma = 2600$.

As is seen from time histories of processes, depicted in Fig. 3, the controlled variables $\psi(t)$, $\omega_1(t)$, $\omega_r(t)$ tend to the desirable (reference) values ψ^*, ω^*, and after the short transient, the sliding mode occurs.

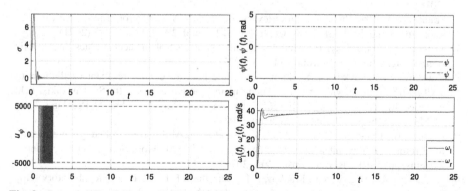

Fig. 3. System (19), (24), $\gamma = 5000$, $\omega^* = 40$ rad/s, $\psi^* = \pi$. Time histories of $\sigma(t)$, $u_\psi(t)$ (left plot) and $\psi(t)$, $\omega_1(t)$, $\omega_r(t)$ (right plot).

5 Conclusion

This paper focuses on the development and study of a phase shift control system for a two-rotor vibration mechatronic setup. The sliding mode motion is achieved through the use of a relay controller in the phase loop, while PI controllers are employed in the velocity control loops. The possibility of sliding mode occurrence in the phase shift loop is examined through both analytical and numerical analysis. The simulation results confirm the appearance of sliding mode motion after a finite transient time and demonstrate the dynamical properties of the closed-loop system.

Future work intends to refine and optimize the control system based on the obtained results and explore additional applications and enhancements for the two-rotor vibration mechatronic setup. The "square-root" multiplier in the control law, inspired by the super-twisting method of [39, 40] also deserves consideration in future studies.

Acknowledgements. This work was supported in part by the St. Petersburg State University grant Pure ID 75207094, by the Leading Scientific Schools of the Russian Federation, project NSh-4196.2022.1.1.

References

1. Pati, C.S., Kala, R.: Vision-based robot following using PID control. Technologies **5**(2), 34 (2017)
2. Aggogeri, F., Borboni, A., Merlo, A., Pellegrini, N., Ricatto, R.: Vibration damping analysis of lightweight structures in machine tools. Materials **10**(3), 297 (2017)
3. Tomchin, D.A., Fradkov, A.L.: Control of rotor passing through the resonance zone on the basis of the high-speed gradient method. J. Mach. Manuf. Reliab. **5**(55), 66–71 (2005)
4. Nonlinear problems of oscillation theory and control theory. Vibration Mechanics: In: Beletsky, V.V., Indeytsev, D.A., Fradkov, A.L. (eds.) Nauka, SPb (2009). (in Russian)
5. Panovko, G., Shokin, A.E.: Experimental analysis of the oscillations of two-mass system with self-synchronizing unbalance vibration exciters. Vibroengineering Procedia **18**(3), 8–13 (2018)
6. Fradkov, A.L., Tomchina, O.P., Andrievsky, B., Boikov, V.I.: Control of phase shift in two-rotor vibration units. IEEE Trans. Control Syst. Technol. **29**(3), 1316–1323 (2021)
7. Zaitceva, I., Andrievsky, B.: Methods of intelligent control in mechatronics and robotic engineering: a survey. Electronics **11**(15) (2022)
8. Gouskov, A., Panovko, G., Shokhin, A.: To the issue of control resonant oscillations of a vibrating machine with two self-synchronizing inertial exciters. In: Sapountzakis, E.J., Banerjee, M., Biswas, P., Inan, E. (eds.) Proc. 14th Int. Conf. on Vibration Problems 2019, LNME, pp. 515–526. Springer, Singapure (2021)
9. Fradkov, A., Tomchina, O., Galitskaya, V., Gorlatov, D.: Multiple controlled synchronization for 3-rotor vibration unit with varying payload. In: 5th IFAC Workshop on Periodic Control Systems, pp. 5–10. Elsevier, Amsterdam (2013)
10. Andrievsky, B., Boikov, V.I., Fradkov, A.L., Seifullaev, R.E.: Mechatronic laboratory setup for study of controlled nonlinear vibrations. In: 6th IFAC Workshop on Periodic Control Systems, pp. 1–6. Elsevier, Amsterdam (2010)
11. Fradkov, A., Gorlatov, D., Tomchina, O., Tomchin, D.: Control of oscillations in vibration machines: start up and passage through resonance. Chaos **26**(11), 116310 (2016)

12. Zaitceva, I., Andrievsky, B.: Real-time reinforcement learning of vibration machine PI-controller. In: 6th Scientific School Dynamics of Complex Networks and their Applications, pp. 307–311. IEEE, New York (2022)

13. Andrievsky, B., Zaitceva, I.: Symmetrical control law for chaotization of platform vibration. Symmetry **14**(11) (2022)

14. Zaitceva, I., Kuznetsov, N.V., Andrievsky, B.: Approach to identifying areas of uncontrolled oscillations in human-machine systems. In: International Russian Smart Industry Conference, pp. 196–201. IEEE, New York (2023)

15. Andrievsky, B., Zaitceva, I., Barkana, I.: Passification-based robust phase-shift control for two-rotor vibration machine. Electronics **12**(4), 1006 (2023)

16. Blekhman, I.I., Yaroshevich, N.P.: Multiple modes of vibration maintenance of rotation of unbalanced rotors. Proceedings of the Academy of Sciences of the USSR. Machine Science **6**, 62–67 (1986). (in Russian)

17. Blekhman, I.I.: Vibrational Mechanics. Phys.-math. lit, Moscow (1994). (in Russian)

18. Blekhman, I.I., Fradkov, A.L. (eds.): Control of Mechatronic Vibrational Units. Nauka, St.Petersburg (2001). (in Russian)

19. Li, L., Chen, X.: Multi-frequency vibration synchronization and stability of the nonlinear screening system. IEEE Access **7**, 171032–171045 (2019)

20. Jia, L., Wang, C., Liu, Z.: Multifrequency controlled synchronization of four inductor motors by the fixed frequency ratio method in a vibration system. Sci. Rep. **13**, 2467 (2023)

21. Zou, M., Fang, P., Hou, Y., Wang, Y., Hou, D., Peng, H.: Synchronization analysis of two eccentric rotors with double-frequency excitation considering sliding mode control. J. Commu. Nonlin. Sci. Numeri. Simul. **92**, 105458 (2021)

22. Andrievsky, B.R., Blekhman, I.I., Blekhman, L.I., Boikov, V.I., Vasil'kov, V.B., Fradkov, A.L.: Education and research mechatronic complex for studying vibration devices and processes. Prob. Mecha. Eng. Reliab. Machi. **4**, 90–97 (2016). (in Russian)

23. Boikov, V.I., Andrievsky, B., Shiegin, V.V.: Experimental study of unbalanced rotors synchronization of the mechatronic vibration setup. Cybernetics and Physics **5**(1), 5–11 (2016)

24. Tomchin, D.A., Fradkov, A.L.: Control of passage through a resonance area during the start of a two-rotor vibration machine. J. Machi. Manuf. Reliabi. **36**(4), 380–385 (2007)

25. Andrievsky, B., Fradkov, A.L., Tomchina, O.P., Boikov, V.I.: Angular velocity and phase shift control of mechatronic vibration setup. In: 8th IFAC Symposium on Mechatronic Systems, pp. 436–441. Elsevier, Amsterdam (2019)

26. Blekhman, I.I.: Vibrational Mechanics: Nonlinear Dynamic Effects, General Approach, Applications. World Scientific, Singapore (2000)

27. Blekhman, I.I.: Synchronization in Nature and Technology: Theory and Applications. ASME Press, New York (1988)

28. Khalil, H.K., Strangas, E.G., Jurkovic, S.: Speed Observer and reduced nonlinear model for sensorless control of induction motors. IEEE Trans. Control Syst. Technol. **17**(2), 327–339 (2009)

29. Joshi, B., Chandorkar, M.: Two-motor single-inverter field-oriented induction machine drive dynamic performance. Sadhana **39**(2), 391–407 (2014)

30. Giri, F.: AC Electric Motors Control: Advanced Design Techniques and Applications. John Wiley & Sons, Ltd., Chichester, UK (2013)

31. Ljung, L.: System Identification: Theory for the User. Prentice Hall, Upper Saddle River, NJ, USA (1999)

32. Fradkov, A.L., Miroshnik, I.V., Nikiforov, V.: Nonlinear and Adaptive Control of Complex Systems. Kluwer, Dordrecht (1999)

33. Fradkov, A.L.: Adaptive control in large-scale systems. Nauka, Moscow (1990). (in Russian)

34. Andrievsky, B., Fradkov, A.: Implicit model reference adaptive controller based on feedback kalman-yakubovich lemma. In: IEEE Conference on Control Applications, pp. 1171–1174. IEEE, Glasgow (1994)
35. Andrievskii, B.R., Fradkov, A.: Method of passification in adaptive control, estimation, and synchronization. Autom. Remote. Control. **67**(11), 1699–1731 (2006)
36. Landau, J.D.: Adaptive control systems. the model reference approach. Dekker, New York, NY (1979)
37. Boiko, I.: Analysis of modes of oscillations in a relay feedback system. In: American Control Conference, pp. 1253–1258. IEEE, Boston (2004)
38. Fradkov, A.: Passification of linear systems with respect to given output. In: 47th IEEE Conference on Decision and Control, pp. 646–651. IEEE, Mexico (2008)
39. Boiko, I.: Discontinuous Control Systems. Frequency-Domain Analysis and Design. Birkhäuser, Boston (2009)
40. Boiko, I.M., Kuznetsov, N.V., Mokaev, R.N., Akimova, E.D.: On asymmetric periodic solutions in relay feedback systems. J. Franklin Inst. **358**(1), 363–383 (2021)
41. Boiko, I.: Input-output analysis of limit cycling relay feedback control systems. In: American Control Conference, pp. 542–546. IEEE, San Diego (1999)
42. Levant, A.: Sliding order and sliding accuracy in sliding mode control. Int. J. Control **58**(6), 1247–1263 (1993)
43. Bartolini, G., Levant, A., Pisano, A., Usai, E.: Adaptive second-order sliding mode control with uncertainty compensation. Int. J. Control **89**(9), 1747–1758 (2016)

GBMILs: Gradient Boosting Models for Multiple Instance Learning

Andrei Konstantinov📵, Lev Utkin📵, Vladimir Muliukha$^{(\boxtimes)}$📵, and Vladimir Zaborovsky📵

Peter the Great St. Petersburg Polytechnic University, 29, Polytechnicheskaya Street, St. Petersburg 195251, Russia
vladimir.muliukha@spbstu.ru

Abstract. An approach based on using the gradient boosting machine for solving the Multiple Instance Learning (MIL) problem under condition of small tabular data is proposed. The MIL deals with labeled objects called bags which consist of several parts of the objects called instances with unknown labels and each bag label depends on the instance labels. Three modifications of the approach are developed and studied. They are determined by different aggregation functions which combine the intermediate predictions of the instance classes in each bag and allow gradient-based optimization through them. The modifications are based on the following aggregation functions: the Hard Max Aggregation, the Simple Attention Aggregation, and the Ensemble of gradient boosting machines in fusion with the Attention Neural Networks. The former two modifications can use an arbitrary decision tree gradient boosting model, which allows iterative training on loss gradients. The later modification simultaneously optimizes an ensemble of parallel gradient boosting models and the parameters of neural network. Numerical experiments with tabular datasets illustrate the proposed modifications of the approach and their superiority comparing to available MIL approaches accompanied by accuracy improvement up to 8%.

Keywords: Multiple Instance Learning · Gradient Boosting Machine · Attention Mechanism · Neural Networks

1 Introduction

The Multiple Instance Learning (MIL) is a framework in machine learning which deals with objects called bags such that each bag consists of some number of instances. An illustrative example of using the MIL is histopathology where the histology images are viewed as bags and separate patches as instances of the bag [1, 2]. A lot of applications can be formalized by means of the MIL, for example, the drug activity prediction [3], the protein function annotation [4], histopathology [2], etc. One of the tasks solved by the MIL is to classify new bags based on training data consisting of a set of labeled bags. To solve the task, it is assumed some relationship between labels of instances and bags, for example, positive bags contain at least one positive instance [5].

A lot of MIL models solving the classification tasks have been proposed [6–8]. We take note of the models based on the attention mechanism [9–12]. These models are the most efficient, but they mainly use neural networks and deal with the image data. However, they may be ineffective when dealing with small tabular data. Therefore, our goal is to devise new methods for the MIL problem, leveraging recent developments in the area of neural networks.

One of the powerful and efficient algorithms for dealing with small tabular data is the Gradient Boosting Machine (GBM) [13]. Its efficiency has been demonstrated in many applications. Therefore, we consider how GBM can be incorporated into MIL. As a result, we propose several modifications, called the Gradient Boosting MIL (GBMIL). The modifications are determined by different aggregation functions which combine the intermediate predictions of the instance classes in each bag. In particular, we propose three modifications based on the so-called Hard Max Aggregation (GBMIL-MAX), on the Simple Attention Aggregation (GBMIL-ATT), and the Ensemble of GBMs implemented by means of the Attention Neural Networks (GBMIL-ANN). The GBMIL-ANN can be regarded as a generalization of the GBMIL-ATT.

Numerical experiments with well-known datasets Musk1, Musk2 [3], Fox, Tiger, Elephant [14] illustrate the proposed models. The above datasets have numerical features that are used to perform tabular data.

The paper is organized as follows. A brief introduction to the MIL and the GBM can be found in Sect. 2. Ideas behind the GBM in the MIL are considered in Sect. 3. Three modifications of the Gradient Boosting MIL are provided in the same section. Numerical experiments illustrating the models are provided in Sect. 4. Concluding remarks can be found in Sect. 5.

2 Preliminaries

2.1 Multiple Instance Learning

MIL is a weakly supervised learning problem because a structure of data in MIL is represented in a form of bags with the class labels such that each bag consists of instances (patches) which usually do not have class labels. For every application, there is a relationship between the instance labels and the corresponding bag label. One of the conventional relationships between the instance classes and the bag class is of the form: at least one positive instance makes the bag positive, and negative bags contain only negative instances [15].

Two tasks can be stated in MIL. According to the first task, we classify each instance to annotate it. The second task is to classify new bags by having a training set of bags. Formally, these tasks can be described as follows. There is a set $\mathcal{D}$ of N bags $\{\mathbf{X}_1, ..., \mathbf{X}_N\}$ with labels $Y_i = f(\mathbf{X}_i) \in \{0, 1\}$, such that each bag, say $\mathbf{X}_i$, consists of n_i instances, i.e., $\mathbf{X}_i = \{\mathbf{x}_1^{(i)}, ..., \mathbf{x}_{n_i}^{(i)}\}$, where each instance $\mathbf{x}_j^{(i)}$ consists of m features, $\mathbf{x}_j^{(i)} \in \mathbb{R}^m$, and has a label $y_j^{(i)} = g\left(\mathbf{x}_j^{(i)}\right) \in \{0, 1\}$. Here f and g are functions of the bag and instance classifiers, respectively. It is usually assumed that negative and positive classes are represented by 0 and 1, respectively. Labels Y_i are known. In contrast to the bag level, labels Y_i are unknown, but the function g is determined during the training process. This is the first task of MIL. The second task is to annotate a new bag $\mathbf{X}$ or to find $f(\mathbf{X})$.

The dataset $\mathcal{D}$ can be represented as:

$$\mathcal{D} = \left\{ \left(\{\mathbf{x}_k^{(i)}\}_{k=1}^{n_i}, y_i \right) \right\}_{i=1}^{N}.$$

Taking into account the conventional relationships between the instance classes and the bag class, the function f is written as:

$$f\left(\{\mathbf{x}_k^{(i)}\}_{k=1}^{n_i} \right) = \max\{g\left(\mathbf{x}_k^{(i)} \right)\}_{k=1}^{n_i}.$$

To find parameters of the model f, we have to minimize the loss function:

$$\mathcal{L} = \frac{1}{N} \sum_{i=1}^{N} l\left(y_i, f\left(\{\mathbf{x}_k^{(i)}\}_{k=1}^{n_i} \right) \right) = \frac{1}{N} \sum_{i=1}^{N} l\left(y_i, \max\{g\left(\mathbf{x}_k^{(i)} \right)\}_{k=1}^{n_i} \right).$$

2.2 A Brief Introduction to GBM

The MIL is a weakly supervised learning problem because a structure of data in MIL is represented in a form of bags with the c Suppose that there is a dataset $\mathcal{D} = \{(\mathbf{x}_1, y_1), ..., (\mathbf{x}_n, y_n)\}$, where $\mathbf{x}_i \in \mathbb{R}^m$, $y_i \in \mathbb{R}$ for the regression and $y_i \in \{0, 1, ..., C-1\}$ for the classification.

GBM [13] tries to iteratively learn a function $F(\mathbf{x})$ on $\mathcal{D}$, which predicts the target value $\tilde{y}$ of a new observation $\mathbf{x}$, by minimizing the loss function:

$$l(F) = \mathbb{E}_{(\mathbf{x},y)} \, l(y, F(\mathbf{x})).$$

The iterative learning improves predictions by means of adding new base learners $h_i(\mathbf{x})$, forming an additive ensemble model of size T:

$$F_0(\mathbf{x}) = \text{const}, \quad F_t(\mathbf{x}) = F_{t-1}(\mathbf{x}) + \gamma_t h_t(\mathbf{x}), \, t = 1, ..., T,$$

where h_t is the i-th base model, for example, a decision tree; γ_t is the learning rate.

The decision tree implementing h_i is built at the i-th iteration on the dataset consisting of residuals $(\mathbf{x}_k, r_k)$, $k = 1, ..., n$, where, for example, $r_k = y_k - F_{i-1}(\mathbf{x}_k)$.

The residual at the t-th iteration $r_i^{(t)}$ for the i-th instance is defined as the partial derivative of the expected loss function:

$$r_i^{(t)} = - \left. \frac{\partial l(y_i, z)}{\partial z} \right|_{z = F_{i-1}(\mathbf{x}_i)}.$$

Hence, the best gradient descent step-size γ_t is:

$$\gamma_t = \underset{\gamma}{\arg\min} \sum_{i=1}^{N} l(y_t, F_{t-1}(\mathbf{x}_i) + \gamma h_t(\mathbf{x}_i)).$$

We study below how GBM can be incorporated into MIL.

3 Gradient Boosting for MIL

The main motivation of applying the GBM with decision trees as base learners to the MIL is that decision trees are an inherently efficient algorithm for dealing with tabular data. Many MIL models, implemented by means of neural networks and successfully dealing with image data, cannot cope with tabular data in many cases. Therefore, we aim to devise new methods for the MIL problem by applying the GBM.

Suppose that we have some differentiable loss function l. The classification function F_T is written as follows:

$$F_T(\mathbf{x}) = \sum_{q=0}^{T} \gamma h_q(\mathbf{x}) = F_{T-1}(\mathbf{x}) + \gamma h_T(\mathbf{x}),$$

where $h_q(\mathbf{x})$ is a regression tree defined as:

$$h_q(\mathbf{x}) = \underset{h \in \mathcal{H}}{\operatorname{argmin}} \sum_{i=1}^{N} \|h_q(\mathbf{x}_i) - r_i\|^2,$$

$$r_i = \left(-\frac{\partial l(y_i, \sigma(z))}{\partial z} \bigg|_{z = F_{T-1}(\mathbf{x}_i)} \right).$$

Here $\sigma(z)$ is the standard sigmoid function. The GBM can be modified for the MIL to handle multiple input points as:

$$\hat{F}_T(\mathbf{x}_1, \ldots, \mathbf{x}_k) = G(F_T(\mathbf{x}_1), \ldots, F_T(\mathbf{x}_k)),$$

where G is a differentiable aggregation function.

A new tree at each iteration is built to optimize the loss function for all bags:

$$h_q(\mathbf{x}) = \underset{h \in \mathcal{H}}{\arg\min} \sum_{i=1}^{N} \sum_{k=1}^{n_i} h_q\left(\mathbf{x}_k^{(i)}\right) - r_k^{(i)2},$$

where:

$$r_k^{(i)} = \frac{\partial l\left(y_i, \sigma\left(G[z_1, \ldots, z_{n_i}]\right)\right)}{\partial z_k} \bigg|_{z_j = F_{T-1}\left(\mathbf{x}_j^{(i)}\right)}.$$

The expression for $r_k^{(i)}$ can be rewritten using the chain rule as:

$$r_k^{(i)} = \frac{\partial l(y_i, \sigma(z))}{\partial z} \bigg|_{z = \hat{F}_{T-1}\left(\mathbf{x}_1^{(i)}, \ldots, \mathbf{x}_{n_i}^{(i)}\right)} \cdot \frac{\partial G(z_1, \ldots, z_{n_i})}{\partial z_k} \bigg|_{z_j = F_{T-1}\left(\mathbf{x}_j^{(i)}\right)}.$$

3.1 Aggregating Functions

It can be seen from the above that an important question is how to choose an aggregating function G. These functions can be regarded as approximations of the maximum operation, which defines the relationship between labels of instances and the corresponding bag containing these instances. Several types of the aggregating functions G have been proposed in literature [6]. They are shown in Table 1 wherein the first column contains abbreviated names of the functions, the second column shows the functions themselves, and the third column contains the partial derivative of the functions. The functions are log-sum-exponential (LSE) [16], generalized mean (GM), noisy-or (NOR) [17], and ISR [17]. Some functions depend on the parameter α. We denote the vector $(z_1, \ldots, z_n)$ as **z**.

It should be noted that there is the boosting implementation for the MIL that uses these approximations [17], but it builds weighted weak classifiers, i.e., the approach does not use the GBM framework, which produces the regression weak models. Therefore, we propose two additional aggregating functions: the Hard Max Aggregation (MAX) and the Simple Attention Aggregation (ATT), which are shown in Table 2 wherein $\mathbb{I}[\cdot]$ is the indicator function.

Table 1. Aggregating functions and the corresponding partial derivatives for the MIL.

Name	Functions $G(z_1, \ldots, z_n)$	Partial derivatives
LSE	$\frac{1}{\alpha}\ln\left(\frac{1}{n}\sum_{i=1}^{n}\exp(\alpha z_i)\right)$	$\mathrm{softmax}(\alpha\mathbf{z})$
GM	$\left(\frac{1}{n}\sum_{i=1}^{n}(z_i)^\alpha\right)^{\frac{1}{\alpha}}$	$G(z)\cdot\frac{(z_i)^{\alpha-1}}{\sum_{i=1}^{n}(z_i)^\alpha}$
NOR	$1-\Pi_{i=1}^{n}(1-z_i)$	$(1-G(z))\frac{1}{1-z_i}$
ISR	$\frac{\zeta}{1+\zeta}, \zeta=\sum_{i=1}^{n}\frac{z_i}{1-z_i}$	$\left((1-G(z))\frac{1}{1-z_i}\right)^2$
LSE	$\frac{1}{\alpha}\ln\left(\frac{1}{n}\sum_{i=1}^{n}\exp(\alpha z_i)\right)$	$\mathrm{softmax}(\alpha\mathbf{z})$

In order to consider how to use the proposed aggregating functions in the GBM for the MIL, we first find the partial derivative of the loss function for computing residuals $r_k^{(i)}$. A natural loss function l for the classification task is the Binary Cross-Entropy represented as follows:

$$l(y, z) = -(y\log(z) + (1 - y)\log(1 - z)).$$

The partial derivative of the loss function applied to the sigmoid of the GBM output is of the form:

$$\frac{\partial l(y, \sigma(z))}{\partial z} = -\sigma(z) \cdot (1 - \sigma(z)) \cdot \left(\frac{y}{\sigma(z)} - \frac{1-y}{1-\sigma(z)} \right).$$
$$= -(y(1 - \sigma(z)) - \sigma(z) + y\sigma(z) = \sigma(z) - y.$$

Table 2. The proposed aggregating functions for the MIL.

Name	Functions $G(z_1, \ldots, z_n)$	Partial derivatives
MAX	$\max\{z_1, \ldots, z_n\}$	$\left(\mathbb{I}[z_i = \operatorname{argmax} \mathbf{z}] \right)_{i=1}^{n}$
ATT	$\mathbf{z}^T \cdot \operatorname{softmax}(\alpha \cdot \mathbf{z})$	$(\operatorname{softmax}(\alpha \cdot \mathbf{z})_i \cdot [1 + \alpha \cdot z_i - \alpha G(\mathbf{z})])_i$

3.2 Hard Max Aggregation

Residuals for the MAX aggregating function can be calculated as follows:

$$r_k^{(i)} = (\sigma(\max \mathbf{z}) - y_i) \cdot \mathbb{I}\left[F_{T-1}\left(\mathbf{x}_k^{(i)} \right) = \max \mathbf{z} \right]$$

$$= \begin{cases} \sigma(\max \mathbf{z}) - y_i, & if \ F_{T-1}\left(\mathbf{x}_k^{(i)} \right) = \max \mathbf{z}, \\ 0, & otherwise. \end{cases}$$

The above expression is equivalent to the instance-level loss calculated for one instance in a bag, which corresponds to $\max F_{T-1}$. However, it is important that we include points with zero residuals to a training set for building the base trees. It can be useful since these points may have already correct predictions which should not be changed by new trees. On the other hand, we can ignore these points during training to implement bagging-like algorithm, where a tree is built at each iteration on a new data subset and support positive bags with more than one positive instance. It yields the new Hard Max GBM modification.

3.3 Simple Attention Aggregation

The idea behind attention aggregation without trainable weights is to compute maximum as a weighted sum of input values, where weights show how relatively large each component is. Particularly, when $\alpha \to +\infty$, we can get:

$$z^T \cdot \operatorname{softmax}(\alpha \cdot z) = \sum_k z_k \cdot (\operatorname{softmax}(\alpha \cdot z))_k \xrightarrow[\alpha \to +\infty]{} z_{\operatorname{argmax} z}.$$

The ATT residuals are obtained as follows:

$$r_k^i = (\sigma(G(\mathbf{z})) - y_i) \cdot (\operatorname{softmax}(\alpha \cdot \mathbf{z})_k \cdot [1 + \alpha(z_k - G(\mathbf{z}))]),$$

where:

$$\mathbf{z} = \left(F_{T-1}\left(\mathbf{x}_j^{(i)} \right) \right)_{j=1}^{n_i}, \ G(\mathbf{z}) = \mathbf{z}^T \cdot \operatorname{softmax}(\alpha \cdot \mathbf{z}).$$

We can analyze the aggregation by considering the following difference:

$$z_k - G(\mathbf{z}) = z_k - \sum_q z_q \cdot \text{softmax}(\alpha \mathbf{z})_q$$

$$= z_k - \sum_q z_q \cdot w_q = z_k(1 - w_k) - \sum_{q \neq k} z_q \cdot w_q.$$

Let us compare it with $-1/\alpha$. Suppose that $z_k - G(\mathbf{z})$ less than $-1/\alpha$. Then we can write for $k : z_k = \max \mathbf{z}$ as follows:

$$z_k(1 - w_k) - \sum_{q \neq k} z_q \cdot w_q \leq -\frac{1}{\alpha},$$

$$z_k \left(\sum_{q \neq k} w_q \right) \leq \sum_{q \neq k} z_q \cdot w_q - \frac{1}{\alpha},$$

$$z_k \leq \sum_{q \neq k} z_q \cdot \frac{w_q}{\sum_{p \neq k} w_p} - \frac{1}{\alpha \cdot (1 - w_k)}.$$

It is guaranteed that there holds:

$$\sum_{q \neq k} z_q \cdot \frac{w_q}{\sum_{p \neq k} w_p} \leq z_k.$$

Hence:

$$z_k \geq z_k - \frac{1}{\alpha \cdot (1 - w_k)} \geq \sum_{q \neq k} z_q \cdot \frac{w_q}{\sum_{p \neq k} w_p} - \frac{1}{\alpha \cdot (1 - w_k)}.$$

The above is equivalent to:

$$z_k - G(\mathbf{z}) \geq -\frac{1}{\alpha},$$

when $w_k < 1$, otherwise we obviously obtain:

$$z_k - G(\mathbf{z}) = 0 > -\frac{1}{\alpha}.$$

For any other values, even for:

$$k : z_k = \min \mathbf{z}, \sum_{q \neq k} z_q \cdot \frac{w_q}{\sum_{p \neq k} w_p} \geq z_k,$$

value $(z_k - G(\mathbf{z}) - 1/\alpha)$ may be smaller or greater than zero. This implies that the component residual may be even inverted.

It should be noted that the ATT aggregation is a generalization for *average* MIL pooling, when $\alpha = 0$. Indeed, there holds:

$$\hat{G}_{\alpha=0}(\mathbf{z}) = \mathbf{z}^T \cdot \text{softmax}(0) = \frac{1}{n} \sum_k z_k.$$

Hence, residuals are of the form:

$$\hat{r}_k^{(i)} = \frac{1}{n_i} \left(\sigma \left(\hat{G}_{\alpha=0}(\mathbf{z}) \right) - y_i \right).$$

If $\alpha \to +\infty$, then we obtain the MAX aggregation. Thus, the ATT aggregation allows us to go smoothly from one pooling to another one by changing α.

3.4 Ensemble of GBMs and the Attention Neural Networks

We propose to replace the introduced ATT aggregating function with a trainable attention neural network. Similarly, to the multiclass classification, an ensemble of GBMs can be built to optimize a common classification loss. In this case, the loss function incorporates the attention-based aggregation of the instance embeddings, where each embedding is obtained by stacking GBM predictions for the corresponding instance.

An ensemble of GBMs can be represented as the following set:

$$\mathcal{F}_T = \left\{ F_T^{(1)}(\mathbf{x}), \dots, F_T^{(E)}(\mathbf{x}) \right\},$$

where E is the embedding dimension.

The ensemble prediction is the vector:

$$\vec{F}_T(\mathbf{x}) = \left(F_T^{(1)}(\mathbf{x}), \dots, F_T^{(E)}(\mathbf{x}) \right).$$

The aggregation model A takes the instance embedding vectors obtained with $\vec{F}_T$ and transforms them to a bag label prediction:

$$A\left(\vec{F}_T\left(\mathbf{x}_1^{(i)}\right), \dots, \vec{F}_T\left(\mathbf{x}_{n_i}^{(i)}\right) \right) \in [0, 1].$$

Let $\mathbf{e}_1^{(i)}, \dots, \mathbf{e}_{n_i}^{(i)}$ be embedding vectors. Then the Attention Neural Network (ANN) is defined as:

$$\text{ANN}\left(\mathbf{e}_1^{(i)}, \dots, \mathbf{e}_{n_i}^{(i)} \right) = \omega \bar{\mathbf{e}} + \beta,$$

where:

$$\bar{\mathbf{e}} = \sum_{k=1}^{n_i} \alpha_k \cdot \mathbf{e}_k^{(i)}, \quad \alpha = \text{softmax}\left(\left(\text{score}\left(\mathbf{e}_k^{(i)}, \mathbf{v} \right) \right)_{k=1}^{n_i} \right),$$

and $\mathbf{v} \in \mathbb{R}^E$ is a *template* trainable vector of parameters, ω, β are parameters of the linear neural network layer, projecting an embedding to the one-dimensional space, and "*score*" is a scoring function, e.g., $\text{score}(\mathbf{a}, \mathbf{b}) = \mathbf{a}^T \mathbf{b}$.

The proposed ANN aggregation is a generalization of the ATT aggregation. Indeed, if $E = 1$, $\mathbf{v} = (\alpha)$ and $\omega = 1$, then these aggregating functions are equivalent. In addition, this method like Attention-based Deep MIL [18] can be regarded as an embedding-level approach, which is preferable in terms of the bag level classification [18]. At the same time, attention weights α allow us to extract information about an instance which significantly affects the prediction and, therefore, to solve the well-known problem of interpreting the obtained predictions.

4 Numerical Experiments

We compare GBMIL with the available MIL models by training all the models on widely used MIL datasets Musk1, Musk2 (drug activity) [3] and Fox, Tiger, Elephant [14]. Numbers of bags N, instances n in each bag and the number of features m in instances in the datasets are provided in Table 3.

Table 3. A brief introduction about datasets for the MIL classification.

Data set	N	n	M
Elephant	200	1391	230
Fox	200	1302	230
Tiger	200	1220	230
Musk1	92	476	166
Musk2	102	6598	166

The following MIL models are used for comparison: mi-SVM [14], MI-SVM [14], MI-Kernel [19], EM-DD [20], mi-Graph [21], miVLAD [22], miFV [22], mi-Net [23], MI-Net [23], MI-Net with DS [23], MI-Net with RC [23], Attention and Gated-Attention [9].

We compare these models with three modifications of GBMIL: GBMIL-ATT, GBMIL-MAX, and GBMIL-ANN.

In experiments, we apply Extremely Randomized Trees (ERT) for initialization because they provide better results.

According to the ERT algorithm, a split point randomly selected for each feature and then the best split among these is selected [24].

We also use in experiments: sigmoid function with the trainable temperature parameter ω, which is initialized with 10, as indicator approximation; softmax operation with the trainable temperature parameter τ, which is is also initialized with 10; the number T of decision trees is 20; the largest depth h of trees is 5; the dimension E of each embedding vector is 4; the number of epochs is 2000; the batch size is 20 and the learning rate is 0.01.

The mean and standard deviation as accuracy measures are computed by using 5-fold cross-validation. Numerical results for datasets Elephant, Fox and Tiger are shown in Table 4.

Table 4. Accuracy measures (the mean and standard deviation) for comparison of the MIL classification models and proposed modifications by using datasets Elephant, For and Tiger.

Model	Elephant	Fox	Tiger
mi-SVM	0.822 ± N/A	0.582 ± N/A	0.784 ± N/A
MI-SVM	0.843 ± N/A	0.578 ± N/A	0.840 ± N/A
MI-Kernel	0.843 ± N/A	0.603 ± N/A	0.842 ± N/A
EM-DD	0.771 ± 0.097	0.609 ± 0.101	0.730 ± 0.096
mi-Graph	0.869 ± 0.078	0.620 ± 0.098	0.860 ± 0.083
miVLAD	0.850 ± 0.080	0.620 ± 0.098	0.811 ± 0.087
miFV	0.852 ± 0.081	0.621 ± 0.109	0.813 ± 0.083
mi-Net	0.858 ± 0.083	0.613 ± 0.078	0.824 ± 0.076
MI-Net	0.862 ± 0.077	0.622 ± 0.084	0.830 ± 0.072
MI-Net with DS	0.872 ± 0.072	0.630 ± 0.080	0.845 ± 0.087
MI-Net with RC	0.857 ± 0.089	0.619 ± 0.104	0.836 ± 0.083
Attention	0.868 ± 0.022	0.615 ± 0.043	0.839 ± 0.022
Gated-Attention	0.857 ± 0.027	0.603 ± 0.029	0.845 ± 0.018
GBMIL-ANN	**0.880** ± 0.041	0.685 ± 0.082	**0.925** ± 0.027
GBMIL-MAX	0.850 ± 0.050	**0.695** ± 0.048	0.913 ± 0.030
GBMIL-ATT	0.875 ± 0.059	0.690 ± 0.080	**0.925** ± 0.048

The best results in tables are shown in bold. Numerical results for datasets Musk1 and Musk2 are shown in Table 5.

One can see from Table 4 that GBMIL models constantly outperform other available models: GBMIL-ANN has the accuracy higher by 1.2% than the most accurate available model for the Elephant dataset, GBMIL-MAX shows 6.5% accuracy improvement for the Fox dataset, GBMIL-ANN and GBMIL-ATT improve accuracy by 8% than the best available model for the Tiger dataset.

It can be seen from Table 5 that the GBMIL models also outperform most available models on Musk1 and Musk2 datasets, showing the best result for Musk1 dataset.

Table 5. Accuracy measures (the mean and standard deviation) for comparison of the MIL classification models and proposed modifications by using datasets Musk1 and Musk2.

Model	Musk1	Musk2
mi-SVM	$0.874 \pm$ N/A	$0.836 \pm$ N/A
MI-SVM	$0.779 \pm$ N/A	$0.843 \pm$ N/A
MI-Kernel	$0.880 \pm$ N/A	$0.893 \pm$ N/A
EM-DD	0.849 ± 0.098	0.869 ± 0.108
mi-Graph	0.889 ± 0.073	$\mathbf{0.903} \pm 0.086$
miVLAD	0.871 ± 0.098	0.872 ± 0.095
miFV	0.909 ± 0.089	0.884 ± 0.094
mi-Net	0.889 ± 0.088	0.858 ± 0.110
MI-Net	0.887 ± 0.091	0.859 ± 0.102
MI-Net with DS	0.894 ± 0.093	0.874 ± 0.097
MI-Net with RC	0.898 ± 0.097	0.873 ± 0.098
Attention	0.892 ± 0.040	0.858 ± 0.048
Gated-Attention	0.900 ± 0.050	0.863 ± 0.042
GBMIL-ANN	$\mathbf{0.905} \pm 0.040$	0.885 ± 0.045
GBMIL-MAX	0.833 ± 0.089	0.845 ± 0.048
GBMIL-ATT	0.863 ± 0.038	0.890 ± 0.038

5 Conclusion

Three modifications of the MIL classification models (GBMIL-ANN, GBMIL-MAX, GBMIL-SM) have been proposed. The proposed models provide better quantitative results for tabular datasets in comparison with many existing MIL models, showing the accuracy improvement up to 8%. From the qualitative point of view, the proposed models take advantage by incorporation of Decision Trees ensembles, widely used for small tabular datasets and constantly evolving, which allows to leverage the recent developments in the regression field and apply them for MIL. The ideas behind the modifications can be regarded as starting points for developing a large class of the efficient MIL models which extend the introduced aggregation operations, especially the operations based on attention mechanisms. The development and the study of these models can be viewed as directions for further research.

Acknowledgments. This work is supported by the Russian Science Foundation under grant 21–11-00116.

References

1. Van der Laak, J., Litjens, G., Ciompi, F.: Deep learning in histopathology: the path to the clinic. Nature Medicine **27**, 775–784 (2021)
2. Yamamoto, Y., Tsuzuki, T., Akatsuka, J.: Automated acquisition of explainable knowledge from unannotated histopathology images. Nature Communications **10**, 1–9 (2019)
3. Dietterich, T., Lathrop, R., Lozano-Perez, T.: Solving the multiple instance problem with axis-parallel rectangles. Artificial Intelligence **89**, 31–71 (1997)
4. Wei, X.S., Ye, H.J., Mu, X., Wu, J., Shen, C., Zhou, Z.H.: Multiple instance learning with emerging novel class. IEEE Trans. Knowle. Data Eng. 33 (2019)
5. Srinidhi, C., Ciga, O., Martel, A.L.: Deep neural network models for computational histopathology: A survey. Medical Image Analysis **67**, 101813 (2021)
6. Babenko, B.: Multiple instance learning: Algorithms and applications. Technical report. University of California, San Diego (2008)
7. Cheplygina, V., de Bruijne, M., Pluim, J.: Not-so-supervised: A survey of semi-supervised, multi-instance, and transfer learning in medical image analysis. Medical Image Analysis **54**, 280–296 (2019)
8. Yao, J., Zhu, X., Jonnagaddala, J., Hawkins, N., Huang., J.: Whole slide images-based cancer survival prediction using attention guided deep multiple instance learning network. Medical Image Analysis **65**, 1–14 (2020)
9. Ilse, M., Tomczak, J., Welling, M.: Attention-based deep multiple instance learning. In: Proceedings of the 35th International Conference on Machine Learning, PMLR, Vol. 80, pp. 2127–2136 (2018)
10. Jiang, S., Suriawinata, A., Hassanpour, S.: Mhattnsurv: Multi-head attention for survival prediction using whole-slide pathology images, arXiv: 2110.11558 (2021)
11. Konstantinov, A., Utkin, L.: Multi-attention multiple instance learning. Neural Computing and Applications **34**, 14029–14051 (2022)
12. Rymarczyk, D., Kaczynska, A., Kraus, J., Pardyl, A., Zielinski, B.: ProtoMIL: multiple instance learning with prototypical parts for fine-grained interpretability, arXiv:2108.10612 (2021)
13. Friedman, J.: Stochastic gradient boosting. Computational statistics & data analysis **38**, 367–378 (2002)
14. Andrews, S., Tsochantaridis, I., Hofmann, T.: Support vector machines for multiple-instance learning. In: Proceedings of the 15th international conference on neural information processing systems, NIPS'02, pp. 577–584. MIT Press, Cambridge, MA, USA (2002)
15. Carbonneau, M.A., Cheplygina, V., Granger, E., Gagnon, G.: Multiple instance learning: a survey of problem characteristics and applications. Pattern Recognition **77**, 329–353 (2018)
16. Ramon, J., Raedt, L.D.: Multi instance neural networks. In: Proceedings of the ICML-2000 Workshop on attribute-value and relational learning, pp. 53–60 (2000)
17. Viola, P., Platt, J., Zhang, C.: Multiple instance boosting for object detection. In: Advances in neural information processing systems, Vol. 18, pp. 1–8 (2005)
18. Ilse, M., Tomczak, J., Welling, M.: Attention-based deep multiple instance learning. In: International conference on machine learning, PMLR, pp. 2127–2136 (2018)
19. Gartner, T., Flach, P., Kowalczyk, A., Smola, A.: Multi-instance kernels. In: Proceedings of ICML, Vol. 2, pp. 179–186 (2002)
20. Zhang, Q., Goldman, S.: Em-dd: An improved multiple-instance learning technique. In: Proceedings of NIPS, pp. 1073–1080 (2002)
21. Zhou, Z.H., Sun, Y.Y., Li, Y.F.: Multi-instance learning by treating instances as non-iid samples. In: Proceedings of ICML, pp. 1249–1256 (2009)

22. Wei, X.S., Wu, J., Zhou, Z.H.: Scalable algorithms for multi-instance learning. IEEE Trans. Neur. Netw. Learn. Sys. **28**, 975–987 (2017)
23. Wang, X., Yan, Y., Tang, P., Bai, X., Liu, W.: Revisiting multiple instance neural networks. Pattern Recognition **74**, 15–24 (2018)
24. Geurts, P., Ernst, D., Wehenkel, L.: Extremely randomized trees. Machine learning **63**, 3–42 (2006)

Approach to Numerical Solution of Nonlinear Optimal Feedback Control Problems

Samir Guliyev[1,2]([⊠]) [iD]

[1] Institute of Control Systems, 68, B. Vakhabzadeh street, Baku AZ1141, Azerbaijan
`azcopal@gmail.com`
[2] Azerbaijan State Oil and Industry University, 20, Azadlyg avenue, Baku AZ1010, Azerbaijan

Abstract. In the paper, we consider optimal feedback control problems for dynamic, in the general case, nonlinear systems with lumped parameters based on continuous and discrete feedback on the object's state. To calculate the values of the feedback control's parameters, we propose to use the measured values of observable components of the phase vector or the object's output at the current and some previous (past) moments of time in order to compensate for the inability to measure all the components of the object's phase state. As a result of this kind of formation of the dependence of the parameters of the synthesized control on a part of the object's state, the process under consideration will be described by ordinary differential equations with time-constant delay arguments in the phase state. The feedback control problem is solved numerically by reducing it to a finite-dimensional optimization problem. To this end, we derive formulas for the gradient of the objective functional of the reduced problem with respect to the optimizable parameters are zonal values of the feedback parameters. These formulas make it possible to formulate necessary first-order optimality conditions, as well as to use them for numerical solution to model problems using first-order optimization methods.

Keywords: Feedback Control · Gradient of Functional · Numerical Optimization Methods · Delay Differential Equations · Zonal Control Actions

1 Introduction

Of constant practical interest among control problems are the problems of synthesizing optimal controls for complex technical objects, for example, manipulation robots, rockets, etc. Feedback control problems within the framework of automatic control and regulation systems have been studied by many authors [1–6]. Interest in this class of problems has increased over the past decades due to the development of technical, computational, and measuring tools for monitoring and controlling technical objects and technological processes. In most cases, linear systems were considered, and in the case of nonlinear systems, the corresponding linearized systems were used. For linear objects with relatively small dimensions of the phase and control vectors, effective state feedback control methods have been developed, which have been widely used in practice in automatic control and regulation systems, as well as in intelligent measuring systems. The works [7, 8] present fairly compact and complete surveys of major results in the field of feedback control and regulation systems. Note that an important role in the development of feedback control systems and their widespread practical implementation belongs to modern technical means of measuring and computing technology, which make it possible to carry out a large amount of measuring and computing work in real time.

The main differences and advantages of the approach proposed in this paper to constructing a feedback control system from the known classical methods are as follows. The approach makes it possible to study objects with both linear and nonlinear dynamics from a unified standpoint. The approach is robust (stable) to errors (noises) in measurements of the current object's state. This is explained by the fact that the parameters of the synthesized values of control actions depend not on the current measured values of the object's state but on the subset (zone) of the set of possible states to which the current state belongs. Feedback control parameters (coefficients of dependence of the control on the state) in each zone are constant and determined from the optimality condition of the given control quality functional. The cases of discrete and continuous feedback are studied, for each of which a piecewise-constant and linear functional dependence of the parameters of zonal control actions on the object's state or output is considered.

The constancy of the parameters of zonal control actions (zonal controls themselves or zonal amplification coefficients with a linear dependence of the control on the object's state or output) ensures the robustness of the control system and feasibility of synthesized control actions with a sufficiently high accuracy and improves technical performance of the equipment involved in the control loop. Examples of objects for which the considered classes of control actions are the most appropriate are pumping and compressor stations in pipeline transport systems of hydrocarbon raw materials, wells in oil and gas fields, and many other technological processes and technical objects. On the one hand, a frequent operational change in the modes of controllable actions for these objects is practically impossible, and on the other hand, it leads to rapid wear of the equipment.

For each class of control actions considered, we obtain formulas for the gradient of the objective functional with respect to the optimizable parameters of synthesized controls. These formulas make it possible to formulate the necessary optimality conditions and to construct numerical solution schemes based on first-order iterative optimization methods. We present the results of numerical experiments obtained by solving test problems.

2   Problem Statement and Solution Scheme

Here we formulate the feedback control problems for nonlinear objects with lumped parameters with various types of feedback on the input and output of the object and on various classes of zonal control functions with inaccurately given information on the values of the object's parameters. Let the controllable object (process) be described by the following nonlinear system of differential equations:

$$\dot{x}(t) = f(x(t), u(t), p), t \in (0, T].$$
(1)

Here $x(t) \in \mathbb{R}^n$ denotes the continuous, piecewise continuously differentiable function of the phase state; T is the duration of the control process; $u(t) \in U$ is the r-dimensional vector of piecewise-continuous control actions, the domain of admissible values of which is a closed convex set $U \subset \mathbb{R}^r$; p is the m-dimensional vector of the object's parameters constant in time, the exact values of which are not known, but they can take values from some predetermined set P; there is given the density (weight) function of the assumed values defined on P:

$$0 \leq \rho_P(p), \ p \in P, \ \int_p \rho_P(p)dp = 1. \tag{2}$$

The vector function $f(x, u, p)$ is continuously differentiable with respect to the first two arguments and continuous with respect to the third argument. Control of the process (1) is carried out taking into account the presence of feedback from the object, while the state vector $x(t)$ can be measured in whole or in part. Assume that observations of the state of the object can be carried out continuously or at discrete moments of time.

Further assume that the initial state of the object $x^0 = x(0)$ is not specified exactly, but there is a set X^0 of possible initial states with the density (weight) function $\rho_{X^0}(x^0)$ defined on X^0:

$$0 \leq \rho_{X^0}(x^0), \ x^0 \in X^0, \ \int_{X^0} \rho_{X^0}(x^0)dx^0 = 1. \tag{3}$$

For each given specific initial condition $x^0 \in X^0$ and specific value of the parameters $p \in P$, we estimate the quality of control over the time interval $[0, T]$ using the following functional:

$$J(u; T, x^0, p) = \int_0^T f^0\big(x(t), u(t)\big)dt + \Phi(x(T), T), \tag{4}$$

where $x(t) = x(t; x^0, p, u)$ is the solution to the system (1) under initial conditions $x(0) = x^0 \in X^0$, control $u(t) \in U$, and the values of the parameters $p \in P$. The process completion time T can be either a given value, as in the case of functional (4), or an optimizable value, as, for example, in optimal fast-action problems. Considering that the initial state and parameter values are not specified exactly but are determined within the accuracy of density functions on the corresponding sets, we evaluate the quality of control by the following average value of the functional (4) over all possible initial states $x^0 \in X^0$ and parameter values $p \in P$:

$$\mathcal{F}(u, T) = \int_{X^0} \int_P J(u; T, x^0, p) \cdot \rho_P(p) \cdot \rho_{X^0}(x^0) \, dp \, dx^0. \tag{5}$$

Note that during the operation of the object, it may be possible to measure the state of only part $\tilde{x}(t) \in \mathbb{R}^\ell$ of the components of the phase vector $x(t)$, $\ell \leq n$, continuously in time. Denote by $X \subseteq \mathbb{R}^n$ and $\tilde{X} \subseteq \mathbb{R}^\ell$ the set of all possible states of the object itself and the set of all possible states of the components $\tilde{x}(t)$ of the object state $x(t)$, respectively, whose dynamics is described by system (1) for different initial states $x^0 \in X^0$, parameter values $p \in P$, and controls $u(t) \in U$ for $t \in (0, T]$. As a rule, for many processes, based on experience and the results of studying the functioning of objects, the set X or $\tilde{X}$ of possible states is known in advance. Control of the dynamics of process (1) is carried out taking into account the presence of feedback on the object's current state $x(t)$ or $\tilde{x}\,(t)$, or on the object's output $y(t)$, which is determined by the nonlinear function of its state $x(t)$:

$$y(t) = \mathcal{G}(x(t)), y \in \mathbb{R}^\nu, \tag{6}$$

where the ν-dimensional observation vector function $\mathcal{G}(x)$ is continuously differentiable with respect to each variable on the set X and, as a rule, $\nu \leq n$. We assume that process (1) is completely observable locally.

Feedback (retrieval of information on the phase state or the object's output) can be carried out both continuously for $t \in (0, T]$ and at discretely given moments of time $\tau_j \in [0, T], j = 0, 1, 2, \ldots, N$. To form the current values of the control actions using feedback, the concept of "zonal control" is introduced. The values of control actions $u(t)$ in the control process will be assigned as described below. Let $Y \subset \mathbb{R}^\nu$ be the set of values of the observable output vector $y(\cdot)$ from (6) for various possible values of the state $x(\cdot) \in X$. Let us divide the sets Y and $\tilde{X}$ into L disjoint open subsets (so-called zones) $Y^i \subset \mathbb{R}^\nu$ and $\Omega_i \subset \mathbb{R}^\ell$, respectively, so that:

$$Y = \bigcup_{i=1}^L \overline{Y}_i, Y_i \cap Y_j = \varnothing, i \neq j, i, j = 1, 2, \ldots, L, \tag{7}$$

$$\tilde{X} = \bigcup_{i=1}^L \overline{\Omega}_i, \Omega_i \cap \Omega_j = \varnothing, i \neq j, i, j = 1, 2, \ldots, L, \tag{8}$$

where $\overline{Y}_i$ and $\overline{\Omega}_i$ are the closures of the sets Y_i and Ω_i, respectively. The boundaries between any two adjacent (having a common boundary) zones Y_i and Y_j are defined by known continuous, almost everywhere differentiable functions $h_{i,j}(y) = -h_{j,i}(y) = 0$, and we assume that $Y_i \subset \{y : h_{i,j}(y) < 0\}$ or $Y_i \subset \{y : h_{j,i}(y) \geq 0\}$. For the first type of feedback control, the values of the control actions $u(t)$ at the current moment of time in the process of controlling the dynamics of the object (1) will be assigned depending on which of the subsets Y_i the observed current value of the output vector $y(t)$ belongs to. For the second type of feedback control, to form the control actions $u(t)$ at the current moment of time, in addition to the state value $\tilde{x}\,(t)$, we use previously measured values $\tilde{x}\,(t-\tau_j), j = 1, 2, \ldots, s$. The choice of delay times $\tau_j, j = 1, 2, \ldots, s$, is done depending on the rate of change of the object's state; namely, at high speeds, it is desirable to choose the quantities τ_j sufficiently small. The choice of these quantities also depends on the accuracy of the measurements; namely, with low accuracy, they are chosen large enough so that the dynamics of the change in the object's state would exceed the measurement accuracy. Then the value of the control at the current moment of time t is built as a linear dependence on the values of the components of the phase variable $\tilde{x}\,(t)$ measured at the moments of time t and $t - \tau_j, j = 1, 2, \ldots, s$:

$$u(t) = \gamma_0^i \tilde{x}\,(t) + \gamma_1^i \tilde{x}\,(t - \tau_1) + \gamma_2^i \tilde{x}\,(t - \tau_2) + \cdots + \gamma_s^i \tilde{x}\,(t - \tau_s), \tilde{x}\,(t) \in \Omega_i, \tag{9}$$

where $\gamma_0^i, \gamma_1^i, \gamma_2^i, \ldots, \gamma_s^i$ are constant matrices of dimension $(r \times \ell)$ defining the optimizable feedback parameters when the components $\tilde{x}\,(t)$ of the phase state belong to the ith zone Ω_i. Such controls will be called zonal. The problem of assigning to each zone Y_i or Ω_i, $i = 1, 2, \ldots, L$, control actions optimal in the sense of functional (5) will be called the feedback zonal control problem. We consider the following variants of the feedback zonal control problem, which differ in the nature of the observation and the type of dependence of the control on the observable state or output vector.

Problem 1. There are given discrete moments of observation time $\xi_j \in [0, T]$, $j = 0, 1, 2, \ldots, N$, such that $\xi_0 = 0$ and $\xi_N = T$, at which it is possible to measure the value of the object's output state $y(\xi_j) = \mathcal{G}(x(\xi_j)) \in Y$. The frequency of these observations should be such, that while the object's state belongs to any zone, at least one observation is made. If this condition is not met, the zones through which the trajectory $y(t)$ did not pass from any starting point, as well as the zones in which no state measurements were made, will not be assigned the values of the zone control parameters. The control values $u(t)$ constant at $t \in [\xi_j, \xi_{j+1})$ are determined depending on the last measured value of the observation vector for the object's current output, namely, depending on which subset (zone) Y_i, $i = 1, 2, \ldots, L$, of the space Y the last measured (observed) output state belonged to. Thus, each subset Y_i has its own constant control value:

$$u(t) = \vartheta^i = \text{const} \in U, y(\xi_j) = \mathcal{G}(x(\xi_j)) \in Y_i, t \in [\xi_j, \xi_{j+1}). \tag{10}$$

If the observed output value $y(\xi_j)$ belongs to the boundary of any zones, then we use the value of the zonal control of the adjacent zone into which the trajectory has passed. Problem 1 consists in finding admissible zonal control values ϑ^i, $i = 1, 2, \ldots, L$, according to (8) that optimize the value of the functional (5). The dimension of the optimizable finite-dimensional vector in this case is $L \times r$.

Problem 2. Control actions are determined by linear functions from the results of observing the parameters of the object's output state at the given discrete moments of time $\xi_j \in [0, T]$, $j = 0, 1, 2, \ldots, N$:

$$u(t) = \alpha_1^i \cdot y(\xi_j) + \beta_1^i, y(\xi_j) = \mathcal{G}(x(\xi_j)) \in Y_i, t \in [\xi_j, \xi_{j+1}). \tag{11}$$

Here α_1^i is the $r \times \nu$ matrix and β_1^i r-dimensional vector constant for $t \in [\xi_j, \xi_{j+1})$. Problem 2 consists in determining the zonal values α_1^i and β_1^i, $i = 1, 2, \ldots, L$. The dimension of the optimizable vector is $L \times r \times (\nu + 1)$.

Problem 3. Continuous measurements of the object's output vector are carried out, and the control actions assume zonal values:

$$u(t) = \theta^i = \text{const} \in U, y(t) = \mathcal{G}(x(t)) \in Y_i, t \in [0, T], i = 1, 2, \ldots, L. \tag{12}$$

Problem 3 consists in determining the admissible zonal control values θ^i, $i = 1, 2, \ldots, L$, that optimize the value of the functional (5). The dimension of the optimizable vector is $L \times r$.

Problem 4. Continuous measurements of the vector of observations of the object's output state are conducted. The control is determined by a linear function of the measured output values:

$$u(t) = \alpha_2^i \cdot y(t) + \beta_2^i, y(t) = \mathcal{G}(x(t)) \in Y_i, t \in [0, T], \tag{13}$$

It is required to find admissible values α_2^i and β_2^i, $i = 1, 2, \ldots, L$, that optimize the value of the functional (5). The number of optimizable parameters is $r \times L \times (\nu + 1)$.

Problem 5. It is assumed in (9) that the values τ_j are sufficiently small, and for $\tilde{x}$ $(t) \in \Omega_i$, the condition $\tilde{x}$ $(t - \tau_j) \in \Omega_i$ is satisfied for at least one index $j \in \{1, 2, \ldots, s\}$. To build the subsets Ω_i constructively, we proceed as described below. Let each of the components $\tilde{x}_s(t)$ of the phase vector $\tilde{x}$ (t) under all possible initial conditions $x^0 \in X^0$, parameters $p \in P$, and controls $u(t) \in U$ belong to some finite interval:

$$\underline{\omega}_k \leq \tilde{x}_k(t) \leq \overline{\omega}_k, t \in [0, T], k = 1, 2, \ldots, \ell. \tag{14}$$

We divide each of the intervals $\left[\underline{\omega}_k, \overline{\omega}_k\right]$ by points $\hat{x}_{k,j}$, $j = 0, 1, .., \ell_k$, such that $\hat{x}_{k,0} = \underline{\omega}_k$ and $\hat{x}_{k,\ell_k} = \overline{\omega}_k$, into ℓ_k subintervals. Let us introduce the notation for ℓ-dimensional parallelepipeds:

$$\Omega_i = \left\{ x \in \mathbb{R}^\ell : \hat{x}_{k,i_k-1} \leq x_k \leq \hat{x}_{k,i_k}, i_k = 1, 2, \ldots, \ell_k, k = 1, 2, ..., \ell \right\}, \tag{15}$$

where $i = (i_1, i_2, \ldots, i_\ell)$ is the m-dimensional multiindex. Substituting the feedback control in (9) using the values of the observed components $\tilde{x}$ (t) at the current and past moments of time into the system (1), we obtain:

$$\dot{x}(t) = f\left(x(t), \gamma_0^i \tilde{x} (t) + \gamma_1^i \tilde{x} (t - \tau_1) + \gamma_2^i \tilde{x} (t - \tau_2) + \cdots + \gamma_s^i \tilde{x} (t - \tau_s), p \right) \tag{16}$$

for $\tilde{x}$ $(t) \in \Omega_i$, $i = 1, 2, \ldots, M$, where M is the total number of zones. The system of differential Eqs. (16) is a system with constant delay arguments in the phase variable [13]. Thus, the original optimal control problem (1)-(5), taking into account the zonal feedback with part of the components of the phase variable in the form (9), is reduced to finding the feedback parameters $\gamma^i = \left[\gamma_0^i, \gamma_1^i, \gamma_2^i, \ldots, \gamma_s^i \right]$, $i = 1, 2, \ldots, M$, that are $(r \times \ell)$-dimensional constant matrices, under which the solutions of the initial-value problems with respect to the system of delay differential Eqs. (16) with the set of initial conditions X^0 and the set of parameters P minimize the functional (5) depending on $\gamma = (\gamma^1, \gamma^2, \ldots, \gamma^M)$ only, i.e., $\mathcal{F} = \mathcal{F}(\gamma, T)$. The dimension of the resulting parametric optimal control problem is equal to $r \times \ell \times M \times (s+1)$, i.e., $\gamma \in \mathbb{R}^{r \times \ell \times M \times (s+1)}$.

All five formulations of the feedback zonal control problems considered above lead to finite-dimensional optimization problems. To solve the first, third, and fifth problems, in the case of a simple construction of the set of admissible controls U (for example, a parallelepiped, a ball, a polyhedron, etc.), it is effective to use first-order numerical optimization methods – gradient projection methods or conjugate gradient projection methods. If the domain of admissible controls has a complex boundary and the projection operator on it is not constructive, then to solve all five problems, one can use sequential unconditional optimization methods (for example, internal and external penalty functions methods) [14]. In the statements of the formulated problems, it is possible to consider the case when the time T is given, and it is also possible that the time T is optimizable.

To construct iterative procedures based on numerical optimization methods, it is important to have exact formulas for the components of the gradients of the objective functional in the space of optimizable parameters of the zonal controls. For this purpose, we derive formulas for the gradients of the functionals of the problems under consideration. The derivation of these formulas is based on the technique of calculating the increment of the objective functional obtained by incrementing an optimizable parameter, as well as the technique of obtaining the necessary first-order optimality conditions for discontinuous systems and systems with variable structure [15–17]. Using these results, we can prove theorems, each of which contains formulas for the components of the gradient of the objective functional with respect to the optimizable parameters in problems 1–5.

Theorem 1. The components of the gradient of the objective functional on the class of controls (11) are determined by the formulas:

$$\frac{\partial \mathcal{F}(u,T)}{\partial \alpha_1^i} = \int_{X^0} \int_P \sum_{j:\mathcal{G}\left(x(\tau_j;x^0,p,u)\right)\in Y_i} \int_{\xi_j}^{\xi_{j+1}} \left[-\psi(t;x^0,p,u) \cdot \frac{\partial f(x(t;x^0,p,u),u,p)}{\partial u} + \right.$$

$$\left. + \frac{\partial f^0(x(t;x^0,p,u),u,p)}{\partial u} \right] dt \times \mathcal{G}\left(x(\xi_j;x^0,p,u)\right) \rho_{X^0}(x^0) \, \rho_P(p) \, dp \, dx^0 / (\text{mes } X^0 \cdot \text{mes } P),$$

$$\frac{\partial \mathcal{F}(u,T)}{\partial \beta_1^i} = \int_{X^0} \int_P \sum_{j:\mathcal{G}\left(x(\tau_j;x^0,p,u)\right)\in Y_i} \int_{\xi_j}^{\xi_{j+1}} \left[-\psi(t;x^0,p,u) \cdot \frac{\partial f(x(t;x^0,p,u),u,p)}{\partial u} + \right.$$

$$\left. + \frac{\partial f^0(x(t;x^0,p,u),u,p)}{\partial u} \right] dt \times \rho_{X^0}(x^0) \, \rho_P(p) \, dp \, dx^0,$$

where $i = 1, 2, ..., L$; $\psi(t; x^0, p, u)$, $t \in [0, T]$, is the solution to the adjoint initial-value problem:

$$\psi(T; x^0, p, u) = -\frac{\partial \Phi(x(T;x^0,p,u),T)}{\partial x},$$

$$\dot{\psi}(t; x^0, p, u) = \frac{\partial f^0(x(t;x^0,p,u),u,p)}{\partial x} - \psi(t;x^0,p,u) \cdot \frac{\partial f(x(t;x^0,p,u),u,p)}{\partial x} + $$

$$+ \sum_{j=1}^{N-1} \int_{\xi_j}^{\xi_{j+1}} \left[\frac{\partial f^0(x(\tau;x^0,p,u),u,p)}{\partial u} - \psi(\tau;x^0,p,u) \cdot \frac{\partial f(x(\tau;x^0,p,u),u,p)}{\partial u} \right] d\tau \times$$

$$\times \alpha_1^i \, \mathcal{G}\left(x(\xi_j;x^0,p,u)\right) \delta(t - \xi_j), \quad t \in [0, T),$$

where $\delta(\cdot)$ is the Dirac delta function.

Theorem 2. For the classes of feedback controls (10)–(13), if the process completion time $T = T(X^0, P)$ is optimizable, then the derivative of the functional (5) with respect to the time T is determined by the formula:

$$\frac{\partial \mathcal{F}(u,T)}{\partial T} = \int_{X^0} \int_P [f^0(x(T;x^0,p,u),u,p) - \psi(T;x^0,p,u) \cdot f(x(T;x^0,p,u),u,p) + $$

$$+ \frac{\partial \Phi(x(T;x^0,p,u),T)}{\partial T} \right] \times \rho_{X^0}(x^0) \, \rho_P(p) \, dp \, dx^0,$$

where $\psi(t; x^0, p, u)$ is the solution of the adjoint problem corresponding to the case of the considered class of feedback controls.

Note that to prove these theorems, we use either the technique of obtaining necessary first-order optimality conditions for discontinuous systems [15, 18] or the technique of obtaining necessary optimality conditions of the first order on the class of piecewise-constant and piecewise-linear functions [9, 16]. To prove Theorem 2, one can use, for example, the scheme applied in [2] for problems with a non-fixed value of the control process completion time.

The quality of the control system with the use of zonal control actions is significantly affected by the structure of the division of the entire set of possible output values Y and the set of phase states $\tilde{X}$ into zones Y_i and Ω_i, $i = 1, 2, ..., L$, respectively. It is clear that increasing the number of zones due to their refinement can only lead to a decrease in the functional value. On the other hand, increasing the number of zones leads to the situation where control actions may change their values more often in time, and, therefore, the robustness property of the control system degrades, which often leads to rapid wear and failure of actuators. Conversely, increasing the size of the zones, i.e., decreasing their number, degrades the controllability of the object, and with a small number of them, the object may become completely uncontrollable. On the other hand, this increases the value of the objective functional, i.e., the quality of control deteriorates. Given the above, an important role is played by the choice of both the number and specifically the structure of the zones Y_i and Ω_i, $i = 1, 2, ..., L$. The following approach is recommended for choosing a rational number of zones and determining the zones Y_i and Ω_i, $i = 1, 2, ..., L$, themselves. For this purpose, the initial value L is selected, and any zones Y_i and Ω_i, $i = 1, 2, ..., L$, that satisfy conditions (7) and (8) are assigned. Having solved the feedback control problem for any strategy of organizing the control, a comparative analysis of the obtained values of the parameters of control actions for all neighboring zones is carried out. If the parameters of the control actions in any adjacent zones differ by a sufficiently small value, then these zones can be combined into one, thus reducing the number L. If the control actions in adjacent zones differ significantly, then each of these adjacent zones should be divided, for example, into two zones, thus increasing the number L and again solving the feedback control problem. The increase in the number of zones should be carried out until the value of the objective functional ceases to change significantly.

3   Results of Numerical Experiments

First, we consider the numerical solution to the feedback control problem for a nonlinear system with feedback on the object's entire state.

Example 1. Let us apply the obtained formulas to the construction of the considered variants of synthesized controls in the example of the following problem. The dimensions of the vectors are as follows: $m = 1$, i.e., $p \in P \subset \mathbb{R}$; $n = 2$, i.e., $x = (x_1, x_2) \in \mathbb{R}^2$; $r = 1$, i.e., $u \in U = [-1, 1] \subset \mathbb{R}$. The system (1) has the following form:

$$\dot{x}(t) = \left\{ \begin{array}{c} \dot{x}_1(t) \\ \dot{x}_2(t) \end{array} \right\} = \left\{ \begin{array}{c} x_2(t) \\ -\sin x_1(t) - px_2(t) + u(t) \end{array} \right\}, t > 0 \qquad (17)$$

The set P consists of three points: $P = \{2.9, 3.0, 3.1\}$. The set X^0 consists of 80 points $x_j^0 \in \mathbb{R}^2, j = 1, 2, \ldots, 80$, uniformly distributed on a circle of radius 2.

$$\Phi\left(x\left(T; x^0, p, u\right), T\right) = R \cdot \left[\min(x_1^2\left(T; x^0, p, u\right) + x_2^2\left(T; x^0, p, u\right) - 0.0001; 0) \right]^2,$$

R is a sufficiently large positive number; $f^0(x(t), u(t), p) \equiv 1$.

Then the objective functional to be minimized, averaged over all possible values of the parameters $p \in P$ and initial points $x^0 \in X^0$, for the problem under consideration will have the following form:

$$\mathcal{F}(u, T) = \frac{1}{240} \sum_{j=1}^{80} \sum_{i=1}^{3} \left[T\left(x_j^0, p_i, u\right) + \Phi\left(x\left(T; x_j^0, p_i, u\right), T\right) \right] \rightarrow \min_{u \in U}. \quad (18)$$

Here, the function $T\left(x_j^0, p_i, u\right)$ determines the time of bringing the object from the point $x_j^0 \in X^0$ to the given neighborhood of the origin for the value of the parameter $p_i \in P$. The entire phase space of all possible states of the vector $x(t)$ is divided into $L = 72$ zones. Zones are obtained using circles of radii 0.1, 0.5, 1.0, 1.5, and 2.0 and straight lines that divide each quarter of the x_1x_2 plane into 18 parts. The zones are numbered counterclockwise, starting from the first quarter, in order of increasing radius, forming six rings. The initial control values in all zones were taken to be equal to 0. The value of the parameter R was successively increased from 10^2 to 10^6. The optimization parameter values were chosen as follows: accuracies for one-dimensional minimization $\delta = 10^{-5}$ and for multidimensional minimization $\varepsilon = 10^{-4}$. The parameter ξ in problems 1 and 2 varied during numerical experiments. The results of solving the first four aforementioned problems are shown in Fig. 1.

Problem 1. In each zone, the control u takes a constant value. Thus, the vectors $\vartheta = \left(\vartheta^1, \vartheta^2, ..., \vartheta^{72}\right)$ and $T = (T_1, T_2, ..., T_{80})$ are optimizable in the problem. Observations of the process state are conducted at moments of time $\xi_i = \xi_{i-1} + \xi, \xi = \text{const}, i = 1, 2, \ldots$. Figure 1(a) shows the optimal trajectories of the system.

Problem 2. In each zone, the control u depends linearly on the state of the system at the current time. Thus, the optimizable vectors are $\alpha_{1,x_1} = \left(\alpha_{1,x_1}^1, \alpha_{1,x_1}^2, ..., \alpha_{1,x_1}^{72}\right)$ and $\alpha_{1,x_2} = \left(\alpha_{1,x_2}^1, \alpha_{1,x_2}^2, ..., \alpha_{1,x_2}^{72}\right), \beta_1 = (\beta_1^1, \beta_1^2, ..., \beta_1^{72})$. The state of the process was observed at the moments of time $\xi_i = \xi_{i-1} + \xi, \xi = \text{const}, i = 1, 2, \ldots$. Figure 1(b) shows the optimal trajectories of the system.

Problem 3. In each zone, the control u takes a constant value. Thus, the vectors $\theta = \left(\theta^1, \theta^2, ..., \theta^{72}\right)$ and $T = (T_1, T_2, ..., T_{80})$ are optimizable in the problem. The state of the process was observed continuously. Figure 1(c) shows the optimal trajectories of the system.

Problem 4. In each zone, the control u depends linearly on the state of the system at the current time. Thus, the optimizable vectors are $\alpha_{2,x_1} = \left(\alpha_{2,x_1}^1, \alpha_{2,x_1}^2, ..., \alpha_{2,x_1}^{72}\right)$ and $\alpha_{2,x_2} = \left(\alpha_{2,x_2}^1, \alpha_{2,x_2}^2, ..., \alpha_{2,x_2}^{72}\right), \beta_2 = (\beta_2^1, \beta_2^2, ..., \beta_2^{72})$. The state of the process was observed continuously. Figure 1(d) shows the optimal trajectories of the system.

Next, we consider the numerical solution to the feedback control problem for the nonlinear system (17) with feedback on the object's output.

Example 2. The object's output state $y(t)$ is observable, which is given by the following non-linear function:

$$y(t) = \mathcal{G}(x(t)) = x_1(t) + x_2(t) + x_1(t) \cdot x_2(t), y(t) \in \mathbb{R}. \quad (19)$$

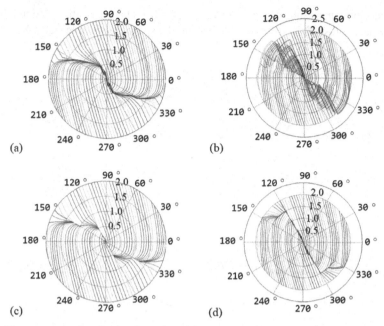

Fig. 1. Phase portrait of optimal trajectories of the system (17) in problems 1–4 for the feedback state problem.

The sets P and X^0 and the objective functional are the same as in the first example. For the set of possible values of the output $y(t)$, the segment $[-5.5, 5.5]$ was chosen as a result of numerical experiments on calculating the state of the system (17) for various admissible values $x^0 \in X^0$, $p \in P$, and $u \in U$. The problem was solved numerically, with the set of possible output values Y divided into $L = 112$ zones. Zones are obtained by dividing the set by points $\{y_i = -5.5 + i \cdot 0.1, i = 0, 1, 2, ..., 110\}$, i.e., $Y_i = (-5.5 + 0.1 \times (i - 1), -5.5 + 0.1 \times i)$. The initial values of the control actions as well as the values of the parameters of the numerical methods involved in the solution to the problems were chosen the same as in Example 1. The results of solving the first four afore-mentioned problems are shown in Fig. 2 in the form of optimal trajectories of the system.

It is of interest to compare the solutions of the feedback zonal control problem with the object's output feedback and state feedback considered in the previous sections. In both problems, the object is described by the same system (17) with the same objective functional (18). As can be seen from Figs. 1(a–d) and 2(a–d), the optimal trajectories in all problems are quite the same, but nevertheless, for almost all possible initial points $x^0 \in X^0$, the times of bringing the object to the neighborhood of the origin of the phase plane are different. The values of the objective functionals also differ; namely, the value of the functional with feedback on the object's output exceeds the value of the functional with feedback on the phase state for all variants of the classes of control functions by approximately 10–15%. It should be noted, of course, that the values of the parameters of the zonal control functions in terms of output and state are completely different, as are the chosen zones (subsets) Y_i, $i = 1, 2, ..., L$, the sets of possible output values Y and the zones (subsets) X_i, $i = 1, 2, ..., L$, from the space of possible states X.

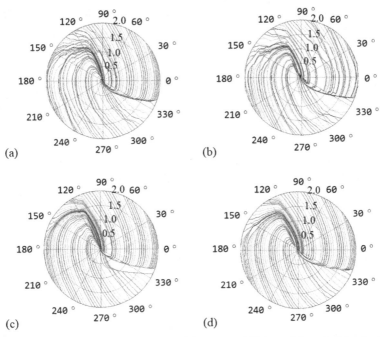

Fig. 2. Phase portrait of optimal trajectories of the system (17) in problems 1–4 for the feedback output problem.

4 Conclusion

The paper has proposed an approach to the optimal feedback control of objects described by nonlinear systems of ordinary differential equations. The difference from the classical methods of optimal feedback control, in which the values of control actions depend on the current state of the process, is as follows: Here, the values of control actions depend on the subset (zone) of states to which the process's current state belongs. The proposed approach is more resistant (stable) to errors in measurements of the current state. With respect to the parameters of the zonal values of the control actions, a finite-dimensional optimization problem is obtained, for whose numerical solution there are ready-made standard software packages. The results of carried out numerical experiments are presented on the example of solving some test problems.

References

1. Desoer, C.A., Vidyasagar, M.: Feedback Systems: Input-Output Properties 1. Academic Press, New-York (1975)

2. Bryson, A.E.: Applied Optimal Control, Estimation and Control, 1st edn. CRC Press, Boca Raton (1975)
3. Egorov, A.M.: Fundamentals of Control Theory. Fizmatlit, Moscow (2004). (In Russ.)
4. Yemelyanov, S.V., Korovin, S.K.: New Types of Feedback. Nauka, Moscow (1997). (In Russ.)
5. Ray, W.H.: Advanced Process Control. Butterworth, Stoneham (1989)
6. Quincampoix, M., Veliov, V.M.: Optimal control of uncertain systems with incomplete information for the disturbances. SIAM J. Control. Optim. **43**(4), 1373–1399 (2004)
7. Polyak, B.T., Scherbakov, P.S.: Robust Stability and Control. Nauka, Moscow (2002). (In Russ.)
8. Polyak, B.T., Khlebnikov, M.V., Rapaport, L.B.: Mathematical Theory of Automatic Control. Lenard, Moscow (2019). (In Russ.)
9. Aida-zade, K.R., Guliyev, S.Z.: A task for nonlinear system control synthesis. Autom. Control. Comput. Sci. **39**(1), 15–23 (2005)
10. Aida-zade, K.R., Guliyev, S.Z.: Zonal control synthesis for nonlinear systems under nonlinear output feedback. J. Autom. Inf. Sci. **47**(1), 51–66 (2015)
11. Guliyev, S.Z.: Synthesis of control in nonlinear systems with different types of feedback and strategies of control. J. Autom. Inf. Sci. **45**(7), 74–86 (2013)
12. Guliyev, S.Z.: Synthesis of zonal controls of nonlinear systems under discrete observations. J. Autom. Control Comput. Sci. Allerton Press **45**(6), 338–345 (2011)
13. Bellen, A., Zennaro, M.: Numerical Methods for Delay Differential Equations, 1st edn. Oxford University Press, Oxford (2003)
14. Nocedal, J., Wright, S.: Numerical Optimization, 2nd edn. Springer, New-York (2006)
15. Aida-zade, K.R., Guliyev, S.Z.: On a class of inverse problems for discontinuous systems. Cybern. Syst. Anal. **4**, 915–924 (2008)
16. Aida-zade, K.R., Handzel, A.V.: An approach to lumped control synthesis in distributed systems. Appl. Comput. Math. **6**(1), 69–79 (2007)
17. David, E.S., Anitescu, M.: Optimal control of systems with discontinuous differential equations. Numerische Math. **114**(4), 653–695 (2010)
18. Aida-zade, K.R., Guliyev, S.Z.: On numerical solution of one class of inverse problems for discontinuous dynamic systems. Autom. Remote Control Pleiades Publishing **73**(5), 786–796 (2012)

Model-Based Policy Optimization with Neural Differential Equations for Robotic Arm Control

Andrey Gorodetskiy[1]([envelope]), Konstantin Mironov[1,2], and Aleksandr Panov[1,2,3]

[1] Center of Cognitive Modeling, Moscow Institute of Physics and Technology, 9, Institutskij per., Dolgoprudny 141701, Russia
gorodetskii.as@phystech.edu
[2] Artificial Intelligence Research Institute, Moscow 105064, Russia
[3] Federal Research Center "Computer Science and Control", 9, 60-letiya Oktyabrya pr., Moscow 117312, Russia

Abstract. Applying learning-based control methods to real robots presents hard challenges, including the low sample efficiency of model-free reinforcement learning algorithms. The widely adopted approach to tackling this problem uses an environment dynamics model. We propose to use the Neural Ordinary Differential Equations to approximate transition dynamics as this allows for finer control of a trajectory generation process. NODE offers a continuous-time formulation that captures the temporal dependencies. We evaluate our approach on various tasks from simulation environment including learning 6-DoF robotic arm to open the door, which represents particular challenges for policy search. The NODE model is trained to predict movement of the arm and the door, and is used to generate trajectories for the model-based policy optimization. Our method shows better sample efficiency on this task comparing to the model-free and model-based baseline. It also shows comparable results on several other tasks. The application of NODE to model-based reinforcement learning enables more precise modeling of robotic system dynamics and enhances the sample efficiency of learning-based control methods. The empirical evaluation on various tasks demonstrates the efficacy of our approach, offering promising prospects for improving the performance and efficiency of real-world robotic systems.

Keywords: Machine Learning · Deep Learning · Manipulation · Reinforcement Learning · Model-Based Control

1 Introduction

Robotic manipulation is often connected to uncertainties and non-deterministic relations within the environment. The dynamics of the manipulators in deterministic and predictable conditions are well explored. Accurate control methods are efficient for these conditions. However, collaborative manipulators often have to operate with various objects of the non-deterministic environment with the unknown parameters. These operations may be executed using policies obtained via deep reinforcement learning (RL), which allows finding high-performance controller from interaction data [1, 2].

A. Ronzhin et al. (Eds.): ICR 2023, LNAI 14214, pp. 258–266, 2023.
https://doi.org/10.1007/978-3-031-43111-1_23

Operating multilink manipulators is challenging for RL due to high number of degree of freedom in the system, high accuracy requirements and continuous-time model of the process [3]. In this work we aim to overcome these challenges by adding continuous-time environment model to policy-based control.

There are several potential advantages of using the Neural Ordinary Differential Equations (NODE) [4] architecture for modeling the environment dynamics in model-based policy optimization [5–7]. First, it can provide a more flexible and expressive model of continuous-time dynamics [8] and allows for the state trajectory to be described as a continuous function, which can better capture the complex relationships. Second, it can be used to model dynamics with varying time scales [9, 10]. Traditional discrete-time models, such as those based on recurrent neural networks, require the time step to be discretized into fixed-size intervals, which can lead to limitations in modeling dynamics with varying time scales. The NODE architecture has been shown to achieve high performance on a variety of tasks, including image classification and time-series prediction [4]. This suggests that it may be a promising approach for modeling environment dynamics in model-based reinforcement learning algorithms.

We propose a new method for policy learning, where model-free RL algorithm is trained on samples from world model, represented by NODE. The method is designed for the challenging task of robotic door opening. Many previous works explored NODE in different settings, but very few considered the task of modeling action-conditioned dynamics [8, 11]. Our contribution consists in, first, use of NODE for modelling continuous-time dynamics of the system under the influence of control inputs, and, second, applying NODE-based action-conditioned dynamics model in model-based RL setting.

The rest paper is organized as follows. In section II we briefly discuss existing works related to model-based policy optimization, neural ordinary differential equations and robotic door opening. Then in short section III we present background statement and notation. Section IV present a description of the proposed approach. In section V we discuss the results of numerical experiments, while section VI includes concluding remarks.

2 Related Work

Model-based policy optimization is a specific approach to model-based reinforcement learning that focuses on optimizing the agent's policy using a model of the environment [12–15]. Recent advances in model-based policy optimization have focused on improving the accuracy and efficiency of learned dynamics models, as well as developing new algorithms that can leverage these models to improve sample efficiency and overall performance. E.g. [16] uses model predictive control in model-based reinforcement learning setting, while [6] learns a world model and uses it for planning.

In [17] authors propose MBPO algorithm that builds a model of the environment to optimize the policy in a sample-efficient manner by alternating between collecting data from the environment and optimizing the policy using the learned model. The algorithm has been shown to achieve state-of-the-art performance on a variety of continuous control tasks. [18, 19] trained one-step policy with the use of dynamics model, represented by Recurrent neural network (RNN).

The use of ODE framework for making model predictions gained massive attention after the work on Neural Ordinary Differential Equations [4]. This framework was used to build dynamics model for model-based RL algorithms [8], including continuous-time setting [7]. A scope of works focuses on modeling dynamics of mechanical systems [20, 21]. Modeling action-conditioned transition dynamics was explored in [11].

As an example use case for manipulation with requirement of dynamic models we consider the task of robotic door opening. The ability to open standard doors in living and office environments is useful for the mobility of robotic systems in human-intended environments. Door and robot may be considered together as a complex underactuated system. The kinematics and dynamics of such a system is represented by a complex model, involving forward kinematics of the robot and inverse kinematics of the door. This model may also include unknown parameters (e.g. size of the door). This property make door opening a theoretically interesting task for evaluating RL approaches. Therefore it was included into meta-world RL benchmark [22]. We may highlight the following significant works applying RL for this task. [23] apply parallelized Normalized Advantage Function Algorithm for training several real robots to solve door opening task. Another work on real-robot RL for door opening is [24], where door-opening task required 17.5 h of real world learning. Some other works consider learning for door opening task in simulation. [25] concentrate on active policy learning with image input and without exact reward models. Experiments on meta world door opening task [22] are provided, while for real world experiments other setups were chosen. [26] apply genetic algorithm to find appropriate parameters of the Deep Deterministic Policy Gradient (DDPG) algorithm. Aforementioned works consider model-free RL for door opening. As an example of utilizing model-based RL we can mention [27], which consider door opening as a sequence of separated tasks (handle approaching, handle rotation, etc.), where each task has own dynamics. The purpose of model learning was to define appropriate embeddings for various subtasks. In our work we consider door opening as an end-to-end task and aim to define learnable model of its continuous dynamics.

3   Background

Reinforcement learning task is formulated as a Markov Decision Process (MDP). MDP is a tuple (S,A,τ,ρ,o), where S – set of states, A – set of actions, τ – transition dynamics, ρ – reward function, ϵ – observation function. Agent starts in environment in some initial state s and have access to corresponding observation $o = \epsilon(s)$. Then it chooses action $a = \pi(a \mid s)$ following policy π, environment transitions to the next state $s' \sim \tau(s,a)$, and agent observes reward $r = \rho(s')$. The goal of agent is to find optimal policy $\pi *$ that maximizes the expected sum of rewards agent would observe during episode.

Model-based reinforcement learning algorithms learn some model E of environment dynamics τ and then use it to search for policy of value functions in a sample-efficient manner, instead of trying to learn them directly from interaction data between agent and environment. In our work we use NODE as a dynamics model.

4   Method

We use model-based policy optimization scheme similar to [17] to train policy entirely on synthetic samples from the environment model, while concurrently optimizing both from scratch (Algorithm 1).

Algorithm 1 General model-based policy optimization

1: Initialize policy π, dynamics model p_θ, buffer for environment samples B_E, buffer for model samples B_π

2: **for** N epochs **do**

3:      sample n transitions from environment under π; add to B_E

4:      Train model p_θ on B_E

5:      **for** M model rollouts **do**

6:          Sample o_t uniformly from the last q records in B_E

7: Perform k-step model rollout starting from $s_t = g(o_t)$ using policy π; add observed transitions to B_π

8:      **end for**

9:      **for** G gradient updates **do**

10:          Update policy parameters on batch from B_π

11:      **end for**

12: **end for**

For policy training, we use off-policy SAC [28] algorithm. Policy π is updated on data from buffer Bπ, which stores only transitions, sampled from the environment model E (Fig. 1). To generate trajectories from environment model, we set it into initial state, and generate a short rollout of fixed length using current policy. Initial states distribution is uniform distribution over the fixed-size chunk of buffer BE, which contains the most recent transitions observed from environment. To compute reward for predicted transitions, we use true reward functions for each env.

To successfully learn a collection of co-dependent models, it's important to balance their sampling and update rates. We fix these as hyperparameters. We build a model of environment dynamics using action-conditioned NODE. It consists of multilayer perceptron (MLP) fθ, observer g and differential equation solver (Eq. 1). MLP learns to predict state derivative ˙s provided state s and action a. Differential equation solver integrates fθ to obtain state trajectory from the initial state s0 and a sequence of actions:

$$\dot{s} = f_\theta(s, a), \quad s = g(o) \tag{1}$$

Observer g is implemented by handcrafted functions that use a subset of agent observation's features to reconstruct states from vector observation o and do not use latents. We use it to simplify prediction task by constructing exhaustively descriptive, minimal, interpretable representations separately for each environment. To interpolate action sequence during the integration of state dynamics we use zero-order hold.

The model is trained using RMSprop by minimizing MSE between predicted and observed trajectories. All trajectories observed from environment are stored in buffer

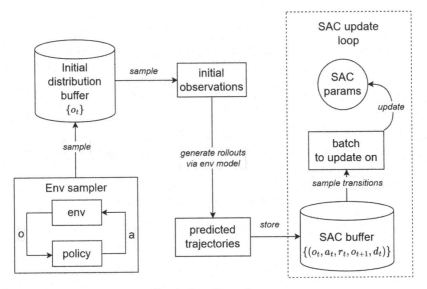

Fig. 1. Sampling scheme.

BEM. We uniformly sample batches of subsequences of fixed length from this buffer to update the model on them. As these subsequences are typically short, we do not use adjoint method and compute gradient using automatic differentiation.

Our method differs from previous works in the choice of dynamics model and training schedule. We use action-conditioned NODE to model environment dynamics. Instead of using encoder, we provide dynamics model with vector states, reconstructed from observations by environment-specific hand coded function, which has no trainable parameters. This function extracts relevant parts of observation which determine their own derivative and are more favorable to predict.

5   Experiments

We train and evaluate the agent in multiple environments and deterministically evaluate it. Environments we use are based on Reacher-v2 from Gym [29], Cheetah-run from DMC [30], and DoorOpen from Metaword [22]. They are built on MuJoCo simulator. Our version of Reacher allows for joint position control to facilitate environment model learning, and DoorOpen uses modified reward function to facilitate policy learning. In all environments we assume that the observed quantities are given and we do not solve the problem of their estimation.

In some of the environments our method exhibit critic divergence, which leads to considerable value overestimation and failure of the learned policy. We hypothesize this is due to specific sampling scheme used to draw transitions from the environment model. This scheme draws a batch of short rollouts from initial states that are chosen from the observed ones. Since the environment model is imperfect, the last state of each of these short rollouts has a considerable chance not to be encountered as a starting state in any transition sampled from environment model. Hence, critic will not be updated in any of these "boundary" states that will accumulate "fake" value from critic updates in other points. The values of boundary states will propagate towards values of observed states, leading to catastrophic overestimation. We validate our hypothesis on simple 1-dimensional environment (Fig. 2) and observe that this effect actually takes place.

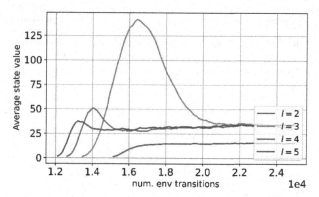

Fig. 2. Demonstration of parasitic value propagation from boundary states in SAC algorithm. Environment is a 1-dimensional segment where agent can walk. The farthest state from the start yields the maximal reward and is reachable in 3 steps. Average value of state value function spikes when the maximum number of steps allowed (l) is 3.

We train and evaluate NODE model on trajectory prediction task using Reacher environment. We collect 1000 trajectories of length 50 using uniform policy and train model on this fixed dataset (Fig. 3a). After 500 iterations, the joint angles prediction error, averaged over prediction horizon of 4 steps, drops below 1 degree. Then we evaluate our MBRL method in Reacher using the same dynamics model configuration (Fig. 3b). Results show that our method outperforms SAC in terms of sample-efficiency, as expected, while successfully solving the task. Dreamer-v3 shows lower performance on Reacher.

We compare our method with Dreamer-v3 [31] in Cheetah environment (Fig. 4). We provide all compared methods with the same vector observations. In this environment our method learns faster on the budget of 10^6 environment samples. However, given additional samples, Dreamer-v3 outperforms our method. We evaluate the proposed method on the door opening task (Fig. 5) in DoorOpen environment. The agent observes position of the end-effector, as well as position and orientation of the handle. Our method demonstrates higher performance than Dreamer-v3. Dreamer-v3 is failed to solve the door opening task with default hyperparameters.

In the challenging DoorOpen environment our method outperforms Dreamerv3 and solves the task. In the Cheetah environment our method shows inferior to Dreamer-v3 performance, but nevertheless learns successful gate.

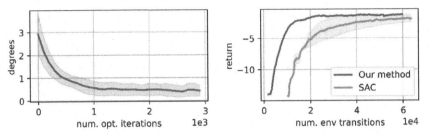

Fig. 3. Method evaluation in the Reacher environment. (a, left)The prediction error of joint angles is consistently below 1 degree over a horizon of 4 steps. (b, right) Our method achieves higher sample efficiency in Reacher environment, requiring 3x fewer samples than SAC.

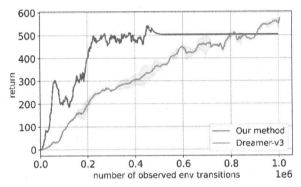

Fig. 4. In the Cheetah-run environment. Our method demonstrates higher sample-efficiency. However, given $2\,10^6$ samples, Dreamer-v3 shows superior performance compared to our method. All compared methods use identical vector observations.

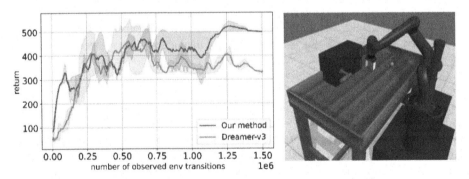

Fig. 5. (left) Our method demonstrates superior performance in the DoorOpen environment compared to Dreamer-v3 with XL (xlarge) model size and default hyperparameters. Notably, the Dreamer-v3 algorithm fails to solve the door opening task. (*right*) Frame from DoorOpen environment.

6   Conclusion

This paper presents the method for model-based policy optimization that successfully solves the door opening task. The main differences from previous works are the training schedule and the use of Neural Ordinary Differential Equations for modeling continuous-time process dynamics.

We evaluate the proposed method on different robotic control tasks and compare to Dreamer-v3 model-based algorithm and SAC model-free algorithm. Our method outperforms these methods for door-opening and show comparable results on other tasks.

References

1. Kalashnikov, D., et al.: Qt-opt: Scalable deep reinforcement learning for vision-based robotic manipulation. arXiv preprint arXiv:1806.10293 (2018)
2. Kalashnikov, D., et al.: Scalable deep reinforcement learning for vision-based robotic manipulation. In: Conference on Robot Learning, pp. 651–673 (2018)
3. Lillicrap, T.P., et al.: Continuous control with deep reinforcement learning. arXiv preprint arXiv:1509.02971 (2015)
4. Chen, R.T., Rubanova, Y., Bettencourt, J., Duvenaud, D.K.: Neural ordinary differential equations. In: Advances in Neural Information Processing Systems, vol. 31 (2018)
5. Ha, D., Schmidhuber, J.: World models. arXiv preprint arXiv:1803.10122 (2018)
6. Hafner, D., et al.: Learning latent dynamics for planning from pixels. In: International Conference on Machine Learning, pp. 2555–2565 (2019)
7. Yildiz, C., Heinonen, M., Lahdesmaki, H.: Continuous-time model-based reinforcement learning. In: International Conference on Machine Learning, pp. 12009–12018 (2021)
8. Du, J., Futoma, J., Doshi-Velez, F.: Model-based reinforcement learning for semi-markov decision processes with neural odes. Adv. Neural. Inf. Process. Syst. 33, 19805–19816 (2020)
9. Rubanova, Y., Chen, R.T., Duvenaud, D.K.: Latent ordinary differential equations for irregularly-sampled time series. In: Advances in Neural Information Processing Systems, vol. 32 (2019)
10. Kidger, P., Morrill, J., Foster, J., Lyons, T.: Neural controlled differential equations for irregular time series. Adv. Neural. Inf. Process. Syst. 33, 6696–6707 (2020)
11. Alvarez, V.M.M., Rosca, R., Falcutescu, C.G.: Dynode: Neural ordinary differential equations for dynamics modeling in continuous control. arXiv preprint arXiv:2009.04278 (2020)
12. Ivashko, A., Safonov, G.: Machine learning model for determination of the optimal strategy in an online auction. Inf. Autom. 22(1), 146–167 (2023). https://doi.org/10.15622/ia.22.1.6
13. Hung, N., Loi, T., Huong, N., Hang, T.T., Huong, T.: AAFNDL – an accurate fake in-formation recognition model using deep learning for the Vietnamese language. Inf. Autom. 22(4), 795–825 (2023). https://doi.org/10.15622/ia.22.4.4
14. Osipov, V., Kuleshov, S., Miloserdov, D., Zaytseva, A., Aksenov, A.: Recurrent neural networks with continuous learning in problems of news streams multifunctional pro-cessing. Inf. Autom. 21(6), 1145–1168 (2022). https://doi.org/10.15622/ia.21.6.3
15. Favorskaya, M., Nishchhal, N.: Verification of marine oil spills using aerial images based on deep learning methods. Inf. Autom. 21(5), 937–962 (2022). https://doi.org/10.15622/ia.21.5.4
16. Nagabandi, A., Kahn, G., Fearing, R.S., Levine, S.: Neural network dynamics for model-based deep reinforcement learning with model-free finetuning. In: 2018 IEEE International Conference on Robotics and Automation (ICRA), pp. 7559–7566 (2018)

17. Janner, M., Fu, J., Zhang, M., Levine, S.: When to trust your model: model-based policy optimization. In: Advances in Neural Information Processing Systems, vol. 32 (2019)

18. Hafner, D., Lillicrap, T., Ba, J., Norouzi, M.: Dream to control: Learning behaviors by latent imagination. arXiv preprint arXiv:1912.01603 (2019)

19. Hafner, D., Lillicrap, T., Norouzi, M., Ba, J.: Mastering atari with discrete world models. arXiv preprint arXiv:2010.02193 (2020)

20. Zhong, Y.D., Dey, B., Chakraborty, A.: Symplectic ode-net: Learning hamiltonian dynamics with control. arXiv preprint arXiv:1909.12077 (2019)

21. Greydanus, S., Dzamba, M., Yosinski, J.: Hamiltonian neural networks. In: Advances in Neural Information Processing Systems, vol. 32 (2019)

22. Yu, T., et al.: Meta-world: a benchmark and evaluation for multi-task and meta reinforcement learning. In: Conference on Robot Learning, pp. 1094–1100 (2020)

23. Gu, S., Holly, E., Lillicrap, T., Levine, S.: Deep reinforcement learning for robotic manipulation with asynchronous off-policy updates. arXiv preprint arXiv:1610.00633 (2016)

24. Zhu, H., Gupta, A., Rajeswaran, A., Levine, S., Kumar, V.: Dexterous manipulation with deep reinforcement learning: efficient, general, and low-cost. In: 2019 International Conference on Robotics and Automation (ICRA), pp. 3651–3657 (2019). https://doi.org/10.1109/ICRA.2019.8794102

25. Singh, A., Yang, L., Hartikainen, K., Finn, C., Levine, S.: End-to-end robotic reinforcement learning without reward engineering. arXiv preprint arXiv:1904.07854 (2019)

26. Sehgal, A., La, H., Louis, S., Nguyen, H.: Deep reinforcement learning using genetic algorithm for parameter optimization. In: 2019 Third IEEE International Conference on Robotic Computing (IRC), pp. 596–601 (2019). https://doi.org/10.1109/IRC.2019.00121

27. Huang, Y., Xie, K., Bharadhwaj, H., Shkurti, F.: Continual model-based reinforcement learning with hypernetworks. In: 2021 IEEE International Conference on Robotics and Automation (ICRA), pp. 799–805 (2021). https://doi.org/10.1109/ICRA48506.2021.9560793

28. Haarnoja, T., Zhou, A., Abbeel, P., Levine, S.: Soft actor-critic: offpolicy maximum entropy deep reinforcement learning with a stochastic actor. In: International Conference on Machine Learning, pp. 1861–1870 (2018)

29. Brockman, G., et al.: Openai gym. arXiv preprint arXiv:1606.01540 (2016)

30. Tunyasuvunakool, S., et al.: dm control: Software and tasks for continuous control. Softw. Impacts **6**, 100022 (2020)

31. Hafner, D., Pasukonis, J., Ba, J., Lillicrap, T.: Mastering Diverse Domains through World Models. arXiv preprint arXiv:2301.04104 (2023)

Monitoring the State of Robotic Systems Based on Time Series Analysis

Viktor Semenov[✉] [iD]

St. Petersburg Federal Research Center of the Russian Academy of Sciences,
39, 14th Line, St. Petersburg 199178, Russia
v.semenov@spcras.ru

Abstract. In view of the close integration of robotic systems into industrial and technological systems, critical infrastructure objects, as well as a significant number of possible entry points, the task of monitoring operational safety for robotic systems is more complex than ensuring information security in classical information systems. The paper presents a method for monitoring the state of robotic systems based on time series analysis. The developed method differs from the existing ones by the combined approach of using an ensemble of parallel classifiers and Fishburn weight coefficients in the security event management system. The time series is composed of a set of informative features, characterizing the functioning of a robotic system. Values for previous discrete time points are ranked using significance weights. The method was approved on a data set of a real industrial system. Due to parallel computing, it was possible to significantly increase the speed of determining the state of robotic systems. The identification precision due to the combined approach increased by 1.45% compared to the best results presented in scientific papers, the recall increased by 4.45% and amounted to 99.85% for both indicators. The results of the study can be applied in monitoring the safety of robotic systems.

Keywords: State Analysis · Robotic Systems · Functional Safety · Identification of Anomalies · Decision Trees

1 Introduction

The merging of information technologies and industrial processes, observed in recent years in the development of technological infrastructure, has led to the transformation of the principles of building production facilities and the widespread use of robotic systems (RS).

At the present stage of RS development, there is an increase in the degree of intelligence of control systems, their autonomy and adaptability, along with this, the volume of processed information transmitted from various sensors is rapidly increasing [1]. These systems are complex and distributed, which also leads to a number of problems associated with their performance and safety [2]. Thus, it is necessary to ensure constant monitoring of the state of the RS, including security assessment, while it is extremely important to take into account the time parameters of potential safety incidents.

Among the main vulnerabilities of the RS, one can distinguish: the possibility of listening to channels, sending "external" packets, physical access of an attacker to the RS, insufficient standardization of intelligent routing algorithms that take into account the state of the network, etc. Figure 1 shows typical destructive effects on RS elements at different levels: physical, network and application levels.

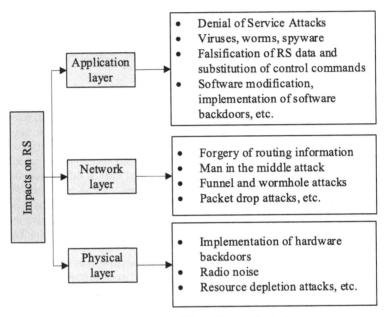

Fig. 1. Security threats at different levels of robotic systems.

Management of security incidents, including their identification, fixation, prediction, is an ongoing complex process of monitoring and analyzing the results of security events and other data. This kind of monitoring is a complex task of dealing with threats and violations of information security, as well as technological failures and failures, complicated by the heterogeneity of industrial network devices and protocols, the amount of data and the speed of their receipt. An additional problem is the need to adapt monitoring tools in dynamically changing conditions. Proceeding from this, a promising task is to develop methods for monitoring the state of RS in order to ensure their comprehensive information security and functional safety, as well as sustainable operation in the presence of information threats and attacks.

Existing methods and technologies are more focused on classical computer or information systems [3–5], which limits the possibility of their application in RS. The solutions currently used [6, 7] do not have sufficient functionality to ensure effective real-time monitoring, which causes a number of problems in ensuring information security and functional safety related to the analysis of the state of RS. In this regard, there is an objective need to develop and adapt the methods of mathematical support for specialized information systems integrated into the RS in order to counteract external and internal destructive influences.

This work is a logical continuation of works [8, 9].

2 Problem Statement

Consider the problem of classifying time series that characterize the state of information security and functional safety of RS. Let there be a time series $\mathbf{X} = \{\{x_1(t_1), x_2(t_1),$ $..., x_S(t_1)\}, \{x_1(t_2), x_2(t_2), ..., x_S(t_2)\}, ..., \{x_1(t_m), x_2(t_m), ..., x_S(t_m)\}\}$, each tuple of which corresponds to a set of characteristics of information or physical processes of the RS at a discrete point in time; $\{c_1, ..., c_l\}$ is the set of RS states, l is the number of identified RS states; $C = \{C_0, C_1\}$ is the set of considered states. Each RS element can be in a dangerous (C_1) or safe (allowed) (C_0) state. $C_0 = \{c_1, c_2, ..., c_k\}$, $C_1 = \{c_{k+1}, c_{k+2}, ..., c_l\}$, k is the number of RS safe states.

It is required to determine the state of the RS (label of class c), to which the input element of the time series belongs. To train the model, it is necessary to obtain a characteristic of the ongoing information and physical processes of each considered state of the RS. The training sample can be formed, for example, using software for automated analysis of network traffic.

The RS state class label c at a discrete time t is described using the method proposed in the paper using a number of the most informative features selected according to [8]:

$$c = \mu\big(a_1\big(x_{t,1}, x_{t,2}, \ldots, x_{t,s}\big), a_2\big(x_{t,1}, x_{t,2}, \ldots, x_{t,s}\big), \ldots, a_n\big(x_{t,1}, x_{t,2}, \ldots, x_{t,s}\big)\big), \\ c \in C, x_{t,i} \in D_f, s << S, \tag{1}$$

where C is the set of RS states under consideration; μ is an aggregating function; $a_1, a_2, ..., a_n$ are classifying algorithms; $x_{t,i}$ is feature values at a discrete point in time; D_f is the set of admissible feature values; s is the number of selected most informative features; S is the total number of available features.

The purpose of this work is to develop a method that provides an increase in the recall and precision of the identification of the state of information security and functional safety of RS through the use in the monitoring system of the values of time series for previous points in time using weighting coefficients of significance.

3 Suggested Method

In this paper, we applied and studied an algorithm based on decision trees, which belongs to the group of logical classifiers [10]. The essence of the algorithm is to build a binary tree, in the internal nodes of which there are predicates, and in the leaves - class labels c_i ($i = 1, ..., l$). The root of the decision trees contains a decision node based on the analysis of the most informative feature, as the removal and further construction of the decision trees, less informative features are used (in descending order of informativeness). Leaf vertices contain the values of the classes determined at the stage of forming the training sample. The choice of predicates was carried out using the informativeness criteria [11].

In a binary decision tree:

- each internal vertex v is assigned a function (or predicate) $\beta_v: \mathbf{X} \to \{0, 1\}$;

- each leaf vertex v is assigned a prediction – one of l possible states of the RS $c_i \in C$.

The predicates β_v compare the value of one of the features with the threshold τ_v:

$$\beta_v(x; j, \tau_v) = \left[x_j < \tau_v\right]. \tag{2}$$

Algorithm $a(x)$, starting from the root vertex v_0, calculates the value of the function β_{v0}. If it is equal to zero, then the algorithm goes to the left child vertex, otherwise to the right one, after which it calculates the value of the predicate at the new vertex and makes the transition either to the left or to the right. The process continues until a leaf top is reached; the algorithm returns the class assigned to this vertex.

Thus, by supplying unknown values at the time t, the constructed algorithm $a(x)$ on the basis of the training set generates an answer – one of the labels of the class $c_i \in C$, associated with the state of the RS.

RS is a complex system, each element of which can be subjected to certain types of destructive influences and attacks. The data coming from various sensors of the RS may have individual properties. In this regard, the problem of identifying the state for classifiers that have their own competencies on subsamples arises.

The time series $\mathbf{X}$ consists of feature values at m moments. According to the bootstrap method, m/n feature vectors are selected equiprobably from the entire set, each of which corresponds to a certain point in time. Note that due to the return, some elements in subsets may be repeated. Denote the new sample by $\mathbf{X}_1$. Repeating the procedure n times, we generate n subsamples $\mathbf{X}_1, \mathbf{X}_2, ..., \mathbf{X}_n$.

We apply n parallel classifiers to increase the speed of obtaining the results. We use the aggregation function μ to improve the stability and accuracy of the algorithms. Principles of constructing an ensemble of parallel classifiers:

- bootstrap generation of n samples with dimension $m/n \times s$ for each classifier a_1–a_n;
- independent training of each elementary classifier (algorithm a_1–a_n defined on its subspace) on a pre-labeled data set (training with a teacher);
- independent classification of each subsample $\mathbf{X}_1, \mathbf{X}_2, ..., \mathbf{X}_n$ on each of the subspaces.
- making a final decision on whether an object belongs to one of the states.

In classical approaches, when using ensembles of classifiers, the final decision on whether the elements of the time series belong to a certain state of the RS is made by one of the following methods.

- Consensus: if all elementary classifiers have assigned the same label to the set of feature values at time t, then such an object will be assigned to the selected class. Consensus is not always reached.
- Simple majority: the object is assigned the label of the class that the majority of elementary classifiers have defined for it.

When using "snapshots" at a discrete point in time, the required recall and precision of identification of the RS state is not always achieved, in addition, in practice, the most important are the values of the states that are close to the current point in time [9]. To increase the recall and precision, it is proposed to introduce the identification time interval (N), which is a sliding window from t_{i-N+1} to the current time t_i, and weight coefficients p_i, taking into account the degree of preference for some identification results over others (Fig. 2).

In the case under consideration, c_b is the safe state of the RS; c_a is the state in which the RS is under attacking informational or physical impact. The weighting factors must meet the following requirements:

- take into account the identification time interval (N), which is the value of the time interval for which the analyzed data is fed to the input of the algorithm that implements the proposed method;
- any coefficient p_{i+1} must be less than p_i ($\forall \, p_{i-1} < p_i$, $i \in [1, N]$).

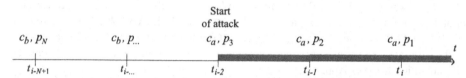

Fig. 2. Time schedule of attack identification which takes into account the coefficients of significance.

For a system of decreasing preference, consisting of N alternatives, it is proposed to use weight coefficients that decrease according to the rule of arithmetic progression. Fishburn weight coefficients are rational fractions, in the numerator of which there are elements of the natural series decreasing by one from N to 1, and in the denominator is the sum of the arithmetic progression of the first N terms of the natural series with a step of 1.

$$r_1 = N, r_i = r_{i-1} - 1, \quad K = \sum_{i=1}^{N} r_i, \quad p_i = \frac{r_i}{K}, \tag{3}$$

where r_i are elements of the natural series; K is the sum of the arithmetic progression of the first N members of the natural series with step 1; p_i is the weight coefficient of the significance of the identification result for a discrete point in time; N is the time interval of identification.

4 Approbation of the Method

4.1 Practical Implementation

For the purpose of practical implementation of the developed method for identifying the state of RS based on the analysis of time series, we will perform a computational experiment on a data set [12]. Researchers from the Singapore University of Technology and Design have simulated various types of attacks on the components of a water treatment test bench. The following attacks were selected for the study: at different levels of the RS; included one or more stages; had different duration and affected different levels of RS; most of the attacks had an impact on the technological process. Table 1 shows the types and number of attacks (the total number is 41).

Table 1. Types of attacks on robotic system.

Attack type	Number of attacks
Single stage single point	26
Single stage multi point	4
Multi stage single point	2
Multi stage multi point	4
Without impact on the technological process	5

From the received network traffic between the SCADA (Supervisory Control and Data Acquisition) system and programmable logic controllers, time series are formed containing information from all available RS sensors. MATLAB R2023a software was used to analyze the time series characterizing the functioning of the RS. The formation of decision trees, their ensembles and subsequent classification was performed using the Classification Learner App.

The initial data for the implementation of the developed method is a numerical two-dimensional array $944\,919 \times 51$. The rows contain the values of the time series recorded once per second, and the columns are sorted by the sources of obtaining information from the RS. The data set is marked by classes (states), each time series is assigned a class label $\{c_1, ..., c_{41}\}$.

At the beginning of the process of monitoring the state of the RS, a training sample is formed from time series composed of the values of the RS functioning parameters and their corresponding state labels (classes). Using the method of uniform random sampling with return, n subsamples are formed.

Algorithms a_1-a_n based on decision trees are trained each on their own subsample independently of each other, the classifiers do not correct each other's errors, but compensate for them when voting. The base classifiers in this case are independent due to training on different subsamples. At the state identification stage, the analyzed indicators for the time interval N, which are a tuple $\mathbf{X}^* = \{\{x_1(t_{i-N+1}), x_2(t_{i-N+1}), ..., x_s(t_{i-N+1})\}, ..., \{x_1(t_{i-1}), x_2(t_{i-1}), ..., x_s(t_{i-1})\}, \{x_1(t_i), x_2(t_i), ..., x_s(t_i)\}\}$, are fed to the input of the above classifying algorithms.

Each algorithm a_1-a_n generates N responses in a given time interval, which are post-processed in the first step using Fishburn weights that give more weight to later identification results. Thus, the class label is determined by weighted generalization of the classification results over time N. The weights p_i for different time points are summed if the predicted classes match. Table 2 shows an example of applying the coefficients calculated by formula (3) for the classifier a_1.

The sum of the coefficients for c_{37} is $\frac{5}{15}$, c_{35} $-\frac{7}{15}$, c_{18} $-\frac{3}{15}$. Taking into account the significance weights, the result will be a label of class c_{35}. If the coefficients before the classes are equal, we will choose the class that was determined for a later point in time.

We will make the final decision by generalizing the results obtained at the previous stage and for each classifier a_1-a_n. The result is determined by a simple majority of the results. Let's use odd n to avoid cases of equal votes for different classes c. The block diagram of the algorithm is shown in Fig. 3.

Table 2. An example of applying weigh coefficients for $N = 5$.

Time	Weight coefficient	Class label
t_i	$\frac{5}{15}$	c_{37}
t_{i-1}	$\frac{4}{15}$	c_{35}
t_{i-2}	$\frac{3}{15}$	c_{35}
t_{i-3}	$\frac{2}{15}$	c_{18}
t_{i-4}	$\frac{1}{15}$	c_{18}

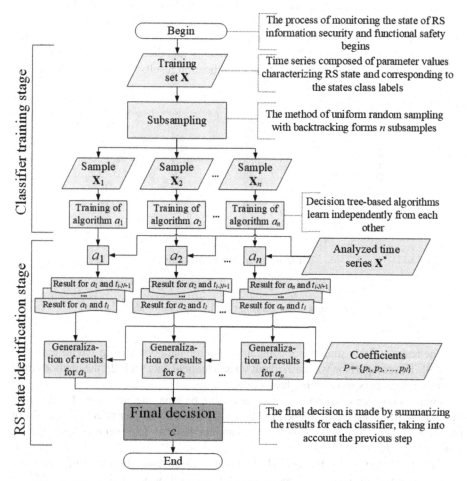

Fig. 3. Block diagram of the algorithm for identifying the state of robotic systems.

4.2 Results

Due to the combined approach, the developed method allowed, without increasing the number of features selected according to [8], to significantly improve the classification quality indicators and the speed of response to information security incidents and physical impacts on the RS. Figure 4 compares the results of applying the proposed approach and the standard method, which does not take into account the degree of preference for identification results at various discrete points in time. For $N = 1$, the solution of the problem is reduced to determining the state of the RS at a discrete time. The application of the developed approach made it possible to increase the F-measure in comparison with the standard method. Based on the analysis of the histogram, we conclude that the optimal value is the value of the identification segment $N = 4$. Note that a further increase in the interval practically does not lead to an increase in the F-measure. The decisive factor for choosing the size of the sliding window N and the number of classifiers n is the maximization of the F-measure of the classification results for the controlled RS.

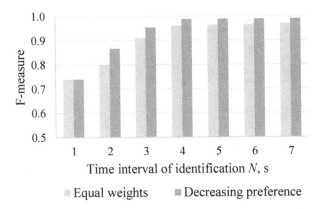

Fig. 4. F-measure under varying the time interval of identification.

The results of this study were compared with the data obtained in scientific papers [13–19]. The comparison was carried out on an identical data set [12], the methods used by other researchers were highlighted (Table 3).

Figure 5 shows a diagram of precision. As can be seen, the precision of identifying the state of RS using the developed method is significantly higher than in the works of other researchers who have used classifiers and methods of data preprocessing that are different in nature.

The developed method also made it possible to increase the recall of identification of the RS state (Fig. 6). Methods with high classification recall are preferable for recognizing previously unknown types of anomalies [20].

Thus, the analyzed works of other researchers are characterized by a relatively low recall of identification of the RS states, which is their significant drawback, since such models can identify a significant number of attacks on RS as safe states.

Table 3. Studies against which the results were compared.

Research authors	Applied method	Abbreviation	Source
Kravchik M., Shabtai A	One-Dimensional Convolutional Neural Networks	1D CNN	[13]
Shalyga D., Filonov P., Lavrentyev A	Multilayered Perceptron	MLP	[14]
	Convolutional Neural Networks	CNN	
	Recurrent Neural Networks	RNN	
Inoue J., Yamagata Y., Chen Y., Poskitt C.M., Sun J	Deep Neural Networks	DNN	[15]
	One-Class Support Vector Machines	OCSVM	
Kravchik M., Shabtai A	Autoencoder	AE	[16]
Elnour M., Meskin N., Khan K., Jain R	Isolation Forests	IF	[17]
Li D., Chen D., Jin B., Shi L., Goh J., Ng S.K	Generative Adversarial Networks	GAN	[18]
Gomez A., Maimo L., Celdran A, Clemente F	Long Short-Term Memory Neural Networks	LSTM NN	[19]

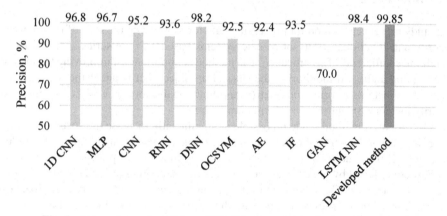

Fig. 5. Comparison of precision of identification of the robotic systems state.

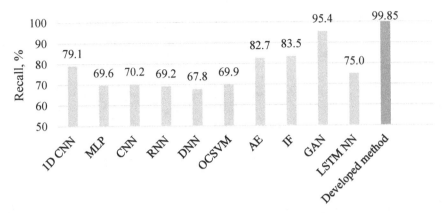

Fig. 6. Comparison of recall of identification of the robotic systems state.

5   Conclusion

The study presents a method for processing data for monitoring the state of information security and functional safety of robotic systems based on time series analysis using weighting coefficients of significance. The method is important for improving the means of providing audit and monitoring the state of an object that is under the influence of threats to violate its information security and functional safety, as well as investigating security incidents in automated information systems.

The proposed method made it possible to significantly increase the speed of identifying the state of elements of robotic systems through the use of an ensemble of parallel classifiers. Errors due to random deviations of the functioning parameters of robotic systems are reduced by generalization and weighted averaging of identification results over a time interval. The identification precision, compared with the best approaches presented in scientific papers, when using the developed method, increased by 1.45%, the recall – by 4.45% and amounted to 99.85% for both indicators. Reducing computational costs and increasing the speed of identifying the state of elements of robotic systems are decisive factors in monitoring and restoring safe operation.

The developed method is a new alternative and addition to existing software and firmware. As further prospects for the study, one can note the development of methods and techniques for counteracting identified violations based on the principle of real-time feedback.

References

1. Shukalov, A.V., Zakoldaev, D.A., Zharinov, I.O., Zharinov, O.O.: Control, computing and communication in industrial cyberphysical systems with feedback. J. Phys: Conf. Ser. **2094**(4), 042036 (2021). https://doi.org/10.1088/1742-6596/2094/4/042036
2. Kotenko, I.V., Kribel, A.M., Lauta, O.S., Saenko, I.B.: Analysis of the process of selfsimilarity of network traffic as an approach to detecting cyber-attacks on computer networks. Electrosvyaz **12**, 54–59 (2020). https://doi.org/10.34832/ELSV.2020.13.12.008

3. Vasilyev, V.I., Vulfin, A.M., Gvozdev, V.E., Kartak, V.M. Atarskaya, E.A.: Ensuring information security of cyber-physical objects based on predicting and detecting anomalies in their state. Syst. Control Commun. Secur. **6**, 90–119 (2021). https://doi.org/10.24412/2410-9916-2021-6-90-119

4. Zegzhda, D.P., Pavlenko, E.Y.: Homeostatic security of cyber-physical systems. Inf. Secur. Prob. Comput. Syst. **3**, 9–23 (2017)

5. Zaitceva, E.A., Zegzhda, D.P., Poltavtseva, M.A.: Applying of graph representation and case-based reasoning for security evaluation of computer systems. Inf. Secur. Prob. Comput. Syst. **2**, 136–148 (2019)

6. Lavrova, D.S.: An approach to developing the SIEM system for the Internet of Things. Autom. Control. Comput. Sci. **50**(8), 673–681 (2016). https://doi.org/10.3103/S0146411616080125

7. Vasiliev, Y.S., Zegzhda, P.D., Zegzhda, D.P.: Providing security for automated process control systems at hydropower engineering facilities. Therm. Eng. **63**(13), 948–956 (2016). https://doi.org/10.1134/S0040601516130073

8. Sukhoparov, M.E., Lebedev, I.S., Semenov, V.V.: Information security state analysis of elements of industry 4.0 devices in information systems. LNCS **12525**, 119–125 (2020). https://doi.org/10.1007/978-3-030-65726-0_11

9. Semenov, V.V.: An approach to the identification of the state of elements in cyber-physical systems based on principal component analysis. Sci. Tech. J. Inf. Technol. Mech. Optics **21**(6), 887–894 (2021). https://doi.org/10.17586/2226-1494-2021-21-6-887-894

10. Kruegel, C., Toth, T.: Using decision trees to improve signature-based intrusion detection. LNCS **2820**, 173–191 (2003). https://doi.org/10.1007/978-3-540-45248-5_10

11. Cagli, E., Dumas, C., Prouff, E.: Convolutional neural networks with data augmentation against jitter-based countermeasures. LNCS **10529**, 45–68 (2017). https://doi.org/10.1007/978-3-319-66787-4_3

12. Goh, J., Adepu, S., Junejo, K.N., Mathur, A.: A dataset to support research in the design of secure water treatment systems. LNCS **10242**, 88–99 (2017). https://doi.org/10.1007/978-3-319-71368-7_8

13. Kravchik, M., Shabtai, A.: Detecting cyber-attacks in industrial control systems using convolutional neural networks. In: Proceedings of the 47th Workshop on Cyber-Physical Systems Security and Privacy, pp. 72–83 (2018).https://doi.org/10.1145/3264888.3264896

14. Shalyga, D., Filonov, P., Lavrentyev, A.: Anomaly detection for water treatment system based on neural network with automatic architecture optimization. arXiv: 1807.07282 (2018). https://doi.org/10.48550/arXiv.1807.07282

15. Inoue, J., Yamagata, Y., Chen, Y., Poskitt, C.M., Sun, J.: Anomaly detection for a water treatment system using unsupervised machine learning. In: Proceedings of the 17th IEEE International Conference on Data Mining Workshops (ICDMW), pp. 1058–1065 (2017).https://doi.org/10.1109/ICDMW.2017.149

16. Kravchik, M., Shabtai, A.: Efficient cyber-attack detection in industrial control systems using lightweight neural networks and PCA. IEEE Trans. Dependable Secure Comput. **19**(4), 2179–2197 (2022). https://doi.org/10.1109/TDSC.2021.3050101

17. Elnour, M., Meskin, N., Khan, K., Jain, R.: A dual-isolation-forests-based attack detection framework for industrial control systems. IEEE Access **8**, 36639–36651 (2020). https://doi.org/10.1109/ACCESS.2020.2975066

18. Li, D., Chen, D., Jin, B., Shi, L., Goh, J., Ng, S.-K.: MAD-GAN: Multivariate anomaly detection for time series data with generative adversarial networks. LNCS **11730**, 703–716 (2019). https://doi.org/10.1007/978-3-030-30490-4_56

19. Gómez, A., Maimó, L., Celdrán, A., Clemente, F.: MADICS: a methodology for anomaly detection in industrial control systems. Symmetry **12**(10), 1583 (2020). https://doi.org/10.3390/sym12101583
20. Gaifulina, D.A., Kotenko, I.V.: Analysis of deep learning models for network anomaly detection in Internet of Things. Inf.-Upravliaiushchie Sist. **1**, 28–37 (2021). https://doi.org/10.31799/1684-8853-2021-1-28-37

Resource-Saving Multiobjective Task Distribution in the Fog- and Edge-Robotics

Anna Klimenko[(⊠)] [iD] and Arseniy Barinov

Institute of IT and Security Technologies, RSUH, 25/2, Kirovogradskaya St.,, Moscow 117534,
Russia
anna_klimenko@mail.ru

Abstract. In the current paper the question of the resource-saving tasks distribution in the robotic groups is under consideration. As a wide range of computational tasks in robotics are performed in a distributed manner, tasks can be assigned to the devices with a relatively low computational capacity. At the same time, data preprocessing, machine learning, SLAM problems are computationally complex, and so the participants of the computational process can be overloaded, while the latter causes the deterioration of average residual life of the computational nodes within the robots. In this paper the problem of resource-saving tasks distribution is formulated as structural-parametric multiobjective one, with paying attention to the workload of those robots in the group, which have to transmit sensor data. The general solution technique is proposed based on global problem decomposition, local time constraints estimations and simulated annealing technique. The a priory time estimations are used according to the tasks graph analysis, as well as time constraints are divided into shares considering the number of transit nodes. Also, some selected experimental results are presented, as well as comparison with the previously conducted results are made.

Keywords: Fog Robotics · Tasks Distribution · Reliability · Distributed Robotics

1 Introduction

Nowadays a problem of resource allocation and task distribution within the robotic groups or swarms is crucial because of the tight connection between robotics and distributed computing. A lot of computationally hard tasks are solved within robot groups or swarms in a distributed manner, for example, as is done in studies [1–3].

As fog robotics is considered as a cornerstone of smart factories, some papers are devoted to the problems of this area, for example [4–6]. Yet very seldom papers are devoted to the reliability issue of the robotic things at the edge or in the fog layers of the network, though edge and fog concepts presuppose data processing by the computational nodes of quite a low performance [7–9].

The need to process large amounts of sensor data in combination with groups of interconnected robots available leads to the issue of sensor data processing somewhere in the robot groups with the only results transmission to the base station (if there any).

© The Author(s), under exclusive license to Springer Nature Switzerland AG 2023
A. Ronzhin et al. (Eds.): ICR 2023, LNAI 14214, pp. 279–288, 2023.
https://doi.org/10.1007/978-3-031-43111-1_25

Such an approach improves the system latency, however, the issue of the need to process the data by the nodes of low performance emerges. At the same time, the decrease of the distance between sensor data source and data processing can provide some additional time to decrease the workload, as well as the shortening of the data transmission route decreases the number of computational process participants.

So, the common problem can be formulated as follows: how to distribute the processing of sensor data through the robot group such as to save as much computational resources as it is possible. Resource-saving is tightly coupled with such reliability parameters as the reliability function, average residual life, failure rate and the workload. In general, the average residual life of the computational node, as an integral part of robot, depends on its workload [10]. So, the optimal workload distribution through the set of robots is a mean to achieve the increase of the robotic computing resources residual life. However, the problem is quite complex and is a structural-parametric one.

In the current paper a problem of resource-saving computational tasks distribution is considered. In our previous study [10] the problem was solved with the application of greedy strategy of tasks distribution within the robot group. Yet, the greedy approach was used for just one task assignment, while the real life conditions presuppose the need to distribute some tasks among the set of robots and so to control their computational resources.

The main contribution of this paper is a new multiobjective model of resource-saving tasks distribution problem. The peculiarity of such task distribution is that multiobjective function vector is formed according the qualitative and quantitative features of computational process participants, representing the individual node preferences as well. So, this determines the structural-parametric property of the problem.

Experimental results conducted show the efficiency of such task distribution: the solution of structural-parametric problem allows to decrease nodes workload and so to improve their reliability function and average residual life. Besides, paying attention to the data transmission routes, which are formed within the robot groups, such routes can be reduced significantly, which also leads to the saving of the computational resources of the robots.

2 Resource-Saving Tasks Distribution: Basic Approach

Reliability function values depend on the failure rate of the computational node, while failure rate is connected to the device temperature and, consequently, workload [11]:

$$\lambda = \lambda_0 \cdot 2^{\frac{\Delta T}{10}}, \tag{1}$$

where: λ is the resulting failure rate, λ_0 is the failure rate under conditions of unloaded device, ΔT is the temperature difference between the temperature of unloaded device and the temperature of loaded one.

Also, the coefficient can be determined, which connects the node temperature and the workload (2):

$$\lambda = \lambda_0 \cdot 2^{\frac{kD}{10}}. \tag{2}$$

Consequently, the reliability function is determined as follows:

$$P(t) = e^{-\lambda t} = e^{-\lambda t \pi \cdot 2^{kD/10}}, \tag{3}$$

where D is the node workload.

Average residual life is estimated as follows:

$$R = \frac{1}{\lambda}. \tag{4}$$

The following "greedy" rule has been formed in [10]:

$$w_{receice} + w_{process} + w_{send} < 2\frac{w_{receive}}{x}. \tag{5}$$

So, for each node it can be esteemed if the data processing is more preferable than data transmission. It is profitable for a node to process data, if inequality (5) is fair.

Yet, there are some weighty drawbacks of this approach:

1. It considers only individual preferences of the nodes. As it is well known, every greedy strategy can lose very good solutions due to its main feature – to choose the best solution on every step.
2. It does not consider data transmission routes, which are loaded with data transmission tasks.

So, this greedy approach seems to be insufficient to distribute tasks properly. At least it is expedient to estimate the overall reliability system state.

Reliability function of the system can be described in terms of consequent – or parallel elements concatenation:

$$P_0(\tau) = 1 - \prod \left(1 - P_j(\tau)\right), P_j(\tau) = e^{-\lambda_j t 2^{\frac{kD_j}{10}}}, \tag{6}$$

where $P_0(\tau)$ is the overall reliability function value for the computational process participants; D is the node workload; k is the coefficient of node temperature increase depending on the current workload; t_{ij} is the moment of assignment of task i to the node j.

The consequent system reliability function is described as follows:

$$P_0(\tau) = \prod \left(P_j(\tau)\right), P_j(\tau) = e^{-\lambda_j \tau 2^{\frac{kD_j}{10}}}. \tag{7}$$

The constraint for this problem is as follows: $\tau \leq t_{decl}$.

Yet, it is hardly possible to describe a random network in this way. So, a new basic function is needed, which could estimate the efficiency of the tasks distribution, including those nodes, which are on data routes.

3   Multiobjective Tasks Distribution: Problem Statement

Consider the network graph $G = <V,U>$, where V is a set of computational nodes, U is a set of ribs. $V = \{v_j\} = \{<j, p_j>\}$, where j is the node identifier, p_j is the node performance.

The user operation is described as an acyclic graph $G' = <T,C>$, which vertexes are assigned to tasks, and ribs are assigned to data transmission between them.

where T is the set of subtasks, C is the set of information connections.

$T = \{t_i\} = \{<i, w_i, d_i>\}$, where i is the subtask identifier, w_i is the computational complexity of the subtask, d_i is the data volume transferred to the network. It must be mentioned that the tasks of data transmission are described in this way as well.

The problem solution is the following tasks assignment:

$$A = \begin{vmatrix} 1 & \ldots\ldots \\ \ldots\ldots\ldots \\ \ldots\ldots & 1 \end{vmatrix}. \tag{8}$$

Assume the case when every participant demands the best individual gain. So, we have m objective functions, which represent "individual good" criteria.

The objective functions can be represented in the following way:

$$P_1(\tau) = e^{-\lambda_j \tau 2^{\frac{kD_1}{10}}};$$
$$\ldots \tag{9}$$
$$P_m(\tau) = e^{-\lambda_j \tau 2^{\frac{kD_1}{10}}};$$

where m is the number of nodes which participate in computation process.

To transfer m-criteria function to the one-criterion function, we use the multiplicative convolution due to that fact that every node reliability function cannot be compensated with the reliability of the other nodes.

The usage of the multiplicative convolution approach allows to assign some preference weights to the chosen nodes:

$$P_0(\tau) = \prod_{i=1}^{m} P_i(\tau)^{\xi_i}, \tag{10}$$

where ξ_i determines the preference of the particular node, which, for example, we'd like to offload.

4   Some Assumptions and General Technique for Resource-Saving Multiobjective Task Distribution

The main particularity of the problem formulated is that it relates to the structural-parametric optimization ones. Indeed, as we consider data routes and workload of the nodes, first we have to form the nodes community which processes data, and after that to analyze all possible routes, which can be used, and find the best one.

So, the general problem is decomposed into two consequently solving problems: the problem of data processing nodes set choice and the one of routes forming with the objective function estimation (10). It is seen that the both of problems are np-hard and hardly can be solved with the usage of classical optimization methods, i.e., brunch-and-bound technique in an acceptable time.

At the same time there are a lot of so-called metaheuristic techniques, such as simulated annealing, genetic algorithms, particle swarm optimization and others. The basic content of iteration, for example, of simulated annealing method contains the following steps [12]:

- to form a solution in a random manner;
- to compare the solution with previously formed "current solution";
- if new solution is better, then it becomes the new current solution with the probability, which is determined by the particular probability law;
- to decrease the temperature variable.

Another particularity of the optimization problem considered is that we have to estimate the workload of the nodes, which can process more than one task or transmit data. The separation between data processing and transmission is the first assumption of the modeling technique proposed, because the mixture of data processing and transmission clutters the estimation model. Then, the workload is calculated based on available time. According to our model task processing/transmission time depends on the selected node computational power, as well as on the remainder of the time for task performing and data transmission according to the time constraint for all the tasks to process. Therefore, the workload depends on the node computational power and time constraints. To estimate the workload of the nodes, we have to esteem the time first, which is available to solve the assigned task.

The way of time periods estimations is the second assumption of this study. The technique of estimations is as follows:

- Consider the task graph and find the critical path;
- For each task, which belongs to the critical path, the available time estimation is got as T_0/N, where N is the number of critical path tasks. Every node on the critical path is marked with its own time estimation.
- For each task, which is not on critical path, the available time is esteemed as $(T_0 - T_{marked})/N_1$, where T_{marked} is the sum of marked tasks time periods, N_1 is the number of unmarked nodes.
- Then the network graph is under consideration. Every data transmission path is analyzed, and when $Task_i$ sends data to $Task_j$, and on the network graph there are nodes between the data source and data sink, time estimation for tasks T_i and T_j is corrected with paying attention to data transmission as follows: every unmarked network node pair, which participates in the process of tasks performing gets the time to process its tasks depending on the data transmission route nodes number, i.e.: T_{marked}/N_{route}.
- So all the network nodes are weighed with the time periods, which are available for computational tasks performing.

One can see that these estimations for time periods are quite rough. However, such time distribution does not conflict with the common trend: with the increase of data route length more and more time from overall time constraint is used for data transfer, and less time is available for tasks performing. This increases the workload of all nodes on the data transmission route.

5 Experimental Comparison of the Greedy and Multiobjective Solutions

According to (5), each node can choose its most beneficial strategy: to process the task or to transmit the data somewhere else. As it was mentioned, data routes are not considered in this greedy approach as well as the reliability features of other nodes do not.

Variable x as a time share to transmit the data is substituted with the following, as we can esteem it with the information about the data channels throughput:

$$t_{process} = t_0 - \sum_{i=0}^{k-1} t_i, \tag{11}$$

where t_i is the data transfer times in the route, t_0 – overall time constraint.

Consider the following task and network graphs (Figs. 1, 2, 3 and 4) (Table 1).

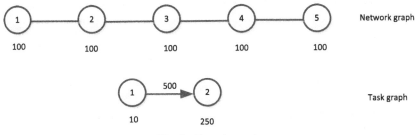

Fig. 1. Experiment 1.

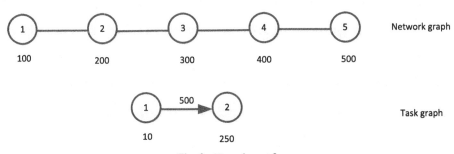

Fig. 2. Experiment 2.

The experimental comparison of the greedy (individual) tasks distribution and the one based on the multiobjective structural-parametric problem solution shows that in the most cases solutions don't contradict, but solution based of multiobjective optimization problem allows to get a precise result for the group of nodes while the greedy approach

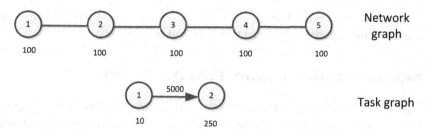

Fig. 3. Experiment 3.

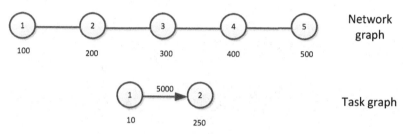

Fig. 4. Experiment 4.

Table 1. The results of greedy and multiobjective techniques comparison.

	Greedy approach	Multiobjective approach
Optimal tasks distribution 1	All nodes prefer to process the task, maximum difference between reliability function value on the node 3	Tasks 0,1 are assigned to the node 1
Optimal tasks distribution 2	All nodes prefer to process the task, maximum difference between reliability function value on the node 1	Tasks 0,1 are assigned to the node 1
Optimal tasks distribution 3	All nodes prefer to process the task, maximum difference between reliability function value on the node 1	Tasks 0,1 are assigned to the node 1
Optimal tasks distribution 4	All nodes prefer to process the task, maximum difference between reliability function value on the node 1	Tasks 0,1 are assigned to the node 1

considers only one node state. The result of experiment 1 shows that with greedy approach there can be situations when the individual preferences of the node contradict with preferences of others and lead to the situation, when one node wins, but others are in situation, which is much worse than they have had before.

6 Experimental Multiobjective Tasks Distribution

Consider the following task and network graph (Fig. 5) We presuppose that node 0 is the starting one and plays the role of fog robotic server. Task 0 is always assigned to the node 0 (Fig. 6).

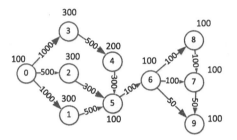

Fig. 5. Task graph.

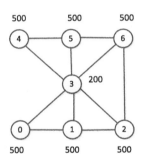

Fig. 6. Network graph.

The first solution is random. After the simulated annealing has been used, with the forming of sets of nodes, the following improved tasks distribution has been provided (Fig. 7).

The results of the experiment illustrate the tasks distribution improvement in the aspect of nodes workload (Fig. 8).

One can see that with the optimization conducted some nodes are out of data routes and have no additional workload, so the data processing time increases significantly because of extra time emergency. Also, one can see that multiobjective tasks distribution and the usage of multiplicative convolution are beneficial for all nodes as individuals, which participate the computational process (workload decrease up to 39% comparing with the random distribution).

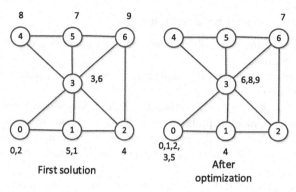

First solution   After
                                  optimization

Fig. 7. Tasks distribution.

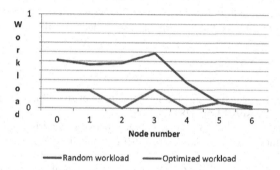

Fig. 8. The workload values with random and optimized tasks distribution.

7 Conclusion

Although there is a wide range of papers devoted to the resource allocation and tasks distribution in robot groups, very seldom publications are devoted to the reliability issue of the computational nodes as the integral parts of robots, although those nodes with low computational complexity can process the large amounts of sensor data. Also, in the robot groups sensor data transmission is used as well, although there can be various cases when it is more profitable to process the data by means of robot group.

Such lack of common strategy in computational tasks distribution with paying attention to the data transmission tasks, lead to the robot computational resources spending and to the decrease of their potential lifetime because of reliability function uncontrolled deterioration.

In this paper we state the problem of resource-saving task distribution. We consider the problem as the multiobjective optimization one, when every node has its own objective function and tries to improve its own workload state. Then this multiobjective function is transformed to the one-criterion optimization problem by the multiplicative convolution.

Formulated problem is a structural-parametric one, and can be decomposed into a range of parametric problems, which are solved with the usage of simulated annealing.

The main results of this paper are as follows:

- multiobjective optimization problem statement for resource-saving tasks distribution within the robot group;
- some techniques of problem solution, including rough time estimations for the task and network graphs;
- experimental comparison of selected cases of the greedy strategy results and of the multiobjective optimization problem ones. The main conclusion is that "greedy" results do not conflict with the optimization problem solution in the most cases, however, sometimes greedy approach leads to the significant deterioration of the solution for the nodes, which participate in data transmission.
- experimental research of tasks distribution among robot nodes according to the techniques proposed shows the positive effect on the individual reliability function values because of the decrease of the data transmission routes and, as a consequence, potential tasks processing time increase. The latter allows to distribute the task computational complexity though time and so to decrease the robot node workload.

References

1. Gul, O.M.: Energy harvesting and task-aware multi-robot task allocation in robotic wireless sensor networks. Sensors **23**(6), 3284 (2023)
2. Zhenwei, Z., Zhao, X., Tao, B., Ding, H.: Distributed gossip-triggered control for robot swarms with limited communication range. IEEE Trans. Industr. Electron. **70**(12), 12511–12521 (2023)
3. Wang, S., Wang, Y., Li, D., Zhao, Q.: Distributed relative localization algorithms for multi-robot networks: a survey. Sensors **23**(5), 2399 (2023)
4. Xu, X., Chai, Z., Xiong, Z., Wu, J.: A scalable resource management architecture for industrial fog robots. In: Liu, X.J., Nie, Z., Yu, J., Xie, F., Song, R. (eds.) ICIRA 2021. LNCS (LNAI), vol. 13013, pp. 67–77. Springer, Cham (2021). https://doi.org/10.1007/978-3-030-89095-7_7
5. Alirezazadeh, S., Correia, A., Alexandre, L.A.: Optimal algorithm allocation for robotic network cloud systems. Robot. Auton. Syst. **154**, 104144 (2022)
6. Matrouk, K., Matrouk, A.: Mobility aware-task scheduling and virtual fog for offloading in IoT-fog-cloud environment. Wireless Pers. Commun. **130**, 801–836 (2023)
7. Maciel, P., et al.: A survey on reliability and availability modeling of edge, fog, and cloud computing. Reliable Intell. Environ. **8**, 227–245 (2022)
8. Baranwal, G., Vidyarthi, D.: TRAPPY: a truthfulness and reliability aware application placement policy in fog computing. J. Supercomput. **78**, 7861–7887 (2022)
9. Montoya-Muñoz, A., Silva, R., Caicedo, M., Fonseca, N.: Reliability provisioning for fog nodes in smart farming IoT-fog-cloud continuum. Comput. Electron. Agric. **200**, 107252 (2022)
10. Klimenko, A.: Model and method of resource-saving tasks distribution for the fog robotics. In: Ronzhin, A., Meshcheryakov, R., Xiantong, Z. (eds) Interactive Collaborative Robotics. ICR 2022. Lecture Notes in Computer Science, vol. 13719, pp. 210–222. Springer, Cham. (2022). https://doi.org/10.1007/978-3-031-23609-9_19
11. Melnik, E., Klimenko, A.: A condition of reliability improvement of the system based on the fog-computing concept. In: Journal of Physics: Conference Series, vol. 1661, p. 012007 (2020). https://doi.org/10.1088/1742-6596/1661/1/012007
12. Manickam, R., Venkateswaran, C., Ramu, K., Prasanth, V., Mathivanan, G.: Application of Simulated Annealing in Various Field (2022). https://doi.org/10.46632/mc/1/1/1

Reliability of Robot's Controller Software

Eugene Larkin[1] [ID], Tatiana Akimenko[1][(✉)] [ID], Alexey Bogomolov[2] [ID],
and Vadim Sharov[1]

[1] Tula State University, 92, Lenina pr., Tula 300012, Russia
tantan72@mail.ru

[2] St. Petersburg Federal Research Center of the Russian Academy of Sciences, 39, 14th Line
V.O., St. Petersburg 199178, Russia

Abstract. The reliability of robots' digital control systems, based on Von Neumann type computer platform is investigated. An approach is proposed for assessing the reliability of a robot control program, based on the analysis of software as a model of a computational process unfolding in real physical time. It is shown that in systems of suchlike class the importance of software in ensuring the reliability of robot operation as a whole increases significantly. It is determined that software failure potential is being laid to the control program at its designing stage due to neglect of such digital controllers properties, as time delays when data processing. The model of control program failures emerging, caused by time factor, is worked out. For delays between transactions estimation the semi-Markov model of poling procedure is used, that permit to estimate probabilities of exceeding data skew, pure lag, and sampling period the threshold, beyond which the control system failure takes place. Using a stochastic matrix, describing poling procedure, probability of failure, caused by transactions order disturbances is estimated. Probabilities and sampling period obtained are used for simulation of failure flow generator, describing reliability of control program.

Keywords: Control Program · Poling · Sampling Period · Transaction ·
Semi-Markov Process · Stochastic Matrix · Failure Flow

1 Introduction

The main feature of robots, as object under control, is their structural complexity, which is understood as a great number of controllable units, as well as links between them [1–3]. Structural complexity of the object under control implies complexity of software, which may be considered as an integral part of the digital controller, ensuring characteristics requirements of the control system as a whole [4–7]. This, in turn, leads to tightening demands for reliability of software embedded on the controller. Leaving aside hardware aspects of controller reliability, soft failures may be considered as a consequence of program developer errors, arising at all stages of program creation, from specification of demands to data processing in the control system, till the embedding of the completed control program into the controller and acceptance test of the system [8–12].

© The Author(s), under exclusive license to Springer Nature Switzerland AG 2023
A. Ronzhin et al. (Eds.): ICR 2023, LNAI 14214, pp. 289–299, 2023.
https://doi.org/10.1007/978-3-031-43111-1_26

In any digital control system algorithm and the program are models of processing data, receiving from sensors subsystem, to compute data, transmitted to actuators. So, errors in the software mean that either an inadequate, or an imperfect model of the computational process was created, which may or may not lead to the failure of the control system as a whole. This is why, when analyzing program reliability one should take into account not only its algorithm semantics, but also the fact, that the program is interpreted by the controller sequentially, command by command, and the interpretation unfolds in the real physical time.

Data processed by the controller is random one, so both the choice of the direction of data processing at program branching points, and the physical time of commands execution, are random values. This fact should be taken into account when developing the data processing model and transforming it to reliability model. For modes of both types the theory of semi-Markov processes is widely used [13, 14]. Therefore, the analysis of the reliability of control programs can be reduced to the transformation of a semi-Markov model, which describes the operation of a digital controller, into a semi-Markov model, which describes its failures due to errors made during programming. Methods for forming a software reliability model for robot control systems are not well developed, which explains the relevance and importance of the research in this domain.

2   Simulation of Robot's Digital Control System

The flowchart of the controllable robot is shown in Fig. 1. [1–7]. System includes robot itself, which is characterized by K-element state vector $x(t) = [x_1(t), ..., x_k(t), ..., x_K(t)]$. Measured robot state on the Interface is transformed to K-element data $x_c(n) = [x_{c,1}(n), ..., x_{c,k}(n), ..., x_{c,K}(n)]$, elements of which together with elements of K-element vector of desired robot states $f(n) = [f_1(n), ..., f_k(n), ..., f_K(n)]$ are processed by controller soft. The result of data processing is the data vector $u_c(n) = [u_{c,1}(n), ..., u_{c,k}(n), ..., u_{c,K}(n)]$, which on the interface is transformed to K-element action vector $u(t) = [u_1(t), ..., u_k(t), ..., u_K(t)]$ of analogue signals, applied to actuators of robot.

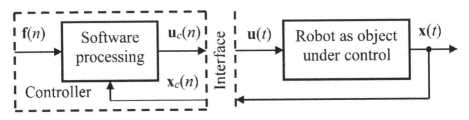

Fig. 1. The control system functional diagram.

States $x(t)$ and actions $u(t)$ are linked with non-linear differential equation system:

$$V\left\{x^{[0(x)]}(t), ..., x^{[m(x)]}(t), ..., x^{[M(x)]}(t),\right.$$

$$\left. u^{[0(u)]}(t), \ \ldots, \ u^{[m(u)]}(t), \ \ldots, \ u^{[M(u)]}(t), \ t \right\} = 0, \tag{1}$$

where $V = (V_1, \ \ldots, \ V_k, \ \ldots, \ V_K)^{\theta}$ is the vector function of vector argument; V_k is the scalar component of vector function; t is the time; $x^{[m(x)]}(t)$ is the $m(x)$-th order derivative of $x(t)$ with respect to time; $u^{[m(u)]}(t)$ is the $m(u)$-th derivative of $u(t)$ with respect to time; $0(x) \leq m(x) \leq M(x)$ and $0(u) \leq m(u) \leq M(u)$ are orders of time derivatives; θ is the transpose sign.

Vector function (1) describes robot operation dynamics, including sensor and actuator subsystems operation, as well as cross links between control contours, which exist on the physical level.

The controller processes data according to the program, in which differentiation and integration operations are substituted by differencing and sunning operations correspondingly. Difference equation takes the form:

$$\mathbf{W}\{\mathbf{u}_c[n - 0(u)], \ \ldots, \ \mathbf{u}_c[n - m(u)], \ \ldots, \ \mathbf{u}_c[n - M(u)],$$

$$\mathbf{x}_c[n - 0(x)], \ \ldots, \ \mathbf{x}_c[n - m(x)], \ \ldots, \ \mathbf{x}_c[n - M(x)], \ n, \ \mathbf{f}(n)\} = 0, \tag{2}$$

where $W = (W_1, \ \ldots, \ W_k, \ \ldots, \ W_K)^{\theta}$ is the vector function of vector arguments; W_k is the scalar component of the vector function; $u_c[n - 0(u)]$ is calculated according the program current value of control data vector; $u_c[n - m(u)]$ is the value of control vector, calculated on previous stages, $m(u)$ discrete times ago; $x_c[n - 0(u)]$ is the current value of data vector describing current robot state; $x_c[n - m(u)]$ is the value of robot state existed $m(x)$ discrete times ago; $M(u)$ and $M(x)$ are maximum values of the difference Eq. (2) order

In accordance with the expression (2) the control program successively, element-by-element receives current information $x_c(n)$ about the robot state, and successively, element-by-element computes vector $u_c(n)$ and transmits it to actuators. Interpretation of control program is carried out cyclically and unfolds in real physical time.

3 Causes of Software Failures

Let us define as reference point, designated the beginning of the cycle, the moment of element $x_1(t)$ digital image $x_{c,1}(n)$ formation, and assume, that all other transactions are generated correspondingly to $x_{c,1}(n)$ with a delay, which is defined by concrete poling procedure, realized in control algorithm. Delays $\tau_{1(x),k(x)}, 2(x) \leq k(x) \leq K(x)$, between inputs of first and other elements of vector $x(t)$ born input data skew. Delays $\tau_{1(u),k(u)}$, $2(u) \leq k(u) \leq K(u)$, between outputs of first and other elements of vector $u(t)$ born output data skew. Both skews influence the control process quality characteristics and should be considered when software failure analysis. Time intervals $\tau_{k(x),l(u)}$ between inputting codes $x_{c,k}(n)$ and outputting codes $u_{c,l}(n)$, where $1 \leq k, \ l \leq K$ give pure lags in control contours, and also should be taken into account when software failure analysis [15–19]. Besides, non-compliance with Nyquist conditions of sampling theorem when organizing poling procedure leads to software failure [20–22].

Common transactions flow, generated by poling procedure, is shown in Fig. 2, where round point arrows designate input data to controller, squire point arrows designate output data from controller. Start of poling procedure is designated as $t_{tr,n} = n\tau_{1(x),1(x)}$. It is linked with the moment of inputting $x_{c,1}(n)$ of vector $\mathbf{x}_c(n)$. The cycle period is designated as $\tau_{tr} = \tau_{1(x),1(x)}$ it lasts from the moment of inputting $x_{c,1}(n)$ till the $x_{c,1}(n+1)$ inputting moment.

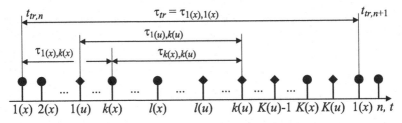

Fig. 2. Transactions flow, generated by control program.

For time intervals estimation the model of controller, as a physical device, operated in a physical time, should be built. For simplicity the model may be represented by transactions operators only. It is assumed that all computations are executed by the proper transaction operator. An adequate model of controller operation when control program interpretation is the semi-Markov process, represented by $Z \times Z$ semi-Markov matrix [13, 14]

$$\boldsymbol{h}(t) = \left[h_{\xi,\zeta}(t)\right] = \left[g_{\xi,\zeta}(t)\right] \otimes \left[p_{\xi,\zeta}\right], \tag{3}$$

where $p_{\xi,\zeta}$ are probabilities of direct switching from the state ξ to the state ζ; $g_{\xi,\zeta}(t)$ is the time density of sojourn the process in the state ξ, when a priory is known, that next state will be the ζ one; $\otimes$ is the sign of direct multiplication of matrices. $\xi, \zeta \in \{1(x), ..., k(x), ..., K(x), 1(u), ..., k(u), ..., K(u)\}; Z = 2K,$; is the common quantity of semi-Markov process states, equal to common quantity of transactions, generated by control program.

Due to the poling procedure is the cyclic one, and during the cycle all transactions should be updated, the structure of semi-Markov process is represented by a complete strongly connected graph with loops, shown in Fig. 3a. Semi-Markov process (3) is the ergodic one, the absorbing or semi-absorbing states are absent in the process. On probabilities of matrix $\left[p_{\xi,\zeta}\right]$ and time distribution densities the following restrictions are lay.

$$0 < T_{\xi,\zeta}^{min \, arg [g_{\xi,\zeta}(t)]_{\xi,\zeta}^{max}}, 1 \le \xi, \zeta \le Z;$$

$$\sum_{\zeta=1}^{Z} p_{\xi,\zeta} = 1; 1 \le \xi \le Z;$$

$$\int_{T_{\xi,\zeta}^{min}}^{T_{\xi,\zeta}^{max}} \int^{=1} g_{\xi,\zeta}(t)dt,$$

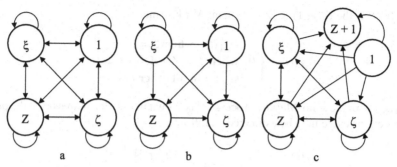

Fig. 3. Structures of semi-Markov processes: a is the initial one; b is the process for estimation of time interval between transactions; c is the process for estimation of polling procedure period.

where $T_{\xi,\zeta}^{min}$ and $T_{\xi,\zeta}^{max}$ are uppermost and lowermost borders of density $g_{\xi,\zeta}(t)$ domain.

For estimation of time interval value from transaction ξ till transaction ζ the ergodic semi-Markov process, shown in Fig. 1a should be transformed into the process,

$$\boldsymbol{h'}(t) = \left[g_{i,j}(t)\right] \otimes \left[p'_{i,j}\right], \tag{4}$$

shown in Fig. 3b, in which state ξ and ζ are starting and absorbing ones correspondingly. The transforming is reduced to recalculation of probabilities according to the formula:

$$p'_{i,j} = \begin{cases} 0, & \text{when } i = \zeta, \text{ or } j = \xi; \\ \dfrac{p_{i,j}}{1-p_{i,\xi}} & \text{in all other cases.} \end{cases}$$

where $1 \le i, j \le Z$.

Time delay is estimated as follows [23]

$$g_{\xi,\zeta}^{\Sigma}(t) = \boldsymbol{I}_{\xi}^{r} \cdot L^{-1}\left[\sum_{i=1}^{\infty}\left\{L[\boldsymbol{h'}(t)]\right\}^{i}\right] \cdot \boldsymbol{I}_{\zeta}^{c} \tag{5}$$

where $L[...]$ and $L^{-1}[...]$ are direct and inverse Laplace transforms, correspondingly; [24–26]; $\boldsymbol{I}_{\xi}^{r}$ is the Z -element row vector, ξ-th element of which is equal to one, and other elements are equal to zero; $\boldsymbol{I}_{\zeta}^{c}$ is the Z -element column vector ζ-th element of which is equal to one, and other elements are equal to zero.

The probability of system failure due to exceeding of delay $\tau_{\xi,\zeta}$ its critical value $\tilde{\tau}_{\xi,\zeta}$ is as follows [27]:

$$q_{\tau,\xi,\zeta} = \int_{\tilde{\tau}_{\xi,\zeta}}^{\infty} g_{\xi,\zeta}^{\Sigma}(t)dt, \tag{6}$$

where ξ, $\zeta \in \{1(x),\ ...,\ k(x),\ ...,\ K(x),\ 1(u),\ ...,\ k(u),\ ...,\ K(u)\}$.

For estimation of transaction cycle period value semi-Markov process (3) should be transformed into the process

$$\boldsymbol{h''}(t) = \left[h''_{\xi,\zeta}(t)\right], \tag{7}$$

where $\mathbf{h}''(t)$ is the $(Z+1) \times (Z+1)$ semi-Markov matrix.

$$h''_{\xi,\zeta}(t) = \begin{cases} h_{\xi,1}(t), & \text{when } \zeta = Z+1 \\ 0, & \text{when } \xi = Z+1, \text{ or } \zeta = 0; \\ h_{\xi,\zeta}(t) & \text{in all other cases}. \end{cases}$$

Structure of the semi-Markov process (7) is shown in Fig. 3c. With use (7) the period of transactions cycle may be estimated as follows

$$g_{tr}(t) = \mathbf{I}_1^r \cdot L^{-1}\left[\sum_{i=1}^{\infty} \{L[\mathbf{h}''(t)]\}^i\right] \cdot \mathbf{I}_{Z+1}^c, \tag{8}$$

where $\mathbf{I}_\xi^r$ is the $(Z+1)$-element row vector, first element of which is equal to one, and all other elements are equal to zeros; $\mathbf{I}_{Z+1}^c$ is the $(Z+1)$-element column vector, $(Z+1)$-th element of which is equal to one, and all other elements are equal to zeros.

The probability of system failure due to exceeding of cycle period τ_{tr} pre-determined critical value $\tilde{\tau}_{tr}$ may be estimated as

$$q_{tr} = \int_{\tilde{\tau}_{tr}}^{\infty} g_{tr,1,1}(t)dt. \tag{9}$$

Programming links missing, leading to transactions order violation is fairly common error when coding control algorithm of a complex multi-contour object that is a robot. When transactions order violation part of vector $x(t)$ elements get processed with algorithm (2) not in the current, but in the next cycle, that may lead or may not lead to system failure. To estimate the probability of failures caused by errors of this type, the task of routing walks through the states of semi-Markov process would be solved.

For solving task, the stochastic matrices concatenation operation should be defined. Stochastic matrices ^1p and ^2p concatenation is the matrix:

$$^1p \& {}^2p = \left[\bigcup_{\psi=1}^{\Psi} {}^1p_{\xi,\psi} \& {}^2p_{\psi,\zeta}\right], \tag{10}$$

where $\&$ is concatenation operation notation; $^1\mathbf{p} = \left[^1p_{\xi,\psi}\right]$ is the $\Xi \times \Psi$ stochastic matrix; $^2\mathbf{p} = \left[^2p_{\psi,\zeta}\right]$ is the $\Psi \times Z$ stochastic matrix.

As it follows from (10), stochastic matrices concatenation operation is performed according to rules of matrices multiplication [28, 29], but instead of multiplication there is concatenation operation, and instead of summation there is operation of strings joint. For the squire stochastic matrix $\left[p_{\xi,\zeta}\right]$ concatenation degree $\left[p_{\xi,\zeta}\right]^{\&i} = \left[p_{\xi,\zeta}\right]^{\&(i-1)} \& \left[p_{\xi,\zeta}\right]$ may be defined. As a result of concatenation exponentiation $\left[p_{\xi,\zeta}\right]^{\&Z}$, strings of Z probabilities designations are formed, located on routes with Z length, leading from the state, with number of the stochastic matrix row to the state with number of the stochastic matrix column Indices of probabilities nomination strings define routes of wandering through semi-Markov process (3) states, and hence determine the transactions sequence in semi-Markov process realizations. From the point of view of software failure, under interest are strings, which begin and end in the first state of semi-Markov process (3), due to other strings do not form required cycles.

In common case component with index 1,1 of matrix $[p_{\xi,\zeta}]^{\&Z}$ is as follows:

$$P_{1,1} = \bigcup_{j=1}^{j} P_{1,1,j}, \tag{11}$$

where $P_{1,1,j}$ is the j-th string of probabilities nominations, which starts and finishes at the state 1; $J = (Z-1)^{(Z-1)}$ is common number of strings.

From J strings $P_{1,1,j}$ of (11), only strings with non-recurring indices describe proper transactions, because during cycle all robot's sensors and actuators must be quested. Common number $\tilde{J} = (Z-1)!$ of such string is defined as quantity of Hamiltonian cycles starting and finishing at the state 1. From $\tilde{J}$ Hamiltonian cycles only $\hat{J} \leq \tilde{J}$ satisfy to restrictions on the wandering routes, imposed by semantic of algorithm (2).

For estimation of probability of Hamiltonian cycle $\bar{P}_{1,1,\hat{j}} = P_{1,\xi(\hat{j})} \&p_{\xi(\hat{j}),\psi(\hat{j})} \&...\&p_{i(\hat{j}),m(\hat{j})} \&...\&p_{\zeta(\hat{j}),1}$ forming probabilities from the string should be transformed to cortege

$$p_{1,\xi(\hat{j})} \&p_{\xi(\hat{j}),\psi(\hat{j})} \&...\&p_{i(\hat{j}),m(\hat{j})} \&...\&p_{\zeta(\hat{j}),1} \rightarrow$$

$$\rightarrow \left(p_{1(\hat{j})}, \ p_{2(\hat{j})}, \ ..., \ p_{l(\hat{j})}, \ ..., \ p_{Z(\hat{j})} \right), \tag{12}$$

where $1(\hat{j}) \leq l(\hat{j}) \leq Z(\hat{j})$ is the index, defining number of elements in the cortege. Probability of failure because or transactions ordering violation is equal to

$$q_{ord} = 1 - \sum_{\hat{j}=1}^{\hat{j}} \prod_{l(\hat{j})=1(\hat{j})}^{Z(\hat{j})} p_{l(\hat{j})} \tag{13}$$

4   Model of Failure Flux Forming

In the roughest version, failures emerging due to investigated above causes can be considered as independent ones. Due to this assumption the probability of software failure is equal to sum of probabilities, i.e.:

$$q = \sum_{\zeta=1}^{Z} \sum_{\xi=1}^{Z} q_{\tau,\xi,\zeta} + q_{tr} + q_{ord}. \tag{14}$$

With use (14) and (8) the semi-Markov model of the software failures generator may be formed:

$$h_{\varphi}(t) = \begin{bmatrix} (1-q) \cdot g_{tr}(t) & q \cdot g_{tr}(t) \\ 0 & 0 \end{bmatrix}. \tag{15}$$

The structure of the model (15) is shown in Fig. 4. The loop in the structure describes the absence of failures during the cycle, arc from the state α_1 to the state α_2 means the failure of control program.

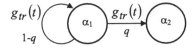

Fig. 4. Model of software failures generator.

Time density from switching on the controller till software failure is as follows:

$$g_\varphi(t) = (1,\ 0) \cdot L^{-1}\left[\sum\nolimits_{i=1}^{\infty} \{L[\mathbf{h}_\varphi(t)]\}^i\right] \cdot \binom{0}{1}. \tag{16}$$

As it follows from (16) time between failures represents by stochastic sum of times, between one, two, etc. cycles. In accordance with [30–33] failure flux may be considered as Poisson one, in which time is distributed according to exponential law:

$$g_\varphi(t) \cong \frac{1}{T_\varphi} \exp\left(-\frac{t}{T_\varphi}\right), \tag{17}$$

where $T_\varphi = \int\limits_0^\infty t \cdot g_\varphi(t)dt$ is the time to failure.

Parameter T_φ can be change to a big side, if robot operating mode allows correction the embedded control program.

5 Example

Let's consider software failure due to missing, when control program design, features of digital control system operation, discussed above. The robot's controllable equipment, including sensors and actuators, is described with the following differential equation system, performed in the form (18):

$$\begin{cases} 2,5 \cdot 10^{-3} \cdot x_1^{(3)}(t) + 0,1 \cdot x_1^{(2)}(t) + x_1^{(1)}(t) = u_1(t) + u_2(t); \\ 6,25 \cdot 10^{-4} \cdot x_2^{(3)}(t) + 0,05 \cdot x_2^{(2)}(t) + x_2^{(1)}(t) = -2,5u_1(t) + 2,5u_2(t), \end{cases} \tag{18}$$

where $x_1(t)$, $x_2(t)$ are state parameters of robot equipment; $u_1(t)$, $u_2(t)$ are control actions.

Control actions, applied to equipment actuators, being computed by controller, is as follows:

$$\begin{cases} u_1(t) = \eta(t) - x_1(t); \\ u_2(t) = \eta(t) - x_2(t), \end{cases} \tag{19}$$

where $\eta(t)$ is the Heaviside function.

Transient processes in the control system are shown in Fig. 5.

Curves in Fig. 5 represent dynamics of the system without lags, data skews, and other errors, introduced by digital controller. Overshooting in the system does not exceed ten percents, and the control overtime is equal to 3 s. Figure 5b shows disturbances emerging at the sampling stage, when Nyquist conditions are violated by poling procedure. In this case in the system occur fluctuations around equilibrium point, which amplitude the greater, the less inertial is the object under control. In the system with delays in feedback circuit overshooting increases up to twenty percent, and control overtime increases to 4 s, which in some cases, may be considered as the system failure. Transactions order violation means that data describing object under control state arrive for processing after the sampling period, that born both data skew, and feedback signal delay (Fig. 5d). In turn, both these factors lead to software failure.

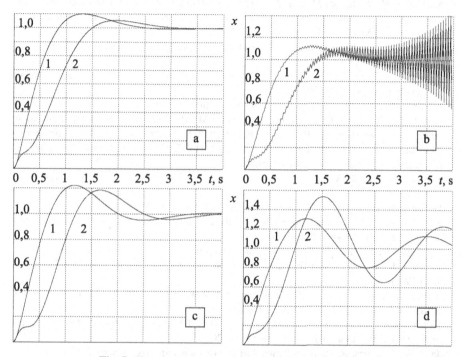

Fig. 5. Transient processes in the digital control system.

6 Conclusion

In such a way, the approach to evaluation of robot's control program reliability, based on analysis of the software as a model of computing process, unfolding in real physical time, is proposed. It is shown how the model of computing process may be transformed into the software failure generator model, which parameters are defined by the soft, embedded onto robot's digital controller. To avoid considered type system failures during robot with installed control program exploiting, it may be recommended at the stage of software design the setting strong limits on the program runtime parameters, especially on the sampling period and delays in feedback contours, for a possibly wide range of robot states. Further investigations in the domain may be directed on working out methods of robot's control software failure-free design.

Acknowledgments. The research was carried out within the grant № 22–26-00808 of Russian Scientific Foundation.

References

1. Siciliano, B., Khatib, O.: Springer Handbook of Robotics. Springer, Berlin (2016)
2. Mehmszow, U.: Mobile Robotics: A Practical Introduction. Springer, London (2003)
3. Kamaldar, M., Mahjoob, M.J., Yazdi, M.H., Vahid-Alizadeh, H., Ahmadizadeh, S: A control synthesis for reducing lateral oscillations of a spherical robot. In: IEEE International Conference on Mechatronics, pp. 546–551 (2011)
4. Landau, I.D., Zito, G.: Digital Control Systems. Design. Identification and Implementation. Springer, London (2006)
5. Aström, J., Wittenmark, B.: Computer Controlled Systems: Theory and Design. Tsinghua University Press, Beijing (2002)
6. Larkin, E.V., Nguyen, V.S., Privalov, A.N.: Simulation of digital control systems by nonlinear objects. In: Dang, N.H.T., Zhang, YD., Tavares, J.M.R.S., Chen, BH. (eds.) Artificial Intelligence in Data and Big Data Processing. ICABDE 2021. Lecture Notes on Data Engineering and Communications Technologies, vol. 124, pp. 711–721. Springer, Cham (2022). https://doi.org/10.1007/978-3-030-97610-1_56
7. Fadali, M.S., Visioli, A.: Digital Control Engineering: Analysis and Design. Academic Press, Cambridge (2012)
8. Dubrova, E.: Fault-Tolerant Design. Springer, New York (2013)
9. Sánchez-Silva, M., Klutke, G.-A.: Reliability and Life-Cycle Analysis of Deteriorating Systems. Springer, Switzerland (2016)
10. O'Conner, P., Kleyner, A.: Practical Reliability Engineering. Willey, Hoboken (2012)
11. Koren, I., Krishna, M.: Fault Tolerant Systems. Morgan Kaufmann Publishers, San Francisco, CA (2007)
12. Zhang, Y., Jiang, J.: Bibliographical review on reconfigurable fault-tolerant control systems. Annu. Rev. Control. **32**(2), 229–252 (2008)
13. Howard R.A.: Dynamic Probabilistic Systems. VOL. 1 Markov Models, Vol. 2 Semi-Markov and Decision Processes. Courier Corporation (2012)
14. Janssen, J., Manca, R.: Applied Semi-Markov processes. Springer, Cham (2006)
15. Pospíšil, M.: Representation of solutions of delayed difference equations with linear parts given by pairwise permutable matrices via Z-transform. Appl. Math. Comput. **294**, 180–194 (2017)
16. Sanz, R., García, P., Fridman, E., Albertos, P.: Robust predictive extended state observer for a class of nonlinear systems with time-varying input delay. Int. J. Control **93**(2), 217–225 (2020)
17. Wu, M., He, Y., She, J.H., Liu, G.P.: Delay-dependent criteria for robust stability of time-varying delay systems. Automatica **40**(8), 1435–1439 (2004)
18. Zhang, X.M., Wu, M., He, Y.: Delay dependent robust control for linear systems with multiple time-varying delays and uncertainties. Control Decision **19**, 496–500 (2004)
19. Wu, R., Fan, D., Iu, H.H.C., Fernando, T.: Adaptive fuzzy dynamic surface control for uncertain discrete-time non-linear pure-feedback mimo systems with network-induced time-delay based on state observer. Int. J. Control **92**(7), 1707–1719 (2019)
20. Hayes, M.H.: Statistical digital signal processing and modeling. Willey, Hoboken (2009)
21. Yeh, Y.C., Chu, Y., Chiou, C.W.: Improving the sampling resolution of periodic signals by using controlled sampling interval method. Comput. Electr. Eng. **40**(4), 1064–1071 (2014)

22. Meyer-Baese, U.: Digital Signal Processing. Springer, Heidelbrg (2004)
23. Larkin, E.V., Bogomolov, A.V., Privalov, A.N.: A method for estimating the time intervals between transactions in speech-compression algorithms. Automatic Documentation Math. Linguist. **51**, 214–219 (2017)
24. Pavlov, A.V.: About the equality of the transform of Laplace to the transform of Fourier. Issues Anal. **23**, 21–30 (2016)
25. Li, J., Farquharson, C.G., Hu, X.: Three effective inverse Laplace transform algorithms for computing time-domain electromagnetic responses. Geophysics **81**(2), E113–E128 (2016)
26. Schiff, J.L.: The Laplace transform: Theory and Applications. Springer, New York (1991)
27. Kobayashi, H., Mark, B.L., Turin, W.: Probability, Random Processes, and Statistical Analysis: Applications to Communications, Signal Processing, Queueing Theory and Mathematical Finance. Cambridge University Press, Cambridge (2011)
28. Petersen, P.: Linear Algebra. Springer, New York (2012)
29. Cherney, D., Denton, T., Thomas, R., Waldron, A.: Linear Algebra. Davis, California (2013)
30. Grigelionis, B.: On the convergence of sums of random step processes to a Poisson process. Theory Probab. Appl. **8**(2), 177–182 (1963)
31. Lu, H., Pang, G., Mandjes, M.: A functional central limit theorem for Markov additive arrival processes and its applications to queuing systems. Queuing Syst. **84**(3), 381–406 (2016)
32. Larkin, E., Bogomolov, A., Gorbachev, D., Privalov, A.: About approach of the transactions flow to Poisson one in robot control systems. In: Ronzhin, A., Rigoll, G., Meshcheryakov, R. (eds.) ICR 2017. LNCS (LNAI), vol. 10459, pp. 113–122. Springer, Cham (2017). https://doi.org/10.1007/978-3-319-66471-2_13
33. Larkin, E., Privalov, A., Bogomolov, A., Akimenko, T.: Model of digital control system by complex multi-loop objects. In: AIP Conference Proceedings, vol. 2700, no. 1. AIP Publishing (2023)

Ontological Approach to the Organization of Computing in Distributed Monitoring Systems with Mobile Components Based on a Distributed Ledger

Eduard Melnik and Irina Safronenkova(✉)

Federal Research Center, The Southern Scientific Center of the Russian Academy of Sciences,
41, Chekhov st., Rostov-on-Don 344006, Russia
safronenkova050788@yandex.ru

Abstract. The implementation of mobile components into monitoring systems has significantly expanded their scope of application. A distributed ledger (DL) allows to synchronize copies of data received from geographically distributed sources. This makes it possible for mobile components to work with the "nearest" copy of the ledger in terms of data access, which reduces the time and energy costs associated with data access. This paper considers issues related to the efficiency of distributed monitoring systems with mobile components based on the concept of fog computing and DL technologies. The problem of organizing the computational process in terms of placement and workload reallocation is highlighted. It is proposed to use the ontological approach in order to reduce the search space of candidate nodes for the placement of computational load. The use of other known methods of placing the computational load is limited by the characteristics of the environment and the system. The core of ontological approach is the ontological model built with the subject domain in mind. Experimental studies have shown that the application of the ontological approach can reduce the search space by 80%. The obtained data are consistent with the results of the experiment conducted for another subject area.

Keywords: Monitoring Systems · Mobile Components · Distributed Ledger · Ontological Model · Latency · Workload Relocation

1 Introduction

The concept of fog computing implies workload relocation closer to the edge of the network in order to reduce the load on the information infrastructure and to reduce the latency of the system [1–3]. This concept fits well with the basic requirements for monitoring systems, for which response time is one of the most important parameters of their functioning [4].

The implementing of mobile components (UAVs, autonomous robots, devices on board the vehicle, mobile devices) in monitoring systems has greatly expanded their scope of application. Distributed data storage in such systems based on a distributed ledger allows to increase the convenience of access to data and in many cases to reduce the load on the network. A DL allows synchronizing copies of data obtained from geographically distributed sources. This enables mobile components to work with the "closest" copy of the ledger in terms of data access, which reduces the time and energy costs associated with data access [5–7].

At the same time, when organizing the computational process, it is necessary to take into account the dynamism of the computing environment implemented on the basis of fog and edge devices, taking into account the peculiarities of the functioning of mobile components. One of the important stages of such organization is the stage of solving the problem of placement and relocation of computational load, which is performed repeatedly [8–10].

The number of relocations affects the following important parameters: the time to solve a functional task and power consumption. The latter is especially relevant for distributed systems with mobile components. It is possible to reduce the number of workload reallocations by selecting such an initial placement of computational task on nodes that would meet a certain level of reliability of computational nodes of the system. In this case, we will understand the reliability as the ability of a computational node to perform an assigned amount of calculations at a certain moment of time. Thus, we can say that providing a certain level of reliability of computational nodes that perform the problem solving, allows to reduce the time of solving the functional task and reduce power consumption, which is an important criterion for the effective functioning of the distributed system with mobile components. In other words, improving the quality of the initial placement of the task by computational nodes allows to increase the efficiency of operation of distributed monitoring systems with mobile components based on a DL.

This paper proposes to use an ontological approach to select the most "suitable" candidate nodes for a particular problem, both for the initial placement and for possible subsequent workload relocations. This approach reduces the search space and shortens the time to make a decision [11]. The use of other known methods of placing the computational load is limited by the characteristics of the environment and the system. The methods and algorithms proposed in [12, 13] do not take into account the influence of the solution time of the problem of moving the workload on the efficiency of solving the user problem. The strategies and approaches proposed in [14–16] have high computational complexity and are not oriented to solving problems of high dimensionality or complex topology. When implementing a LDG-method [17], the time to obtain a solution may be unacceptably long due to numerous information exchanges. The constraint forming method for solving the problem of computational load reallocation in a distributed system [18] does not take into account the presence of mobile components and DL nodes.

2 Ontological Approach to the Organization of Computations in Distributed Systems

The idea of using ontologies to reduce the search space is not new. For example, it was proposed to use domain ontology models to reduce the search space when solving the workload relocation problem in a distributed system [11, 18].

The method within the ontological approach, aimed at reducing the search space and including an ontological model of the subject area, is performed in 6 steps (Fig. 1):

- Step 1. Input data, containing information about the transferred subgraph of the problem and about the resources of the candidate nodes.
- Step 2. Carry out ontological analysis procedure.
- Stage 3. Forming limited space of candidate nodes.
- Step 4. Simulation procedure of computational workload allocation on the limited set of nodes.
- Step 5. Solving the problem of workload relocation on the limited set.
- Step 6. Obtaining the result of the problem of workload relocation.

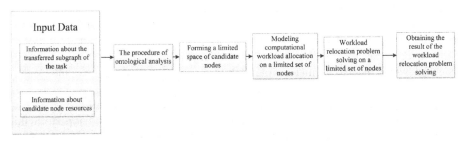

Fig. 1. Ontological method for reducing the search space of candidate nodes.

The ontological analysis procedure is based on the domain ontological model, which reflects the information about the computing nodes involved in the distribution of workload of the system and in the direct solution of the functional task of the system, as well as information about the information flows inherent in this system. Accordingly, to form a domain ontological model describing the specifics of functioning of distributed systems with mobile components, implemented using fog computing and DL technologies, it is necessary to conduct a comprehensive analysis of this subject area.

3   Development of a Domain Ontological Model

3.1   Methodology for the Development of a Domain Ontological Model

The development of a domain ontological model involves performing the following steps, according to [19]:

- identifying the domain and scope of the ontology;
- consideration of options for reuse of existing ontologies;
- listing important terms in the ontology;
- definition of classes and class hierarchy;
- definition of class properties - slots;
- definition of slot facets;
- creation of instances.

3.2 Analysis of the Subject Area of Operation of a Distributed Monitoring System with Mobile Components Based on a Distributed Ledger

To design a domain ontological model it is necessary to carry out a comprehensive analysis of the area under consideration, in this case it is the area of operation of a distributed monitoring system with mobile components based on a DL.

The concept of a scheme for collecting, processing, transmitting and storing data in such a distributed system has the form shown in Fig. 2 [20].

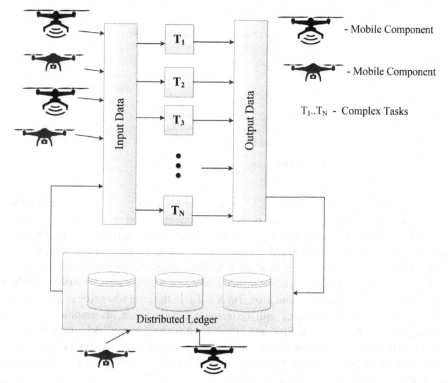

Fig. 2. The concept of functioning of a distributed monitoring system with mobile components based on a DL.

The data arriving at the input of the distributed system consists of a set of data collected and, in most cases, preprocessed by mobile components, as well as data that are copies of the DL data.

Once the data arrive, their subsequent processing takes place, which is the process of solving a set of complex tasks $(T_1, T_2,...T_N)$. To solve complex tasks we split them into subtasks and then assign them to computational nodes, and in some cases such nodes can be DL nodes $(L_1, L_2,...,L_N)$, which is not desirable, and the priority of assigning subtasks to nodes is taken into account in the proposed approach, which will be described below. A group of computing nodes, calculating a particular task, passes the result of the obtained solution (output) data to the "closest" node of the DL, as shown in Fig. 3.

For example, the result of solving problem T_1 will be transmitted to nodes L_1 and L_2 of the DL, while the results of solving subtasks T_2 and T_3 will be transmitted to nodes L_1 and L_2, respectively.

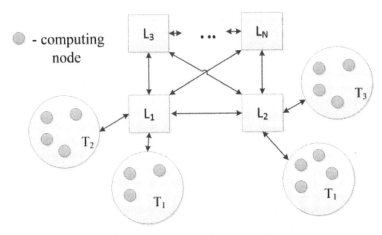

Fig. 3. The computational process schemes.

Let us consider various scenarios for the implementation of the computational process in a monitoring system with mobile components based on distributed ledger.

Scenario 1. Let the computational process (solution of some functional problem T_2) involve only "edge" components of the system. In this case, the result of solving some problem is transmitted to the "closest" node of distributed ledger is node L_1.

Scenario 2. Let a group of computational nodes, for which node of distributed ledger L_1 is "closest", solve some computational task is T_2. In the case where the computational node (group) needs in accordance with the mission to collect data, geographically remote from the node of distributed ledger, which was for him the "closest" is L_1 until this node has not changed its position in space, then in terms of reducing the time costs of data transfer, the node must transfer data to the node of distributed ledger is L_3, which is for him at the moment is the "closest" (Fig. 4).

Then the node of DL L_3 synchronizes the data on those nodes of DL that need the data. Thus, to synchronize the data, the nodes of DL located in the "fog" layer are included in the computational process.

Based on the scenarios described above, we can conclude that two levels can be distinguished in the process of organizing the computational process:

- The "edge" layer level, when the computational process is performed at the level of mobile components and other "edge" devices;
- The level of the "fog" layer, when to organize the computational process it is necessary to include DL nodes, which are not "closest" to the group of computing devices involved in solving the problem.

The following key concepts and their characteristics were identified in the process of analyzing the subject area:

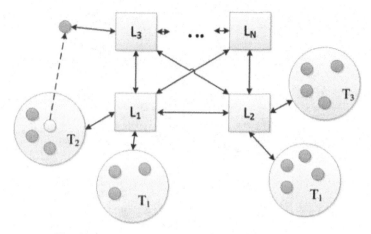

Fig. 4. Computational process according to Scenario 2.

- the structure of the task graph;
- the method of cutting the task graph: longitudinal (cutting into graph branches) and transverse (cutting into tiers of the graph);
- information flows: volume of transmitted data, frequency of transmitted data;
- communication channels: latency, bandwidth;
- node-candidate: energy resource, bandwidth, distance from the source/receiver of data, mobility of the candidate node, "edge" level latency;
- DL candidate node: energy resource, bandwidth, distance from data source/receiver, candidate node mobility, link latency, "fog" level latency.

3.3 Domain Ontological Model of Distributed Monitoring System Functioning with Mobile Components Based on DL Technologies

Based on this analysis and the ontology development methodology described above, a domain ontological model for the operation of a distributed monitoring system with mobile components based on DL technologies was developed. The developed model is shown in Fig. 5.

On the basis of the developed domain ontological model, which allows to describe the features of functioning of the distributed monitoring system with mobile components based on a DL, in accordance with the basic principles of distributed computing, taking into account the characteristics of the functioning environment, a software model has been obtained.

The specified software model allowed us to conduct a series of experiments.

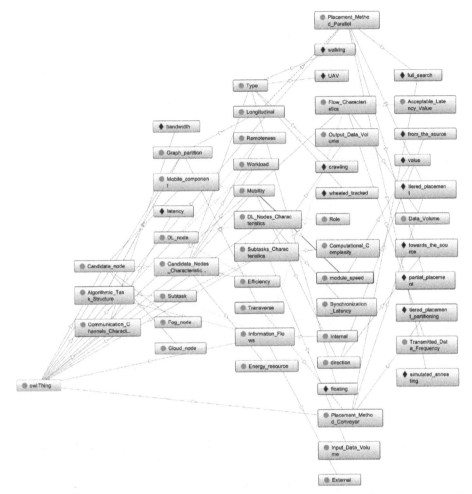

Fig. 5. Domain ontological model for the operation of a distributed monitoring system with mobile components based on DL technologies.

4 Experimental Studies

The aim of the experimental study: to investigate the effectiveness of the developed software model depending on the initial number of candidate nodes for different cutting methods (longitudinal and transverse).

The effectiveness criterion of the developed software model will be understood as a reduction in the number of candidate nodes after the ontology analysis procedure in comparison with the initial number of candidate nodes. The effectiveness of the proposed method is calculated by the formula (1):

$$\Delta = \frac{F_{init} - F_{fin}}{F_{init}} \times 100\%, \tag{1}$$

where F_{init} is initial number of candidate nodes to place computational load;

F_{fin} is final number of candidate nodes to place computational load after ontology analysis procedure.

By the depth of the fog layer we will mean the maximum distance, measured in hops, from the leader node to the computational node to which some of the computational load can be transferred.

Scenario 1 consists of computational experiments on the implementation of the ontological analysis procedure on the set of computational nodes, the depth of which lies in the range from 1 to 5 hops (see Fig. 6, 7).

Scenario 2 consists of computational experiments on the implementation of ontology analysis on the set of computational nodes, the depth of which is between 1 and 30 hops (see Fig. 8, 9).

The varied parameter is also the initial number of candidate computational nodes, F_{init}.

$F\_fin\_\{1;5\}\_l$ – selected nodes after ontological analysis at layer depth $\{1;5\}$ hop for the longitudinal method of graph cutting.

$F\_fin\_\{1;30\}\_l$ – selected nodes after ontological analysis at layer depth $\{1;30\}$ hop for the longitudinal method of graph cutting.

$F\_fin\_\{1;5\}\_t$ – selected nodes after ontological analysis at layer depth $\{1;5\}$ hop for the transversal method of graph cutting.

$F\_fin\_\{1;30\}\_t$ – selected nodes after ontological analysis at layer depth $\{1;30\}$ hop for the transversal method of graph cutting.

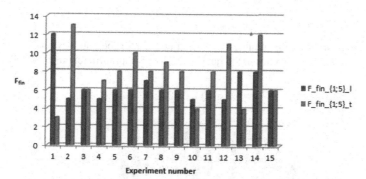

Fig. 6. Diagram showing the number of selected nodes after the ontology analysis procedure, when $F_{init} = 100$, the depth lies in the range from 1 to 5 hops, different methods of task graph cutting.

According to formula (1), the effectiveness of the proposed method can be estimated at 80%, which means reducing the search space by 5 times. The overall effect of reducing the decision time for the selection of candidate nodes depends on the time complexity of the optimization algorithm used.

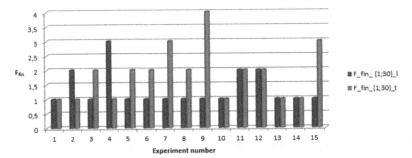

Fig. 7. Diagram showing the number of selected nodes after the ontology analysis procedure, when $F_{init} = 100$, the depth lies in the range from 1 to 30 hops, different methods of task graph cutting.

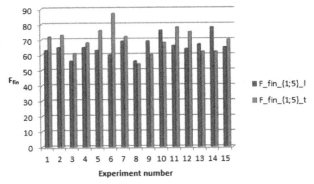

Fig. 8. Diagram showing the number of selected nodes after the ontology analysis procedure, when $F_{init} = 1000$, the depth lies in the range from 1 to 5 hops, different methods of task graph cutting.

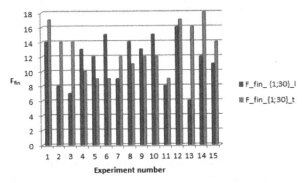

Fig. 9. Diagram showing the number of selected nodes after the ontology analysis procedure, when $F_{init} = 1000$, the depth lies in the range from 1 to 30 hops, different methods of task graph cutting.

5 Results

The obtained results of the experimental studies demonstrate the promising use of the ontological approach to the selection of candidate nodes for placement and redistribution of computational load in distributed monitoring systems with mobile components based on the concept of fog computing and DL, and also agree well with the results obtained in earlier studies [13, 14].

6 Conclusion

In this paper, we examined issues related to the organization of the computational process in monitoring systems with mobile components, implemented using the concept of fog computing and distributed ledger technologies, in terms of solving the problem of placement and redistribution of the computational load. To solve this problem, it was proposed to use ontological approach to reduce the search space, which has shown its effectiveness in solving large dimension optimization problems.

Domain ontological model of distributed monitoring systems that takes into account the specifics of mobile components functioning, as well as the characteristics of the environment and data access organization on the basis of a distributed ledger was developed. Experimental studies have shown the applicability of the ontological method and the adequacy of the developed ontological model to the considered subject area.

Acknowledgments. This study is supported by the GZ SSC RAS N GR project 122020100270–3.

References

1. Moura, J., Hutchison, D.: Fog computing systems: state of the art, research issues and future trends, with a focus on resilience. J. Netw. Comput. Appl. **169**, 102784 (2020)
2. Movahedi, Z., Defude, B., Hosseininia, A.M.: An efficient population-based multi-objective task scheduling approach in fog computing systems. J. Cloud Comput. **10**(1), 1–31 (2021)
3. Abdali, T.A.N., Hassan, R., Aman, A.H.M., Nguyen, Q.N.: Fog computing advancement: concept, architecture, applications, advantages, and open issues. IEEE Access **9**, 75961–75980 (2021)
4. Abreha, H.G., Cano, C.J.B., De La Oliva, A., Cominardi, L., Saloa, A.A.: Self-Adaptive Monitoring in Fog Computing by Leveraging Machine Learning. Technical Report (2020)
5. Distributed Ledger Technology, Blockchains and Identity. A Regulatory Overview. https://www.gsma.com/identity/wp-content/uploads/2018/09/Distributed-Ledger-Technology-Blockchains-and-Identity-20180907ii.pdf. Accessed 30 May 2023
6. Lücking, M., et al.: The merits of a decentralized pollution-monitoring system based on distributed ledger technology. IEEE Access **8**, 1–17 (2020)
7. Clark, N., Maglaras, L., Kantzavelou, I., Chouliaras, N., Ferrag, M.A.: Blockchain technology: security and privacy issues. In: Patnaik, S., Wang, T.-S., Shen, T., Panigrahi, S.K. (eds.) Blockchain Technology and Innovations in Business Processes. SIST, vol. 219, pp. 95–107. Springer, Singapore (2021). https://doi.org/10.1007/978-981-33-6470-7_6
8. What is fog computing? What is Fog Computing? - Definition from IoTAgenda, techtarget.com Accessed 30 May 2023

9. Hurbungs, V., Bassoo, V., Fowdur, T.P.: Fog and edge computing: concepts, tools and focus areas. Int. J. Inf. Technol. **13**, 511–522 (2021)

10. Li, G., Yan, J., Chen, L., Wu, J., Lin, Q., Zhang, Y.: Energy consumption optimization with a delay threshold in cloud-fog cooperation computing. IEEE Access **7**, 159688–159697 (2021)

11. Klimenko, A.B., Safronenkova, I.B.: A Technique of workload distribution based on parallel algorithm structure ontology. Adv. Intell. Syst. Comput. **1046**, 37–48 (2019)

12. Yin, L., Luo, J., Luo, H.: Tasks scheduling and resource allocation in fog computing based on containers for smart manufacturing. IEEE Trans. Industr. Inf. **14**(10), 4712–4721 (2018)

13. Jamil, B., Shojafar, M., Ahmed, I., Ullah, A., Munir, K., Ijaz, H.: A job scheduling algorithm for delay and performance optimization in fog computing. Concurrency Comput. Pract. Experience **32**(7), e5581 (2020)

14. Sun, Y., Lin, F., Xu, H.: Multi-objective Optimization of resource scheduling in fog computing using an improved NSGA-II. Wireless Pers. Commun. **102**, 1369–1385 (2018)

15. Wang, J., Li, D.: Task scheduling based on a hybrid heuristic algorithm for smart production line with fog computing. Sensors **19**(5), 1023 (2019)

16. Ghenai, A., Kabouche, Y., Dahmani, W.: Multi-user dynamic scheduling-based resource management for Internet of Things applications. In: 2018 International Conference on Internet of Things, Embedded Systems and Communications (IINTEC), Hamammet, Tunisia, pp. 126–131 (2018)

17. Melnik, E.V., Klimenko, A.B., Ivanov D.Y.: The model of the problem of forming communities of information and control system devices in fog computing environments. In: XIII All-Russian Meeting on Management Problems-2019, pp. 2979–2984. Tula State University, Tula (2019)

18. Klimenko, A., Safronenkova, I.: An ontology-based approach to the workload distribution problem solving in fog-computing environment. In: Silhavy, R. (ed.) CSOC 2019. AISC, vol. 985, pp. 62–72. Springer, Cham (2019). https://doi.org/10.1007/978-3-030-19810-7_7

19. Noy, N., McGuinness, D.: Ontology development 101: a guide to creating your first ontol-ogy. Stanford knowledge systems laboratory Technical report KSL-01–05 and Stanford Medical Informatics Technical report SMI-2001–0880 (2001)

20. Kapustyan, S. G., Orda-Zhigulina, D. V., Orda-Zhigulina, M. V., Prakapovich, R. A., Sychev, U. A.: Model of multi-robotic complex at the base of distributed registry for monitoring and diagnostics system. In: Silhavy, R. (ed.) CSOC 2021. LNNS, vol. 228, pp. 659–669. Springer, Cham (2021). https://doi.org/10.1007/978-3-030-77448-6_64

Improved Model of Greedy Tasks Assignment in Distributed Robotic Systems

Anna Klimenko$^{(\boxtimes)}$ (iD)

Institute of IT and Security Technologies, RSUH, 25-2, Kirovogradskaya Street,
Moscow 117534, Russia
anna_klimenko@mail.ru

Abstract. The problem of computations efficiency estimation is a topical one nowadays because of cost and various constraints, including energy consumption, resource spending, data transmission constraints, etc. Taking into account the tight connection between distributed robotic systems and IoT concepts, including fog and edge, the problem of computational resource spending is considered as one of the efficiency criteria. In the current paper the improved model for computational tasks distribution efficiency estimation is presented and discussed. As the failure rate of the node depends on the workload, we consider the strategy, when each node can choose its regime - to transmit or to process data. The decision depends on the estimation inequality, which includes such parameters as computational complexities of data processing, data transmission and time share of the data transmission in the overall time constraint for the tasks performing. The model developed allows to implement the greedy strategy of tasks distribution, in which every robotic device chooses the best individual state and differs from the previously presented model by more precise estimations of the data transmission. Also, some selected experimental results are presented, pros and cons of such greedy approach are discussed.

Keywords: Distributed Robotics · Tasks Distribution · Reliability · Fog Robotics

1 Introduction

The latest trends in robotics, such as increase of the robotic things interconnection level, an application of machine learning techniques at the robotic edge, tasks offloading and the virtualization, make robotics and IoT much more connected than ever. Such intersection of domains brings the well-known problems of IoT edge-cloud continuum to the distributed robotics. Having the robot limited on-board computational capacity, the problems of energy consumption, optimal resource allocation and tasks distribution take place as well, especially for complex computational tasks – mapping, learning, routing. Such problems are considered in [1–3].

In this paper a problem of computational resource spending for the distributed robotic systems, including fog- and edge ones, is considered. As every robot in the system has its own computing power, it can be considered as computational node/device with its

© The Author(s), under exclusive license to Springer Nature Switzerland AG 2023
A. Ronzhin et al. (Eds.): ICR 2023, LNAI 14214, pp. 311–321, 2023.
https://doi.org/10.1007/978-3-031-43111-1_28

own performance, failure rate, reliability function and average residual life. As is shown in [4], the non-optimal tasks distribution causes the average residual life to decrease and, consequently, the decrease of the expedient exploitation time of the device. It can be explained in a way as if some robotic nodes in the distributed robotic system process more data than others, it is presupposed that their lifetime shortens faster than it could. So, the problem of tasks distribution through the robotic system is topical and supposed to be solved.

The major contribution of this paper is an improved model of tasks distribution efficiency estimation, which differs from the previously presented model by the new parameter addition. This parameter is the throughput of the data route, and its usage allows to estimate the time, which is used for the data transfer and data processing more precisely.

2 Robotics and Distributed Computing Domains Intersection

A lot of problems in contemporary robotics are solved in a way as ones of distributed computing are.

For example, the study [5] is one of the early ones in this field and uses the robotic cluster to solve complex tasks with the performance objective function. In this work SLAM problem is solved by the distributed robotic system, combined to the cluster of computational nodes. Multi-robot SLAM is solved in [6], and edge-cloud SLAM algorithm is proposed in [7] as well. SLAM problem in the aspect of edge- and cloud computing, including the tasks offloading issues, is considered in [8].

Routing is another complex computational problem, which often relates to the TSP or M-TSP [9]. Earlier the distributed computing was used to increase the accuracy and decrease the solution time of the TSP [10]. One more example of routing is [11], as well as [12]. In the study [13] computationally heavy routing task for the robot group is solved in a distributed manner.

Yet, another emerging area of the edge- and fog- concepts application in the distributed robotics relates to the machine learning. Some studies consider offloading strategies in general [14–16], while some works are devoted to the robots learning processes [17–20]. Some studies also relate to the distributed tasks processing, including the following [21, 22].

So, the following general conclusions can be made:

- The areas of robotics, fog- and edge- computing have been intersected and now are coupled tightly.
- Numerous problems of robotics are solved with the usage of distributed computing mechanisms, including learning, SLAM, routing, and many others.
- Despite of intensive usage of robots with limited computational capacity, no attention has been paid to the problem of resource-saving.

The latter relates to the average residual life/reliability/failure rate of a computational robot part, i.e., affects the time of expedient device exploitation.

Our previous study considers the model for the task distribution in the resource-saving way [21].

Reliability function value depends on the failure rate of the computational node, while failure rate is connected to the device temperature and, consequently, workload:

$$\lambda = \lambda_0 \cdot 2^{\frac{\Delta T}{10}}, \tag{1}$$

where λ is a resulting failure rate, λ_0 is the failure rate under conditions of unloaded device, ΔT is the temperature difference between the temperature of unloaded device and the temperature of loaded one.

Also, the coefficient can be determined, which connects the node temperature and the workload:

$$\lambda = \lambda_0 \cdot 2^{\frac{kD}{10}}. \tag{2}$$

Consequently, the reliability function is determined as follows:

$$P(t) = e^{-\lambda t} = e^{-\lambda t \cdot 2^{kD/10}}, \tag{3}$$

where D is the node workload.

Average residual life is estimated as follows:

$$R = \frac{1}{\lambda}. \tag{4}$$

Consider the node workload for the node 3 (Fig. 2) as follows (for the case when the node transits some data):

$$D = \frac{w_i}{p_j t_{transfer}}, \tag{5}$$

where w_i is the computational complexity of the task, $t_{transfer}$ is the time needed for the data transfer.

Consider the data processing shift discussed in [21], where the data transmission to the cloud takes place (Fig. 1).

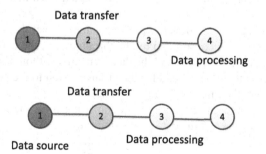

Fig. 1. Data processing shift illustration.

With the data processing shift the workload of the processing node is:

$$D = \frac{w_i}{p_j t_{process}}. \tag{6}$$

Obviously, with the data shift $t_{process}$ is bigger than $t_{transfer}$, and so D decreases. And, finally the following "greedy" rule has been formed in [21]:

$$w_{receice} + w_{process} + w_{send} < 2\frac{W_{receive}}{x}, \tag{7}$$

where x is the time fraction for the time of data transfer process of the particular node.

However, at least one drawback of this model can be considered, that is the absence of estimations of time fraction x, which is needed for data transfer. Of course, this model is sufficient to prove the expediency of the data processing near the data source, yet, the accuracy of the estimations does not allow to use this model, for example, when we have a route consisted of robots, as well as we cannot get accurate estimations of how long the data will be transferred through this route.

In this paper an improved model is presented, which considers the network through-put parameter. It allows to get more precise estimation of expediency of the data processing on the particular node.

3   Tasks Distribution Efficiency Estimation

Consider the robotic network as a set of connected robots, which have to transfer some data to the base station for processing. It is obvious that sometimes data have to be send through some intermediate robotic nodes – or, vice versa – to be processed somewhere in the robotic group, while the base station gets the results only. When data are processed somewhere in the robotic group, this data processing can be distributed among the robots with low computational capacity – actually, it reduces the robotic group latency. Computing resources of robots are spent much faster, and there is a need to search a kind of equilibrium between computational resource spending and the system latency. However, there is a possibility to save some extra-time and use it for data processing distribution to prevent the computational resource spending, and, as a result, there must be the estimation method to choose what it is better for the particular robot: to transmit data or to process.

As is mentioned earlier, the workload of the computational nodes can be estimated as is in Eqs. (5, 6).

Consider the route for data transfer, presupposing the fact that the velocity of the data transfer by the node is constrained by the throughput of the network channel. So, if we have some nodes in the route, and the data transmits without accumulation on the nodes, we can esteem the time needed for data transmission to the processing node, as well as we can esteem the time for data processing.

Assuming the t_0 as the tasks processing completion time, the following describes the data transmission time and the data processing time:

$$t_{process} = t_0 - \sum_{i=0}^{k-1}\sum t_{max}, \tag{7}$$

where t_{max} is the minimum of the data transfer velocity in the route.

Then, the workload of the data processing on the node k is as follows:

$$D_k = \frac{w_{receive} + w_{op} + w_{send}^{res}}{p_k(t_0 - (k-1)t_{max})}, \tag{8}$$

where $w_{receive}$ is the computational complexity of the data receive procedure; W_{op} is the computational complexity of the data processing; w^{res}_{send} is the computational complexity of the sending of the data processing result; P_k is the performance of the node k; t_0 is the time constraint; t_{max} is the maximum time of the data transfer in the route.

The workload of the node, which just transmits the data is as follows:

$$D'_k = \frac{2w_{receive}}{P_k t_{max}}. \tag{9}$$

Taking into account the Eqs. (2, 3), it is expedient to process the data on the node k, when the following inequality is fair:

$$D_k < D'_k, \tag{10}$$

$$\frac{w_{receive} + w_{op} + w^{res}_{send}}{(t_0 - (k-1)t_{max}} < \frac{2w_{receive}}{t_{max}}. \tag{11}$$

So, for the node k, having the information about the minimum node throughput, the data processing becomes expedient, when the inequality (11) is fair.

In case when every node accumulates data and then sends it further, the Eq. (11) transforms into the following one:

$$\frac{w_{receive} + w_{op} + w^{res}_{send}}{(t_0 - \sum_{j=1}^{i-1} t_j)} < \frac{2w_{receive}}{t_i}, \tag{12}$$

where t_i is the time of data transfer of the selected node in the route, t_j is the time of data transfer of the previous node in a route.

It must be mentioned that according to the inequality (11) the maximum increase of the reliability function is when the nearest to the data source node processes a task. It can be checked, if we transform the Eq. (11) into the non-linear integer optimization problem, with the objective function as is shown in Eq. (13):

$$\frac{2w_{receive}}{t_{max}} - \frac{w_{receive} + w_{op} + w^{res}_{send}}{(t_0 - (k-1)t_{max}.} \rightarrow max. \tag{13}$$

So, the inequalities (11, 12) allow to estimate the node's proficiency in case of data transmission or, vice versa, data processing.

If a node estimates its preferences in this way, it takes a task for a processing, or transmits data somewhere else to the nodes, which are farer from data source.

Such approach forms a kind of "egoistic" strategy, in which every node choses the best individual strategy without paying attention to other nodes state and workload. It must be mentioned as well, that within such strategy the node can choose from "data transmission" and "data processing" only and has very limited knowledge about the set of nodes, which participate in computational process. However, such "egoistic" approach is quite suitable for single-node offloading, or when there is a need to select the processing node for the consequently upcoming tasks.

Next section contains the experimental results for estimation of developed estimation application prospects.

4 Experimental Results

To check the possibility of inequality (11) application to the tasks assignment in the resource-saving manner, consider the following data transfer routes within the robot group/distributed robotic system (Figs. 2, 3).

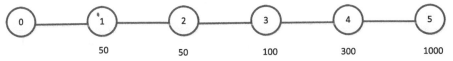

Fig. 2. Network route structure №1.

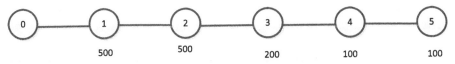

Fig. 3. Network route structure №2.

Consider the node 0 as a data source, nodes 1–5 as nodes which are capable of data processing and weighed with their performances.

The aim of the experiment is to check if our estimation allows to assign the data processing task in an optimal way according to the given parameters.

4.1 Experiment 1. Small Data Volume to Transmit, Route №1

We consider the following variable values: $w_{receive} = 50$; $w_{op} = 200$; $w_{send} = 50$; $t_0 = 320$ (modeling units); the ribs of the graph is weighed with the following: 100, 100, 50, 35, 10 (modeling units), which determine the data transfer velocity between the nodes. For this case the following values of Eq. (11) are got (Table 1).

One can see that with the given values of variables nodes 2, 3, 4 suppose that it is more profitable for them to transfer the data somewhere else than to process it, taking into account data transfer delays. So, data processing can be assigned to the node 1 or to the node 5. Despite that fact that node 5 is the most distant one from the data source, it is suited for data processing due to its performance, which is the highest within the node set.

4.2 Experiment 2. Large Data Volume to Transmit, Route №1

We consider the following variable values: $w_{receive} = 5000$; $w_{op} = 200$; $w_{send} = 50$; $t_0 = 500$ (modeling units); the ribs of the graph is weighed with the following: 100, 100, 50, 35, 10 (modeling units), which determine the data transfer velocity between the nodes. One can see that this case is for the large data volume processing and transfer (Table 2).

The results conducted are quite interesting because of the nodes overloading in the data transmission regime. One can see that if the data are transmitted with the

Table 1. Results of experiment 1.

Δ_1	Data transfer workload, node1	Data processing workload, node1	Data transfer R, node1	Data processing R, node1
0.0625	0.02	0.01875	9330.33	9370.838
Δ_2	Data transfer workload, node 2	Data processing workload, node 2	Data transfer R, node 2	Data processing, R, node 2
−0.0303	**0.026667**	**0.05**	**9117.225**	**8408.964**
Δ_3	Data transfer workload, node 3	Data processing workload, node 3	Data transfer R, node 3	Data processing R, node 3
−0.1470	**0.04**	**0.042857**	**8705.506**	**8619.728**
Δ_4	Data transfer workload, node 4	Data processing workload, node 4	Data transfer R, node 4	Data processing, R, node 4
−0.1587	**0.014815**	**0.028571**	**9499.516**	**9057.237**
Δ_5	Data transfer workload, node 5	Data processing workload, node 5	Data transfer, R, node 5	Data processing, R, node 5
1.42857	0.012	0.01	9707.306	9659.363

Table 2. Results of experiment 2.

Δ_1	Data transfer workload, node1	Data processing workload, node1	Data transfer, R, node 1	Data processing, R, node 1
89.5	**2**	**0.21**	–	**4829.682**
Δ_2	Data transfer workload, node 2	Data processing workload, node 2	Data transfer, R, node 2	Data processing, R, node 2
120.20	**2.666667**	**0.35**	–	**2973.018**
Δ_3	Data transfer workload, node 3	Data processing workload, node 3	Data transfer, R, node 3	Data processing, R, node 3
217.79	**4**	**0.21**	–	**4829.682**
Δ_4	Data transfer workload, node 4	Data processing workload, node 4	Data transfer R, node 4	Data processing R, node 4
423.44	**1.481481**	**0.081395**	–	**7542.022**
Δ_5	Data transfer workload, node 5	Data processing workload, node 5	Data transfer R, node 5	Data processing R, node 5
975.58	1	0.024419	312.5	9188.536

maximum velocity of the channel (and this allows to save time for data processing), the computational devices are overloaded, though all of the nodes successfully process the same large data volumes. Such situation is a good proof for fog concept application and its benefits from the resource-saving.

4.3   Experiment 3. Small Data Volume to Transmit, Route №2

We consider the following variable values: $w_{receive} = 50$; $w_{op} = 250$; $w_{send} = 50$; $t_0 = 500$ (modeling units); the ribs of the graph is weighed with the following: 10, 35, 50, 100, 100 (modeling units), which determine the data transfer velocity between the nodes. One can see that this case is for the large data volume processing and transfer (Table 3).

Table 3. Results of experiment 3

Δ_1	Data transfer workload, node 1	Data processing workload, node 1	Data transfer, R, node 1	Data processing, R, node 1
3.7444	0.008889	0.0014	9696.631	9951.597
Δ_2	Data transfer workload, node 2	Data processing workload, node 2	Data transfer, R, node 2	Data processing, R, node 2
1.6386	**1.638655**	**0.004706**	–	**9946.823**
Δ_3	Data transfer workload, node 3	Data processing workload, node 3	Data transfer, R, node 3	Data processing, R, node 3
0.5641	0.564103	0.02	9330.33	9851.362
Δ_4	Data transfer workload, node 4	Data processing workload, node 4	Data transfer, R, node 4	Data processing, R, node 4
0.1358	0.01	0.011475	9659.363	9610.097
Δ_5	Data transfer workload, node 5	Data processing workload, node 5	Data transfer, R, node 5	Data processing, R, node 5
−0.1475	**0.01**	**0.011475**	**9659.363**	**9610.097**

It is seen here that such strategy can produce not a good solution: while node 5 supposes that it will better for it to transfer data somewhere else, this can lead to the solution loss, because the farer node has less time for the data processing than its predecessor. Also, node 2 is overloaded with the data transfer regime, because of high channel throughput and, according to our assumption, the need to transmit the data as fast as it is possible.

4.4   Experiment 4. Large Data Volume to Transmit, Route №2

We consider the following variable values: $w_{receive} = 5000$; $w_{op} = 250$; $w_{send} = 50$; $t_0 = 500$ (modeling units); the ribs of the graph is weighed with the following: 10, 35, 50, 100, 100 (modeling units), which determine the data transfer velocity between the nodes. One can see that this case is for the large data volume processing and transfer (Table 4).

With the need to transfer a large amount of data, it is seen that with the high performance of the nodes it is profitable to process the data. Nodes 3, 4, 5 are overloaded for the data transmission regime, while data processing is preferable.

Table 4. Results of experiment 4

Δ_1	Data transfer workload, node 1	Data processing workload, node 1	Data transfer, R, node 1	Data processing, R, node 1
433.844	0.888889	0.0212	459.292	9291.607
Δ_2	Data transfer workload, node 2	Data processing workload, node 2	Data transfer, R, node 2	Data processing, R, node 2
224.477	0.470588	0.023297	1957.466	9224.333
Δ_3	Data transfer workload, node 3	Data processing workload, node 3	Data transfer, R, node 3	Data processing, R, node 3
121.685	**2**	**0.065432**	–	**7971.038**
Δ_4	Data transfer workload, node 4	Data processing workload, node 4	Data transfer, R, node 4	Data processing, R, node 4
86.9135	1	0.17377	312.5	5475.822
Δ_5	Data transfer workload, node 5	Data processing workload, node 5	Data transfer, R, node 5	Data processing, R, node 5
82.6229	1	0.17377	312.5	5475.822

So, as a result, the greedy approach of tasks assignment can be formulated. The initial conditions are as follows:

- The unit, which holds the control center functions, have to assign the new task to the one of the nodes within the given distributed robotic system;
- The system of robots is distributed geographically such as the routes of data transmission can be formed;
- The amounts of data to transfer, the computational complexities of tasks, the network throughput are known as well.

The scenario of the tasks assignment is as follows:

1. The robot, which receives some sensor data, requests its neighbours for free resources to perform a new task;
2. For all answers the estimations (11–12) are made;
3. The robot with the highest estimation value is chosen.

The similar strategy can be applied to the situation when some tasks must be offloaded from one robot to another. The robot requests its neighbours and offloads its task to that one, which has the maximum result of estimation inequality (11).

5 Conclusion

In this paper the previously developed model for resource-saving tasks assignment is enhanced and specified with the new parameter related to the time of data transfer. This new model does not conflict with the previous one, clarifying the way to estimate the data transmission time.

Greedy approach to the tasks assignment, as experimental results have shown, is applicable to the process of tasks offloading or single/consequent tasks assignment in the distributed robotic systems.

Yet, as every greedy approach, the developed model and strategy have some drawbacks:

- There can be solutions, when the refusal of the particular robot to perform the task leads to the loss of potentially acceptable task distribution;
- as only one robot is considered for making a solution, to process or to transmit data, other robots workload and resources are out of consideration, and potentially this leads to the uncontrolled resource spending among other robots, if, for example, there are more than one data transmission routes.

The latter is an important feature of the developed approach: individual profit does not guarantee the common one.

Besides, such strategy does not take into account the length of data transfer route: with the growth quantity of robots in the routes, more robots have to perform an additional task of data transfer, which is quite complex in case of large sensor data volumes. It leads to the following decision making: to use n nodes with workload $D1$, or to use n-k nodes with workload $D2$, $D2 > D1$. Such issues demand further consideration and research.

References

1. Avgeris, M.: dynamic resource allocation and computational offloading at the network edge for internet of things applications. PhD thesis (2021)
2. Afrin, M., Jin, J., Rahman, A., Gasparri, A., Tian, Y.-C., Kulkarni, A.: Robotic edge resource allocation for agricultural cyber-physical system. IEEE Trans. Netw. Sci. Eng. **9**(6), 3979–3990 (2022). https://doi.org/10.1109/TNSE.2021.3103602
3. Natsuho, S., Ohkawa, T., Amano, H., Sugaya, M.: Power consumption reduction method and edge offload server for multiple robots. In: Zhang, L.-J. (ed.) EDGE 2021. LNCS, vol. 12990, pp. 1–19. Springer, Cham (2022). https://doi.org/10.1007/978-3-030-96504-4_1
4. Melnik, E., Klimenko, A.: A condition of reliability improvement of the system based on the fog-computing concept. J. Phys. Conf. Ser. **1661**, 012007 (2020). https://doi.org/10.1088/1742-6596/1661/1/012007
5. Gouveia, B.D., Portugal, D., Silva, D.C., Marques, L.: Computation sharing in distributed robotic systems: a case study on SLAM. IEEE Trans. Autom. Sci. Eng. **12**, 410–422 (2015)
6. Zhong, S., Qi, Y., Chen, Z., Wu, J., Chen, H., Liu, M.: DCL-SLAM: a distributed collaborative LiDAR SLAM framework for a robotic swarm. arXiv:2210.11978 (2022). https://arxiv.org/abs/2210.11978
7. Lv, T., Zhang, J., Chen, Y.: A SLAM algorithm based on edge-cloud collaborative computing. J. Sens. **2022**, 1–17 (2022). https://doi.org/10.1155/2022/7213044
8. Huang, P., Zeng, L., Chen, X., Luo, K., Zhou, Z., Yu, S.: Edge robotics: edge-computing-accelerated multi-robot simultaneous localization and mapping. IEEE Internet Things J. **9**, 1 (2022)
9. Liu, C., Zhang, Y.: Research on MTSP problem based on simulated annealing. In: ICISS 2018: Proceedings of the 2018 International Conference on Information Science and System, pp. 283–285 (2018). https://doi.org/10.1145/3209914.3234638

10. Nishi, T., Mori, Y., Konishi, M., Imai, J.: An asynchronous distributed routing system for multi-robot cooperative transportation. In: 2005 IEEE/RSJ International Conference on Intelligent Robots and Systems, IROS, pp. 1730–1735 (2005). https://doi.org/10.1109/IROS.2005.1545268

11. Camisa, A., Testa, A., Notarstefano, G.: Multi-robot pickup and delivery via distributed resource allocation. IEEE Trans. Robot. **39**, 1106–1118 (2022)

12. Guo, Y., Wang, Y., Qian, Q.: Intelligent edge network routing architecture with blockchain for the IoT. Chin. Commun. 1–14 (2023)

13. Seisa, A., Satpute, S., Nikolakopoulos, G.: A Kubernetes-based edge architecture for controlling the trajectory of a resource-constrained aerial robot by enabling model predictive control (2023)

14. Wu, S., Xue, H., Zhang, L.: Q-learning-aided offloading strategy in edge-assisted federated learning over industrial IoT. Electronics **12**(7), 1706 (2023)

15. Zhao, P., Yang, Z., Mu, Y., Zhang, G.: Selfish-aware and learning-aided computation offloading for edge-cloud collaboration network. IEEE Internet Things J. **10**(11), 9953–9965 (2023)

16. Yang, Z., Zhong, S.: Task offloading and resource allocation for edge-enabled mobile learning. Chin. Commun. **20**, 326–339 (2023)

17. Felbrich, B., Schork, T., Menges, A.: Autonomous robotic additive manufacturing through distributed model-free deep reinforcement learning in computational design environments. Constr. Robot. **6**, 1–23 (2022)

18. Esteves, L., Portugal, D., Peixoto, P., Falcao, G.: Towards mobile federated learning with unreliable participants and selective aggregation. Appl. Sci. **13**, 3135 (2023). https://doi.org/10.3390/app13053135

19. Jayaratne, M., Alahakoon, D., Silva, D.: Unsupervised skill transfer learning for autonomous robots using distributed growing self organizing maps. Robot. Auton. Syst. **144**, 103835 (2021). https://doi.org/10.1016/j.robot.2021.103835

20. Gamboa, J., Alonso-Martin, F., Marques, S., Sequeira, J., Salichs, M.: Asynchronous federated learning system for human-robot touch interaction. Expert Syst. Appl. **211**, 118510 (2023)

21. Klimenko, A.: Model and method of resource-saving tasks distribution for the fog robotics. In: Ronzhin, A., Meshcheryakov, R., Xiantong, Z. (eds.) Interactive Collaborative Robotics. ICR 2022. Lecture Notes in Computer Science, vol. 13719. Springer, Cham (2022). https://doi.org/10.1007/978-3-031-23609-9_19

22. Meshcheryakov, R.: Information processing methods in Ergatic robotic systems: In: International Conference Engineering and Telecommunication (En&T), Dolgoprudny, Russian Federation, pp. 1–4 (2021). https://doi.org/10.1109/EnT50460.2021.9681750

Construction of a Three-Dimensional UAV Movement Planner When the Latter Moves in Conditions of Difficult Terrain

Vladimir Kostyukov$^{(\boxtimes)}$ ⓘ, Igor Evdokimov, and Vladislav Gissov

Joint Stock Company "Scientific-Design Bureau of Robotics and Control", Taganrog 347900, Russia
wkost-einheit@yandex.ru

Abstract. The known methods of planning the routes of movement of robotic platforms based on cellular decomposition of the area of movement in a three-dimensional formulation are severely limited in speed. Therefore, the construction of high-speed planning algorithms in a three-dimensional mapped environment is an urgent task. This article proposes a method for planning the movement of robotic platforms in this environment, combining the use of the well-known Dijkstra algorithm for constructing a two-dimensional projection curve with subsequent projection reconstruction and multi-stage correction of the target spatial piecewise polyline curve. The restoration of the original spatial curve by its two-dimensional projection onto the horizontal plane is performed on the basis of a given discrete elevation map of the motion area, and the specified adjustment is made taking into account the requirements, firstly, the minimality of the total length of the final piecewise polyline, and, secondly, taking into account the specified known kinematic limitations of the apparatus. The algorithm for the synthesis of a spatial curve is detailed for the common case when obstacles are represented in the form of rectangular cylinders with polygonal generators. The effectiveness of the developed global scheduler algorithm is confirmed by the results of numerical modeling.

Keywords: Methods of Planning Robot Movements · Complex Mapped Environment · Smoothing of Piecewise Linear Trajectory · Kinematic Limitations of the Robot

1 Introduction

The construction of a software trajectory of a robotic platform moving in a three-dimensional mapped environment can be carried out using a wide range of displacement planning algorithms, among which cellular decomposition methods can be distinguished, primarily Dijkstra algorithms, A* [1, 2], D* [3]. Dijkstra's algorithm allows us to obtain the optimal path up to the quantization error of the grid structure. Methods A*, D* are not optimal.

A common disadvantage of algorithms based on the cellular decomposition method is a high demand for memory, as well as a sharp increase in computational complexity with an increase in the number of partition cells. To reduce the memory requirements of the A* algorithm and its computational complexity, such modifications as the algorithm with iterative deepening [4], A* with memory restriction [5], hierarchical A* [6], A* with dynamic change of edge weights [7, 8] have been developed. Nevertheless, when solving the problems of path planning in three dimensions, even existing modifications of these algorithms are not enough to ensure the required performance.

Algorithms based on the methods of potential fields [9–12] allow to increase the speed by orders of magnitude, but their disadvantage is the possibility of the existence of local minima of the potential function, which entails the problem of providing an exit from the corresponding areas of looping. There are known approaches [12, 13] that offer certain algorithms for detecting and exiting local minima zones, but what they have in common is the lack of a sufficient experimental base confirming their operability.

This problem can be leveled to a large extent by applying the method of unstable modes based on the use of the dynamics of the object when planning to bypass sudden obstacles, and the stability of the corresponding control algorithms in which such a scheduler is implemented is shown [14, 15]. However, this method is highly dependent on the adequacy of the used dynamic model of a moving object and the accuracy of setting its parameters.

The second problem of the algorithms of the potential fields method is the formation of a non-smooth trajectory as a result of their application, often including areas with oscillations [16–19]. To solve this problem, a method of two-stage smoothing of trajectories with harmful (noise) oscillations in two dimensions is proposed in [12]. In the same work, an algorithm is proposed for finding a special time parametric representation of the target trajectory.

The approach to planning movements in three dimensions developed in this article combines the use of Dijkstra's algorithm for constructing a two-dimensional projection curve and a number of algorithms presented below for restoring the target spatial curve and correcting it in order to minimize its length in compliance with the existing kinematic limitations of the apparatus.

2 Problem Statement

Suppose there is some terrain map and a height map linked to it, constructed with a given discreteness. The initial S and target G points of the route are given. There are also obstacles presented in the form of cylindrical areas with polygonal sections, and the guides of these cylinders are all orthogonal to the horizontal plane.

Restrictions are set on: a) the height of the flight above the terrain; b) the kinematic characteristics of the device: horizontal and vertical components of linear velocities, pitch angle, maximum curvature of the spatial trajectory.

It is required to construct the target trajectory of the vehicle from the starting point to the target one, taking into account the above restrictions, so that the length of this curve is as small as possible. At the same time, the optimization problem is not supposed to be solved in a strict formulation. At the output of the scheduler, nodes of the resulting spatial piecewise polyline curve and linear velocity vectors in them should be formed.

Figure 1 shows a fragment of a three-dimensional terrain map, where green parallelepipeds represent relief elements taking into account a given elevation map, a rectangular cylinder with a polygonal section shows an obstacle. The target trajectory of movement from the starting point (located in the lower left corner) to the target point is also shown.

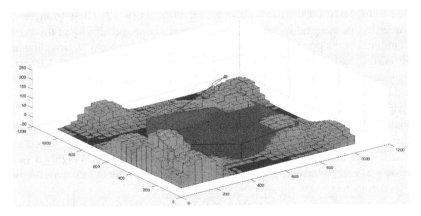

Fig. 1. To the problem statement.

3   Generalized Global Scheduler Algorithm

When constructing the global trajectory of the UAV in conditions of complex terrain, we will start from the possibility of constructing an appropriate two-dimensional trajectory is a projection curve along which the projection of the origin of the coordinates of the local system of the device moves on a conditional horizontal plane. Let's consider a generalized algorithm of the global scheduler. The three-dimensional target spatial trajectory is constructed in two stages.

At the first stage, a two-dimensional projection of the desired spatial trajectory is constructed using Dijkstra's algorithm. The resulting piecewise polyline trajectory is further minimized in length using a special algorithm. Such optimization can be performed using a modified Ramer-Douglas-Pecker method.

The second stage of the global algorithm involves the generation of the corresponding spatial piecewise polyline according to its two-dimensional projection, as well as its necessary subsequent correction. For each node of the curve, the corresponding target height is found, taking into account the heights of those relief elements whose two-dimensional projections border on this point.

After obtaining the resulting optimized piecewise polyline, it is necessary to smooth it. To do this, a modified Dubins method can be used, which consists in replacing the circular arc of parts of rectilinear segments adjacent to each given internal node of the polyline, as well as constructing a time parametric representation of the smoothed trajectory, taking into account the peculiarities of the change in the trajectory velocity of the apparatus when passing curved sections of the trajectory [12].

After the smoothing stage, the global algorithm takes into account the kinematic limitations of the movement of the device along the linear velocity vector and pitch angle.

4 Algorithm for Thinning a Piecewise Polyline and Reducing its Total Length

The points obtained after the global planning stage on a two-dimensional map are passed to this function. Next, the segments connecting the corresponding pairs of such points are iteratively considered, and a piecewise polyline is sought that would contain some nodes of the original one, would be as short as possible and would not intersect any of the obstacles.

The algorithm divides the piecewise polyline into two parts at the current iteration each time. The input of the algorithm is the coordinates of all points between the first A_1 and the last A_N point of the polyline. The points A_1 and A_N remain unchanged. After that, the algorithm finds a point A_k $(1 < k < N)$ that is furthest from the segment connecting these two extreme points. If such a point is located at a distance less than some positive, sufficiently small value $\varepsilon > 0$, then the algorithm outputs a piecewise polyline $A_1A_kA_N$, which smoothes the original curve with the accuracy of ε.

If the distance is greater than ε, then the algorithm recursively calls itself on the set from the initial A_1 to the given A_k and from the given A_k to the end point A_N (in this case, this point A_k will be marked for preservation).

At the end of all recursive calls, the output polyline is constructed only from those points that were marked for saving.

At each step, a check is made for the intersection of the current piecewise polyline with two-dimensional obstacles. If an intersection is detected, the simplification of the function is canceled on its corresponding linear section.

The considered algorithm is a modification of the existing Ramer-Douglas-Pecker algorithm.

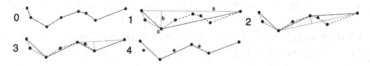

Fig. 2. Modified Ramer-Douglas-Pecker Method.

From the comparison of the initial and final piecewise polylines shown in Fig. 2, it can be seen that as a result of this algorithm, it was possible to reduce the number of nodes from eight to five with a noticeable decrease in the length of the original curve, but without losing its qualitative behavior.

5 Modified Dubins Method

After constructing a spatial piecewise polyline trajectory, it is necessary to smooth it, which can be effectively performed using the modified Dubins method, which also allows to give smooth parametric time representations for both the target curve and its corresponding trajectory velocity. In [12], such a method is considered for two measurements. This algorithm is a modification of the well-known Dubins method, which reduces to the conjugation of adjacent rectilinear segments of a piecewise polyline by arcs of circles [20].

The problem of obtaining smooth trajectories often arises when planning methods involving obtaining spatial trajectories in the form of individual points. Various techniques are used to smooth out such trajectories. For example, the D* algorithms are characterized by smoothing of trajectories due to continuous linear interpolation of weights at the boundary of each cell, which, in general, leads to a significant increase in their operation time [18].

When planning the movement of the device, it is necessary to smooth out to exclude discontinuities of the derivatives of each of the coordinates in their parametric time representation.

In this regard, the task arises of smoothing the initial piecewise linear trajectory in such a way as to exclude or minimize the stops of the device in the vicinity of the specified nodal points of the trajectory, which are impossible for some types of devices. To solve this problem, the use of the Bezier curve [21] is not suitable since it does not make it possible to simulate motion with deceleration in sections of the trajectory with increased curvature. Below we consider the modified Dubins method in two dimensions, and then generalize it to the case of three.

Let be given: nodes of a piecewise linear trajectory $\{A_i\}, i = 1, 2, ..,N;$; the target speed of the vehicle on linear sections of the trajectory (cruising) speed is V_k, the degree of decline of η velocity at the conditional maximum rotation of the trajectory (by π rad); the minimum radius of curvature of the arc at the vertex of the original piecewise polyline Rmin determined by the kinematic constraints of the apparatus. At the output, it is required to obtain the nodes $\{B_k\}, j = 1, 2, ..,K$ (K < = N) of the target smooth trajectory and the linear velocity vectors of the apparatus $\{V_j\}, j = 1, 2, ..,K$ in them in accordance with the specified speed limits are V_k and η.

Figures 3 shows a fragment of a smooth curve constructed using the quadratic-linear smoothing algorithm considered below for the above case of a piecewise linear curve.

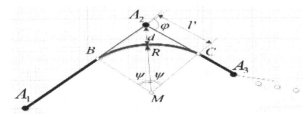

Fig. 3. Key geometric constructions of the modified Dubins method. Geometry of the problem of determining the arc of the conjugation circle.

The key point of the algorithm is the time parametric representation of the BC arc section obtained in [12]:

$$x(t) = x_M + R\cos(s_c(t - t_l) + \alpha), \ y(t) = y_M + R\sin(s_c(t - t_l) + \beta), \quad (1)$$

$$s_c(t) = \{(a(\varphi)\Delta t/\pi) \sin[\pi(t - t_l)/\Delta t] + b(\varphi)(t - t_l)/R\} \quad (2)$$

Here $a(\varphi)$, $b(\varphi)$ there are some functions of the angle of rotation of the curve at a given node, determined by the specified requirements for the decline of the cruising speed of the device during rotation; R is the radius of curvature of the arc circle, which replaces parts of two straight segments adjacent to this node; t_l is the time of the beginning of the movement along the arc BC; Δt is half the time of the passage of the arc; $s_c(t)$ is there is an angular distance traveled along the circumference of the arc to the moment of time t, and $s_c(0) = 0$. The angles α, β are determined from the condition that the arc passes from B to C along the shortest path is along the smaller of the two possible arcs of the resulting circle.

On each linear section, the device moves at a constant cruising speed V, and when entering a turn, there is a cosine decrease in speed to a certain level, depending on φ.

After finding the time parametric representation of the desired curve, the target nodes $\{B_k\}, k = 1, 2, .., K$ and the corresponding velocity vectors $\{V_k\}, k = 1, 2, .., K$. can be automatically obtained using finite difference formulas.

In order to find time parametric representations of all sections of the original piecewise polyline in the same way, it is necessary to first determine transition points of type B and C (see Fig. 3) linear segments in an arc for each node of the piecewise polyline in accordance with the specified minimum allowable radius of rounding Rmin.

This algorithm is transferred to a spatial piecewise polyline curve by introducing a local coordinate system for each triple of its nodes, finding a section of a smooth curve for this triple in the above way, and then recalculating the obtained time parametric representation of the curve sections into the base coordinate system.

6 Trajectory Correction Algorithm Taking into Account Kinematic Constraints

We will take into account the kinematic limitations of the apparatus in terms of speed and pitch angle.

Let us have arrays of coordinates of nodes $\{B_k\}, k = 1, 2, .., K$ at time points $\{t_k\}, k = 1, 2, .., K$, and $t_1 = 0$ is the initial moment of motion when the device should be at the starting point B_1 of its trajectory, and the moment $t_K = T$ corresponds to the moment of being in the target point B_K.

It is necessary to adjust the array $\{B_k\}, k = 1, 2, .., K$ in such a way as to obtain some new array $\left\{\tilde{B}_k\right\}, k = 1, 2, .., K$, so that the following inequalities are met:

$$v_{gor,k} \equiv \left| \left(\tilde{B}_k - \tilde{B}_{k-1} \right)_{gor} \right| / (t_k - t_{k-1}) \leq v_{gor,max}, \ v_{gor,k} \geq v_{gor,min} \quad (3)$$

$$v_{ver,k} \equiv \frac{\left(\tilde{B}_k - \tilde{B}_{k-1}\right)_{ver}}{(t_k - t_{k-1})} : \begin{cases} \left|v_{ver,k}\right| \leq v_{ver,l,max}, \, if \left(\tilde{B}_k - \tilde{B}_{k-1}\right)_{ver} \geq 0, \\ \left|v_{ver,k}\right| \leq v_{ver,s,max}, \, otherwise, \end{cases} \quad (4)$$

where $v_{gor,max}$, $v_{gor,min}$ are maximum and minimum permissible horizontal speeds; $v_{ver,l,max}$, $v_{ver,s,max}$ are maximum permissible vertical ascent and descent speeds; $(\bullet)_{gor}$, $(\bullet)_{ver}$ are operators for taking the horizontal component of the linear velocity vector and the vertical projection of this vector.

Further, for any linear section $\tilde{\boldsymbol{B}}_{k-1}\tilde{\boldsymbol{B}}_k$, the position of which relative to the conditional horizon plane is characterized by the pitch angle ϑ_k:

$$\vartheta_k \equiv \begin{cases} \vartheta_{0k}, \, if \left(\tilde{\boldsymbol{B}}_k - \tilde{\boldsymbol{B}}_{k-1}\right)_{ver} \geq 0, \\ -\vartheta_{0k}, \, otherwise, \end{cases} \quad (5)$$

where $\vartheta_{0k} = \boldsymbol{acos}\left(\left|\left(\tilde{\boldsymbol{B}}_k - \tilde{\boldsymbol{B}}_{k-1}\right)_{gor}\right| / \left|\tilde{\boldsymbol{B}}_{k-1}\tilde{\boldsymbol{B}}_k\right|\right)$ is a module of the current pitch angle. The restriction condition for this angle must be met:

$$\vartheta_k : \begin{cases} \vartheta_k \leq \vartheta_{pr,l}, \, if \left(\tilde{\boldsymbol{B}}_k - \tilde{\boldsymbol{B}}_{k-1}\right)_{ver} \geq 0, \\ \left|\vartheta_k\right| \leq \vartheta_{pr,s}, \, otherwise. \end{cases} \quad (6)$$

In the last expression, $\vartheta_{pr,l}$ and $\vartheta_{pr,s}$ are the maximum permissible pitch angles when ascending and descending, respectively.

To make adjustments according to formulas (3)–(6), the following sequence of actions is proposed.

If in the case of $v_{ver,k} > 0$ is performed $v_{ver,k} > v_{ver,l,max}$, then we limit $v_{ver,k}$ and simultaneously make a primary correction of the pitch angle:

$$\tilde{v}_{ver,k} = v_{ver,l,max}, \quad (7)$$

$$\tilde{\vartheta}_k = arctg\left(\tilde{v}_{ver,k} / v_{gor,k}\right). \quad (8)$$

If $\left|v_{ver,k}\right| < v_{ver,l,max}$, then the pitch angle at this stage is taken as the initial: $\tilde{\vartheta}_k = \vartheta_k$.

Similarly, the vertical component of the speed is adjusted when the conditions are met: $v_{ver,k} < 0$, $\left|v_{ver,k}\right| > v_{ver,s,max}$:

$$\tilde{v}_{ver,k} = sign\left(v_{ver,k}\right)v_{ver,s,max}. \quad (9)$$

Here and below in this paragraph, the "tilde" sign will mean the adjusted value.

After that, we make a secondary adjustment of the pitch angle, directly based on the inequality (3). The pitch angle correlates with the horizontal and vertical components of the velocity. Therefore, if inequality (3) is not met, then the pitch angle can be adjusted either by changing the horizontal velocity or by changing the vertical one.

First, to satisfy the inequality (6), we will try to change the horizontal velocity, leaving the vertical, calculated earlier in (10), the same. In this case, when $\tilde{\vartheta}_k = \pm \vartheta_{pr}$ the required horizontal velocity must be equal to:

$$v_{gor0,k} = \left| \tilde{v}_{ver,k} \right| / tg(\vartheta_{pr}), \tag{10}$$

where $\vartheta_{pr} = \vartheta_{pr,l}$ is for the case of lifting, and $\vartheta_{pr} = \vartheta_{pr,s}$ for the case of lowering the height.

However, in this case, the inequality for the horizontal velocity (8) may not be fulfilled, which will force us to switch to the option of changing the vertical velocity to ensure the desired pitch angle, namely, its reduction compared to the value in (7). In the latter case, the vertical velocity adjusted at this stage is equal to:

$$\tilde{v}_{ver,k} = v_{gor,k} tg\left(\tilde{\vartheta}_k\right), \tag{11}$$

with simultaneous execution $\tilde{\vartheta}_k = \pm \vartheta_{pr}$.

After the adjustments, the vertical component of the velocity and the pitch angle are within the acceptable ranges.

In general, there remains the possibility that the horizontal velocity does not belong to a given range in accordance with inequalities (3).

If inequality (3) is not fulfilled, we adjust the horizontal and vertical components of the velocity as follows:

$$\begin{cases} \tilde{v}_{gor,k} = v_{gor,min} if\, v_{gor,k} \le v_{gor,min}, \\ \tilde{v}_{gor,k} = v_{gor,max}, \tilde{v}_{ver,k} = \tilde{v}_{gor,k} tg\left(\tilde{\vartheta}_k\right) if\, v_{gor,k} \ge v_{gor,max}. \end{cases} \tag{12}$$

It is obvious that the last correction does not lead to the exit of the vertical component of the velocity from its permissible range given by the inequality (3).

Thus, the linear velocity vector and the pitch angle are corrected.

Then it remains to determine the adjusted position of the second point $\tilde{B}_k$:

$$\tilde{B}_k = \begin{bmatrix} B_{k-1}(1) + \tilde{v}_{gor,k}(t_k - t_{k-1})(B_k(1) - B_{k-1}(1)) / \left| \left(\tilde{B}_k - \tilde{B}_{k-1} \right)_{gor} \right| \\ B_{k-1}(2) + \tilde{v}_{gor,k}(t_k - t_{k-1})(B_k(2) - B_{k-1}(2)) / \left| \left(\tilde{B}_k - \tilde{B}_{k-1} \right)_{gor} \right| \\ B_{k-1}(3) + sign(\tilde{\vartheta}_k)\tilde{v}_{ver,k}(t_k - t_{k-1}) \end{bmatrix}. \tag{13}$$

Let's consider the algorithm for accounting for kinematic constraints in its entirety.

We organize a search of the original set of nodes $\{B_k\}, k = 1, 2, .., K$, set at points in time $\{t_k\}, k = 1, 2, .., K$. We will not adjust the position of the first node. First, we find the corrected position of the second node by the first node $\tilde{B}_2$, using the previously considered methodology for taking into account speed limits and pitch angle restrictions (3)–(8) and equality (13). Next, we find the adjusted position of the third node in the same way $\tilde{B}_3$.

Next, we proceed to the analysis of the three nodes with numbers $k = 2, 3, 4$, and speeds in them. We adjust the speed in the 4th node according to criteria (3)–(6), and Eq. (13). Repeat these steps for all three nodes $\tilde{B}_{k-2}, \tilde{B}_{k-1}, \tilde{B}_k$ by $k = 3, 4, \dots, K$.

7 Simulation Results

Let's consider an example of building a target trajectory using the global scheduler algorithm described in the previous paragraphs. Calculations will be made in the Matlab application.

The initial data for the test example is as follows. The positions of the start and target points: $A = [0, 185534, 200], m$; $B = [389621, 779243, 50]$, m; recommended absolute altitude of the UAV - Hrec $= 150, m$; maximum absolute altitude of the UAV flight - Hmax $= 400, m$; required height adjustment from the terrain - $\Delta H_{rec} = 50$, m; kinematic constraints: $[\vartheta_{pr,l}, \vartheta_{pr,s}, v_{ver,l,max}, v_{ver,s,max}, v_{gor,min}, v_{gor,max}] = [1.0472,$ rad; 1.0472, rad; 5, m/s; 5, m/s; 10, m/s; 40, m/s].

Figures 4, 5, and 6 show in the corresponding scenes the trajectories obtained at the considered five stages of this algorithm.

Figure 4a below shows a piecewise polyline curve (in purple) obtained after applying the modified Ramer-Douglas-Pecker method. This curve has a length that is 6.8% less than the length of the original curve (shown in blue) entering the algorithm input.

The results of the reconstruction of the heights of the preliminary spatial piecewise polyline trajectory according to the specified two-dimensional projection are shown in Fig. 4b. Here the desired curve is represented by a blue solid curve.

Figure 5 shows the resulting spatial curve obtained after working out the correction module taking into account kinematic constraints discussed earlier.

Finally, Fig. 6 shows the resulting piecewise polyline curve obtained as a result of the operation of the entire global scheduler algorithm.

The results of numerical modeling carried out according to the global planning algorithm discussed in the previous sections are adequate to physical representations of the behavior of the UAV when moving over a complex terrain in conditions of cylindrical obstacles with complex generators, taking into account restrictions on the limit values of the key kinematic characteristics of the device.

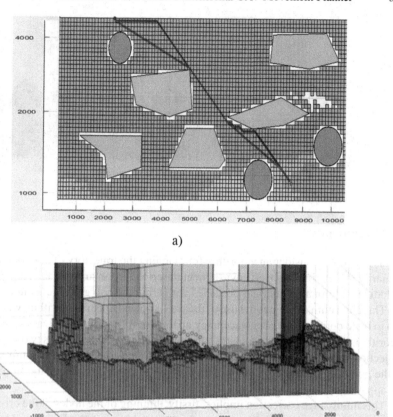

a)

b)

Fig. 4. Work of the scheduler at the first stage of the algorithm. Curve after optimization of a two-dimensional piecewise polyline (a) and reconstruction of the heights of the preliminary spatial piecewise polyline trajectory (b)

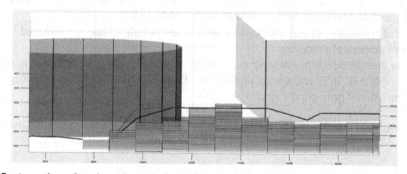

Fig. 5. A section of a piecewise polyline adjusted after the kinematic constraints accounting module.

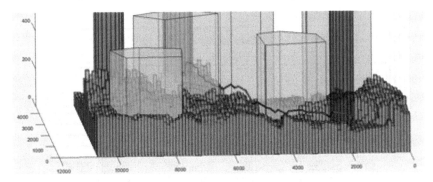

Fig. 6. The resulting piecewise polyline curve.

8 Conclusion

In this paper, we consider an algorithm for planning the trajectory of a robotic platform, primarily a UAV, in a mapped environment described by an array of terrain heights and including additional cylindrical obstacles with arbitrary polygonal generators.

This algorithm combines the use of the well-known Dijkstra algorithm, which allows you to build optimal routes with accuracy up to the error of grid quantization, and special algorithms for reconstructing a spatial piecewise polyline curve from its two-dimensional projection with multi-stage correction according to the criterion of the minimum length of the polyline, followed by taking into account the specified kinematic limitations of the apparatus.

This multi-stage correction implies, firstly, thinning of the nodes of the original two-dimensional piecewise polyline obtained after working out the Dijkstra algorithm, in order to initially reduce the length of the curve; secondly, smoothing of the intermediate piecewise polyline is performed using the modified Dubins method, which implies obtaining smooth to the first derivative of time parametric representations of the corrected curve. Finally, consideration of the kinematic limitations of the apparatus and the corresponding final correction of the curve is made at the final stage and includes consideration of the limit values of the horizontal and vertical components of the linear velocity and acceleration vectors, as well as the pitch angle.

The effectiveness of the developed global scheduler algorithm is confirmed by the results of numerical modeling.

Note that the developed algorithm can be generalized to the case of dynamic obstacles. To do this, it is enough to replace the Dijkstra algorithm used to generate a two-dimensional projection trajectory with D*.

Acknowledgements. The study was supported by the Russian Science Foundation Grant No. 22-29-00370, https://rscf.ru/project/22-29-00370/.

References

1. Hart, P.E., Nilsson, N.J., Raphael, B.A.: Formal basis for the heuristic determination of minimum cost paths. IEEE Trans. Syst. Sci. Cybernet. **4**(2), 100–107 (1968)

2. Piskorsky, D.S., Abdullin, F.H., Nikolaeva, A.R.: Optimization of the A-star path planning algorithm. Bull. SUSU. Comput. Technol. Control, Radio Electron. **20**(1), 154–160 (2020). (In Russ.)
3. Stentz, A.: Optimal and efficient path planning for partially known environments. In: Intelligent Unmanned Ground Vehicles. The Springer International Series in Engineering and Computer Science, vol. 388, pp. 203–220 (1997)
4. Wang, Q., Hao, Y., Chen, F.: Deepening the IDA* algorithm for knowledge graph reasoning through neural network architecture. Neurocomputing **429**, 101–109 (2021)
5. Zhou, R., Hansen, E.A.: Memory-bounded {A*} graph search. In: The Florida AI Research Society Conference (FLAIRS), pp. 203–209 (2002)
6. Holte, R., Perez, M., Zimmer, R., MacDonald, A.: Hierarchical A*: searching abstraction hierarchies efficiently. In: AAAI/IAAI, vol. 1, pp. 530–535 (1996)
7. Liu, B., Xiao, X., Stone, P.: A lifelong learning approach to mobile robot navigation. IEEE Robot. Autom. Lett. **6**(2), 1090–1096 (2021)
8. Chen, B.Y., Chen, X.W., Chen, H.P., Lam, W.H.: Efficient algorithm for finding k shortest paths based on re-optimization technique. Transp. Res. Part E: Logistics Transp. Rev. **133**, 101819 (2020)
9. Khatib, O.: Real-time obstacle avoidance for manipulators and mobile robots. Int. J. Robot. Res. **5**(1), 90–98 (1986)
10. Platonov, A.K., Karpov, I.I., Kirilchenko, A.A.: The method of potentials in the problem of laying a route. M.: Preprint of the Institute of Applied Mathematics of the USSR Academy of Sciences, p. 27 (1974). (In Russ)
11. Filimonov, A.B., Filimonov, N.B.: Issues of motion control of mobile robots based on the potential guidance method. Mechatron. Autom. Control **20**(11), 677–685 (2019). (In Russ.)
12. Kostyukov, V.A., Medvedev, M., Pshikhopov, V.H.: Planning the movement of ground robots in an environment with obstacles: an algorithm for constructing smoothed individual trajectories. Mechatron. Autom. Control **24**(1), 33–45 (2022). (In Russ.)
13. Pshikhopov, V.K.H., et al.: Path planning for vehicles operating in uncertain 2D environments. Elsevier, Butterworth-Heinemann, p. 312 (2017)
14. Pshikhopov, V., Medvedev, M.: Decentralized management of a group of homogeneous moving objects in a two-dimensional environment with obstacles. Mechatron. Autom. Control **17**(5), 346–353 (2016). (In Russ.)
15. Pshikhopov, V., Medvedev, M.: Group control of the movement of mobile robots in an uncertain environment using unstable modes. Comput. Sci. Autom. **5**(60), 39–63 (2018)
16. Gaiduk, A.R., Martyanov, O.V., Medvedev, M., Pshikhopov, V.H., Hamdan, N., Farhud, A.: Neural network control system for a group of robots in an uncertain two-dimensional environment. Mechatron. Autom. Control **21**(8), 470–479 (2020). (In Russ.)
17. Nazarahari, M., Khanmirza, E., Doostie, S.: Multi-objective multi-robot path planning in continuous environment using an enhanced genetic algorithm. Expert Syst. Appl. **115**, 106–120 (2019)
18. Hoy, M., Matveev, A.S., Savkin, A.V.: Algorithms for collision-free navigation of mobile robots in complex cluttered environments: a survey. Robotica **33**(3), 463–497 (2015)
19. Shlyakhov, N.E., Vatamaniuk, I.V., Ronzhin, A.L.: Review of the methods and algorithms of a robot swarm aggregation. Mechatron. Autom. Control **18**(1), 22–29 (2017)
20. Sapronov, L., Lacaze, A.: Path planning for robotic vehicles using generalized Field D. In: Unmanned Systems Technology X, vol. 6962, pp. 447–458. SPIE (2008)
21. Grigor'ev, M.I., Malozemov, V.N., Sergeev, A.N.: Bernstein polynomials and composite Bézier curves. Comput. Math. Math. Phys. **46**, 1872–1881 (2006)

Identification of the Quadcopter Rotational Dynamics for the Tilt Angle

Vadim Alexandrov$^{(\boxtimes)}$ ⓘ, Ilya Rezkov ⓘ, Dmitrii Shatov ⓘ, and Yury Morozov ⓘ

V.A. Trapeznikov Institute of Control Sciences of Russian Academy of Sciences, 65, Profsoyuznaya Street, Moscow 117997, Russia
va.alexandrov@yandex.ru

Abstract. The pitch and roll angles of the quadcopter attitude are controlled by torque arising from the difference in thrust of different rotors. Rotational dynamics of the quadcopter as a rigid body is considered. The pitch and roll angles that form the quadcopter tilt angle have similar dynamics for the case of symmetric quadcopter frame, so the pitch angle is studied separately in the paper. The finite frequency identification approach is used to find the transfer function from the experimental flight data. The approach needs data, when sine wave test signals are fed to the system input. In the case of the unstable loop of the quadcopter tilt angle, the closed loop identification procedure is used where the test signal is added to the setpoint of the operating controller. As a result, a more complex model is identified than is commonly used. Moreover, the nonlinear model of the quadcopter pitch angle is considered, taking into account the translation velocity. Parameters of this model are estimated from the same experimental data using the nonlinear grey-box model parameters identification procedure. The transfer function founded from this model confirms the structure of the transfer function obtained via the finite frequency identification procedure.

Keywords: System Identification · Robotic System · Quadcopter Dynamics · Transfer Function · Nonlinear Model · Closed Loop Identification

1 Introduction

The identification of robotic systems is an important problem to obtain a system model from experimental data for simulation and control design purposes. So, some parameters of the differential equations system that describes the quadcopter flight dynamics cannot be obtained from its design, which leads to the need for experimental studies. Several control loops operate simultaneously to provide the quadcopter flight. The model identification for altitude control loop has been studied in [1, 2]. The transfer function from the horizontal projection of a full thrust to the horizontal velocity of the quadcopter was experimentally identified, and aerodynamic drag was detected in [3]. The horizontal part of thrust is determined by the quadcopter tilt angle, which is a combination of pitch and roll angles. The pitch and roll angles control is one of the main loops for quadcopter flight control that provides the direction and value of the horizontal velocity.

© The Author(s), under exclusive license to Springer Nature Switzerland AG 2023
A. Ronzhin et al. (Eds.): ICR 2023, LNAI 14214, pp. 334–344, 2023.
https://doi.org/10.1007/978-3-031-43111-1_30

The problem of quadcopter model identification was studied in several research using the CIFER software, where the special test signal called frequency sweep is applied to the real quadcopter, then the corresponding frequency response is found, and coefficients of the linearized quadcopter models are identified. In [4] the linearized quadcopter model in form of the several transfer functions was identified, in particular, for pitch and roll angular velocities there were obtained the third order systems with pure differentiation plus time delay and the poles were stable, one was real, and the rest were complex conjugate. The oscillating second order transfer function was identified in [5] for roll and pitch loops, when looking for a low order model. The authors of [6] identified quadcopter model in state-space form basing on the results of transfer function identification. In [7] the rotors dynamics as the first order with delay is added into the state-space quadcopter model.

The article [8] develops a method of linear model identification in state-space form for a multirotor vehicle based on the equation-error maximum likelihood estimator which reduces to least-square approach applied to experiment data in time domain. The real-time identification method for a quadcopter model was proposed in [9]. Here, the recursive Fourier transform coupled with least-square estimation was used to find the state-space model coefficients estimates. The proposed method uses multisine excitation signal added to the full motor command, which is similar to our identification approach. A survey of the quadcopter model identification is in [10]. Thus, finding a practically acceptable linear model for the nonlinear dynamics of the quadcopter is a non-trivial problem.

Identification of the quadcopter rotational dynamics model from the control signals, which provide the torques related to the body frame axes, to the Euler angles of pitch and roll is the purpose of the paper. Only the pitch angle loop is considered because the roll angle loop dynamics is similar. The yaw dynamics, which is the third Euler angle, is not considered in the paper. Section 2 describes the application of the finite-frequency identification approach [11] for finding transfer functions of the linearized models from control signal to the pitch angle. The structure of the nonlinear model and its parameters evaluation are considered in Sect. 3. Conclusions are presented in Sect. 4.

2 Finite Frequency Identification Case

The experimental quadcopter [1] is the frame S500, 10-inch propellers, the onboard flight controller Pixhawk 4 and the standard ArduPilot software suite. Control signals for each motor for symmetric X-frame type quadcopter are formed as

$$
\begin{aligned}
u_1 &= u_F - 0.5u_{roll} - 0.5u_{pitch} + u_{yaw}, \\
u_2 &= u_F + 0.5u_{roll} + 0.5u_{pitch} + u_{yaw}, \\
u_3 &= u_F + 0.5u_{roll} - 0.5u_{pitch} - u_{yaw}, \\
u_4 &= u_F - 0.5u_{roll} + 0.5u_{pitch} - u_{yaw},
\end{aligned}
\tag{1}
$$

where u_F is the control value for thrust providing the altitude hold, u_{roll}, u_{pitch}, and u_{yaw} are controls for torques related to body frame axes x, y and z. It is assumed that

$$
u_{1,\dots,4} \in [0, 1],
$$

and these values are then scaled for transmission to the motors controllers called electronic speed controllers (ESC).

Our experimental quadcopter is almost symmetrical (see Fig. 1). Only the position of the battery along the x axis forms some difference between the x and y axes. Therefore, the rotational dynamics around y axis only will be considered below. The roll loop dynamics is similar to the pitch's one, and yaw loop is not considered in the paper. Note, that the Euler's angles values are not measured directly, but obtained from the extended Kalman filter implemented in ArduPilot flight software for onboard control system.

Thus, the identification problem is to find a transfer function from control u_{pitch} to the pitch angle θ.

The finite-frequency identification approach is based on analysis of the experimental data when the sine wave test signals on several different frequencies from wide enough range are fed to the system input. The quadcopter cannot be tested in open loop mode, since even in manual flight mode the attitude controllers must be active to provide horizontal stabilization. In the case of closed loop identification [1–3] the sine wave test signals are added to the controller setpoint. The preinstalled AltHold flight mode of ArduPilot onboard control system is used for the test. In this mode the throttle is automatically controlled to maintain the current altitude [12], and the attitude controller provides the desired values of pitch and roll angles and yaw angular velocity.

The required values of the pitch, roll and yaw angles θ^*, φ^*, ψ^* for attitude controllers in our identification experiment of the pitch angle loop should be the follows one:

$$\begin{aligned}
\theta^* &= \eta_i \sin(\omega_i(t - t_0)), \\
\varphi^* &= 0, \\
\psi^* &= 0,
\end{aligned} \tag{2}$$

Fig. 1. Body frame axes for X-frame type quadcopter.

where η_i and ω_i are amplitude and frequency of the test signal ($i = 0, .., n_\omega$, where n_ω is a number of the test frequencies from a given test set that are fed consequently to the system input), t is time and t_0 is the start time of the experiment on the current frequency. Then, u_{pitch}, u_{roll} and u_{yaw} are the outputs of the corresponding controllers that stabilize the roll and yaw angles values and provide the sinusoidal variation of the pitch angle. Authors' procedures are added to the open-source onboard software to form the test signals (2) and collect the experimental data.

The finite-frequency identification procedure consists of two steps: 1) obtaining estimates of frequency response for several test frequencies ω_i and 2) finding estimates of coefficients of the identified transfer function using the frequency response estimates. The frequency response estimates are obtained as

$$P(j\omega_i) = \alpha_i + j\beta_i = \frac{\alpha_{y_i} + j\beta_{y_i}}{\alpha_{u_i} + j\beta_{u_i}}, i = 1, .., n_\omega, \tag{3}$$

where α_i and β_i are called the frequency parameters, which are found using output α_{y_i}, β_{y_i} and input α_{u_i}, β_{u_i} values estimated during experiments by Fourier filter formulae [1, 2, 11]:

$$\hat{\alpha}_{y_i} = \frac{2}{\eta_i T_i} \int_{t_0}^{t_0+T_i} \theta(t) \sin(\omega_i(t - t_0))dt,$$

$$\hat{\beta}_{y_i} = \frac{2}{\eta_i T_i} \int_{t_0}^{t_0+T_i} \theta(t) \cos(\omega_i(t - t_0))dt,$$

$$\hat{\alpha}_{u_i} = \frac{2}{\eta_i T_i} \int_{t_0}^{t_0+T_i} u_{pitch}(t) \sin(\omega_i(t - t_0))dt, \tag{4}$$

$$\hat{\beta}_{u_i} = \frac{2}{\eta_i T_i} \int_{t_0}^{t_0+T_i} u_{pitch}(t) \cos(\omega_i(t - t_0))dt,$$

$$i = 1, \ldots n_\omega,$$

where $T_i = 2\pi q/\omega_i$ is the filtration time (experiment duration), where $q \in \mathbb{N}$ is the number of periods of the test frequency. Examples of the test data for the pitch loop are shown in Figs. 2, 3. The frequency parameters values obtained from experimental flights are presented in Table 1.

Table 1. Experimentally obtained frequency parameters estimates.

i	Frequency, ω_i, rad/s	Real part, $\hat{\alpha}_i$	Imaginary part, $\hat{\beta}_i$
1	20.11	−22.07	16.41
2	16.01	−41.46	25.09
3	12.03	−80.72	36.01
4	8.00	−204.60	55.70
5	5.33	−390.45	122.72
6	4.00	−451.59	392.35
7	3.50	−399.43	331.84
8	3.00	−398.90	420.68
9	2.00	−117.65	418.49
10	1.00	−5.24	194.18

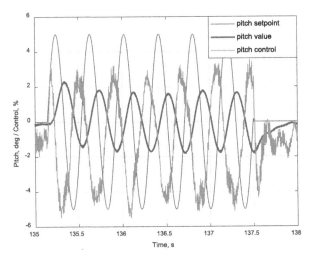

Fig. 2. Sine wave test with frequency 16 rad/s.

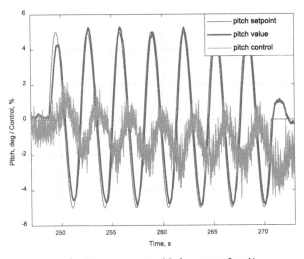

Fig. 3. Sine wave test with frequency 2 rad/s.

The second part of the finite-frequency identification procedure is to find a transfer function from obtained frequency parameters. The order of the identified transfer function should be less than the number of experimentally obtained frequency response estimates in Table 1. Then, the solution of the overdetermined system of algebraic equations provides estimates of the transfer function coefficients by the least squares criterion. If the transfer function order is unknown, then one can start with the most possible transfer function order and then decrease the order until there are no obviously cancellable poles and zeros in the identified transfer function left.

The result for the pitch data from Table 1 is:

$$P_1(s) = \frac{2828 \cdot (s - 0.156)}{(0.046s + 1)(0.18s + 1)(s^2 - 3.79s + 12.9)}. \tag{5}$$

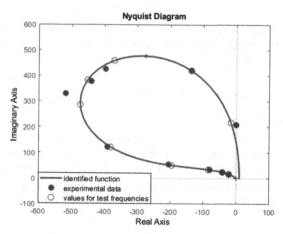

Fig. 4. Frequency response of identified pitch model (7) and points from experiments.

This transfer function determines the model structure and serves as an initial point for the optimization procedure that tries to find a better result for criterion [2]:

$$\min_{\chi} \sum_{i=1}^{n_\omega} \frac{\left| P_{id}(j\omega_i) - \left(\hat{\alpha}_i + j\hat{\beta}_i\right) \right|}{\left| \hat{\alpha}_i + j\hat{\beta}_i \right|}, \tag{6}$$

where $P_{id}(j\omega_i)$ are the frequency parameters values calculated using the identified transfer function, $\hat{\alpha}_i$ and $\hat{\beta}_i$ denote the experimentally determined according to (3), (4) estimates of the frequency parameters, χ is the variables vector.

The identified according to criterion (6) transfer function is:

$$P_2(s) = \frac{2654 \cdot (s + 0.045)}{(0.048s + 1)(0.16s + 1)(s^2 - 3.86s + 12.4)}. \tag{7}$$

It is shown in Fig. 4 that frequency response of the obtained function (7) matches the experimental data from Table 1.

The structure of the identified transfer function (7) is unexpected. Therefore, a more detailed analysis of the quadcopter rotational dynamics is carried out below.

3 Nonlinear Model Identification

The first principles consideration of the quadcopter rotational dynamics as a rigid body [10] for the separate pitch loop under assumption that the roll and yaw angles φ, ψ and the corresponding angular velocities ω_x, ω_z are equal zeros (i.e. interactions are not taken into account) provides the differential equations:

$$\dot{\theta} = \omega_y, \tag{8}$$

$$\dot{\omega}_y = \frac{1}{I_y}\tau_{pitch}, \tag{9}$$

where θ is the pitch angle, ω_y is the angular velocity around y axis, I_y is the body rotational inertia around the y axis, and τ_{pitch} is the torque from a difference of the rotors angular velocities $\Omega_{1,...,4}$:

$$\tau_{pitch} = K_\tau\left(\Omega_2{}^2 + \Omega_4{}^2 - \Omega_1{}^2 - \Omega_3{}^2\right), \tag{10}$$

where K_τ is a proportional gain.

Electronic speed controllers (ESC) of type BLHeli32 are installed on the experimental quadcopter, so the rotors angular velocities values Ω_i are measured. The transfer function from the controls u_i, $i = 1, .., 4$ that are described by (1) to the rotor angular velocities Ω_i for (10) can be identified from the data of the Sect. 2 experiments via the finite-frequency identification procedure. The first order function with time delay is obtained:

$$P_\Omega(s) = \frac{967.4}{0.044s + 1}e^{-0.0042s} \tag{11}$$

The Nyquist plot of (11) with the experimental points is shown in Fig. 5.

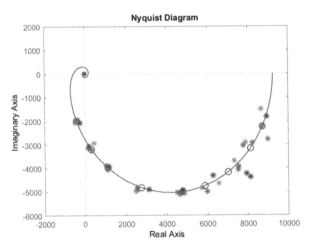

Fig. 5. Frequency response of identified the rotor angular velocity model (11) and points for each rotor from experiments.

This result is quite in line with expectations. The small delay is the sum of the cycle time of the flight controller 0.0025 s and certain delay in ESC. The gain of (11) corresponds to the rotor angular velocity in rad/s and $u_i \in [0, 1]$.

Further, the static tests were made using weighing-machine to find relations between the control u_F, average rotor angular velocity $\overline{\Omega}$ and thrust. These tests have confirmed that the ESC controller provides the rotor angular velocity proportional to the control value with the gain approximately equal to the gain in (11). Thrust is close to quadratic dependence on the rotor velocity with the gain $K_F = 0.0000115$. It is known that the gain K_τ for torque is the product of this value and the lever of the rotors, which is measured as 0.17 m. Thus,

$$K_\tau = 1.955 \cdot 10^{-6} \tag{12}$$

and τ_{pitch} can be simulated by (10), where Ω_i are integrated from (11), while u_i are determined by (1), u_F corresponds to hovering and u_{roll}, u_{yaw} assumed to be zero.

Thus, the system of Eqs. (1), (8) – (11) is a simple model for the pitch loop dynamics, where the only parameter I_y is undefined. The function *nlgreyest* from Matlab System Identification Toolbox with *fmincon* search method is used to estimate nonlinear grey-box model parameters. The experimental data are obtained in the closed loop system, which model structure should be defined for the estimation procedure. The ArduPilot cascaded control system with proportional controller for the angle and PID controller with a filter for the angular velocity is added to the estimated system. The parameters of P and PID controllers are known. The input experimental data for the estimated system is the setpoint for the pitch angle. The outputs, which are used to compare results of experiment and simulation, are the pitch angular velocity ω_y and control u_{pitch}. It is important for the case of closed loop system to use the experimental and simulated control values u_{pitch} for comparison, since the controller will provide a match of the controlled output for a wide range of parameters and model structures. The data set of 64000-time instances of 160 s with test sine waves from 8 to 1 rad/s is used. Results of identification procedure *nlgreyest* are shown in Fig. 6, where it is seen that for obtained value $I_y = 0.0116$ the simulated values of control u_{pitch} does not correspond at all to the experimental data. Therefore, the Eq. (9) does not represent all acting torques, and more complex dynamics should be considered.

The translational velocity is taken into account in the model identified in [6–8]. Moreover, one can include all other state variables in the Eq. (9) so as not to restrict the possible identified model. Thus, instead of (9), the differential equation for the pitch angular velocity, considered separately, has the form:

$$\dot{\omega}_y = p_1 \tau_{pitch} - p_2 \omega_y - p_3 \theta - p_4 v_x, \tag{13}$$

where v_x is the translational velocity, keeping in mind that for simplicity $\varphi = 0$, $\psi = 0$ are assumed, i.e., v_x is only determined by the pitch angle. Note that it is assumed that a positive value of the translational velocity corresponds to a positive value of the pitch angle. The dynamics of additional state variable v_x is defined by the horizontal force, which is the product of the Earth gravity and the tilt angle tangent under condition of zero vertical velocity, and the drag approximation [3]:

$$\dot{v}_x = 9.81 \cdot \tan\theta - p_5 \cdot |v_x| v_x, \tag{14}$$

where p_5 is the aerodynamic parameter. It is shown in [3] that this parameter is not a constant, and evaluation is made for operating points with pitch angle values of 5

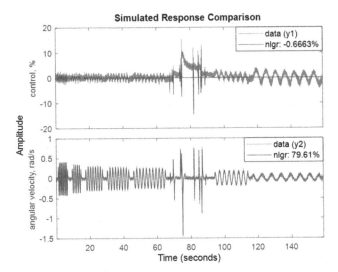

Fig. 6. Comparison of simulated (nlgr) and experimental (data) values of control u_{pitch} and pitch angular velocity ω_y for identified parameter of (9).

and 8 degrees. The estimate for the operating point corresponding to the identification experiment should be made here.

Thus, the parameters $p_{1..5}$ of the system (1), (8), (10), (11), (13), (14) should be identified. The function *nlgreyest* for the closed loop system with the same as above input and outputs data finds the parameters values:

$$p_{1..5} = [87.44, 2.87, -2.98, 13.87, 0.21]. \tag{15}$$

A good match of the simulated system and the experimental data can be seen in Fig. 7.

This nonlinear model can be linearized, when $\tan\theta \approx \theta$ is assumed for small angles. The transfer function for linearization of (14) in the operating point $\theta = 1°$ is:

$$P_{v_x}(s) = \frac{13.73}{s + 0.267}. \tag{16}$$

Torque τ_{pitch} is related to control u_{pitch} through (11) multiplied by $4K_\tau\overline{\Omega}_0$ as a linearization of (10), where $\overline{\Omega}_0 \approx 586\,\mathrm{rad/s}$ is an average rotor angular velocity for hovering. Then, the transfer function from u_{pitch} to the pitch angle θ in degrees for the operating point $\theta = 1°$ is:

$$P_3(s) = e^{-0.0042s} \cdot \frac{3102 \cdot (s + 0.267)}{(0.044s + 1)(0.14s + 1)\left(s^2 - 4.02s + 26.52\right)}. \tag{17}$$

The structures of the transfer functions (17) and (7) differ only in a small delay, revealed during the identification of the transfer function (11) for the rotor angular velocities. It should be noted that some parameters of the obtained transfer functions (17) and (7) differ significantly. Nevertheless, the identified transfer function structure of the tilt angle dynamics model is confirmed.

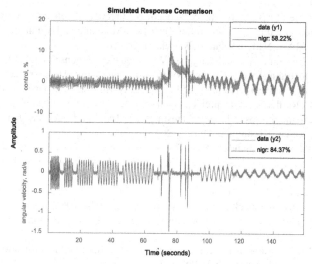

Fig. 7. Comparison of simulated (nlgr) and experimental (data) values of control u_{pitch} and pitch angular velocity ω_y for identified parameters of (13).

4 Conclusion

The finite-frequency identification approach allows finding the transfer function under the assumption that the system is linear, or the control test signals, and measured output values vary in a small neighborhood of the desired operating point, so the system can be linearized. It is important that this does not require prior knowledge of the mathematical model of the plant. In the presented study, the identified structure is confirmed via consideration of the nonlinear model of the rotational dynamics of the quadcopter tilt angle based on the first principles. The study will be continued to refine the model parameters and obtain their values for various conditions.

Acknowledgements. Research partially supported by RSF, project No. 23-29-00588, https://rscf. ru/en/project/23-29-00588/.

References

1. Alexandrov, V.A., Rezkov, I.G., Shatov, D.V.: Identification of the quadcopter vertical translation dynamics. In: 28th Mediterranean Conference on Control and Automation (MED), pp. 363–368. IEEE, Saint-Raphael, France (2020)
2. Alexandrov, V., Rezkov, I., Shatov, D.: Linearized model identification for quadcopter vertical translation dynamics. In: 25th International Conference on System Theory, Control and Computing (ICSTCC), pp. 278–283. IEEE, Iasi, Romania (2021)
3. Alexandrov, V., Rezkov, I., Shatov, D.: Finite-frequency identification of the quadcopter translation dynamics. In: 24th International Conference on System Theory, Control and Computing (ICSTCC), pp. 471–476. IEEE, Sinaia, Romania (2020)

4. Wei, W., Tischler, M.B., Schwartz, N., Cohen, K.: Frequency-domain system identification and simulation of a quadrotor controller. In: AIAA Modeling and Simulation Technologies Conference, AIAA, National Harbor, Maryland (2014)

5. Sakulthong, S., Tantrairatn, S., Saengphet, W.: Frequency response system identification and flight controller tuning for quadcopter UAV. In: Third International Conference on Engineering Science and Innovative Technology (ESIT), IEEE, North Bangkok, Thailand (2018)

6. Niermeyer, P., Raffler, T., Holzapfel, F.: Open-loop quadrotor flight dynamics identification in frequency domain via closed-loop flight testing. In: AIAA Guidance, Navigation, and Control Conference, AIAA, Kissimmee, Florida (2015)

7. Cho, S.H., Bhandari, S., Sanders, F.C., Tischler, M., Cheung, K.K.: System identification and controller optimization of coaxial quadrotor UAV in Hover. In: AIAA Scitech 2019 Forum, AIAA, San Diego, California (2019)

8. Cunningham, M.A., Hubbard, J.E., Jr.: Open-loop linear model identification of a multirotor vehicle with active feedback control. J. Aircraft **57**(6), 1044–1061 (2020)

9. Alabsi, M.I., Fields, T.D.: Real-time closed-loop system identification of a quadcopter. J. Aircraft **56**(1), 324–335 (2019)

10. Zhang, X., Li, X., Wang, K., Lu, Y.: A survey of modelling and identification of quadrotor robot. Abstract Appl. Anal. Article ID 320526 (2014)

11. Alexandrov, A.G., Orlov, Y.: Comparison of the two methods of identification under unknown-but-bounded disturbances. Autom. Remote Control **66**(10), 1647–1665 (2005)

12. ArduPilot Altitude hold mode. https://ardupilot.org/copter/docs/altholdmode.html. Accessed 21 June 2023

Development of a Firmware for Multirotor UAV Flight Controller Implemented on MCU MDR 32

Daniyar Wolf(ID), Vadim Alexandrov(ID), Dmitrii Shatov(✉)(ID), Ilya Rezkov(ID), Peter Trefilov(ID), and Roman Meshcheryakov(ID)

V.A. Trapeznikov Institute of Control Sciences of RAS, 65, Profsoyuznaya St., Moscow 117997, Russia
dvshatov@gmail.com

Abstract. The paper is devoted to study unmanned aerial vehicle (UAV) flight operational features and UAV's automatic control system operating in manual mode (it processes pilot's control commands). The analysis of operation in special cases and conditions is carried out for the aircraft equipped with a radio-operating human-controlled system and automatic flight control system. The main goal of the research is to develop fully functional flight controller the flight controller based on the domestic made microcontroller unit (MCU) MDR 32. The main novelty is that board LDM-BB-K1986BE92QI with the MDR32F9Q2I microcontroller core is used as a hardware base for the flight controller. The development of hardware and software are described separately including some features that was used to overcome several limitations of the selected MCU. The base flight controller firmware modules, functions and algorithms are described. A sample quadrotor based on the S550 frame was assembled using the developed flight controller to carry out testing flights. Two test experiments are presented: the first one is a checking of the flight controller base functionality (parameters configuration and calibration) and the second one is a test flight performed by a pilot.

Keywords: Aerial Vehicle · Quadrotor · Flight Controller · Euler's Angles · Attitude Control · Manual Control Mode

1 Introduction

Developing of manned/unmanned vehicles is accompanied by wide using of automation tools, the main of which is a flight controller that is a software and hardware complex implementing the vehicle control system. Known flight controllers use different hardware and differ also in firmware parts, which implement corresponding software logic and have various application areas.

There are dozens of onboard firmware for UAV's. All of them have their own pros and cons depending on the specific flight task, so it is impossible to select "the best flight controller firmware". The existing firmware can be divided into three groups: the first ones are intended to acrobatic flights (drones races), the second group is for

A. Ronzhin et al. (Eds.): ICR 2023, LNAI 14214, pp. 345–356, 2023.
https://doi.org/10.1007/978-3-031-43111-1_31

freestyle flights (manual control) and the rest ones are for autonomous flights using GPS navigation (automatic control).

The following firmware can be considered as the most popular for autonomous flights:

1. Ardupilot [1] – perhaps this is the most popular open-source firmware for autonomous navigation with GPS. The autopilot has been actively developed for many years and is now considered as one the most reliable solutions for both flight enthusiasts and professionals when it comes to automatic flights.
2. Pixhawk [2] – this is professional open-source autopilot developed by high qualified engineers from industry together with scientists. The firmware is supported by active community and provides control of all kinds of vehicles (ground, aerial and undewater) in several mentioned modes (race, freestyle and automatic). The corresponding flight controller is part of the PX4 ecosystem that contains open hardware standard (pixhawk), mavlink and uavcan/cyphal communication protocols, software for mission planning (groundcontrol) and other useful issues.
3. iNav [3] – this autopilot is intended to automatic navigation and autonomous tasks like flight through given points and return to home (RTH). The firmware is branch from the project Cleanflight, so is Betaflight, that is why they have a lot of similar functions, even user interface of configurator looks similar. However, besides multirotors iNav also supports fixed-wing aircrafts and radio-controlled cars. The iNav project uses all the GPS capabilities for mission planning (waypoints), it is constantly evolving and improving. Yet its development lags the latest flight characteristics achieved by Betaflight, when it comes to freestyle and racing drones. iNav supports several, but not all Betaflight flight controllers.

In general, a flight controller consists of a processor for computing (MCU), a gyroscope and an accelerometer installed on a printed circuit board. Processors in flight controllers are called microcontrollers. They store and execute autopilot firmware.

Most modern firmware is implemented on 32-bit microcontrollers of STM32x family, due to their extensive computing capabilities and a lot of useful free software. Companies, that develop flight controllers, use actively such microcontrollers because they have significant computing resources and a numerous set of functions required to effective control of UAV. In present, there are five main series of STM32 processors: F1, F3, F4, F7 and H7, which differ by size of memory and computing power.

The Atmel controller series such as ATMEGA2560 and ATMEGA32U-2 are also used by minor part of developers for implementation of flight controllers firmware. However, software support of these controllers is limited and underdeveloped in comparison to the STM32x series. This means that flight controllers developers on Atmel microcontrollers face limitations in available functions and tools which complicates the development of complex and advanced unmanned systems.

As a result, STM32 controllers, supported by extended functionality and turnkey solutions in forms of libraries and frameworks, are chosen preferably by developers for their flight controllers projects. For software developers this allows to focus on implementation of applied functions instead of low-level programming of standard functions.

Necessity of flight controller onboard firmware development on base of a domestic made MCU is caused by political and economic situation. Current conditions in the world motivate researchers groups to create their own scientific and engineering projects in this area. Without a doubt, such separate technological base allows to strengthen strategic independence. An autopilot firmware development is bounded by the technical capabilities of the microelectronic base, so such a high-tech software development at the level of aerial vehicle control systems will allow to build feedback with manufactures of domestic microelectronics.

Novelty of the paper results on one side lies in the use of the domestic MCU as a hardware base for the flight controller. Such choice requires development a lot of software, since the known autopilots are not compatible with this selected microcontroller. Thus, the other part of novel results consists of engineering and programming features developed and implemented in the flight controller firmware. The paper goal is to present development of the whole quadrotor construction and hardware-software complex "aircraft – onboard computing system – autopilot – operator – environment – disturbances". This complex allows to carry out advanced and complementary research on design of future and existing UAV's and their automatic control systems with adjustment to domestic microprocessor technology.

2 Problem Statement

The practical application of the flight automatic control methods is impossible without information about the model of aircraft characteristics (in general, non-stationary) and model of the pilot's actions (commands). In this relation, it is necessary to use theoretical and practical approaches to determine mathematical models accounting aerodynamic characteristics and to estimate their affect on the flight dynamics.

The general considered problem is to develop cyberphysical system operating in conditions of an aerial environment. In particular, an aerodynamic system of quadrotor UAV is considered. The certain problem is to design automatic attitude control system that stabilizes UAV at Euler's angles – roll, pitch, and yaw.

3 Model of the Flight Controller

At first, the flight controller development was reduced to modeling the pilot behavior at the aircraft control problem in several certain situations. Such a model was designed for 4 control channels: throttle, roll, pitch, and yaw.

The automatic control system of aerial vehicle should simultaneously reject disturbances caused by several sources: asymmetry of structural elements of the aircraft, nonideal work of the propulsion system and its motors, effect of wind action and so on. Design of such control system is the main problem of aerodynamic system control.

The considered problem is solved using classical feedback approach with PID control law, that allows to obtain desired time performance (system reaction time on disturbances and pilot commands). This quality index is crucially important for aircrafts, having very fast dynamics and usually unstable in open loop state, and should be selected at the stage of initial design research.

In the present time, the several approaches are widely used to model pilot's control actions: structural, optimal, neural network and fuzzy-logic based [4–6]. Design of universal model fit for flight study of different situations with further formalization implies great difficulties and requires additional research, so at the stage of initial R&D, the simple approximation base model was used.

To create a specific model for the rather special situations, a structural model of pilot's actions [7] was chosen. The structure of the pilot's actions model significantly depends on the character of the special situation caused by a disturbing factor.

From the considered special situations (for roll, pitch and yaw), the following pilot actions were selected:

- a time delay with control intervention (a pilot intervenes in the control by tilting the joystick sticks intended to control the axes X for roll, Y for pitch and Z for yaw after the time t spent since the situational factor occurs).
- rejection of disturbances in angular velocities (ω_x, ω_y, ω_z) and angles (roll φ, pitch θ and yaw γ). After tilting the corresponding control stick the pilot holds it in fixed position until the value the angle (or angular velocity) returns to the initial one.
- stabilization of motion parameters (corrective tilting of the control stick is intended to stabilize zero (or desired) values of the roll, pitch and yaw angles and the corresponding angular velocities).

The dynamics of the roll φ and pitch θ angles are practically the same, so further the control of the pitch angle is only considered. The control loop for the roll angle for a practically symmetrical quadrotor will have the same structure and controller parameters as the pitch one. According to the Newton-Euler's formalism the rotational dynamics on pitch angle is described as follows [8]:

$$\begin{cases} \dot{\omega}_y = \omega_x \omega_z \frac{I_z - I_x}{I_y} + \frac{1}{I_y} \tau_{pitch}, \\ \dot{\theta} = \omega_y \cos\varphi - \omega_z \sin\varphi, \end{cases} \tag{1}$$

where ω_x, ω_y, ω_z are the angular rotational velocities relative the quadrotor mass center, I_x, I_y, I_z are the moments of inertia, τ_{pitch} is the torque relative to the Y axis. It is assumed that in (1) the angular velocities ω_x, ω_y and the angle φ are close to zero. Then, the reduced dynamics, that relates torque τ_{pitch} with control signal u_{pitch}, is determined by the first order time lag [9, 10], so the linearized transfer function from control u_{pitch} to the corresponding angle θ is the following:

$$P(s) = \frac{K_\theta}{s^2 (T_\Omega s + 1)}, \tag{2}$$

where s is the Laplace variable, K_θ is the proportional gain, T_Ω is the time constant. One can note that the value of T_Ω in (2) is rather small: its value, obtained from the experiments, is estimated as less than 0.1 s. However, this lag cannot be discarded, since it is required to design the fast closed loop system to provide stability of the system with two integrators, in the that case the value T_Ω cannot be considered as small and omitted.

The control loop for the pitch angle is designed in the well-known form of a backstepping system, that consists of two loops: the inner on the angular velocity and the external on the pitch angle. The block diagram of the control loop is presented in Fig. 1. The inner loop implements a PID controller of the angular velocity that generates the control u according to the following equation:

$$u = C(s)e_{\omega_y}, \; C(s) = \frac{K_p + \frac{K_i}{s} + K_d s}{T_f s + 1},$$

where $C(s)$ is the PID controller transfer function with coefficients K_p, K_i, K_d for the corresponding proportional, integral and differential parts, T_f is the filter time constant, $e_{\omega_y} = \omega_y{}^* - \omega_y$ is the tracking error, where the desired setpoint value $\omega_y{}^*$ is generated by an output of the proportional (P) controller on the pitch angle:

$$\omega_y{}^* = K_{p_\theta} e_\theta = K_{p_\theta}(\theta^* - \theta),$$

where θ^* is the setpoint value of the pitch angle and θ is its current value, K_{p_θ} is the coefficient of the P controller. The diagram also shows PWM's that produce signals for motors, P(s) that simplified denotes the real control plant and gyroscope that measures the angular velocities.

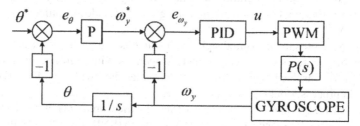

Fig. 1. The block diagram of the pitch angle control system.

In the case $\theta^* = 0$ (if pilot does not set the desired pitch angle), the control system operates in a stabilization mode that rejects the external disturbances and parametric uncertainties which could disturb the horizontal attitude of the quadrotor.

The control system for the roll angle φ is designed in a similar way. The yaw angle γ control operates according to a simplified variant only with a PI controller for the corresponding angular velocity ω_z (without design of a backstepping control system), which is due to the control plant slower dynamics for this Euler's angles component.

4   Design of the Flight Controller Hardware

It follows from the mathematical model of the flight controller that UAV is a complex of complicated interconnected systems, which are hard to describe and implement during real design process even in simplified approximate degree. The UAV operating performance is mainly determined by the separation structure of control functions, information transmission from an operator to computing system of the flight controller and an instant processing of the inner and external disturbances effects.

A pilot located onboard of an aircraft can solve the disturbance rejection problem using his own acceleration senses, that is described with previously introduced terms «the reaction time» and «the special situation». The first one is determined as the elapsed time from special situation initialization till the beginning of the pilot actions intended to reject disturbing factor called the special situation. It is known that the average reaction time on such situations varies in range 100–300 ms. If the pilot control the aircraft remotely, he does not receive any acceleration senses and cannot react on special situations, so the main problem of design is reduced to replace the pilot actions (with the same or higher reaction time) with an automatic system based on a cyberphysical mathematical model, which is then implemented in available domestic made MCU providing modern technology level. The functional diagram of the designed model and corresponding control system is shown in Fig. 2, where $r(t)$ denotes the setpoint signal of the considered loop, $y(t)$ is respectively the measured output and control signal $u(t)$ that is fed through PWM Generator to electric speed unites (ESC) and then to motors, a_x, a_y, a_z are the projections of the accelerometer output.

The MCU implements system, that allows to replace the pilot and stabilize the quadrotor horizontal attitude [11, 12]. The angular velocities for pitch and roll are separately controlled by two PID controllers (Fig. 2 presents a generic structure of the quadrotor hardware and its operation scheme), which generate control signals that are added by mixer to the whole motors control signal (it includes throttle, pitch, roll and yaw controls).

The feedback uses the measured signal y(t) which is generated by a sensor. Modern equipment for gyroscopes and accelerometers operates with high rate of information transmission, for instance, sensor MPU6050 provides data with rate 400 kHz, so the MCU should processes data with the same rate.

Another two important characteristics of inertial measurements unit (IMU) are the maximum sampling frequency and signal-to-noise ratio (SNR) regardless of mechanical vibrations and electromagnetic interference. The wide usage among aircraft modelists has got microchip MPU6000 that supports sampling frequency up to 8 kHz and provides good noise immunity. To a lesser extent, the IMU's are used MPU6500, MPU9250 and ICM20689 providing higher transmitting rates at the cost of worse SNR.

The abroad autopilots usually operate using reaction time in range 2–5 ms. Resuming, the minimum clock rate of the MCU processor should be selected not lower than 50 MHz. Another requirement on quadrotor MCU is the present of PWM channels. Both described conditions hold for microchip of MDR32F9Q21 series that provides three timers with 4 channels supporting PWM operating mode. However, in real application it occurs, that only the third timer can be used for this purpose.

A hardware part of the flight controller is shown in Fig. 2. The actuators consist of motors with the ESC's. UAV control signals from a pilot are received via a radio channel by a communication device (receiver), then fed to the microcontroller (MC) inputs by a bus (the information channel can be any – PWM, PPM, IBUS, SBUS, etc.). After that the MC transforms them either directly into pulse-width modulation (PWM) signals fed to ESC 1–4 which set the corresponding rotation speed of the electric motors M1–4 or uses in control logic as setpoints for the angles control loops.

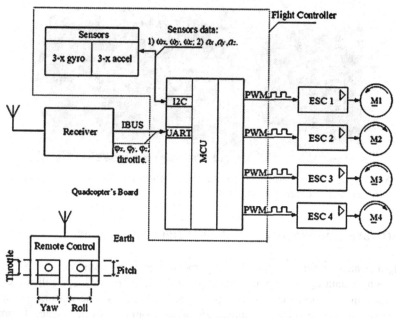

Fig. 2. The flight controller connections scheme including MCU, ESC's, motors, sensors and a receiver.

An experimental sample of the flight controller is a microcontroller device consisting of a circuit board with electronic elements placed on it according to Fig. 2. The microcontroller itself is placed on the debug board LDM-BB-K1986BE92QI manufactured by "PKK Milandr". The core of the MDR32F9Q2I microcontroller is built using ARM Cortex-M3 technology with the LQFP-64 form factor and 128 KB FLASH memory and 32 KB SRAM memory. Operating clock rate is 80 MHz (the autopilot operates on the frequency 72 MHz). Operating temperature range of the MK is −40...+85 °C. Also, a module for a 3-axis gyroscope and accelerometer GY-521 MPU-6050 is placed on the board (see Fig. 3). The board and pins protection is provided by a 3D printed bath of the appropriate sizes.

Fig. 3. Appearance of the experimental sample of the flight controller based on a domestic made MCU: A) in a protective cover; B) on the UAV board.

5 Software Implementation of the Flight Controller

The flight controller firmware architecture consists of three main systems: propulsion control, sensor data processing and automatic attitude control. The propulsion control system contains functions performing operations with motors. The sensors system collects data about angular velocities and accelerations from gyroscope and accelerometer, processes it to calculate the Euler's angles, stores all data in logs. The attitude control system consists of the functions, that implement pitch, roll and yaw control loops, and performs stabilization in a given by a pilot attitude.

In turn, each system consists of subsystems (modules):

1. information collection modules (Sensors);
2. attitude calculation module (with IMU);
3. automatic attitude control modules: PID, Mixer, Motors controller;
4. external control commands receiving module: IBUS, SBUS, etc.;
5. low-level drivers that provide communication exchange (UART, I2C);
6. the core of the system with a resource manager.

Structure and interconnections of the flight controller software modules and blocks are presented in Fig. 4. The software implementation of the flight controller allows to select the reaction time in the range 2–4 ms, which corresponds to the similar characteristics of the well-known firmware such as Ardupilot and Pixhawk. The subsystem for planning input and output data processing is implemented in the special class, called task scheduler. The subsystems of the UART and I2C drivers level implement the necessary communication between the receiver, the MPU6050 sensor with the MPU and IBUS subsystems. The IMU subsystem is a module that collects data from the MPU6050 sensor using the I2C protocol. This module solves the following tasks: 1) using the I2C driver module, it accesses the memory registers containing the sensor measurments; 2) it converts the received data to the required measure units (m/s^2 for an accelerometer, rad/s for a gyroscope); 3) calculates the Euler's angles values (in degrees).

Sensor measurements are read at a frequency of 250 to 500 Hz, depending on the selected operating mode of the system core. The separate control loops are implemented with the PID control in backstepping structure for angles pitch and roll, and with the

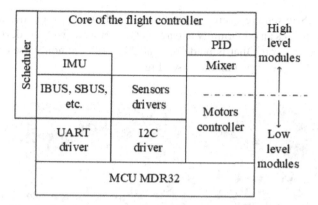

Fig. 4. Software architecture of the developed flight controller.

simple PI control for yaw angular velocity. The setpoints in these loops are the desired angles values for pitch and roll and the angular velocity for yaw. The information transmission rate between the Motors controller module and ESC's meets the condition of dShot600 standard. The software that implements the autopilot functions is developed in C++ using object-oriented programming paradigm for the above architecture of the flight controller device. The program satisfies the requirements of the RTOS level system for domestic made microcontrollers and has the following characteristics [13–15]:

- the ensured response time to the inner and external situations (noise from the equipment, the peripheral device, the data processing subsystems and etc.);
- the presence of a subsystem for planning the input information processing and forming the control signals;
- increased requirement for reaction time to external and internal events (receiving external measurements and control signals time, the input signals processing time and time for generating control signals);
- the presence of a special subsystem for generating motors control signals, considering the hardware capabilities of the used MCU.

At this stage of development, there is no user interface to confige the flight controller settings.

6   Experimental Testing

The main quadrotor load-bearing frame was assembled from the S550 frame. The frame is made up of four beams connected cruciformly. Electric motors of the 2212 series, providing 920 rpm, were chosen as propulsors. Propellers with 9.4″ blade in 5″ increments have a total thrust of about 4 kg with 4S Li-Po battery. This load capacity is enough to provide power to drive the assembled test platform weighing 1560 g, including the battery. To control the motors, ESC's with a power of up to 30 A and the SimonK firmware preinstalled were used. To receive signals and control the quadrotor, the FS-iA6B receiver was chosen, which works with the control panel using the IBUS protocol.

The FLYSKY FS-i6 remote control joystick was used to control the quadrotor. Thus, this test setup provides an opportunity to carry out experiments with the developed flight controller using quadrotor that is made of available and commonly used components that can be purchased on open markets (see Fig. 5).

Fig. 5. The experimental quadrotor setup: A) Appearance UAV on the ground; B) UAV in flight controlled by the developed flight controller.

The flight controller was tested for automatic flight stabilization in manual control mode, the experiments were performed in the following sequence:

1. Configuration of the flight controller parameters and calibration actions: tuning the PID controller coefficients and determining the bounds of stabilization control, calibration of the accelerometer, gyroscope and ESC's.
2. Testing flight in manual control mode: the angles setpoints for the desired attitude are set by a pilot using joystick, then the stabilization control quality (in terms of control errors and reaction time) is estimated using logs data.

Tests from the first category allows to prepare the quadrotor for takeoff. Without their implementation, it is impossible to proceed to flights, since the quadrotor is unstable in the open loop state and overturns without stabilization in the horizontal attitude (on the pitch and roll angles). The PID controllers parameters were found using a combination of the heuristic and analytical approaches: the controllers coefficients were designed using the Ziegler–Nichols method, the range bounds on the permissible automatic control values were determined empirically based on the results of the intermediate tests, the frequency of control discreteness was determined as the maximum available, taking into account the flight controller hardware capabilities. Calibration of sensors and ERS is performed automatically when the flight controller is initialized.

The second experiments category is the manually controlled flight: the pilot uses a joystick to control the throttle control and Euler angles channels, determining the desired flight trajectory. Test flights carried out at the ICS RAS testing area showed good controllability of the UAV in this mode on all channels. Figure 6 shows the experimental data plot during the flight: the change in pitch angle θ in blue, the desired pitch angle value of the pitch angle θ^* in red, and the corresponding values of the angular and desired angular velocities ω_y in green and ω_y^* in blue color respectively.

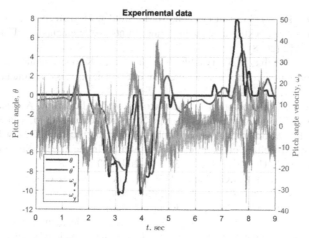

Fig. 6. The pitch angle and the corresponding angular velocity, and the corresponding desired values of these signals during the test flight.

7 Conclusion

The paper presents results of the flight controller development basing in domestic made MCU MDR32 series, which is a new engineering result. A fully functionalautopilot firmware has been developed that implements the standard function of free flight under the control of a pilot, which operates similarly to well-known common flight controllers firmware. The article describes new hardware and software solutions that have been developed and implemented to take into account the specifics of the selected processor module.

The experimental study of the flight controller shows that it provides good attitude automatic stabilization and therefore comfort takeoff, flighting, and landing characteristics in manual control mode. The testing setup was designed from the commonly used components, and it can be considered as a standard one, so the developed flight controller might be used in practice as a firmware for wide range of UAV.

Currently, the functionality of the developed hardware and software is being expanded. The hardware improvement of the flight controller is aimed to increasing the degree of UAV's autonomy by means of placing on the circuit board and integration in the flight controller a barometer, magnetometer, and GPS sensors, lidar, radar, etc. The final purpose of this research is to create a fully functional quadrotor flight controller intended for all kinds of applications, including usage in advanced group control systems [16].

References

1. Ardupilot Homepage. https://ardupilot.org. Accessed 23 May 2023
2. Pixhawk Homepage. https://docs.px4.io. Accessed 23 May 2023
3. iNav Homepage. https://github.com/iNavFlight/inav. Accessed 23 May 2023

4. van der El, K., Pool, D.M., van Paassen, M.M., Mulder, M.: Effects of preview on human control behavior in tracking tasks with various controlled elements. IEEE Trans. Cybern. **48**(4), 1242–1252 (2018)

5. Efremov, A.V., Tyaglik, M.S., Tyaglik, A.S., Irgaleev, I.K.: Developing the mathematical model of a pilot in a control manual preview tracking task. Russ. Aeronaut. **62**, 394–400 (2019)

6. Verezschikov, D.V., Voloschin, V.A., Ivaschkov, S.S., Vasiliev, D.V.: Application of fuzzy logic to create a simulation model of the pilot's control actions. In: MAI Proceedings (99). (in Russian). http://trudymai.ru/published.php?ID=91926. Accessed 23 May 2023

7. Natalijn, V.M.: Modelling of the Pilot Control Actions in the Special Situations. Sci. Bull. Moscow State Tech. Univ. Civ. Aviat. **138**, 205–209 (2009). (in Russian)

8. Alexandrov, V.A., Rezkov, I.G., Shatov, D.V. Identification of the quadcopter vertical translation dynamics. In: Proceedings of the 28th Mediterranean Conference on Control and Automation, pp. 363–368. IEEE, Saint-Raphaël (2020)

9. Alexandrov, V.A., Rezkov, I.G., Shatov, D.V.: Linearized model identification for quadcopter vertical translation dynamics. In: Proceedings of the 25th International Conference on System Theory, Control and Computing, pp. 278–283. IEEE, Iași (2021)

10. Mikrin, E.A., Zubov, N.E., Lapin, A.V., Ryabchenko, V.N.: Analytical formula of calculating a controller for linear SIMO-system. Differ. Eqn. Control Process. **1**, 1–11 (2020). (in Russian)

11. Wolf, D.A., Alexandrov, V.A., Rezkov, I.G.: Automation of the UAVs pilot's behavior using a native microcontroller. Industr. Autom. Control Syst. Controllers **3**, 9–16 (2023). (in Russian)

12. Lipovii, D.A., Maltsev, A.C.: Development of a flight controller architecture for a quadrocopter based on a single-board computer raspberry pi. Bull. Novosibirsk State Univ. Ser.: Inf. Technol. **18**(3), 19–33 (2020). (in Russian)

13. Wolf, D.A.: Software implementation of group control of collector motors. In: Proceedings of the 33rd International Scientific and Technical Conference "Extreme Robotics", pp. 206–212. RTC, St. Petersburg (2022). (In Russian)

14. Mamchenko, M.V., Romanova, M.A. Trefilov, P.M.: Algorithm for sensor data merging using analytical module for priority sensor selection. In: Proceedings of the 2020 International Conference on Industrial Engineering, Applications and Manufacturing. IEEE, Sochi (2020). https://ieeexplore.ieee.org/document/9111978

15. Mamchenko, M.V., Romanova, M.A. Trefilov, P.M.: An algorithm for evaluating the measured values of dynamic objects under the influence of external factors. In: Proceedings of the 2020 International Russian Automation Conference, pp. 1069–1073. IEEE: Sochi (2020)

16. Kutakhov, V.P., Meshcheryakov, R.V.: Group control of unmanned aerial vehicles: a generalized problem statement of applying artificial intelligence technologies. Control Sci. **1**, 55–60 (2022)

Autonomous Landing Algorithm for UAV on a Mobile Robotic Platform with a Fractal Marker

Dmitry Anikin, Artem Ryabinov$^{(\boxtimes)}$, Anton Saveliev , and Alexander Semenov

St. Petersburg Federal Research Center of the Russian Academy of Sciences (SPC RAS), 39, 14th Line, St. Petersburg 199178, Russia
ryabinov.a@iias.spb.su

Abstract. This article describes experiments related to the simulation of automatic landing of UAV on a mobile robotic platform using computer vision and a control system based on PID and polynomial regulators within the Gazebo environment. Algorithm has been developed to generate control inputs for maintaining the velocities of the UAV based on the data from the computer vision system and feedback from onboard sensor devices. A series of experiments were conducted at altitudes ranging from 5 to 20 m, which allowed for identifying limitations that affect the successful landing of the UAV. Measurements were taken of the landing time and landing error, calculated as the distance between the platform center and the UAV's center of mass upon completion of the landing. The average landing time and error ranged from 19.64 s and 0.16 m at an initial altitude of 5 m to 121.01 s and 0.27 m at an initial altitude of 20 m. Analysis of the obtained results revealed that both the average error and landing time increase with the initial altitude, which is associated with the accuracy of marker recognition at altitudes above 15 m. The obtained results can be valuable for further improvement of systems for automatic landing of UAVs on mobile platforms.

Keywords: Unmanned Aerial Vehicle · Quadcopter · Marker Detection · Automated Landing · Computer Vision · Navigation

1 Introduction

In the modern world, autonomous control systems and unmanned aerial vehicles (UAVs) and specifically quadcopters are gaining increasing popularity and are being used in various fields of activity, including industry [1], transportation [2], and the agricultural sector. The applications of quadcopters include monitoring and surveillance of territories, such as detecting forest fires, environmental pollution zones, and more.

One of the most challenging tasks faced by developers of multirotor UAVs is the creation of a reliable automatic landing system to a predefined point. Most modern commercial and open-source autopilot systems allow for landing based on GPS. However, in certain situations, such as landing in urban areas or near tall buildings, the GPS signal may be unavailable or inaccurate, leading to landing errors. Furthermore, often, the landing needs to be performed not on a stationary target but on a moving object (e.g., another robotic platform).

In light of these challenges, the use of computer vision technologies for landing purposes becomes particularly promising. The goal of this research is to develop and test algorithms that generate control inputs for UAVs based on computer vision for the automatic landing of UAVs onto a predefined ground robotic platform (GRP) at various flight altitudes. To achieve this goal, experiments were conducted to simulate the automated landing of a quadcopter model [3], equipped with an autopilot system and a video camera, onto a GRP equipped with a fractal ArUco marker [4]. Corresponding high-level autopilot algorithms were developed and tested, integrated into low-level software representing the Pixhawk PX4 autopilot [5]. The simulation was conducted using the Gazebo environment [6], with initial heights of 5, 10, 15, and 20 m. The research includes quantitative measurements of spatial errors and time associated with the landing process. The results of the performance analysis of the system under various conditions can be valuable for the developers of control and landing systems for UAVs in various practical applications [7, 8].

The structure of this article is organized as follows: Sect. 1 provides a literature review, including an analysis of related research studies. Section 2 describes the methods, algorithms, and environments used for conducting the experiments. Section 3 presents the description and results of the experiments. Section 4 analyzes the obtained experimental data and draws conclusions. Finally, Sect. 5 provides an overall conclusion, and suggests avenues for further development of the study.

2 Analysis of Existing Research

The authors of the study [9] propose an approach based on computer vision that enables an unmanned aerial vehicle (UAV) to detect, track, and land on a mobile ground robotic platform using ArUcO markers. The authors did not provide the landing time results and spatial error during landing. The UAV reached a maximum height of 4 m.

The authors of the study [10] present a fully autonomous vision-based system that addresses limitations posed by wind disturbances by tightly integrating localization, planning, and control. The approach proposed in this work employs an extended Kalman filter with simulated GPS measurements for platform position, orientation, and velocity estimation at a large distance between the platform and the UAV. In close proximity to the platform, fiducial AprilTags are utilized for estimation. The flight height was set at 0.5 m, and the landing duration was 5.7 s for a static platform and 11.5 s for a moving platform. The authors did not specify the spatial error of the landing.

The study [11] presents a method for autonomous landing that can be implemented on a micro-UAV. The approach requires broadband feedback control loops to ensure safe landing in the presence of various uncertainties and wind disturbances. The authors demonstrate the system architecture, including dynamic modeling of the UAV, implementation of a Kalman filter for optimal mobile platform localization, and the development of model predictive control for UAV guidance. Simulations were conducted with and without wind conditions. The flight height was set at 3 m, and the wind speed was 5 m/s. In the simulation without wind, the spatial error was 0.21 m, and the landing time was 44.25 s. In the simulation with wind, the error was 0.37 m, and the landing time was 105.24 s.

The authors of the study [12] propose an autonomous landing system using a composite landmark. In this system, a circular landmark with notches and a two-dimensional landmark are combined to provide visual localization over a wide range. Real-world experiments were also performed in an open area. The maximum flight height was 5 m. The proposed method achieved continuous localization results within a range of 0.5 m to 6 m, with a localization error of 0.1–0.6 m. The maximum average positional error was 0.32 m, with an 80% probability of successful landing. The landing time was 19.5 s.

In the study [13], a custom visual serving controller is employed to guide the UAV, generating control commands for linear velocities based on relative position data obtained by processing frames from an onboard camera mounted on a stabilizer. The authors do not provide information about the flight height, consider only the reflection of sunlight as an external disturbance, and do not specify the error. The study mentions a landing speed of 6.5 s after detecting the marker. In the simulation, out of 19 landing attempts, 17 were successful, and in real-world conditions, out of 22 attempts, 19 were successful. Unsuccessful attempts were attributed to sunlight reflection, which hindered marker recognition.

The authors of the paper [14] propose a system that enables tracking and landing of a UAV on a ground vehicle. The system utilizes vision-based input without external localization, where the UAV observes the motion of the UGV, predicts its movement, and generates a smooth approach trajectory to the predicted position. Experiments were conducted in the Gazebo simulation environment using the Rotors simulator. The flight altitude was set at 3 m, and the landing time took 13.5 s for linear motion and 13 s for a curved trajectory. The authors do not specify the error.

In the paper [15], a solution for high-precision landing based on marker usage is presented. The flight altitude was set at 20 m, with an average error of 11 cm, and the landing time took 162 s with a wind speed of 2.7 m/s.

The authors of the paper [16] propose a developed system for autonomous landing of a multi-rotor aerial vehicle (MAV) on a moving platform based on a vision-based tracking device. The system combines GPS positions of the MAV and the platform for MAV navigation when the marker is outside the camera's detection range or in the camera's blind spot. The flight altitude of the MAV was set at 4 m, and the landing time took 35 s with an error of 30 cm.

After analyzing the proposed solutions, it was concluded that many papers do not specify the spatial landing error. Additionally, almost all works focus on landing at low altitudes (up to 6 m). Therefore, this study will present a comprehensive testing of the developed algorithms, considering both the landing time and the spatial landing error using statistical analysis methods. This will allow conclusions to be drawn not only regarding the performance but also the accuracy of the developed solutions.

3 Materials and Methods

3.1 Used Models

The experiments were conducted in the Gazebo simulation environment. The modified model of the Clearpath Husky UGV [17] was used as the Unmanned Ground Vehicle (UGV), on which a fractal ArUco marker with a size of 1×1 m and five levels of nesting was placed (see Fig. 1a, b).

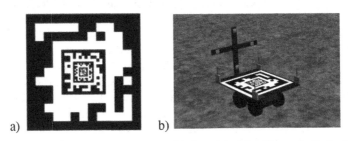

a)   b)

Fig. 1. a) Fractal ArUco marker, b) Modified model of the Clearpath Husky UGV.

This feature allows for efficient marker detection at various distances compared to a standard marker. The platform moves at a constant speed of 1 m/s along a fixed curved trajectory. The 3DR Iris quadcopter model [3], provided by the PX4 SITL simulation is used in this work. Additionally, a lower RGB camera with a resolution of 640×480 and a frame rate of 30 frames/second is mounted on the model. The technical specifications of the UAV are:

- Mass: 1.535 kg;
- Moments of inertia around the X, Y, and Z axes: 0.019125 kg m^2, 0.29125 kg m^2, 0.055255 kg m^2, respectively;
- Maximum rotor speed: 1100 RPM;
- Dimensions: 47 cm $\times$ 47 cm $\times$ 11 cm.

3.2 The Landing Control Algorithm

The landing control algorithm involves guiding the UAV to the center of the platform by setting linear velocities along the X, Y, and Z axes using the landing controller, which communicates with the autopilot (refer to Fig. 2).

The landing controller consists of two adaptive height-proportional-integral-derivative (PID) controllers that generate linear velocities along the X and Y axes, and a logarithmic polynomial (LP) controller that generates linear velocities along the Z axis based on the relative coordinates $\Delta r = [\Delta x, \Delta y, \Delta z]^T$. The vector of output linear velocities V_{sp} is passed to the input of the cascaded autopilot controller system. The velocity PID controller generates the necessary accelerations a_{sp} to achieve the desired velocities. The accelerations are transformed into a quaternion representing the UAV's position in the air, denoted as q_{sp}, , which is then passed to the proportional (P) controller for attitude control. The output of the attitude PID controller is a vector of required

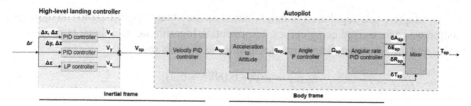

Fig. 2. UAV Controller System.

angular velocities Ω_{sp}. The angular velocities are used to generate virtual commands, which are normalized values of the throttle δR_{sp}, aileron δA_{sp}, and elevator δE_{sp}. These commands are processed by a mixer, which generates the propeller torques [18].

The proportional-integral-derivative (PID) controller is described by the following expression [19]:

$$u(t) = K_p e(t) + K_i \int_0^t e(t)dt + K_d \frac{de(t)}{dt}, \tag{1}$$

where: $e(t)$ is the error signal; K_p is the proportional gain, K_i is the integral gain, K_d is the derivative gain, t is time.

To discretize the continuous PID controller, the integral term is approximated using the trapezoidal rule, and the derivative term is approximated using finite differences:

$$\frac{de(t)}{dt} \approx \frac{e_{i-1} - e_i}{\Delta t}, \tag{2}$$

$$\int_0^t e(t)dt = \frac{1}{2} \sum_{i=1}^n (e_{i-1} + e_i)\Delta t, \tag{3}$$

where: Δt is the discretization step, i is the current step number, n is the last step number.

To reduce derivative noise and smooth the control signal, a low-pass filter with an infinite impulse response is applied to the derivative part:

$$E_i = (1 - r)E_{i-1} + r\frac{e_{i-1} - e_i}{\Delta t}, \tag{4}$$

where: E_i is the filtered derivative component, r is the smoothing coefficient.

The tuning of the PID controller was performed empirically by observing the response of the UAV to individual control signals. As a result, the following coefficients were determined (see Table 1).

Table 1. Coefficients of the tuned adaptive height PID controller.

Height, meters	Kp	K_i	Kd
20	0.305	0.0325	0.0025
5	0.5	0.0705	0.0005

For adaptive self-regulation of height based on the obtained coefficients, an approximation was constructed using curves. Exponential, logarithmic, and linear curves were tested, and the exponential approximation showed the best results.

$$K_p(z) = exp(-0.098z - 0.2), \tag{5}$$

$$K_i(z) = exp(-0.154z - 1.878), \tag{6}$$

$$K_d(z) = exp(0.321z - 9.21), \tag{7}$$

where z is the current altitude of the UAV in meters. The final control law takes the following form:

$$V_{x,y} = K_p(z)e_i + K_i(z) \cdot \frac{1}{2} \sum_{i=1}^{n} (e_{i-1} + e_i)\Delta t + K_d(z)E_i, \tag{8}$$

where e_i is value of the error signal; z is current altitude of the UAV in meters; E_i is value of the filtered derivative component of the controller.

The generation of linear velocity along the Z-axis is based on the logarithm of a polynomial function of normalized distance in the vertical plane [20].

$$V_z = V_{z0} \log_n \left(1 + ax + bx^2\right), \tag{9}$$

where $x = \frac{R_z}{R_{z0}}$;
V_{z0} is initial descent velocity; n is logarithm base; a, b is coefficients determining the velocity profile; R_{z0} is initial distance along the Z-axis; R_z is current distance along the Z-axis.

According to this law, the approach speed logarithmically decreases to zero as the distance to the landing site approaches zero (see Fig. 3).

The maximum descent speed is calculated using the following formula:

$$V_{zmax} = V_{z0} \cdot \log_n \left(1 - \frac{a^2}{4b}\right), \tag{10}$$

where V_{z0} is initial descent velocity; n is logarithm base; a, b are coefficients determining the velocity profile.

The landing algorithm is schematically represented as follows (see Fig. 4).

After the marker enters the camera's field of view, the PID controllers generate control signals for following the visual target. The altitude of the UAV remains constant during this movement (the descent rate is zero). When the UAV reaches a distance of 45 cm from the center of the platform, the descent process begins. The process ends when the descent altitude becomes less than 10 cm, at which point the motors are turned off, and the copter lands completely.

In case the platform goes out of the camera's field of view, after three seconds, the UAV ascends at a rate of 5 m/s in order to reacquire the platform. If the platform is not detected again within two seconds, an emergency return to the initial GPS position is initiated to perform a new maneuver.

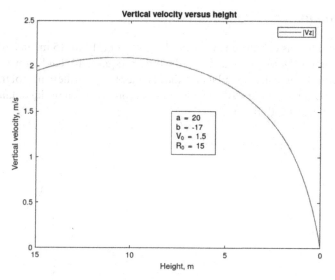

Fig. 3. Descent velocity dependence on altitude.

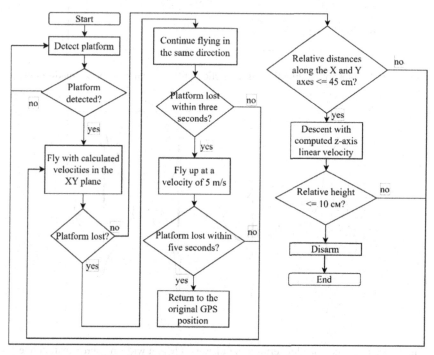

Fig. 4. Block diagram of the landing algorithm.

4   Experiments

Testing of landing was conducted at various heights: 5 m, 10 m, 15 m, and 20 m, with a total of 40 attempts. During each attempt, the time τ required for landing was measured, as well as the error ε, which is calculated as the distance between the center of the platform and the center of mass of the UAV. The graphical representation of the obtained results is presented in Fig. 5 and Fig. 6.

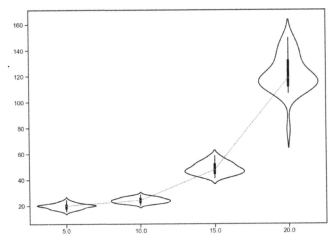

Fig. 5. Violin plots of landing time as a function of height with an approximation line.

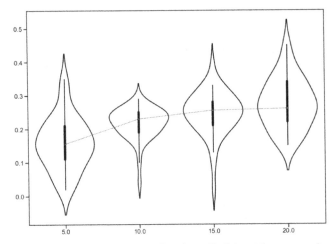

Fig. 6. Violin plots of landing error as a function of height with an approximation line.

The provided graphical representations allow us to observe an increase in both landing time and error with an increase in initial height. For each height, the mean value and standard deviation of the landing time and error were calculated. Additionally, for each height, the increments in landing time and error, $\Delta\tau$ and $\Delta\varepsilon$, were calculated as the difference between the corresponding mean values at the current and previous heights. The results of the experiments are presented in Table 2.

Table 2. Coefficients of the tuned adaptive height PID controller.

Height, m	Success rate	τ, sec	ε, m	$\Delta\tau$, sec	$\Delta\varepsilon$, m
5	100%	19.64 ± 2.108	0.16 ± 0.078	0	0
10	100%	24.08 ± 2.019	0.22 ± 0.047	4.44	0.06
15	100%	48.51 ± 4.526	0.25 ± 0.066	24.43	0.03
20	82.50%	121.01 ± 14.188	0.27 ± 0.074	72.5	0.02

It can be observed that the height of 15 m is the highest at which stable landing on the platform was achieved in 100% of cases. As the initial height increases, the time required for landing significantly increases. The error also increases, but not to the same extent.

5   Analysis of Obtained Results

An empirical assessment of the graphical representation of the obtained results allows for clear conclusions regarding the nonlinear relationship between the landing time (τ) and the initial height of the UAV. This can also be observed from the non-uniform increase in the values of $\Delta\tau$.

As for the landing error (ε), although the average error value increases with the initial height, this increase is not significant. To determine the impact of landing height on the error, statistical tests will be conducted. First, it is necessary to determine whether the error value samples obtained during the experiments follow a normal distribution. For this purpose, the classical Shapiro-Wilk test will be used [21]. The Shapiro-Wilk test returns a p-value, which indicates the probability of obtaining such or more extreme results, given that the null hypothesis of data normality is true. If the p-value is less than the chosen significance level (we consider the most common significance level of 0.05), the null hypothesis is rejected, and it is concluded that the data does not follow a normal distribution. Table 3 presents the p-values of the Shapiro-Wilk test for the landing error samples at different heights.

Table 3. Results of the Shapiro-Wilk test for landing error samples at different heights.

Height, meters	5	10	15	20
p-value	0.46	**0.0006**	**0.029**	0.49

The obtained p-values for heights of 10 and 15 m indicate that the data obtained in the corresponding experiments does not follow a normal distribution. In such cases, nonparametric methods are necessary for statistical analysis of the impact of landing height on the error. In this study, we will perform pairwise tests using the Mann-Whitney U test [22]. The Mann-Whitney test allows us to assess whether there are statistically significant differences between two groups of data, without assuming a normal distribution. During the analysis, pairwise comparisons of the ε samples were conducted for each landing height of 5, 10, 15, and 20 m. The null hypothesis assumed no statistically significant differences between these samples. As a result, p_ε values were obtained, which indicate the level of statistical significance of the differences between the samples. In this case, the null hypothesis is rejected if the obtained p-value is less than or equal to 0.05. Table 4 presents the results of the test.

Table 4. Results of pairwise Mann-Whitney U test for landing error at different heights.

Height, meters	5	10	15	20
5	–	2.09E−05	5.08E−07	6.04E−08
10		–	0.003	0.0004
15			–	0.091

The obtained results allow us to conclude that there is a statistically significant increase in landing error with increasing height, except for the increase from 15 to 20 m. The most significant differences are observed when comparing the error at the initial height of 5 m. Thus, the conducted research leads to the following conclusions:

1. The developed algorithm enables automated landing using a marker at different heights. The maximum height for marker recognition is 20 m, but periodic failures in marker recognition occurred, and any fluctuations of the UAV could affect the detection performance. In the worst cases, this resulted in the inability to perform the landing and the need for a repeated maneuver. Stable marker recognition and landing were achieved at heights of 15 m and below.
2. Increasing the initial landing height leads to a significant increase in landing time and a slight increase in error. If high precision and speed of landing are required, the algorithm should be used at heights not exceeding 5 m.
3. Increasing the height to 15 m allows for stable landing, but the landing time increases by almost 2.5 times compared to the landing from a height of 5 m.

6 Conclusion

This article presents the examination and testing of an algorithm for automated landing of UAVs on a moving platform in the Gazebo simulation environment, measuring landing time and spatial error on different initial altitudes. The average landing time and error ranged from 19.64 s and 0.16 m at an initial altitude of 5 m to 121.01 s and 0.27 m at an initial altitude of 20 m. The obtained results demonstrate the effectiveness of the algorithm and its stable performance in landings up to 15 m. To improve performance at higher altitudes, potential enhancements can be considered, such as improving detection algorithms, using more accurate and sensitive cameras, and employing additional sensors. Furthermore, improvements in UAV stabilization systems can be explored to reduce oscillations and enhance landing precision.

Future work aims to expand this research by conducting simulation modeling with the influence of external factors on the UAV that can impact the algorithm's effectiveness, such as wind, lighting conditions, and precipitation.

The investigations conducted in this study open up new possibilities for autonomous UAV landings in constrained areas using computer vision. The experimental results can be valuable for the design and development of automatic landing systems for UAVs at various heights and under heterogeneous conditions.

References

1. Saveliev, A., Lebedev, I.: Method of autonomous survey of power lines using a multi-rotor UAV. In: Ronzhin, A., Pshikhopov, V. (eds.) Frontiers in Robotics and Electromechanics. Smart Innovation, Systems and Technologies, vol. 329, pp. 359–376. Springer, Singapore (2023). https://doi.org/10.1007/978-981-19-7685-8_23
2. Saveliev, A., Lebedeva, V., Lebedev, I., Uzdiaev, M.: An approach to the automatic construction of a road accident scheme using UAV and deep learning methods. Sensors 22(13), 4728 (2022)
3. PX4 User Guide. Gazebo Vehicles. https://docs.px4.io/v1.12/en/simulation/gazebo_vehicles.html#quadrotor. Accessed 14 Mar 2023
4. Romero-Ramire, F.J., Munoz-Salinas, R., Medina-Carnicer, R.: Fractal markers: a new approach for long-range marker pose estimation under occlusion. IEEE Access 7, 169908–169919 (2019)
5. Software Overview PX4 Autopilot. https://px4.io/software/software-overview. Accessed 14 Mar 2023
6. About Gazebo. Gazebo Official Website. https://gazebosim.org/about. Accessed 14 Mar 2023
7. Basan, E., Peskova, O., Silin, O., Basan, A., Abramov, E.: Data generation for modeling attacks on UAVs for the purpose of testing intrusion detection systems. Inform. Autom. 21(6), 1290–1327 (2022). https://doi.org/10.15622/ia.21.6.8
8. Sevostyanova, N., Lebedev, I., Lebedeva, V., Vatamaniuk, I.: An innovative approach to automated photo-activation of crop acreage using UAVs to stimulate crop growth. Inform. Autom. 20(6), 1395–1417 (2021). https://doi.org/10.15622/ia.20.6.8
9. Morales, J., Castelo, I., Serra, R., Lima, P.U., Basiri, M.: Vision-based autonomous following of a moving platform and landing for an unmanned aerial vehicle. Sensors 23(2), 829 (2023)
10. Paris, A., Lopez, B.T., How, J.P.: Dynamic landing of an autonomous quadrotor on a moving platform in turbulent wind conditions. In: 2020 IEEE International Conference on Robotics and Automation (ICRA), pp. 9577–9583. IEEE (2020)
11. Feng, Y., Zhang, C., Baek, S., Rawashdeh, S., Mohammadi, A.: Autonomous landing of a UAV on a moving platform using model predictive control. Drones 2(4), 34 (2018)
12. Xing, B.Y., Pan, F., Feng, X.X., Li, W.X., Gao, Q.: Autonomous landing of a micro aerial vehicle on a moving platform using a composite landmark. Int. J. Aerosp. Eng. 2019, 1–15 (2019)
13. Keipour, A., et al.: Visual servoing approach to autonomous UAV landing on a moving vehicle. Sensors 22(17), 6549 (2022)

14. Acuna, R., Zhang, D., Willert, V.: Vision-based UAV landing on a moving platform in gps denied environments using motion prediction. In: 2018 Latin American Robotic Symposium, 2018 Brazilian Symposium on Robotics (SBR) and 2018 Workshop on Robotics in Education (WRE), pp. 515–521. IEEE (2018)

15. Wubben, J., et al.: A vision-based system for autonomous vertical landing of unmanned aerial vehicles. In: 2019 IEEE/ACM 23rd International Symposium on Distributed Simulation and Real Time Applications (DS-RT), pp. 1–7. IEEE (2019)

16. Zhao, Z., et al.: Vision-based autonomous landing control of a multi-rotor aerial vehicle on a moving platform with experimental validations. IFAC-PapersOnLine **55**(3), 1–6 (2022)

17. Husky UGV - Outdoor Field Research Robot by Clearpath. https://clearpathrobotics.com/husky-unmanned-ground-vehicle-robot/. Accessed 17 Mar 2023

18. Controller Diagrams - PX4 User Guilde. https://docs.px4.io/main/en/flight_stack/controller_diagrams.html. Accessed 17 Mar 2023

19. Denisenko, V.V.: PID controllers: principles of construction and modification. Mod. Autom. Technol. **4**, 66–75 (In Russ.)

20. Gautam, A., Ratnoo, A., Sujit, P.B.: Log polynomial velocity profile for vertical landing. J. Guid. Control. Dyn. **41**(7), 1617–1623 (2018)

21. Shapiro, S.S., Wilk, M.B.: An analysis of variance test for normality (complete samples). Biometrika **52**(3/4), 591–611 (1965)

22. Mann, H., Whitney, D.: Controlling the false discovery rate: a practical and powerful approach to multiple testing. Ann. Math. Stat. **18**(1), 50–60 (1947)

Curl-Free Vector Field for Collision Avoidance in a Swarm of Autonomous Drones

Tagir Muslimov$^{(\boxtimes)}$ [ID]

Ufa University of Science and Technology, 12, K. Marx St., Ufa 450008, Russia
tagir.muslimov@gmail.com

Abstract. To perform complex tasks, drones must have the ability to move autonomously. Ensuring collision avoidance is very important for the safe movement of autonomous drones indoors. FIRAS function-based potential field method is the standard for collision avoidance as implemented in isolated drones. However, its use in an autonomous swarm can be problematic. Its complex interconnected structure causes one of the known issues when there are multiple simultaneously active control objectives. They are intra-swarm collision avoidance and reaching the target relative distance (normally referred to as formation control). This paper shows that with collision avoidance active, the standard potential field method will cause a local minima-like effect in an autonomous swarm. To prevent it, this paper proposes a modified curl-free vector field-based algorithm. This modification enables extended lateral circular motion to prevent swarm members from getting stuck in a local minimum. Stability theory methods are invoked to show that the formation remains stable when running the proposed algorithm. Comparative numerical experiments were run on a drone swarm model in MATLAB/Simulink to illustrate the functioning of this algorithm. To prove the proposed method effective, the paper presents simulation results for standard vs modified potential field.

Keywords: Potential Field Method · Indoor Drones · Swarm Control · Collision Avoidance · Multi-UAV System

1 Introduction

Research into controlling swarms of autonomous robots is commonplace and of great interest [1]. A variety of research problems have drawn attention, including distribution of tasks between swarm members [2] and novel types of robots for better swarm efficiency [3]. Consensus-based formation control, including that of autonomous unmanned aerial vehicles (drones) is a closely related topic [4, 5]. Yet, controlling a swarm or a decentralized formation of autonomous drones is a complex problem if it involves avoidance of collision with a diverse set of obstacles [6]. That is critical where drones must be moving safely in a confined space. In such cases, avoiding drone-to-drone collision avoidance becomes especially relevant due to limited flight space.

A. Ronzhin et al. (Eds.): ICR 2023, LNAI 14214, pp. 369–379, 2023.
https://doi.org/10.1007/978-3-031-43111-1_33

Isolated drone movement amidst obstacles is a well-researched problem with a variety of solutions, e.g., those based on rapidly exploring random trees (RRT) [7]. Potential field is another classical method; it was originally proposed to enable isolated robots to navigate safely through stationary obstacles. However, this method has recently found uses in controlling formations of mobile ground robots or drones where they should avoid collisions within the team [8, 9]. One possible implementation of the potential field method consists in splitting the flight space for each drone into individual regions with a version of the potential function for each [10, 11]. This approach has been proven effective when controlling a formation in a stationary-obstacle environment. However, if the swarm has to move cohesively with respect to intra-formation target points, then a conflict of control objectives might arise. This conflict causes drones to become 'stuck', an effect similar to that of local minima, which is typical of the classical potential field method.

Thus, the goal hereof was to address this issue. To do so, the paper proposes curl-free vector field-based modification. A similar approach has been proposed in [12, 13]. However, paper [12] demonstrated using it to avoid collision of two drones facing each other in flight on a collision course. Paper [13] considers a multi-obstacle flight zone but the obstacles are static. In [14], a curl-free vector field was used to create a circular formation that preserves its arrangement around the target while tracking the trajectory. This paper is about a modification for cases where the swarm has to reach preset relative distances whilst prioritizing formation control. We further demonstrate the theoretical foundations and the numerical simulation to prove this approach effective.

2   Curl-Free Vector Field-Based Approach to Drone Swarm Control

2.1   Drone Swarm System Model

The proposed model is based on an assumption that each micro-quadcopter in the system is receiving data respective of the adjacent aircraft and of the global coordinate system. Assume that the internal control loop (the autopilot) stabilizes the UAV. This can be verified by means of a test flight that performs hovering at the same spot as well as manual control by entering movement commands in four directions and commands to increase or decrease the altitude. The external control loop tracks the predetermined trajectory using special-purpose software. Control is proved by a central computer; however, quadcopters can only access local data on the adjacent aircraft, which makes the formation decentralized. Thus, the high-level control dynamics can be utilized to develop and implement swarm control.

The swarm control model has a fairly standard description, see e.g. [15] for a general overview. Consider a swarm of N micro-quadcopters, each referred to as an 'agent'. For high-level control, assume that each quadcopter is a system in n-dimensional space that has the following single-integrator dynamics:

$$\dot{p}_i = u_i, \quad i = 1, 2, \dots, N,$$

where $p_i \in \mathbb{R}^n$ is the aircraft's attitude, $u_i \in \mathbb{R}^n$ is the ith quadcopter's control.

Let us introduce the notation: $\Delta_{ij} \in \mathbb{R}^n$ is the desired relative distance between the ith and the jth agent. Apparently, for the swarm to operate correctly, the condition $\Delta_{ij} = -\Delta_{ji}$ must be satisfied for each ith and jth agent pair except when $i = j$. For any i, the condition $\Delta_{ii} = 0$ must be satisfied.

As a problem, swarm formation control can be worded as follows.

Control Objective. Consider a swarm of N agents (quadcopters). For each ith agent, synthesize such control $u_i^{formation}(t)$ that for $t \geq 0$, the attitude satisfies the condition: $\lim_{t \to \infty} (p_j(t) - p_i(t)) = \Delta_{ij}$ $\forall i, j, i \neq j$.

Classical papers on the topic usually show how this could be achieved by using a control algorithm that relies on relative attitude mismatch:

$$u_i^{formation} = k_f \sum_{j=1}^{N} (p_j - p_i - \Delta_{ji}), \tag{1}$$

where k_f is the positive tunable coefficient.

We can analyze unidimensional ($n = 1$) formation control for a single axis. That analysis could be easily reapplied to a multidimensional case ($n \geq 1$).

Swarm system dynamics can be written as a matrix using the Laplacian matrix L as follows:

$$\dot{\mathbf{p}} = -k_f \mathbf{L} \mathbf{p} + \mathbf{b},$$

where $\mathbf{p} = \begin{bmatrix} p_1, p_2, \ldots, p_N \end{bmatrix}^T$, $\mathbf{b} = \begin{bmatrix} b_1, b_2, \ldots, b_N \end{bmatrix}^T$, $b_i = -k_f \sum_{j=1}^{N} \Delta_{ji}$, $\mathbf{L} \in \mathbb{R}^{N \times N}$ is the Laplacian matrix that represents a graph of agent-agent interaction in the swarm. By default, the matrix $\mathbf{L}$ is written as $\mathbf{L} = \mathbf{D} - \mathbf{A}$, where $\mathbf{D} \in \mathbb{R}^{N \times N}$ is a matrix where the diagonal element i corresponds to the in-degree of the ith vertex (the number of edges coming into that vertex); $\mathbf{A} \in \mathbb{R}^{N \times N}$ is the adjacency matrix of the interaction graph. For example, for a fully connected interaction structure the elements of the matrix $\mathbf{L}$ would be written as

$$l_{ij} = \begin{cases} -1, & i \neq j \\ N-1, & i = j \end{cases}.$$

Such Laplacian matrix only has one zero eigenvalue; other eigenvalues are positive and identical.

This UAV swarm control model has been modified using an artificial potential field. We named the complete potential field-based swarm control algorithm APFfSwarm (Artificial Potential Field for Swarm).

2.2 Control Algorithm for Collision Avoidance

Consider a case of swarm movement with formation control and collision avoidance. The artificial potential field $U_r^{APFfSwarm}$ for the swarm control algorithm is proposedly written as the sum of the formation control field and curl-free vector field as follows:

$$U_r^{APFfSwarm} = U_r^{Form}(\mathbf{q}_i, \mathbf{q}_j) + U_r^{CAfM}(\mathbf{q}_i, \mathbf{q}_j) + U_r^{CAfS}(\mathbf{q}_i, \mathbf{d}_{obst}),$$

where $U_r^{Form}(\mathbf{q}_i, \mathbf{q}_j)$ is the component that controls making the formation; $U_r^{CAfM}(\mathbf{q}_i, \mathbf{q}_j)$ is the component that controls collision avoidance for moving obstacles (i.e., copter-to-copter collision avoidance); $U_r^{CAfS}(\mathbf{q}_i, \mathbf{q}_j)$ is the component that controls collision avoidance for stationary obstacles; $\mathbf{q}_i \triangleq \left[p_i^x \ p_i^y \right]^T$ and $\mathbf{q}_j \triangleq \left[p_j^x \ p_j^y \right]^T$ are the coordinates in the inertial coordinate system (ICS).

The component $U_r^{Form}(\mathbf{q}_i, \mathbf{q}_j)$ is defined as $U_r^{Form}(\mathbf{q}_i, \mathbf{q}_j) \triangleq k_f \frac{1}{2} \sum_{j=1}^{N} \|\mathbf{q}_j - \mathbf{q}_i - \Delta_{ji}\|_2^2$ given (1), where $\Delta_{ji} \triangleq \left[\Delta_{ji}^x \ \Delta_{ji}^y \right]^T$ specifies the desired formation in the horizontal plane.

The components $U_r^{CAfM}(\mathbf{q}_i, \mathbf{q}_j)$ and $U_r^{CAfS}(\mathbf{q}_i, \mathbf{d}_{obst})$ are defined as follows:

$$U_r^{CAfM}(\mathbf{q}_i, \mathbf{q}_j) = \begin{cases} \frac{1}{2} k_{r_i}^m \left(\frac{1}{d(\mathbf{q}_i, \mathbf{q}_j)} - \frac{1}{d_o} \right)^2, & \text{if } d(\mathbf{q}_i, \mathbf{q}_j) \le d_o \\ 0, & \text{if } d(\mathbf{q}_i, \mathbf{q}_j) > d_o \end{cases},$$

$$U_r^{CAfS}(\mathbf{q}_i, \mathbf{d}_{obst}) = \begin{cases} \frac{1}{2} k_{r_i}^s \left(\frac{1}{d(\mathbf{q}_i, \mathbf{d}_{obst})} - \frac{1}{d_o} \right)^2, & \text{if } d(\mathbf{q}_i, \mathbf{d}_{obst}) \le d_o \\ 0, & \text{if } d(\mathbf{q}_i, \mathbf{d}_{obst}) > d_o \end{cases},$$

where $k_{r_i}^m$ and $k_{r_i}^s$ are the positive tunable coefficients; d_o is the radius of the area around the drone where the repulsion components begin to take effect; U_r^{CAfS} is defined similarly to U_r^{CAfM} but uses $\mathbf{d}_{obst}$ (the distance to the nearest point of a stationary obstacle) instead of $\mathbf{q}_j$.

For the ith UAV agent, define Control Algorithm 1 based on the control law $\mathbf{f}_i^{APFfSwarm}$, which consists of several components:

If $d(\mathbf{q}_i, \mathbf{q}_j) \le d_o$, then

$$\begin{aligned} \mathbf{f}_i^{APFfSwarm} &= \mathbf{f}^{escape}(\mathbf{q}_i, \mathbf{q}_j) + \mathbf{f}^{CAfM}(\mathbf{q}_i, \mathbf{q}_j) + \mathbf{f}^{CAfS}(\mathbf{q}_i, \mathbf{d}_{obst}) \\ &= -\nabla_{\mathbf{q}_i - \mathbf{q}_j} U_r^{CAfM}(\mathbf{q}_i, \mathbf{q}_j) \mathbf{R}_{\varsigma_{ij}}(\mathbf{q}_i - \mathbf{q}_j) \\ &\quad -\nabla_{\mathbf{q}_i - \mathbf{d}_{obst}} U_r^{CAfS}(\mathbf{q}_i, \mathbf{d}_{obst}) \mathbf{R}_{\varsigma_{obst}}(\mathbf{q}_i - \mathbf{d}_{obst}) \\ &\quad +\mathbf{f}^{escape}(\mathbf{q}_i, \mathbf{q}_j) \end{aligned}$$

else

$$\mathbf{f}_i^{APFfSwarm} = \nabla U_r^{Form}(\mathbf{q}_i, \mathbf{q}_j)$$

end

The matrices $\mathbf{R}_{\varsigma_{ij}}$ and $\mathbf{R}_{\varsigma_{obst}}$ are defined as follows:

$$
\mathbf{R}_{\varsigma_{ij}}\left(\mathbf{q}_i - \mathbf{q}_j\right) = \begin{cases} \begin{bmatrix} 0 & 1 \\ -1 & 0 \end{bmatrix} & \textit{if } \varsigma_{ij} = -1 \\[2mm] \begin{bmatrix} 0 & -1 \\ 1 & 0 \end{bmatrix} & \textit{if } \varsigma_{ij} = 1 \end{cases};
$$

$$
\mathbf{R}_{\varsigma_{obst}}\left(\mathbf{q}_i - \mathbf{d}_{obst}\right) = \begin{cases} \begin{bmatrix} 0 & 1 \\ -1 & 0 \end{bmatrix} & \textit{if } \varsigma_{obst} = -1 \\[2mm] \begin{bmatrix} 0 & -1 \\ 1 & 0 \end{bmatrix} & \textit{if } \varsigma_{obst} = 1 \end{cases}.
$$

Here, ς_{ij} and ς_{obst} are the parameters that, in the program code, set the copter rotation direction for collision avoidance maneuvers; $\mathbf{f}^{escape}\left(\mathbf{q}_i, \mathbf{q}_j\right) \triangleq \mu_i \sum_{j \neq i}(\mathbf{q}_j - \mathbf{q}_i)/\|\mathbf{q}_j - \mathbf{q}_i - \boldsymbol{\Delta}_{ji}\|_2^2$ is the vector that enables both UAVs to leave the safety zone and continue swarming, μ_i is a tunable positive coefficient. Assume that $\mu_i = \mu_j$. The vector $\mathbf{f}^{escape}\left(\mathbf{q}_i, \mathbf{q}_j\right)$ is based on the final positions of the swarm formation; this allows to make the formation faster.

Let us demonstrate how this algorithm guarantees Lyapunov stability. For space considerations, consider that drones only encounter moving obstacles. Adjustment for stationary obstacles would only require a slight modification. Choose the following Lyapunov function:

$$
\mathbb{V} = \begin{cases} \frac{1}{2}\kappa\sum_{i=1}^{N}\sum_{j \neq i} U_r^{CAfM}\left(\mathbf{q}_i, \mathbf{q}_j\right), & \textit{if } d\left(\mathbf{q}_i, \mathbf{q}_j\right) \leq d_o \\[2mm] \frac{1}{2}\sum_{i=1}^{N}\left(\mathbf{q}_i - \frac{1}{k_f N}\mathbf{b}_i\right)^T\left(\mathbf{q}_i - \frac{1}{k_f N}\mathbf{b}_i\right), & \textit{if } d\left(\mathbf{q}_i, \mathbf{q}_j\right) > d_o \end{cases},
$$

where $\kappa \in \mathbb{R}_{>0}$ is a positive coefficient.

A derivative of the function $\mathbb{V}$ can be written as follows:

$$
\dot{\mathbb{V}} = \begin{cases} \frac{1}{2}\kappa\sum_{i=1}^{N}\sum_{j \neq i} \dot{U}_r^{CAfM}\left(\mathbf{q}_i, \mathbf{q}_j\right) & \textit{if } d\left(\mathbf{q}_i, \mathbf{q}_j\right) \leq d_o \\[2mm] \sum_{i=1}^{N}\left(\mathbf{q}_i - \frac{1}{k_f N}\mathbf{b}_i\right)^T \dot{\mathbf{q}}_i, & \textit{if } d\left(\mathbf{q}_i, \mathbf{q}_j\right) > d_o \end{cases}.
$$

Consider the case $d\left(\mathbf{q}_i, \mathbf{q}_j\right) \leq d_o$ using Control Algorithm 1. The derivative $\dot{U}_r^{CAfM}\left(\mathbf{q}_i, \mathbf{q}_j\right)$ can be written as

$$
\dot{U}_r^{CAfM}\left(\mathbf{q}_i, \mathbf{q}_j\right) = \left(\nabla_{\mathbf{p}_{ij}} U_r^{CAfM}\right)^T \dot{\mathbf{p}}_{ij},
$$

where $\mathbf{p}_{ij} \triangleq \mathbf{q}_i - \mathbf{q}_j$. Let us introduce the notation $U_r^{CAfM}\left(\mathbf{q}_k, \mathbf{q}_l\right) \triangleq U_{r,kl}^{CAfM}$. If $d\left(\mathbf{q}_i, \mathbf{q}_j\right) \leq d_o$, then, in view of the control algorithm, the Lyapunov function's derivative is written as follows:

$$
\frac{1}{2}\kappa\sum_{i=1}^{N}\sum_{j \neq i}\dot{U}_r^{CAfM}\left(\mathbf{q}_i, \mathbf{q}_j\right) = \kappa\sum_{i=1}^{N}\sum_{j \neq i}\left\{\left(\nabla_{\mathbf{p}_{ij}} U_{r,ij}^{CAfM}\right)^T\left(\begin{array}{c} \mathbf{f}^{escape}\left(\mathbf{q}_i, \mathbf{q}_j\right) \\ -\nabla_{\mathbf{p}_{ij}} U_{r,ij}^{CAfM} \mathbf{R}_{\varsigma_{ij}}\left(\mathbf{q}_i - \mathbf{q}_j\right) \end{array}\right)\right\}.
$$

This equation transforms as

$$\frac{1}{2}\kappa \sum_{i=1}^{N}\sum_{j\neq i} \dot{U}_r^{CAfM}\left(\mathbf{q}_i, \mathbf{q}_j\right) = \kappa \sum_{i=1}^{N}\sum_{j\neq i}\left\{\begin{array}{c} -\mu_i K_{escape}\left[\begin{array}{c}\left(p_j^x - p_i^x\right)^2 + \\ \left(p_j^y - p_i^y\right)^2\end{array}\right] \\ + \underbrace{\begin{array}{c} K\left(p_i^y - p_j^y\right)\left(p_i^x - p_j^x\right) \\ -K\left(p_i^y - p_j^y\right)\left(p_i^x - p_j^x\right)\end{array}}_{=0}\end{array}\right\}$$

$$= \kappa \sum_{i=1}^{N}\sum_{j\neq i}\left\{-\mu_i K_{escape}\left[\begin{array}{c}\left(p_j^x - p_i^x\right)^2 + \\ +\left(p_j^y - p_i^y\right)^2\end{array}\right]\right\}.$$

The following notation is used:

$$K_{escape} \triangleq \mu_i\left(\frac{1}{d\left(\mathbf{q}_i, \mathbf{q}_j\right)} - \frac{1}{d_o}\right)\frac{1}{d^3\left(\mathbf{q}_i, \mathbf{q}_j\right)\|\mathbf{q}_i - \mathbf{q}_j - \Delta_{ji}\|_2^2} \geq 0,$$

since $d\left(\mathbf{q}_i, \mathbf{q}_j\right) \leq d_o$; and $K \triangleq \left(k_{r_i}^m\right)^2\left(\frac{1}{d\left(\mathbf{q}_i, \mathbf{q}_j\right)} - \frac{1}{d_o}\right)^2\frac{1}{d^6\left(\mathbf{q}_i, \mathbf{q}_j\right)} \geq 0.$

In the case of the other criterion of the collision danger area, the following can be noted. For example, given that $\left(p_j^x - p_i^x - \Delta_{ji}^x\right) \wedge \left(p_j^y - p_i^y - \Delta_{ji}^y\right) < 0$, as the copters are in the 'risk-of-collision zone', as aircraft-to-aircraft distances are below the algorithm's threshold whilst they are in the zone.

If $d\left(\mathbf{q}_i, \mathbf{q}_j\right) > d_o$, then the reasoning is partly similar to the one in [15]; however, it is modified to account for the copter's position outside the danger zone and for the system model's greater dimensionality. Note that the vector $\mathbf{b}$ is an eigenvector for the Laplacian matrix $\mathbf{L}$ with the corresponding eigenvalue N: $\mathbf{Lb} = N\mathbf{b}$. The Lyapunov function's derivative $\dot{V}$ is then written as:

$$\dot{V} = \sum_{i=1}^{N}\sum_{j\neq i}\left(\mathbf{q}_i - \frac{1}{k_f N}\mathbf{b}_i\right)^T\left(-k_f\left(\mathbf{q}_i - \mathbf{q}_j\right) + \mathbf{b}_i\right)$$

$$= -k_f\sum_{i=1}^{N}\sum_{j\neq i}\left(\mathbf{q}_i - \frac{1}{k_f N}\mathbf{b}_i\right)^T\left(\left(\mathbf{q}_i - \mathbf{q}_j\right) - \frac{1}{k_f}\mathbf{b}_i\right)$$

$$= -k_f\left(\mathbf{q} - \frac{1}{k_f N}\mathbf{b}\right)^T\left(\mathbf{L} \otimes \mathbf{I}_2\right)\left(\mathbf{q} - \frac{1}{k_f N}\mathbf{b}\right) \leq 0,$$

where $\mathbf{I}_2$ is a second-order unit matrix. We used the following notation:

$$\mathbf{q} \triangleq \left[\left[p_1^x\ p_1^y\right]^T, \dots, \left[p_N^x\ p_N^y\right]^T\right]^T \text{ and } \mathbf{b} \triangleq \left[\left[b_1^x\ b_1^y\right]^T, \dots, \left[b_N^x\ b_N^y\right]^T\right]^T,$$

$$b_i^x \triangleq -k_f\sum_{j=1}^{N}\Delta_{ji}^x \text{ and } b_i^y \triangleq -k_f\sum_{j=1}^{N}\Delta_{ji}^y.$$

We thus conclude that the derivative along the trajectories of the system for the Lyapunov function is negative semidefinite. Thus, given that the function $\mathbb{V}$ is positive definite, Lyapunov stability is ensured. Therefore, drones will not collide in motion because the Lyapunov function is limited for limited states. A collision event implies that $d\left(\mathbf{q}_i, \mathbf{q}_j\right)$ is zero, in which case the Lyapunov function's value would tend to infinity.

3 Numerical Simulation Results and Discussion

To visualize the effectiveness of the curl-free vector field for collision avoidance between swarming UAVs (i.e., moving obstacles), we simulated a specific case. The swarm was reduced to 4 UAVs; the final geometry of the formation was preset. Initial positions were picked to force UAV#4 to overtake UAV#3 in order to make the for-mation. Formation-making and trajectory-following coefficients were picked to have such a ratio as to cause such overtaking to result in the collision of the involved UAVs if collision avoidance were not engaged.

Numerical simulation shows that the standard FIRAS function-based potential field fails to prevent such collision. The distance between UAV#3 and UAV#4 begins to shorten drastically upon entering the 'risk-of-collision zone'; it goes below 0.1 as a result, which creates a high risk of collision. Such UAV behavior is attributable to the fact that the term whose purpose is to make the formation actually causes UAVs to come too close to each other. The reason is that the formation-making action actually involves closing on, and overtaking another aircraft, which is necessary to shape the final geometry. At this point, UAVs #3 and #4 are virtually on the same line of movement; the standard FIRAS function-based potential field cannot generate a sufficient control action to initiate a lateral evasive maneuver. The situation is somewhat similar to local minima problem.

It is a completely different outcome with the proposed curl-free vector field-based algorithm. This approach prevents UAVs from 'getting stuck' in the longitudinal axis and generates a control action that enables a lateral evasive maneuver, allowing the UAV to keep a safe distance.

Figure 1 shows the swarm's trajectories (Fig. 1a) and the distance between UAV#3 and UAV#4 (Fig. 1b), no collision avoidance algorithm. It also shows the distance from each UAV to a small obstacle near point (6; 6), which is used as reference (Fig. 1c). This distance was for testing whether the formation's final geometry matched the preset. The collision event (zero distance between UAVs #3 and #4) is clearly seen.

Figure 2 compares two algorithms: the FIRAS function-based one to the left and the proposed curl-free vector field-based one to the right. Figures 2a and 2b show the swarm trajectories. Figures 2c and 2d show the distances between UAV#3 and UAV#4. Figures 2e and 2f show each drone's distance to the reference. As repulsion forces cause a substantial increase in speed, the distance dot plot is discontinuous in the 'risk-of-collision' zone. However, note that at some point, the distance between UAVs #3 and #4 goes below 0.1 when using the standard potential field. The alternative, curl-free vector field prevents the value from ever going below 0.7.

The comparative graphs also visualize the difference in movement trajectories as produced by the two algorithms. The distance-to-reference graph demonstrates that the final geometry was also attained.

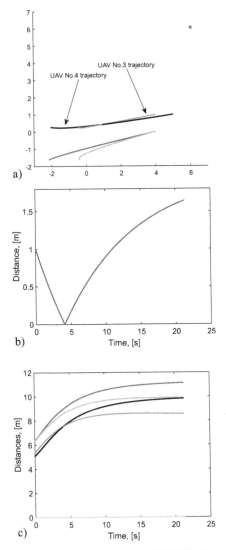

Fig. 1. Swarm trajectories, distance between UAV#3 and UAV#4, distances to the reference point.

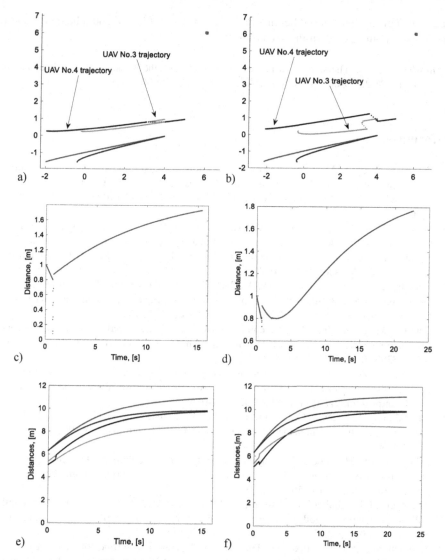

Fig. 2. Collision avoidance algorithm comparison.

4   Conclusion

This paper investigates a drone swarm system model that enables avoidance of collision with various types of obstacles. To that end, we implemented a curl-free vector field-based modification. Focus was made on drone-to-drone collision avoidance, representing moving obstacles. The paper proves the algorithm to be Lyapunov-stable. A MATLAB/Simulink simulation was run and proved the proposed method effective. Its results demonstrate that the method addresses the potential field's weakness in swarm control. This weakness lies in causing a local minima-like effect of 'getting stuck'. The model and approach proposed herein are sufficiently versatile and could be modified to handle more complex swarming scenarios.

Acknowledgements. The study was funded by a grant from the Russian Science Foundation (RSF) (project № 22-79-00168), https://rscf.ru/en/project/22-79-00168/.

References

1. Zakiev, A., Tsoy, T., Magid, E.: Swarm robotics: remarks on terminology and classification. In: Ronzhin, A., Rigoll, G., Meshcheryakov, R. (eds.) ICR 2018. LNCS (LNAI and LNB), vol. 11097, pp. 291–300. Springer, Cham (2018). https://doi.org/10.1007/978-3-319-99582-3_30

2. Petrenko, V., Tebueva, F., Antonov, V., Ryabtsev, S., Sakolchik, A., Satybaldina, D.: Evaluation of the iterative method of task distribution in a swarm of unmanned aerial vehicles in a clustered field of targets. J. King Saud Univ.-Comput. Inf. Sci. **35**, 283–291 (2023). https://doi.org/10.1016/j.jksuci.2023.02.022

3. Darush, Z., Martynov, M., Fedoseev, A., Shcherbak, A., Tsetserukou, D.: SwarmGear: heterogeneous swarm of drones with reconfigurable leader drone and virtual impedance links for multi-robot inspection (2023). http://arxiv.org/abs/2304.02956

4. Popov, A.M., Kostrygin, D.G., Shevchik, A.A., Andrievsky, B.: Speed-gradient adaptive control for parametrically uncertain UAVs in formation. Electron. **11**, 4187 (2022). https://doi.org/10.3390/ELECTRONICS11244187

5. Muslimov, T.Z., Munasypov, R.A.: Multi-UAV cooperative target tracking via consensus-based guidance vector fields and fuzzy MRAC. Aircr. Eng. Aerosp. Technol. **93**, 1204–1212 (2021). https://doi.org/10.1108/AEAT-02-2021-0058

6. Izhboldina, V., Lebedev, I.: Group movement of UAVs in environment with dynamic obstacles: a survey. Int. J. Intell. Unmanned Syst. **11**, 256–284 (2022). https://doi.org/10.1108/IJIUS-06-2021-0038

7. Pshikhopov, V., Medvedev, M., Kostjukov, V., Houssein, F., Kadhim, A.: Trajectory planning algorithms in two-dimensional environment with obstacles. Inform. Autom. **21**, 459–492 (2022). https://doi.org/10.15622/ia.21.3.1

8. de Angelis, E.L., Giulietti, F., Rossetti, G.: Multirotor aircraft formation flight control with collision avoidance capability. Aerosp. Sci. Technol. **77**, 733–741 (2018). https://doi.org/10.1016/J.AST.2018.04.002

9. Karkoub, M., Atınç, G., Stipanovic, D., Voulgaris, P., Hwang, A.: Trajectory tracking control of unicycle robots with collision avoidance and connectivity maintenance. J. Intell. Robot. Syst. **96**, 331–343 (2019). https://doi.org/10.1007/s10846-019-00987-2

10. Qiao, Y., et al.: Formation tracking control for multi-agent systems with collision avoidance and connectivity maintenance. In: Drones 2022, vol. 6, p. 419 (2022). https://doi.org/10.3390/DRONES6120419

11. Wang, N., Dai, J., Ying, J.: UAV formation obstacle avoidance control algorithm based on improved artificial potential field and consensus. Int. J. Aeronaut. Sp. Sci. **22**, 1413–1427 (2021). https://doi.org/10.1007/S42405-021-00407-6/

12. Choi, D., Lee, K., Kim, D.: Enhanced potential field-based collision avoidance for unmanned aerial vehicles in a dynamic environment. In: AIAA Scitech 2020 Forum. American Institute of Aeronautics and Astronautics, Reston, Virginia (2020). https://doi.org/10.2514/6.2020-0487

13. Choi, D., Kim, D., Lee, K.: Enhanced potential field-based collision avoidance in cluttered three-dimensional urban environments. Appl. Sci. **11**, 11003 (2021). https://doi.org/10.3390/APP112211003

14. Dang, A.D., La, H.M., Nguyen, T., Horn, J.: Formation control for autonomous robots with collision and obstacle avoidance using a rotational and repulsive force–based approach. Int. J. Adv. Robot. Syst. **16**, 172988141984789 (2019). https://doi.org/10.1177/1729881419847897

15. Toksoz, M.A., Oguz, S., Gazi, V.: Decentralized formation control of a swarm of quadrotor helicopters. In: 2019 IEEE 15th International Conference on Control and Automation (ICCA), pp. 1006–1013. IEEE (2019). https://doi.org/10.1109/ICCA.2019.8899628

Author Index

A. Ronzhin et al. (Eds.): ICR 2023, LNAI 14214, pp. 381–382, 2023.
https://doi.org/10.1007/978-3-031-43111-1